STUDENT WORKBOOK AND STUDY GUIDE

for use with

LAW FOR BUSINESS

Fifth Edition

A. James Barnes
Terry M. Dworkin
Eric L. Richards

Prepared by

Frona Powell
Indiana University

IRWIN
Burr Ridge, Illinois
Boston, Massachusetts
Sydney, Australia

Printed in the United States of America.

ISBN 0-256-11595-8

2 3 4 5 6 7 8 9 0 MG 0 9 8 7 6 5 4

CONTENTS

CHAPTER 1
INTRODUCTION TO THE LAW

Outline

I. Introduction

II. The Nature of Law

    A. Definition of the Legal System is not a simple one. Law is an institution within American society that changes and evolves to reflect, influence, and interact with other social institutions within society.

    B. Functions of Law include keeping the peace, enforcing standards of conduct, maintaining order, facilitating planning, and promoting social justice

III. Classifications of Law

    A. Substantive law and procedural law. Substantive law sets out rights and duties; procedural law establishes the rules under which substantive rules of law are enforced. Note, however, that the distinction is not always so clear. For example, is a rule requiring an indigent defendant be supplied with an attorney a procedural or substantive rule?

    Texas v. Johnson, 109 S.Ct. 2533 (U.S. Sup. Ct. 1989) is an example of a question of substantive law—in this case, the U.S. Supreme Court held prosecution of a defendant for desecrating the American flag violated the defendant's first amendment.

    B. Criminal law and civil law.

        1. Criminal law defines the duty of individuals to society; Breach of that duty results in prosecution by the government against an individual.

        2. Civil law defines duties owed by individuals to other individuals. (Examples include negligence and contract law.)

IV. The American Legal System

    A. Law and Government: The law establishes the government and also limits the power of that government.

    B. Constitutional powers and limitations include the Bill of Rights (first 10 amendments to the U.S. Constitution), and the system of "Checks and Balances" between the three branches of government.

V. Sources of Law

    A. Federal and State Sources include constitutions, treaties, statutes, administrative rules and decisions, executive orders, and court decisions.

    B. Court Decisions—Nature of Common Law. The United States is a "common law" country, sharing the English common law system with other English-speaking countries. Under these system, court decisions have the force of law, and the decision of a court is binding on lower courts within its jurisdiction. The principle that a court should follow precedent (or a prior judicial decision on point in the present case) is called the principle of stare decisis.

    Hallstrom v. Tillamook County, 110 S. Ct. 304 (U.S. Sup. Ct. 1989) is an example of the U.S. Supreme Court's interpretation of federal legislation.

VI. How the Law Changes

    A. One of the important principles underlying the Common Law, and its principle of stare decisis is the belief that law should be predictable. However, the Common Law must also be adaptable in order to respond to changing social and political realities.

    B. Today, business managers must be familiar with basic principles of statutory and common law affecting business. Not only will this help them avoid costs associated with litigation or penalties associated with violating public law, it can also help managers minimize legal risks and consequences.

Learning Objectives

1. You should understand the basic functions law serves.
2. You should understand the differences between civil law and criminal law.
3. You should understand the basic idea of checks and balances and be able to give some examples of its operation.
4. You should know what the Supremacy Clause of the Constitution is and the effect it has on state law.
5. You should be thoroughly familiar with the different sources of law.
6. You should understand the three ways in which courts make law.
7. You should be aware of the ways in which the law ensures predictability while still remaining adaptable to changing circumstances.
8. You should consider the interaction between law and ethics and corporate social responsibility

Learning Hints

1. Substantive law sets forth rules spelling out the rights and duties which govern citizens in our society. Procedural law sets forth the rules governing the behavior of our government as it establishes and enforces the rules of substantive law.
2. A civil action is a lawsuit between two private parties (one of whom may be the government). In a criminal action, the government is basically acting in a prosecutorial role and is enforcing the criminal law, a body of law set up to punish breaches of duty to society at large.
3. In a civil suit, the plaintiff is the party who is suing and the defendant is the party being sued. In a criminal suit, the party who is being prosecuted is the defendant. In criminal cases, however, the government (which brings the criminal case against the defendant) is not usually referred to as the plaintiff.
4. The Constitution can limit Congress's law-making power in two ways: by specifically listing Congress's powers and saying that Congress shall have these powers and no others, and by imposing certain independent checks on Congress when it exercises its legitimate powers, such as the requirement that citizens be given due process of law. At the present time, the second sort of limitation on Congressional power is much more important than the first.
5. The Taxing Power is a source of regulatory power because of the effect that taxation can have on socially disfavored activities. Therefore, it is often said that "the power to tax is the power to destroy." Also, various tax deductions and tax credits can have a regulatory effect by encouraging certain kinds of activities, and denying tax deductions discourages other kinds of activities.
6. Delegation is a process whereby the legislature effectively "hands over" some of its power to legislate to a subordinate body. The rules issued by the subordinate body are valid because the legislature has given that body power to issue them. Among the sources of law discussed in the text, administrative rules and decisions and executive orders clearly result from a legislative delegation of lawmaking power.
7. Law and equity used to be dispensed in separate courts, and the test for obtaining equitable relief was whether the plaintiff lacked an adequate remedy at law. Today, law and equity are usually dispensed within the same courts. Also, equitable remedies and equitable concepts are sometimes applied in what seem to be "law" cases.
8. As the text stresses, the doctrine of stare decisis, while appearing to be very rigid, actually permits considerable change in the common law. This is because it is theoretically possible to distinguish every past case, or precedent, from the case being decided. The power to determine what are appropriate distinctions of past cases rests with the courts.
9. Law is a means by which society attempts to control certain kinds of behavior. Rules of ethics and morality are concerned with questions of right and wrong. In many cases, law reflects a society's moral or ethical belief. However, there are cases where law may not. In these cases, should a person follow the law or his own ethical belief? What are the ethical and social ramifications of your answer?
10. A significant distinction between criminal and civil law is the purpose of the legal action. In a civil case, the purpose is generally to deter certain conduct through punishment. In civil cases,

the purpose is generally to <u>compensate</u> a person who has been injured by another's wrongful act.

True-False

In the blank provided, put "T" if the statement is True or "F" if the statement is False.

T   1. Money awards in civil cases are called "damages."

F   2. Substantive law is concerned with the rules determining what cases a court can decide and how a judgment by a court is enforced.

F   3. The Bill of Rights consists of the first 25 @X = amendments to the U.S. Constitution.

T   4. A court has the power to interpret and apply statutory law.

T   5. The power of judicial review is not specifically granted by the U.S. constitution.

T   6. Criminal cases are initiated by society through government employees, not by the private parties who are the victims of crime.

F   7. "Checks and balances" are present only between state governments and the federal government, and do not exist within the federal government itself.

T   8. Court interpretations of the amount of protection offered by the Constitution to business activities have changed over time.

T   9. A treaty may override a conflicting statute enacted by Congress.

F   10. Governmental units within a state, such as cities and counties, also have the power to pass binding legislation.

Multiple Choice

Circle the best answer.

1. The law is a set of principles, rules, and standards of conduct:
   a. Which have general application in society;
   b. Which have been adopted by proper authority;
   c. Which imposes a penalty for their violation;
   d. All of the above are correct.

2. The First Amendment's guarantee of "free speech" in the U.S. Constitution:
   a. Is an example of substantive law;
   b. Is a right or privilege protected by the bill of rights;
   c. Does not apply to state action;
   d. Both (a) and (b) are correct.

3. A duty to carry out a contractual promise:
   a. Is a duty established by criminal law;
   b. Is a duty established by civil law;
   c. Is an example of procedural law;
   d. Both (a) and (c) are correct.

4. Most federal regulations that affect business are based on power given to Congress under:
   a. The bill of rights;
   b. The commerce clause;
   c. Federal criminal law statutes;
   d. State statutes.

5. Which of the following is <u>not</u> a function of a court?
   a. To determine the meaning of statutes;
   b. To make common law;
   c. To enact statutes;
   d. To review the constitutionality of acts of the legislative branch.

3

6. Which statement regarding American law is false?
   a. The rule of <u>stare decisis</u> did not originate in America, but was developed within the English common-law system.
   b. The law of equity developed because sometimes the legal remedies available to the plaintiff were inadequate.
   c. A federal or state statute can be defeated by an inconsistent treaty provision.
   d. American judges neither make nor change law.

7. The common law:
   a. exists only at the federal level.
   b. exists only in situations which are governed by statutes or other positive law.
   c. will prevail over a conflicting constitutional provision.
   d. is judge-made law which develops through the use of <u>stare decisis</u>.

8. Executive orders:
   a. exist only at the federal level.
   b. will defeat inconsistent statutes.
   c. are issued by administrative agencies.
   d. usually result from a delegation of power by the legislature.

9. Administrative agencies have the power to make law because:
   a. the state and federal constitutions give them this power.
   b. the English common law tradition dictates that they have this power.
   c. Congress or a state legislature has delegated this power to them.
   d. Administrative agencies cannot make law.

10. The doctrine of <u>stare decisis</u>:
   a. is a technique courts use to overturn actions of Congress.
   b. compels a court in one state to follow the decisions of courts in a different state.
   c. means that precedent cases are never overruled.
   d. states that a case should be decided the same as a similar prior case.

Short Essay

1. In 1965, Berry pleaded guilty in the State of X to a charge of felony theft. The court never entered judgment against him. In 1966, after a policeman noticed that Berry was wearing a concealed gun, Berry was arrested and convicted of violating the X state statute which makes it a crime for a convicted felon to possess a handgun. Berry appealed his conviction, arguing that he did not violate this statute because he had never been convicted of a felony. The appellate court disagreed, saying that in a debate on the floor of the Senate, "Congress made it clear that it was intent on preventing those with criminal backgrounds from possessing firearms." Which method of statutory interpretation did the appellate court use? Explain.

2. Explain how the doctrine of <u>stare decisis</u> not only produces stability and predictability in the common law, but also enables the common law to evolve to meet changing social conditions.

3. Describe the functions that law performs in American society today.

4. Briefly explain three techniques of statutory interpretation used by courts in determining legislative intent.

CHAPTER 2
DISPUTE SETTLEMENT

Outline

I. Means of Dispute Settlement
  A. Negotiation
  B. ADR (Alternative Dispute Resolution)
  C. Mediation
  D. Arbitration
  E. Mini/Summary Trial

II. The Courts
  A. Courts must have Jurisdiction
     Venue is where, within a jurisdiction, a suit must be heard.
  B. State Courts
     1. Inferior Courts: Not courts of record
     2. Trial Courts
     3. Courts of Appeals
  C. Federal Courts
     1. Trial court is the District Court
     2. Courts of Appeals
     3. U.S. Supreme Court

III. The Adversary System
     1. Functions of the Judge
     2. Functions of Procedure (The Pleadings, Discovery)
     3. The Appeal

Learning Objectives

1. You should know the differences between negotiation, mediation, fact-finding, and arbitration as methods of settling disputes outside the court system.
2. You must know what is required for the two types of federal court subject-matter jurisdiction: diversity jurisdiction and federal question jurisdiction.
3. You should be able to name and describe all of the procedural steps in a civil lawsuit.
4. You should know the difference between the burden of proof in a criminal case and the burden of proof in a civil case.
5. You should know the permitted grounds and procedures for appealing the decisions in civil lawsuits.
6. You should know the theory behind the adversary system, and how the judge and the lawyers function in this system.
7. You should understand the principle of federal supremacy and the U.S. Supreme Court's ultimate power to declare a federal or state law unconstitional.
8. You should understand the principle of personal and subject matter jurisdiction and distinguish it from venue.

Learning Hints

1. Most cases are heard in state (rather than federal) courts. An important distinction between state inferior courts and state trial courts of general jurisdiction is the fact that inferior courts are not courts of record. This means that in many instances, an appeal from a state inferior court will result in a new trial at the state trial court level.

2. In most cases, there are two aspects to jurisdiction. The first is the ability of the court to hear a particular kind of case—this is referred to in the textbook as "subject-matter jurisdiction." For example, a state may set up special courts to handle only a certain type of case, such as special divorce, probate, and juvenile courts. The other aspect of jurisdiction is the territorial or geographical reach of the court. This issue arises mainly during discussions of the state courts, for federal courts have nationwide jurisdiction.

3. In federal cases brought under diversity jurisdiction, the amount involved must be at least $50,000. There is no minimum amount of money which is required for federal question jurisdiction to exist.

4. Many civil lawsuits may be brought either in a state trial court or in a federal District Court. For example, a lawsuit against a driver from another state for an amount over $50,000 can be brought in either state trial court or in federal District Court. The existence of this choice creates strategic questions for the plaintiff's lawyer. Keep in mind also that the defendant may ask to have a case filed in state trial court removed to federal District Court.

5. With very few exceptions, cases do not begin in appellate courts. Appellate courts are usually limited to correcting alleged errors of law (not fact) made at the trial court level.

6. Be aware of the ways in which the basic state court structure or heirarchy parallels the basic federal court structure or heirarchy.

7. The summons and the complaint, while often served on the defendant together, are not the same, and serve very different functions.

8. Many cases are disposed of by the motion to dismiss described on page 32. The most common form of the motion to dismiss goes to the legal sufficiency of the complaint, and states that even if the facts stated in the complaint are true, the plaintiff still cannot recover because there is no legal remedy for such a situation. For this reason, it is often said that the motion to dismiss amounts to saying "So what?" to the plaintiff's complaint.

9. The motion for a directed verdict and the motion for judgment notwithstanding the verdict are both ways of asking the judge to decide the case instead of the jury. Basically, both assert that no reasonable jury could decide in favor of the other party. The existence of these motions reveals the American legal system's ambivalence about juries, because if all juries were reasonable, the motions would not be necessary.

10. Generally speaking, the appellate courts only review legal errors that one party claims were made by the trial court—not errors in deciding questions of fact. Legal errors include at least the following: lack of jurisdiction, rulings during discovery, rulings on motions to dismiss, evidentiary rulings at trial, rulings on motions for directed verdict and motions for judgment notwithstanding the verdict, and the judge's findings of law (if there was no jury present at the trial).

True-False

In the blank provided, put "T" if the statement is True or "F" if the statement is False.

_____ 1. Alternative dispute resolution mechanisms are usually cheaper and less complicated than a trial by a court.

_____ 2. Generally, appellate courts hear witnesses and re-try the facts to determine whether to grant relief on appeal.

_____ 3. Federal trial courts are called "district courts."

_____ 4. Most cases reach the U.S. Supreme Court on writ of certiorari.

_____ 5. In a federal case, the plaintiff must state the basis for the court's jurisdiction in the complaint.

_____ 6. Mediation is a means of dispute settlement in which the mediator's function is only to make negotiation more productive; no binding decision is rendered by the mediator.

_____ 7. All cases brought in the federal District Courts must be for $50,000 or more.

_____ 8. The adversary system is based on the idea that truth is best discovered through the presentation of competing ideas.

_____ 9. Cases heard in the federal courts must involve either a federal question or situations in which there is diversity of citizenship between the parties.

_____ 10. In a civil case, the plaintiff must prove his case beyond a reasonable doubt in order to win.

Multiple Choice

Circle the best answer.

1. Venue concerns:
   a. the power of a court to hear a case;
   b. the place where the case will be heard;
   c. the kind of court (inferior, trial, or appellate) which may hear the case;
   d. whether the case should be filed in state or federal court.

2. An example of an inferior court is:
   a. a state trial court;
   b. a district court;
   c. a municipal court;
   d. an appellate court.

3. Which of the following generally occurs last?
   a. Filing the complaint;
   b. Filing the answer
   c. Discovery
   d. Serving the summons.

4. The standard of proof in a civil case is:
   a. By a preponderence of the evidence;
   b. Beyond a reasonable doubt;
   c. Beyond any doubt;
   d. By a substantial certainty.

5. Which of the following motions is generally made at trial?
   a. Motion to dismiss for failure to state a claim;
   b. Motion to dismiss for lack of jurisdiction;
   c. Motion for a directed verdict;
   d. Motion for summary judgment.

6. Which of the following is an advantage of arbitration as a means of dispute settlement?
   a. Because lawyers are not permitted to participate in arbitration, fewer petty technical objections are raised.
   b. Arbitration proceedings are usually less formal and more speedy than court proceedings.
   c. Arbitrators are more fully trained in the law than are judges.
   d. The wisdom of arbitration awards can be fully scrutinized by an appeal to the courts.

7. Federal question jurisdiction:
   a. is a type of jurisdiction possessed by state trial courts.
   b. is the most common form of U.S. Supreme Court jurisdiction.
   c. requires that the amount in controversy be at least $10,000.
   d. is jurisdiction over questions arising under federal laws, treaties, and the U.S. Constitution.

8. The primary way a case can be appealed to the U.S. Supreme Court is:
   a. through a writ of certiorari.
   b. by asserting the right of appeal.
   c. by demonstrating the existence of a federal question.
   d. All of the above

9. Sally Student, a citizen of Indiana, is denied admission by Holy Roller University in Oklahoma on the ground that she is female and the Holy Rollers believe that God does not approve of women going to college. Sally wants to sue Holy Roller University for sex discrimination in violation of the U.S. Constitution and to allege damages of $95,000. Which of the following would be an <u>incorrect</u> statement about where Sally can file her lawsuit?
   a. Sally can sue either in federal District Court or in state court.
   b. Sally can sue in federal District Court under that court's diversity jurisdiction.
   c. Sally can sue in federal District Court under that court's federal question jurisdiction.
   d. Sally must sue in state court because the amount in controversy in her lawsuit is not enough for federal court jurisdiction to exist.

10. The role of the judge in the adversary system is:
   a. to direct the search for truth.
   b. to request necessary evidence.
   c. to question witnesses.
   d. to act as a referee.

Short Essay

1. What are the basic steps in a civil lawsuit?

2. State the tests for federal diversity jurisdiction and the tests for federal question jurisdiction.

3. What are the advantages of using alternative dispute resolution mechanisms over the use of the judicial system?

CHAPTER 3

BUSINESS ETHICS AND CORPORATE SOCIAL RESPONSIBILITY

Outline

I. The Profit Maximization Criterion: An objective promoted on the ground that it efficiently allocates a society's resources.

    A. Criticisms: Sometimes social values outweight allcational efficiency.

    B. Market Forces and Corporate Responsibility: "Alar and Apples" is an example of consumer boycott of a product in an attempt to change corporate behavior.

II. The Law as a Corporate Control Device

    A. Corporate Influence on the Law: corporations may utilize political and social power to influence legislation

    B. Conscious Law breaking: Ford Motor Co. v. Durrill is an example of a case where plaintiffs recovered substantial punitive damages (reduced by the appellate court to $10 million) for offensive conduct in the "Ford pinto" case.

    C. Problem of Unknown Harms: After the fact legal action may not compensate for harms that occurred in the past.

    D. Problem of Irrational Corporate Behavior: A corporation may not respond sensibly to legal threats.

    E. "Risky Shift": Decisions by a team may accept a level of risk greater than that of an individual.

    F. Ford v. Revlon, Inc. is an example of a case where a company incurred liability for disregarding company policy for protecting its employees from sexual harassment.

III. The Dilemmas of Ethical Corporate Behavior

    A. How do we define Ethical Behavior? In Auto Workers v. Johnson Controls, the Supreme Court held that a company's fetal-protection policy illegally discriminates on the basis of sex.

    B. Corporate Codes: Following the Exxon Valdez oil spill, the company adopted a harsh position prohibiting alcohol and drug abusers from returning to critical jobs after treatment.

    C. Changes in Corporate Procedure to Encourage Responsible Decision-making.

Learning Objectives

1. You should consider the relationship between corporate decision-making, ethical theory, and the function of law.

2. You should be able to identify procedural steps that enhance or improve responsible corporate decision-making.

3. You should become familiar with the major arguments in favor of profit-maximization as the proper ethical stance for corporations to take.

4. You should be aware of the major weaknesses of the profit-maximization stance, including, for instance, the inherent limits on the law as a corporate control device.

5. You should understand what corporate or industry codes of conduct are, and should be aware of the competing views concerning whether these codes are meaningful and significant.

6. You should understand the chief obstacle to implementation of the ethical, socially responsible stance: the problem of diversity among persons concerning what is and is not ethical.

7. You should become familiar with the major proposals for revisions in the customary forms of corporate governance, as well as with the strengths and weaknesses of the respective proposals.

8. You should develop an awareness of, and sensitivity for, the sorts of issues that may embroil corporate managers in controversy over what course of action to take where corporate interests and societal interests do not appear to coincide.

Learning Hints

1. Ethical guidance for responsible corporate decision-making may result from the values of an individual, collective values of society, corporate codes of conduct, and other considerations.

Sometimes these values conflict, and it is necessary to determine which value should take priority. Ethical theory helps in analyzing an ethical problem, although the result reached in a particular problem may differ depending on the ethical theory applied.

2. Corporations may be regarded as leading actors on the world economic stage. Despite their instrumental role in a productive economic system, corporations have been the targets of criticism throughout their history. The frequently heard charge that corporations do not have a "soul" is nothing new.

3. Although the <u>profit-maximization</u> stance and the <u>ethical</u> stance may be presented as competing responses to the question concerning how corporations should be run, the supposed difference between the two sometimes may be more imaginary than real. For instance, if a corporation engages in behavior that is widely thought to be ethical or socially responsible, the corporation's public image is enhanced and the corporation may become more profitable as a result.

4. Corporate interests indeed have significant effects on the development and content of law. Nevertheless, in view of the dramatic increase in government's regulation of business over the past quarter-century, it would not be accurate to regard the law as a mere pawn of the business community.

5. The law does not always provide a ready answer to ethical dilemmas that corporate managers may face. Our system of lawmaking, which includes statutory law, common law, and administrative law, is such that law dealing with a particular problem or concern generally is not created until after the problem or concern has caused some damaging effects. Many of the difficult decisions faced by corporate managers involve a problem whose resolution a certain way would benefit the corporation but would cause damage to parties outside the corporate structure. If such damage has not occurred before, clear legal standards concerning the problem probably have not yet been developed. This means that corporate managers may be on their own in deciding what course of action to pursue. Whether they choose a proper course of action is another question, the answer to which may not become apparent—if at all—until one has the benefit of hindsight.

6. A recurring problem associated with the premise that corporations should act in an "ethical" manner is the difficulty of determining whose particular notions of what is ethical should govern. Although different persons sometimes agree about whether a certain course of conduct would be ethical, they cannot always be expected to do so. "Ethical" is a nebulous term whose meaning, when applied to particular sets of circumstances, varies from person to person and group to group.

7. Despite their failings and frequent inadequacies as regulators of corporate behavior, the law and the marketplace appear destined to remain the primary regulators of this behavior—at least for the foreseeable future. Neither the law nor the marketplace is likely to provide a comprehensive guide to what is appropriate decisionmaking by corporate officials.

True-False

In the blank provided, put "T" if the statement is True or "F" if the statement is False.

_____ 1. In cases where the behavior of a corporation shocks the conscience, courts may award substantial punitive damages, in addition to compensatory damages, to punish wrongful conduct by corporate officers or employees.

_____ 2. The tendency for group members to internalize the group's values and perceptions and to suppress critical thought is called "risky shift."

_____ 3. A corporate policy which excludes women with child-bearing capacity from lead-exposed jobs does not illegally discriminate against women.

_____ 4. One recommendation for making coporations more sensitive to outside concerns is to give shareholders greater power within the corporation, but it is unlikely that greater shareholder control will lead to greater corporate social responsibility.

_____ 5. Constituency values are those values expressly stated in a corporate policy manual.

_____ 6. One problem with the idea that the law can be an effective corporate control device is the fact that business has a significant voice in determining the content of the law.

_____ 7. Proposals for changes in corporate management structure are largely procedural suggestions designed to give corporations the means to anticipate problems before they arise.

_____ 8. Industry codes of ethical conduct are laws passed by Congress or state legislatures in an effort to specify what is and is not an ethical practice in a given industry.

Multiple Choice

Circle the best answer.

1. As a result of the Exxon Valdez disaster:
   a. Exxon adopted a policy prohibiting alcohol and drug abusers who have completed treatment from working for the corporation in critical jobs like piloting a ship;
   b. Exxon adopted a policy prohibiting alcohol and drug abusers who have completed treatment from working for the corporation in any capacity.
   c. Exxon adopted a treatment policy that may illegally discriminate against the handicapped.
   d. Both (b) and (c) are correct.

2. Which of the following is not a limit on the law's ability to control corporate behavior?
   a. corporations may influence the content of law;
   b. corporations may consciously break the law;
   c. the harms caused by the corporation may be unkown at the time they occurred;
   d. corporations, unlike individuals, always act rationally.

3. The tendency of persons acting as part of a group to make group decisions that involve higher levels of potentially adverse consequences than they would accept as individuals is an organizational phenomenon known as
   a. "groupthink."
   b. "collective buck-passing."
   c. "bureaucratic inertia."
   d. "risky shift."

4. According to those who adhere to the "corporate social responsibility" viewpoint, the main problem with proposals for increasing shareholders' power to influence corporate policy is
   a. that as a group, shareholders probably are at least as strongly profit-oriented as managers are.
   b. that individual shareholders have different ideas about what is ethical behavior.
   c. that virtually all shareholders lack the business sophistication necessary for the making of sound judgments.
   d. that such proposals have little relevance because shareholders already have substantial power in that regard today.

5. Which of the following is an inaccurate statement concerning the use of the law as a device for controlling corporate behavior?
   a. The law is not always an adequate means of checking harm-producing corporate behavior because legal rules prohibiting such behavior often are not developed until after harm has resulted from the behavior.
   b. Conscious lawbreaking by corporations undermines the effectiveness of the law as a device for controlling corporate behavior.
   c. Even critics of using the law as device for controlling corporate behavior concede that the law may be effective in this respect because corporations, as profit-maximizers, can be counted upon to respond sensibly to legal threats.
   d. The substantial political influence of corporations allows them to help shape the law so that it reflects their interests; as a result, the applicable legal rules may be less effective as a check on arguably inappropriate corporate behavior than they otherwise would be.

6. One viewpoint in the debate over corporations' obligations, if any, toward society is that aside from the basic duty to obey the law, the only ethical obligation corporate managers should have is to maximize profits and thereby ensure efficient allocation of scarce resources. Which of the following is the most effective argument against this viewpoint?
   a. That profit-maximization in fact does not produce allocational efficiency.
   b. That some values may be more important than allocational efficiency.
   c. That allocational efficiency is not a very important social value.
   d. That the whole argument is merely academic, because corporations do not allocate resources efficiently anyway.

7. Which of the following is the most common criticism leveled at industry codes of conduct by those who adhere to the "corporate social responsibility" viewpoint?
   a. That corporations and other business entities do not pay attention to these codes, so they have very little practical significance.
   b. That they often are enacted to give the impression that the firms subject to them are acting responsibly, and to forestall legislation that might impose even stricter standards.
   c. That they impose unrealistically high standards on the firms subject to them.
   d. That they unreasonably restrict profit-maximization.

8. Which of the following is not among the changes in corporate governance urged by those who wish to have corporate decisionmaking be more "responsible" and reflective of a variety of values?
   a. A change in the composition of corporate boards of directors.
   b. Adoption of internal information flow procedures for ensuring that relevant external information reaches the proper corporate department.
   c. Establishing educational and licensing requirements for certain corporate employment positions.
   d. A reduction in the amount of policy shaping that shareholders can bring about.

9. Defenders of profit-maximization as the appropriate standard to govern corporate behavior
   a. maintain that the law has rather limited ability to deter inappropriate corporate behavior.
   b. take the position that laws having an adverse effect on a corporation's profits should not be obeyed.
   c. maintain that market forces and other private activity of citizens generally will force corporations to behave in a responsible fashion.
   d. maintain what is set forth in each of the above answers.

10. Which of the following is the strongest argument against profit-maximization as the appropriate standard to govern corporate behavior?
    a. Profit-maximization is an inherently unethical idea.
    b. Profit-maximization is a shortsighted approach that tends to emphasize short-term profits at the expense of long-term allocational efficiency and long-term societal objectives.
    c. Profit-maximization is a concept guaranteed to lead to disputes among directors, officers, and shareholders.
    d. Profit-maximization, when pursued as a corporate strategy, inevitably leads to a greater disparity of wealth among the groups comprising our society, and invariably leads to corporations taking undue advantage of those who are outside the corporate circle.

Short Essay

1. Kleenco has been told by its legal department that the EPA has identified a byproduct ("DDP") produced in an essential production process at the plant as a "probable human carcinogen." No current environmental regualtions requires special treatment for DDP, so Kleenco has been releasing 1,000 tons of it into the air along with other unregulated substances. At this point, only a handful of Kleenco's upper management is even aware of the emission of DDP from the plant. It would cost Kleenco at least $500,000 to install equipment to recover DPP and dispose of it safely. What should Kleenco do? Discuss using a profit maximization criterion.

2. Behemoth, Inc., which considers itself a socially responsible firm, defines "social responsibility" as behavior that properly accommodates the interests of its various constituencies. The following constituencies are those to which Behemoth considers itself responsible: its workers; consumers of its products; its shareholders; and the communities where its plants are situated. Assuming whatever facts are necessary to complete your answer, identify three situations in which the interests of two or more of these constituencies would clash, and discuss what the particular clashes would be.

3. You are a high-ranking officer of a tobacco company whose cigarettes are sold throughout the United States and in various other countries. Approximately fifteen percent of your firm's cigarette sales during 1990 were made in Nation A. Your company's competitors also sell large amounts of cigarettes in Nation A. Although all packages of cigarettes sold in the United States must bear certain health-related warnings as specified by federal law, neither United States law nor the law of Nation A requires that packages of cigarettes sold in Nation A bear any warnings about the health hazards posed by smoking. During the past several years, your company's sales in Nation A have increased significantly. Overall cigarette consumption in that country (including not only your company's cigarettes but also those sold by your competitors) has increased dramatically during the same time frame. You are faced with deciding whether your firm should voluntarily begin placing health-related warnings on packages of cigarettes sold in Nation A. What constituencies stand to be affected, and how are they likely to be affected, by a decision either way on this issue? What course of action do you believe should be taken? Why that course of action?

4. You are a high-ranking officer of Griese Corp., which operates a large chain of fast food restaurants. Griese restaurants "deep fry" a variety of foods in beef tallow. The same is true of numerous other competing fast food restaurants. Some competitors, however, have ceased using beef tallow in response to scientific studies indicating that regular consumption, over a period of years, of foods deep fried in beef tallow may be harmful to the health of some persons. Assume, for purposes of this question, that the conclusions drawn in the scientific studies are correct. Assume, also, that there thus far has been only moderate public attention devoted to the beef tallow issue, and that the cost of using something other than beef tallow for frying would necessitate a price increase of approximately three to five cents per food item. Do you urge your fellow officers to authorize a shift away from the use of beef tallow? State the reasons for your answer.

5. You are a director of a large corporation that has a thriving business in the United States and an extremely profitable business in a foreign country. Many persons in the United States and around the world believe that the government of the other nation adheres to an invidious policy of racial discrimination and perpetuates a system that treats members of a certain racial minority as second-class citizens. Much of the work your firm does there is on contracts with the government of that nation. Recently, your firm has drawn considerable public criticism because of its business ties there. What competing interests must be considered by the board of directors when it considers what course of action to pursue with regard to business relations with the foreign government? What course of action do you urge the board of directors to pursue? Why that course of action?

CHAPTER 4
CRIMES

Outline

I. The Nature of Crimes: Crimes are public wrongs and prosecutions are brought by the state rather than an individual party.

   A. Kinds of crimes: Felonies and misdemeanors

   B. The Essentials of Crime: The state must prove a statute existed at the time the act was committed, that defendant's acts violated that statute, and defendant had the capacity to form a criminal intent.

     Northern Virginia Chapter, ACLU v. Alexandria, Va. is a case where a court held an ordinance unconstitutional because it restricted a constitutionally protected activity.

   C. Criminal Procedure: Our system has procedural safeguards to protect the accused.

     1. In Michigan Department of State Police v. Sitz, the court determined that sobriety checkpoints do not unconstitutionally invade a driver's right to privacy. The court was required to balance the constitutional protection against unreasonable searches against the government's interest in controlling the problem of drunken driving.

II. Crimes and Business

   A. Personal liability for corporate executives has been imposed under the theory this will deter violation of laws.

     Example: In Illinois v. Chicago Magnet Wire Corp., a corporation and its officers were subject to state criminal prosecution in a case where the officers were also subject to sanctions under federal law (OSHA).

   B. Other issues include Problems with Individual Liability, and Application of RICO (Racketeer Influenced and Corrupt Organizations Act) to businesses.

     Example: In H.J. Inc. v. Northwestern Bell Telephone Co., the U.S. Supreme Court held that a single fraudulent scheme by a business can constitute a pattern of racketeering activity under RICO.

Learning Objectives

   1. You should be able to distinguish the parties involved in civil and criminal actions, the standard of proof, and the burden of proof required in each action.

   2. You should be familiar with the rationales for punishment underlying criminal law.

   3. You should know the essentials of crime and be able to explain constitutional protections which apply in criminal prosecutions.

   4. You should know the general difference between a felony and a misdemeanor.

   5. You should know the rules surrounding the three major types of criminal incapacity: intoxication, infancy, and insanity.

   6. You should be familiar with the more important procedural protections that our legal system has developed to protect the accused.

   7. You should understand the trends and problems for the criminal justice system as it deals with white-collar crime.

   8. You should understand the purpose of RICO and its application to business and corporate executives.

Learning Hints

   1. One important difference between criminal and civil law is the purpose or function of the action. An important purpose of criminal prosecution is to punish, in order to deter similar activity in the future. The purpose of civil law, on the other hand, is to compensate the plaintiff for injury caused by the wrongful act of the defendant.

   2. An essential requirement of a crime is that there be a statute in effect at the time the defendant's act occurred which prohibited that activity. A statute passed after the act occurred

cannot be the basis of a criminal prosecution under the constitutional prohibition against <u>ex post facto</u> laws.

3. The postponement of trial or sentencing, or the acquittal of the defendant, on the basis of the defendant's insanity does not necessarily mean that the defendant will be released from custody. In many such cases, the defendant is committed to an institution for psychiatric treatment.

4. Remember that whether a given act is classified as criminal or not is a social question, and that only the legislature can criminalize behavior in the U.S.

5. The protections provided for persons accused of crime are designed to prevent innocent people from being convicted of crimes they did not commit, and also represent the appropriate role of government in a democracy.

6. White-collar crimes are usually characterized by non-violence and deceit, but they do cost the public billions of dollars a year, and often maim and kill.

True-False

In the blank provided, put "T" if the statement is True or "F" if the statement is False.

_____ 1. A serious offense, such as murder, rape, or arson, is called a felony.

_____ 2. A person can be convicted of violating a statute which is enacted after the defendant's act but before the time for prosecution expires.

_____ 3. Mens rea refers to a defendant's intention to commit a crime.

_____ 4. The fourth amendment prohibits any search or seizure of a criminal defendant unless a warrant is obtained.

_____ 5. If a defendant is subject to prosecution under federal law for committing an illegal act, he cannot be tried for violating state law for those actions.

_____ 6. Sometimes voluntary intoxication diminishes the extent of the defendant's criminal liability, but it is not a complete defense to criminal liability.

_____ 7. Many prosecutions of white-collar criminals are controversial because it is often difficult to prove criminal intent on the part of high-level corporate executives.

_____ 8. Some criminal statutes impose liability on a corporate executive for the acts or omissions of other corporate employees without requiring proof of criminal intent or knowledge on the part of any corporate employee.

_____ 9. RICO has been applied for the most part as intended by Congress: solely to the activities of those engaged in organized crime.

_____ 10. There are no common law crimes today.

_____ 11. The state must overcome the presumption of innocence by proving every element of the offense charged against the defendant by a preponderance of the evidence.

_____ 12. The new federal sentencing guidelines specifically require stiffer penalties for white-collar crime.

Multiple Choice

Circle the best answer.

1. The Organized Crime Control Act of 1970:
   a. Is generally limited to prosecution of organized crime and does not apply to white-collar crime;
   b. Contains broad language which has resulted in its application to businesses;
   c. Not only prohibits engaging in a racketeering activity, but also prohibits <u>conspiring</u> to engage in such activity;
   d. Both (b) and (c) are correct.

2. Mike was arrested for loitering under the provisions of an anti-drug statute which prohibited "being in the same general location for at least 15 minutes during which he had two or more face-to-face encounters that lasted no more than two minutes, while exchanging money." Mike's best defense is:
   a. He lacked the capacity to commit the offense;
   b. Prosecution is prohibited under the constitutional prohibition against ex post facto laws;
   c. The statute violates the first amendment of the U.S. Constitution;
   d. None of the above is a good defense to prosecution under this ordinance.

3. The standard of proof in a criminal case is:
   a. by a preponderance of the evidence;
   b. beyond a reasonable doubt;
   c. "more likely than not";
   d. by a substantial certainty.

4. If a defendant was insane at the time of committing an illegal act:
   a. He lacks the capacity to commit the crime;
   b. In some states, he may be found guilty but mentally ill;
   c. He cannot formulate premeditation required by some criminal statutes;
   d. All of the above are correct.

5. Recent Sentencing Guidelines adopted by congress:
   a. permit flexibility and judicial discretion in sentencing those convicted of federal crimes;
   b. have been held unconstitutional by the courts;
   c. specifically mandate stiffer penalties for white-collar crime;
   d. require that federal courts use sentencing patterns consistent with those used by state courts in which the federal court sits.

6. The essential elements of a crime under our legal system generally do not include:
   a. proof of a prior statutory prohibition of the act.
   b. proof beyond a reasonable doubt that the defendant committed every element of the criminal offense prohibited by the statute.
   c. proof beyond a reasonable doubt that the defendant was aware of the criminal statute he violated.
   d. proof that the defendant had the capacity to form a criminal intent.

7. Which is a true statement about the insanity defense?
   a. A defendant who is found "guilty but mentally ill" is set free after the jury renders this verdict.
   b. If a defendant who receives the death penalty is found to be legally insane at the time he is to be executed, he may not be executed until his sanity is restored.
   c. A defendant who is found to be legally insane at the time of sentencing may still be sentenced, as long as the sentence is not carried out until his sanity is restored.
   d. The only type of insanity which will provide a legal defense is the defendant's inability to control his behavior to resist the impulse to commit the crime.

8. Which of the following pieces of evidence would a court be required by the Fifth Amendment to exclude from the evidence admitted at trial?
   a. Samples of the defendant's hair which were clipped from his head by the arresting officers without his consent
   b. The defendant's confession to the commission of the crime, which occurred after he was arrested and advised of his Miranda rights
   c. Fingerprints of the defendant obtained through governmental compulsion
   d. None of the above

9. The primary way our system minimizes the risk of convicting an innocent person is:
   a. the mens rea requirement.
   b. the ex post facto law.
   c. the irresistible impulse rule.
   d. the presumption of innocence.

10. Which of the following is <u>not</u> a type of incapacity recognized by our legal system?
    a. Insanity
    b. Infancy
    c. Severe depression
    d. Intoxication

Short Essay

1. Jane was a passenger in her boyfriend's (Jack's) car when he was arrested for criminal trespass. The statute made it a criminal offense to knowingly or intentionally trespass upon the land of another. Jack had taken a short cut through the back of a neighbor's property in his car when the arrest occurred. Explain <u>two</u> defenses to prosecution that <u>Jane</u> may raise in this case.

2. Briefly explain the constitutional protection against <u>ex post facto</u> laws.

3. What problems does imposing individual criminal responsibility on persons in business pose for prosecutors?

4. What types of legal liability does a business face under RICO?

CHAPTER 5
INTENTIONAL TORTS

Outline

I. Intentional Torts: Torts are private wrongs

A. Kinds of Damages include compensatory and punitive damages.

B. Kinds of Torts include Intentional, Negligence, and Strict Liability.

II. Battery: Intentional harmful or offensive touching. Assault is putting another in apprehension of an imminent battery.

Example: Kathleen K. V. Robert B. is a case where sexual contact based on misinformed consent constitutes battery.

III. False Imprisonment: Wrongful confinement without the other's consent.

IV. Intentional Infliction of Mental Distress: Defendant's conduct must be outrageous and produce severe emotional distress.

Example: Wilson v. Pearce, holding that a campaign of harassment by one neighbor against another constituted intentional infliction of emotional distress.

V. Defamation: Injury to a person's reputation by publication of untrue statement of facts.

A. The U.S. Supreme Court has held that a public figure or public official must prove actual malice in the publication of the defamatory statement by a media defendant in order to recover damages for this tort.

Example: Hustler Magazine Inc. v. Falwell, where the U.S. Supreme Court held that the "malice" standard required of public figures should be extended to suits alleging intentional infliction of emotional distress as a result of a defamatory publication.

VI. Invasion of Privacy: A relatively recently development in tort law protecting a persons reasonable expectation of privacy.

Example: Jenkins v. Bolla, a case where publication of prior criminal conviction by a newspaper did not constitute invasion of plaintiff's privacy.

VII. Malicious Prosecution/wrongful use of civil proceedings

Example: Wilson v. Pearce, holding that a plaintiff may prove malicious prosecution if he proves that defendant brought the earlier case maliciously, without probable cause, and the earlier case ended in his (plaintiff's) favor.

VIII. Interference with Property Rights

A. Trespass: Entry by a person onto land in the possession of another. The knowing deposit of microscopic particles by a lead smeltering plant on a neighbor's property was held not to constitute trespass in Bradley v. American Smelting and Refining Company.

B. Trespass to personal property may constitute conversion.

Learning Objectives

1. You should distinguish a civil action from a criminal action. You should understand that an intentional tort may also give rise to criminal prosecution because the same act may violate criminal law.

2. You should understand the rationale underlying a different standard of proof in tort cases than in criminal cases.

3. You should distinguish battery from assault.

4. You should understand the concept of consent, and how it may constitute a defense in some intentional tort cases.

5. You should understand that there are three broad categories of intentional torts: interference with personal rights, interference with property rights, and interference with economic relations.

6. You should know the difference between libel and slander, when proof of actual damages is required in each type of case, and the various defenses and privileges available to the defendant in a defamation suit.

7. You should know the four different types of invasion of privacy.
8. You should be familiar with each of the specific intentional torts, including interference with economic relations, discussed in the textbook.

Learning Hints

1. Sometimes an action can give rise to both a civil action and a criminal prosecution, as in the case of battery. However, in a civil case, the burden is on the plaintiff to prove each and every element by a preponderance of the evidence.
2. Because the standard of proof is different in a civil case and less stringent, a civil judgment holding a defendant liable for committing an intentional tort is generally <u>not</u> admissible in a subsequent criminal prosecution of the defendant for the same act.
3. Because the standard of proof is different in a criminal case, and <u>more</u> stringent than in a civil case, evidence that a defendant has been convicted of a crime <u>is generally admissible</u> in a civil case for damages arising form the same act.
4. Assault and battery differ in that assault does not require physical contact with the plaintiff or anything connected with the plaintiff, and battery does not require awareness or apprehension of a threat to physical safety. If A makes threatening gestures toward B, there may be an assault, but there is no battery. Likewise, if A sneaks up behind B and knocks B unconscious without B ever having been aware of the threat, there is battery, but there is no assault. In most battery cases, however, assault is also present.
5. In considering the confinement element of false imprisonment, keep in mind that confinement must involve a substantial restriction of the confined person's freedom of movement of which he is aware, and there must be no reasonable escape route available.
6. Problems sometimes arise in trying to decide whether a statement is libel or slander. Some have suggested that embodiment in some permanent form (not merely putting the statement in writing) should be the test for libel. Thus, some courts have found that pictures, signs, movies, and statues were libelous. While broadcast defamation is generally considered to be libel, in many states the status of radio and television broadcasts is still unclear.
7. The reason the plaintiff must prove actual damages in most slander cases but in relatively few libel cases is that the law perceives libel as being more damaging to reputation than slander. The actual damages which must be proved in most slander cases are fairly specific; e.g., lost business, lost job opportunities, lost profits.
8. In some intentional infliction of emotional distress cases problems arise because the plaintiff is extremely susceptible emotionally; i.e., the plaintiff is not a person "of ordinary sensibilities." Generally, these overly sensitive plaintiffs cannot recover—unless the defendant was aware of their heightened susceptibility.
9. The four types of invasion of privacy are four separate torts, not four elements of the tort of invasion of privacy. Therefore, the plaintiff need only prove one of the four to recover for invasion of privacy.
10. Truth is a complete defense in defamation cases, but is <u>not</u> a defense in invasion of privacy cases.

True-False

In the blank provided, put "T" if the statement is True or "F" if the statement is False.

_____ 1. A defense to both assault and battery is <u>consent</u> by the plaintiff.

_____ 2. A person may be sued for both defamation and false imprisonment as a result of the same incident, if the plaintiff can establish the elements of each tort.

_____ 3. If a person is prosecuted for a crime as a result of an act, he cannot be sued for damages arising from the same act in a civil proceeding.

_____ 4. A media defendant is not liable for defamation if the plaintiff cannot prove it acted with "actual malice," even if the plaintiff is not a public official or public figure.

_____ 5. In general, a person is only liable for invasion of privacy if the plaintiff's expectation of privacy was a reasonable one.

_____ 6. There can be no liability for false imprisonment if the plaintiff had a reasonable escape route.

_____ 7. Trespass to land is limited to intentional physical entry of one person's land by another person.

_____ 8. All courts require that the defendant's conduct be outrageous before the plaintiff can recover for intentional infliction of mental distress.

_____ 9. Punitive damages are used to punish the defendant and deter the defendant and others like him from engaging in behavior that is particularly offensive.

_____ 10. Truth is a complete defense to a defamation suit.

Multiple Choice

Circle the best answer.

1. The standard of proof in a civil case to recover damages for battery is:
   a. Beyond a reasonable doubt;
   b. By a preponderance of the evidence;
   c. By a reasonable certainty;
   d. Probable cause.

2. Intentional infliction of mental distress is:
   a. An intentional tort;
   b. A strict liability tort;
   c. A new developing tort whose dimensions are still evolving;
   d. Both (a) and (c) are correct.

3. A person who is wrongfully detained on suspicion of shoplifting may bring an action for:
   a. abuse of process;
   b. malicious prosecution;
   c. false imprisonment;
   d. all of the above.

4. One difference between libel and slander is:
   a. Libel requires proof of publication but slander does not;
   b. Libel refers to written publications while slander includes spoken communication like television and radio;
   c. Proof of special damages are required in cases of slander;
   d. All of the above are correct.

5. A person may be liable for trespass:
   a. If he puts or places something on the land of another;
   b. If he stays on the property of another after permission to do so has been denied by the owner;
   c. Both of the above are correct.
   d. None of the above are correct.

6. A falsely tells B's customers that B's goods are worthless and that they should break their sales contracts with B. A's actions could be:
   a. disparagement.
   b. interference with contractual relations.
   c. interference with economic expectations.
   d. All of the above.

7. The National Hairball, a tabloid sold at supermarket checkout counters, publishes a story stating that Frank Sinatra has AIDS. Sinatra does not really have this disease. If Sinatra sues the Hairball for defamation:
   a. he will lose unless he can prove actual damages.
   b. he will be required to prove actual malice on the Hairball's part.
   c. he will lose if only 10 copies of the Hairball were sold.
   d. the Hairball would be liable for defamation even if the story were true.

8. The tort of false imprisonment:
    a. can occur even if the confinement is only partial.
    b. does not apply where the confinement is for a few minutes only.
    c. applies even where the defendant is unaware that he is being confined.
    d. does not apply if the plaintiff has consented to the confinement.

9. Fatcat Oil Corporation mistakenly drills at the wrong angle and its oil well begins pumping oil which is actually contained in land owned by its neighbor, the Slick Oil Company. Which is a false statement abut Fatcat's liability?
    a. Slick can recover under a trespass to land theory.
    b. Fatcat is liable for conversion.
    c. Slick can recover the reasonable value of the oil from Fatcat.
    d. Slick cannot recover under a trespass to land theory because Fatcat made an honest mistake.

10. Statutes giving merchants a conditional privilege to stop persons suspected of shoplifting:
    a. do not protect merchants who stop and search customers on a random basis.
    b. are probably redundant, since the common law gave merchants a similar privilege.
    c. will not protect merchants from tort liability if the search reveals that the customer is innocent of any wrongdoing.
    d. protect merchants from liability for negligence, but not from liability for intentional torts.

Short Essay

1. Shirley, enraged by her grade on a business law exam, throws a punch at her professor. Her professor ducks, and she unintentionally strikes Pinky, another student who was standing behind the professor and who never saw the punch coming. Shirley may be liable to whom for what torts? Explain.

2. At a small dinner party, Bert Blabbermouth, a college professor, tells his guests that Navin Nerdly, an obscure professor of folklore, is having a homosexual affair with a student. Nerdly hears about the story and, despite the fact that his job and general reputation are in little danger, sues Bert for defamation and invasion of privacy. Assuming the story is true, discuss Nerdly's chances of recovery under each theory.

3. X is sound asleep in his first floor dorm room with the window open. Y decides to play a practical joke on X and locks the bedroom door, but changes his mind ten seconds later and unlocks the door. Later Y confesses to X, who gets mad and sues Y for false imprisonment. Give three reasons why Y is not liable for false imprisonment.

4. Bob borrowed his roommate's bike (with his roommate's permission.) Bob needed money for tuition so he sold the bike to another friend, Fred, who did not know the car belonged to Bob's roommate. When his roommate discovered what Bob had done he was furious and demanded $1000 for the bike, which is twice the value of the bike. Is Bob required to pay? Discuss.

CHAPTER 6
NEGLIGENCE AND STRICT LIABILITY

Outline

I. Negligence: Unintentional breach of duty resulting in harm to another

A. Standard of reasonableness is flexible, but objective, standard.

Example: <u>Eimann v. Soldier of Fortune Magazine</u>. @D = In the blank provided, put "T" if the statement is True or "F" if the statement is FalseCourt held that magazine was not liable to. plaintiff under negligence for running an advertisement resulting in a man hiring another to kill his wife.

B. Negligence <u>per se</u> results when a defendant breaches a statutory duty, and the harm the statute was designed to prevent occurs to one the statute was designed to protect.

Example: <u>Ford v. Gouin</u>. Court held that a defendant was not negligent per se for driving a boat too close to a riverbank because the plaintiff was not within the class of persons the statute was designed to protect.

C. Plaintiff must prove breach of duty, causation in fact, and proximate cause.

1. Proximate cause generally requires that the harm occurring to plaintiff was foreseeable. *Example:* <u>Exxon Corporation v. Tidwell</u>, where service station was liable for harm caused to plaintiff by the criminal conduct of a third party.

2. <u>Res Ipsa Loquitur</u> is a doctrine creating an inference of negligence. *Example:* <u>Clark v. Norris</u>, holding this doctrine did not apply.

II. Injury to Plaintiff: Negligent Infliction of Mental Distress

Courts are increasingly permitting parties to recover for emotional distress resulting from witnessing harm to another. *Example:* <u>Quesada v. Oak Hill Improvement Company</u>

III. Defenses to Negligence:

A. Contributory negligence (abolished in most states) in favor of Comparative negligence

B. Assumption of the Risk: Requires proof that plaintiff voluntarily assumed a known risk. *Example:* <u>Exxon Corporation v. Tidwell</u>, holding service station employee did not voluntarily assume the risk of danger of assault by a third party.

IV. Strict Liability

A. Traditionally, strict liability imposed for abnormally dangerous or ultrahazardous activities.

Example: <u>Klein v. Pyrodyne Corporation</u>, holding that conducting fireworks display is an abnormally dangerous activity for which a defendant may be held strictly liable (liability without fault.)

Learning Objectives

1. You should know the elements of a negligence action.

2. You should know the factors which must be considered when the "reasonable person" standard is used in a negligence case.

3. You should understand the elements of the doctrines of negligence <u>per se</u> and <u>res ipsa loquitur</u> and when each doctrine is used.

4. You should understand the problem for which the concept of "proximate cause" was developed, and the various definitions of proximate cause used by the courts.

5. You should understand the operation of the defenses of contributory negligence and assumption of risk.

6. You should know the two types of comparative negligence (pure and mixed) and how comparative negligence differs generally from contributory negligence.

7. You should understand the difference between intentional infliction of emotional distress and negligent infliction of emotional distress.

8. You should understand strict liability, when it is applied, and the effect it has upon the defenses of contributory negligence and assumption of risk.

9. You should distinguish negligence from intentional torts, and distinguish the tests of causation used in each instance.

Learning Hints

1. Negligence is a fact-sensitive determination requiring a judge or jury to balance considerations of what is a reasonable act under a particular circumstance. For example, a person may drive a reasonable speed on a bright clear sunny day, but driving that same speed may be unreasonable at night during a blinding snowstorm.

2. Negligence is tested by an objective standard which examines the defendant's behavior—not by a subjective standard which examines the defendant's mental state. The behavior required for negligence is the failure to act as a reasonable person would have acted in the circumstances.

3. The reasonable person standard is very flexible, and this flexibility is necessary because of the variety of situations to which negligence must be applied. Among the factors which are considered under the reasonable person standard are the reasonable foreseeability of the harm resulting from the defendant's behavior, the likely severity of this reasonably foreseeable harm, the social utility of the defendant's conduct, and the ease or difficulty of avoiding the risk of harm associated with the defendant's conduct. For example, negligence might not be present if the harm is too unforeseeable or too trivial, if the defendant's activity is extremely valuable to society, or if there was little that the defendant could have done to avoid the risk of harm.

4. Negligence per se is an alternative way of establishing breach of duty. It requires proof of three things: violation of a statute; a plaintiff who suffers harm of a sort the statute was intended to prevent; and a plaintiff who is within the class of persons intended to be protected by the statute. Of course, it is sometimes difficult to ascertain the intent of the legislature with regard to the second and third elements of proof.

5. Causation in a negligence case has two separate elements. One is causation in fact, where the court asks if the injury to the plaintiff would have occurred without the defendant's breach of duty. If the answer is "yes," the test is not met and the defendant is not liable. Assuming that the answer is "no" and causation in fact exists, the next question is whether the injury to the plaintiff is too remote for the defendant to fairly be held liable. This is the problem of proximate causation. Most American courts use some test of reasonable foreseeability as the test for proximate cause.

6. The test of proximate cause, unlike the test of cause in fact, is a question of law for a judge. Consequently, a court may determine that an intervening cause (for example, an assault by a third party against the plaintiff) was not the proximate or legal cause of the injury to the plaintiff, even though it was the cause in fact of his injuries.

7. Like negligence, contributory negligence is also an objective standard of behavior, which asks roughly what the reasonably self-protective person would have done to prevent harm to himself in the situation.

8. Assumption of risk is the knowing and voluntary acceptance of a risk of harm to oneself. Unlike contributory negligence, it is tested by a subjective standard of what the plaintiff actually knew and intended.

9. Strict liability is "liability without fault" in the sense that it imposes liability on the defendant regardless of his intent, recklessness, or negligence. This does not mean, however, that strict liability is automatic liability, for there must be a determination that the innocent defendant should bear this risk of harm rather than the innocent plaintiff who has been injured.

10. In some states, contributory negligence or comparative negligence is not a defense to strict liability. However, assumption of the risk may be a defense in such cases, or may be treated as a factor in a comparative fault analysis.

True-False

In the blank provided, put "T" if the statement is True or "F" if the statement is False.

_____ 1. Negligence requires proof that the defendant acted intentionally in causing harm to the plaintiff.

_____ 2. Most states have abandoned contributory negligence in favor of a comparative fault standard in negligence cases.

_____ 3. Cause in fact requires the plaintiff to prove that "but for" the negligence of the defendant, the harm that occurred to plaintiff would not have occurred.

_____ 4. If a defendant engages in an ultrahazardous activity, he may be liable to plaintiff for harm occurring as a result of that activity, even if the defendant was not negligent in conducting the activity.

_____ 5. Res Ipsa Loquitur is a legal test used to determine whether a particular activity is ultra-hazardous or abnormally dangerous.

_____ 6. In a negligence per se case, the plaintiff must be within the class of persons the statute is intended to protect.

_____ 7. In negligence cases, the defendant is liable for all consequences of his negligence, no matter how bizarre or remote.

_____ 8. A foreseeable intervening force will not excuse the defendant from liability.

_____ 9. Where the defendant has been reckless, assumption of risk will not be a good defense.

_____ 10. A relationship between the parties can impose a duty of care on one of them not to injure the other.

_____ 11. "Last clear chance" is a doctrine whereby the plaintiff can escape the defense of contributory negligence by showing that the accident could have been avoided if the defendant had exercised reasonable care to prevent it after the plaintiff put himself in danger.

_____ 12. Strict liability for ultrahazardous activities is only imposed where the defendant acted recklessly.

Multiple Choice

Circle the best answer.

1. Which of the following relationships may impose a special duty on a defendant with regard to a plaintiff that might not otherwise exist?
   a. landlord/tenant;
   b. common carrier and passenger;
   c. innkeeper and customer;
   d. all of the above;
   e. none of the above.

2. The general test of proximate cause is:
   a. res ipsa loquitur;
   b. "but for" test;
   c. foreseeability
   d. "last clear chance."

3. A defense requiring proof that the plaintiff voluntary engaged in an activity he knew to be dangerous:
   a. is called "assumption of the risk";
   b. is called "contributory negligence";
   c. has been abolished in most states today;
   d. Both (a) and (c) are correct.

4. Strict liability for ultrahazardous activities:
   a. Requires proof that defendant failed to act as a reasonable person;
   b. Requires proof that plaintiff undertook a known risk;
   c. Is unconstitutional;
   d. None of the above is correct.

5. When a defendant's behavior indicates a "conscious disregard for a known high degree of probable harm to another," and a plaintiff is injured as a result, the plaintiff may recover damages under which of the following theories?
   a. Recklessness;
   b. Negligence;
   c. Negligence per se;
   d. Res Ipsa Loquitur.

6. Nebbish is walking down the street and is struck on the head by a 100-pound bag of limestone which falls from an open second story window of a building owned by Bloated Corporation. All of the evidence about the accident is in Bloated's control and all of its employees testify that they have no idea why the bag fell out of the window. Nebbish's best strategy would be:
   a. to try to directly prove that Bloated was negligent.
   b. to use the doctrine of negligence <u>per se</u>.
   c. to use the doctrine of <u>res ipsa loquitur</u>.
   d. to sue Bloated's employees instead of Bloated Corporation.

7. On a windy day and in the middle of a drought, A decides to burn leaves. The wind picks up a burning leaf, carries it half a mile, and deposits it on a puddle of gasoline. The gas ignites, causing a fire which spreads to B's house a mile away. B sues A in negligence. B will have trouble proving:
   a. proximate cause.
   b. causation in fact.
   c. breach of duty.
   d. actual injury.

8. Which is a true statement about negligent infliction of mental distress?
   a. A plaintiff must prove that the defendant's conduct was outrageous in order to recover.
   b. No court will permit recovery by a plaintiff who cannot prove an impact with his person.
   c. Courts are increasingly allowing third parties to recover for emotional distress resulting from witnessing harm caused to another person by the defendant's negligent acts.
   d. All courts require that this emotional distress result in physical symptoms or injury.

9. Del was driving toward a busy intersection when he momentarily bent over to adjust the radio in his truck. He ran a red light and hit another car, which hit a utility pole and knocked out electricity to all homes and businesses in a 3-mile radius. Electrical service was not restored for 48 hours due to a strike by utility company linemen. Susie Homemaker sues Del because all of the food in her refrigerator spoiled due to the power outage. What result?
   a. Del will be liable to Susie because a person is liable for all consequences of his negligence.
   b. Del will not be liable to Susie because he did not actually foresee that it was dangerous to look away from the intersection.
   c. Del will be liable to Susie because he could have foreseen that his inattention would cause her food to spoil.
   d. Del will not be liable to Susie because his conduct was not the proximate cause of her damages.

10. Which of the following statements concerning the standard of a "reasonable person" is <u>not</u> correct?
    a. The reasonable person standard is a flexible one, allowing consideration of all the circumstances surrounding a particular accident;
    b. The reasonable person standard is an objective standard;
    c. The reasonable person standard is a subjective one, and is based on what a particular defendant actually believed to be reasonable under the circumstances;
    d. Whether a person owes a particular duty to another may depend on the special relationship between the parties.

Short Essay

1. Assume that there was an ordinance in Smallville requiring all residents to shovel snow from the sidewalk in front of their property. Jake failed to shovel snow and his neighbor, 90 year old Mr. Peepers, was injured when he slipped and fell on the sidewalk. Under these circumstances, Peepers should be able to establish duty and breach of duty under what theory? What must he prove?

2. Assume the facts above. What two elements of <u>causation</u> must Peeper establish in order to recover damages from Jake? What must he prove to be successful?

3. X is driving at 90 miles per hour on a narrow, curving road in the rain. Without looking, Y walks across the road directly into X's path and is struck by X's car. Y sues X for negligence. Assuming that X's behavior was a breach of duty, what defense should X allege against Y? What doctrine might Y use to overcome this defense? What would you have to know in order to determine if this doctrine will wipe out X's defense?

4. What is the difference between the "cause in fact" and the "proximate cause" of an injury?

5. State X passes a statute banning the sale of ZAP, a new and powerful elephant tranquilizer which has become very popular among druggies of all ages. Repeated use of ZAP destroys brain cells and reduces its users to vegetables, which is why State X has banned its sale. Dave Dealer sells some ZAP to Steve Simple, an accountant. Steve goes to work after taking a few hits of Dave's ZAP and becomes so disoriented that he is unable to work. Due to his ZAPPED-out mental state, Steve causes his employer to lose several thousand dollars. The employer discovers the source of Steve's problems and sues Dave for its losses under the doctrine of negligence per se. If you were Dave's lawyer, what would you argue to convince a judge that Dave is not liable to Steve's employer under the doctrine of negligence per se?

CHAPTER 7
THE NATURE AND ORIGINS OF CONTRACTS

Outline

I. What is a Contract? A legally enforceable promise

   A. Elements: agreement supported by consideration, voluntarily entered into by parties with capacity, for a legal purpose

   B. Development of contract law: The law has evolved from a free-market theory to a developing concept of protecting consumers and workers

II. The Uniform Commercial Code (UCC) governs contracts for the sale of goods.

   Example: Gall v. Allegheny County Health Department: The UCC's implied warranty of merchantability applies to water because water is a "good".

III. Types of Contracts

   A. Valid contract meets the legal requirements for a contract.

   B. Unenforceable contracts meet legal requirements but will not be enforced by a court.

   C. Voidable contract may be canceled by one or both parties.

   D. Unilateral contract is a contract with only one promise by one party (for example, an offer for a reward); a Bilateral contract consists of promises by both parties.

   E. A contract or contract term may be express or implied.

IV. Equitable concepts important to contract law

   A. Quasi-contract: A contract implied in law to avoid unjust enrichment by one party at the expense of another.

      Example: Darling v. Standard Alaska Production Co., enumerating the three elements required for quasi-contract.

   B. Promissory Estoppel: a doctrine permitting a plaintiff to recover reliance damages from a defendant who makes a promise that he knows will induce reliance, in cases where the plaintiff actually and reasonably relies on the promise to his detriment.

      Example: Bellios v. Victor Balata Belting Co., holding that a promise of employment can result in an award of damages under the theory of promissory estoppel, even in the case of an employment at will contract.

Learning Objectives

1. You should understand the evolution of contract theory from a laissez faire perspective to a consumer-protection perspective.

2. You should be able to identify the elements of a contract.

3. You should understand the requirement of an agreement, and the necessity of a "meeting of the minds," in order to create a valid contract.

4. You must know the difference between bilateral and unilateral contracts.

5. You must know the difference between void and voidable contracts.

6. You must know the difference between express and implied contracts.

7. You must know the difference between executed and executory contracts.

8. You must be familiar with quasi-contract, and the difference between a contract implied in law and one implied in fact.

9. You must be familiar with promissory estoppel and, as your study of contracts proceeds, with the situations where promissory estoppel can substitute for some required element of a contract.

10. You should understand the significance of the Uniform Commercial Code and the circumstances in which it applies.

Learning Hints

1. Probably the most important social factor underlying the change from nineteenth century contract law to twentieth century contract law was the rise of the large private group, mainly the corporation. This development produced countless disparities of bargaining power and resulting injustices when such groups contracted with individuals or smaller groups. The response to this was government intervention, often to set the terms of the contract in order to protect the weaker party to the contract.

2. One of the most significant changes in modern contract law has been the adoption of the Uniform Commercial Code, which is in effect in all states but Louisiana. This Code changes the common law rules in some important respects.

3. The Uniform Commercial Code (UCC) applies to any contract for the sale of goods. It is <u>not</u> limited to contracts where the parties are merchants.

4. An unenforceable contract cannot serve as the basis for a lawsuit by either party to the contract because it cannot be enforced. However, it is technically still a contract, even though unenforceable, and may be valid for other purposes. For example, the fact that a contract is unenforceable will not block a suit for intentional interference with contractual relations (Chapter 3) because technically a contract exists, though it be unenforceable, and can be interfered with.

5. Among the things that might happen when a contract is voidable are that the party with the power to avoid the contract (such as a party who has been defrauded) may choose to go ahead and perform the contract and bind the other party to the contract; the party with the power to avoid the contract may refuse to perform the contract and assert a defense if sued by the other party to the contract; the party with the power to avoid the contract may choose to rescind if the contract is executed; i.e., has already been performed. Rescission is a remedy whereby the court effectively cancels the transaction and restores each party to his pre-contract position.

6. It is sometimes said that the term "void contract" is a contradiction in terms because such an agreement is not a contract at all.

7. Perhaps the most important feature of an express contract is that the parties have stated its terms <u>in words</u>, either oral or written.

8. Note that technically a contract is executed only when all parties have fully performed.

9. Quasi-contract is a strange legal fiction which is applied in a variety of different situations. All of the situations involve the idea of <u>unjust enrichment</u>, because they all involve a benefit conferred on the defendant by the plaintiff (the enrichment), with the defendant's knowledge at the time the benefit was conferred, under circumstances where it would be unjust for the defendant not to pay the plaintiff for the benefit.

10. Under Article 2 of the Uniform Commercial Code, "goods" are moveable, tangible objects. In every contract problem, you must first ask yourself whether the contract is one for the sale of goods or not. If it does involve the sale of goods, the UCC rule will apply (if there is one that covers the situation). If the contract is not for the sale of goods, or it is for the sale of goods but no UCC rule covers the situation, common law contract rules will apply instead. As you will see in the later contracts chapters, common law contract rules and UCC rules are sometimes very different.

True-False

In the blank provided, put "T" if the statement is True or "F" if the statement is False.

_____ 1. An enforceable contract may exist even without proof that the parties intended to create a contract or even reached an agreement.

_____ 2. A contract which has not been voluntarily entered into may not be enforceable.

_____ 3. Today, because a large number of agreements are based on form contracts, courts are more likely to protect consumers who may not understand technical "fine print" language in standardized contract forms.

_____ 4. The Uniform Commercial Code only applies in cases where both parties are merchants.

_____ 5. Under the doctrine of promissory estoppel, a person may recover damages for relying on a promise that might be unenforceable under traditional contract law.

_____ 6. A unilateral contract involves the exchange of a promise for a promise.

_____ 7. Quasi-contract applies even when the party being enriched is not aware of the enrichment at the time it is received.

_____ 8. An unenforceable contract lacks the basic elements necessary for a contract.

_____ 9. A contract is void if one of the contracting parties can avoid it.

_____ 10. Courts treat contracts as bilateral rather than unilateral whenever it is possible to do so.

Multiple Choice

Circle the best answer.

1. Which of the following statements concerning the Uniform Commercial Code is correct?
    a. Only a minority of states today have adopted the UCC;
    b. The UCC only applies to contracts for the sale of goods between merchants;
    c. The UCC avoids the problem of promoting higher standards of fair dealing by only imposing a duty of good faith on contracts between merchants.
    d. None of the above is correct.

2. A voidable contract:
    a. Is not enforceable by either party;
    b. May be enforceable by one party;
    c. Is an illegal contract;
    d. None of the above is correct.

3. When all parties have performed their duties under a contract, the contract is:
    a. executory;
    b. voidable;
    c. executed;
    d. void.

4. Mike went to his dentist for treatment. Neither party discussed the payment terms. Later, Mike's dentist sent him a bill for dental services. Mike is obligated to pay the dentist's bill under which of the following theories?
    a. quasi-contract;
    b. promissory estoppel;
    c. contract implied in fact;
    d. contract implied in law.

5. A person who is unjustly enriched at the expense of the other party may be obligated to pay the reasonable value of the goods or services he received under which of the following theories?
    a. quasi-contract;
    b. promissory estoppel;
    c. contract implied in fact;
    d. none of the above.

6. Mrs. Smith promises to pay Johnny $10 if he will mow her lawn next Saturday. This is a(n):
    a. bilateral contract.
    b. unilateral contract.
    c. executed contract.
    d. implied contract.

7. Which of the following contracts will be governed by Article 2 of the UCC?
    a. A sale of stock on the stock exchange
    b. The construction of a house by a professional builder
    c. A sale of ball bearings
    d. A sale of an acre of land

8. Promissory estoppel generally applies where a party:
   a. has been unjustly enriched.
   b. has inferior bargaining power.
   c. is a merchant.
   d. relies in a significant and foreseeable way on a promise.

9. The Restatement (Second) of Contracts:
   a. was a major influence on the drafters of the U.C.C.
   b. bears the strong imprint of common law contract principles.
   c. has been adopted by the legislatures of most states.
   d. does not have the force of law.

10. Rho Alpha Tau Sigma fraternity ordered 100 Halloween masks from Costume Delights. Costume Delights acknowledged the order and agreed to fill it. Costume Delights delivered the masks, but the RATS have not paid for them yet. The contract between Costume Delights and the RATS is:
    a. unilateral, valid, and executory.
    b. bilateral, express, and executory.
    c. bilateral, implied, and executed.
    d. bilateral, express, and executed.

Short Essay

1. Ralph's Roofing entered into a contract with Frank Folz to put a new roof on Frank's house at 711 South Maple Street for the unreasonable sum of $3,750. By mistake, Ralph's workmen replaced the roof on George Gump's house at 811 South Maple Street. Gump knew that Ralph's men were making a mistake, but said nothing because he needed a new roof. If Ralph's sues Gump for the sum of $3,750, what result and why?

2. Assume the facts above. Assume, however, that Gump was on vacation in Florida when the workman arrived and replaced the room on his house. Might this change your answer? Why or why not?

3. Marlon Shadd told Tomontra Mangrum that he would take her to his high-school prom. As a result, Tomontra's mother bought Tomontra a new dress, purse, and shoes. However, on the appointed night, Shadd did not show up. Tomontra's mother wants to sue Shadd to recover the money she spent on prom preparations. Under what theory can she recover?

4. What is the important legal difference between a void contract and a voidable contract?

CHAPTER 8
CREATING A CONTRACT: OFFERS

Outline

I. An agreement, or "meeting of the minds" may be defined as an Offer + Acceptance.

II. What is an Offer? An offer is the manifestation of a willingness to enter into a contract.

    A. Requires a present intent to offer, which is definite, and is communicated to the offeree.

    Example: Saunder v. Baryshnikov, holding that a promise which is too indefinite or vague to establish material details of the agreement will not be enforceable.

III. Special Problems

    A. Advertisements: Are generally not treated as offers.

    B. Rewards: Offer for a reward is an offer for a unilateral contract.

    C. Auctions: Generally an auction is a request for bids

IV. What terms are included?

    A. If the offeree read the terms or a reasonable person should have notice, the offeree is bound.

    Example: Izadi v. Machado (Gus) Ford, Inc.. The fine print in part of an advertised offer is not enforceable, especially where submicroscopic print is contradictory to other language in the offer.

V. Termination of the Offer

    A. By its terms. *Example:* Newman v. Schiff

    B. Lapse of reasonable time, revocation prior to acceptance.

        1. Exception: Option contracts which require new consideration

        2. Exception: Estoppel

    C. Unilateral Contract offers: Cannot be revoked if the offeree has begun performance.

    D. Revocation: Must be received to be effective.

    Example: Madaio v. McCarthy, holding that an offer may be revoked until accepted

    E. Rejection by the Offeree terminates the Offer

    Example: Estate of Chosnyka v. Meyer

    F. Death or Insanity of either party; destruction of subject matter; intervening illegality also terminate offers.

Learning Objectives

    1. You should understand the meaning of an offer, offeror, and offeree, and the requirements for an effective offer: intent, definiteness, and communication to the offeree.

    2. You should understand how courts use offer and acceptance to define an agreement and "meeting of the minds."

    3. You should learn how courts judge whether a person intended to enter an contract.

    4. You should know what factors the courts consider when deciding whether a given term was included in the offer (and therefore in the contract).

    5. You should know the different actions which terminate an offer.

    6. You should know the exceptions to the general rule that the offeror can revoke his offer at any time before it is accepted by the offeree.

    7. You should know the meaning of the term "estoppel" and how it relates to the resolution of problems concerning offers.

    8. You should know the rules governing when the offeror may revoke an offer for a unilateral contract.

    9. You should understand the difference between an acceptance and counter-offer.

Learning Hints

1. "Offer" and "acceptance" are words used by courts to describe a factual situation requiring proof of a statement indicating a present intent to enter into a contract.

2. In order to determine whether there is a legally effective offer, courts must determine the intention of the offeror. This intention, however, is determined by using an objective, rather than subjective, test. Thus, if a reasonable person would believe that an offeror had indicated a present willingness to enter into a bargain, the court may determine that an offer was made, even though the offeror denies any such intention.

3. Keep in mind that the words "offer" and "acceptance" used in contract law have special technical, legal meanings that may be different from the way these words are used in everyday speech. For example, advertisements often use the word "offer," but we have seen that advertisements are generally presumed not to be offers.

4. When you make an offer to another person, you give that person the power to legally bind you to a contract obligation merely by accepting your offer. For this reason, courts will not imply an offer lightly.

5. There are three elements of an offer: an objective manifestation of a present intent to contract, the use of reasonably definite terms, and the communication of the offer to the offeree.

6. Advertisements are generally presumed not to be legally binding offers, even if the advertiser uses the word "offer." This means that the person who reads the advertisement cannot bind the advertiser merely by appearing and saying "I accept." The person who reads the ad is treated as the offeror, not as an offeree.

7. One of the exceptions to the general rule that the offeror can revoke any time before acceptance is the situation when parties have entered an option contract. An option contract is an agreement in which the offeree has paid the offeror something to keep the offer open for a certain period of time. During that period of time, the offeror cannot revoke. If the offeree decides to accept the offer during that period of time, the offeror must go through with the deal. However, the offeree has no obligation to accept during the duration of the option.

8. A request for bids is treated as a request for offers. Bids are generally treated as offers, which the other party may accept or reject. However, this rule may be changed by statute. For example, many states have statutes prescribing the manner and effect of bids made by governmental units.

True-False

In the blank provided, put "T" if the statement is True or "F" if the statement is False.

_____ 1. The person who makes an offer is called the offeree.

_____ 2. In order to determine intention to make an offer, courts used a test of subjective intent.

_____ 3. Under common law, and offer which is indefinite as to one or more material terms is still enforceable if the parties intended to contract.

_____ 4. An acceptance which changes a material term of the offer is treated as a counter-offer and constitutes a new offer.

_____ 5. In general, an advertisement is not an offer but a request for an offer.

_____ 6. As a general rule, offerors have the power to revoke their offers at any time prior to acceptance.

_____ 7. Advertisements of merchandise to the public can be offers to sell if the terms are very specific and the ad requires some extraordinary act to accept.

_____ 8. Grumbling acceptances and inquiries are interpreted as rejections, and under common law contract rules, they terminate offers.

_____ 9. A makes an offer to B to enter a contract. Before B can accept, a statute is enacted which makes the contract illegal. A's offer is terminated.

_____ 10. An advertisement of a reward is an example of an offer for a unilateral contract.

Multiple Choice

Circle the best answer.

1. Which of the following does not terminate an offer?
   a. Death or insanity of the offeror;
   b. Death or insanity of the offeree;
   c. Rejection by the offeree;
   d. All of the above terminate an offer.

2. Bob offered to sell Bill his (Bob's) pedigreed poodle. After Bill accepted the offer, Bob argued that he had not really intended to sell, and therefore was not bound by contract. Which of the following statements concerning Bob's offer is correct?
   a. Unless Bob actually, subjectively, intended to sell, there is no contract.
   b. Whether Bob made an offer will depend on an objective test—if a reasonable person in Bill's position would believe an offer had been made, there is a contract.
   c. Under common law rule, even if Bob's offer were indefinite as to all material terms, there is a still a contract if Bill intended to accept the offer.
   d. None of the above statements is correct.

3. An advertisement for an auction "without reserve," means:
   a. The seller is required to accept the final offer—the highest bid;
   b. The seller is not required to accept the final offer—the highest bid;
   c. The seller may withdraw the item from auction even after hammering down the sale;
   d. The buyer may revoke his acceptance at any time prior to paying for the goods.

4. If an offeror stipulates in his offer the time the offer terminates:
   a. The stipulation is not enforceable unless reasonable;
   b. The stipulation is not enforceable if it exceeds three months;
   c. The stipulation is not enforceable unless both parties agree;
   d. The stipulation is enforceable because the offeror is the "master of the offer."

5. An offer for a reward is an offer for:
   a. A bilateral contract;
   b. a unilateral contract;
   c. a voidable contract;
   d. an auction.

6. Ace was considering selling his 1964 Buick to Wilbur for $400. Ace told Bart of his plan. Without Ace's knowledge or consent, Bart immediately went to Wilbur and told Wilbur that Ace was planning to offer his car to Wilbur. Wilbur then telephoned Ace and said "I accept." What result?
   a. Wilbur and Ace have a contract because Wilbur accepted Ace's offer.
   b. Wilbur and Ace have a contract under the doctrine of promissory estoppel.
   c. Wilbur and Ace do not have a contract because Ace did not communicate his offer to Wilbur.
   d. Wilbur and Ace do not have a contract, but Bart and Wilbur do.

7. Alfred wrote Bob a letter, offering to sell him three parcels of land at $20,000 each if he bought all three at once. Bob answered in a return letter that he would buy only two parcels of the land for $15,000 each, and that he wanted Alfred to fence the land. What result?
   a. There is a contract to buy two parcels of land at $15,000, and Alfred must fence the land.
   b. There is a contract to buy two parcels of land at $15,000, but Alfred does not have to build a fence.
   c. Bob has rejected Alfred's offer.
   d. There is a contract, and Alfred can sue Bob for an additional $10,000.

8. In the fall of 1981, Farmer Hicks wrote to City Slicker, a food wholesaler, and offered to sell Slicker his entire crop of persimmons for $500. Slicker did not reply, and Hicks did not contact him again. In the fall of 1982, however, persimmons were scarce, and Slicker wrote Hicks, "I hereby accept your offer."
   a. There is a contract because Hicks never said how long his offer would remain open and never revoked his offer before Slicker accepted it.
   b. There is a contract if Slicker subjectively intends to contract.
   c. There is no contract because Hicks' offer was terminated by the passage of a reasonable time before Slicker accepted it.
   d. There is no contract to sell Slicker the entire crop for $500, but Hicks must sell Slicker persimmons at the new market price.

9. Paul Promoter offers a prize of $3,000 to the winner of the Macho Marathon. Halfway through the race, Paul posts himself along the side of the road with a sign saying "I revoke the offer of a prize—stop at once!" Phil Phleet presses on to the end anyway, comes in first, and sues for the prize money. What result?
   a. Paul has the right to revoke his offer at any time prior to acceptance by full performance.
   b. Where performance takes time to complete, courts will generally declare the offer to be irrevocable until a reasonable time for completion has passed. Therefore, Paul is contractually obligated to pay Phil the prize.
   c. Phil did not accept Paul's offer before beginning to perform, so no valid contract ever existed.
   d. Phil can only recover if he can prove he did not see or understand Paul's sign.

10. State University approaches Professor MBA and tells him that if he will move to Stateville, the University will hire him. MBA quits his tenured position at the University of Chicago, moves himself and his family to Stateville, and sells their Chicago home. Just before the semester is to begin, State University refuses to hire MBA. MBA sues. What result?
   a. MBA can force State to hire him because they both made binding promises and therefore entered a bilateral contract.
   b. MBA can recover from State under a quasi-contract theory.
   c. MBA can force State to hold open its offer for a reasonable time.
   d. MBA may be able to recover the damages he incurred under a promissory estoppel theory if his reliance on State was reasonable.

Short Essay

1. Jeremy ran an advertisement in the local newspaper as follows: "Lost Cat—Reward! I will pay $20.00 to anyone who finds my lost cat Ralphie, a large tiger-striped yellow cat with a collar. Call 333-3333 and leave message." One week later, Buffy found Ralphie and returned him to Jeremy. Jeremy, however, refuses to pay. Is he required to do so? Why?

2. Fly-By-Night Contractors, a general construction company, wanted to obtain a contract to build the new Chemistry Building at Easy University. It obtained a subcontract bid of $150,000 for the plumbing work from Sludge Plumbing Company. Fly-By-Night used this bid in calculating its own bid for the general contract. Fly-By-Night had the lowest bid and won the general contract. Sludge now wants to back out of its bid, saying it cannot perform for less than $170,000. What is Fly-By-Night's best argument that Sludge should not be able to withdraw its subcontract bid of $150,000?

3. John offered to sell his house to Mary, but before Mary could accept, John's house burned down. What is the legal status of John's offer? Why?

CHAPTER 9
CREATING A CONTRACT: ACCEPTANCES

Outline

I. What is an Acceptance? An acceptance is an expression of present willingness to enter into a bargain based on the terms of an offer.

A. Requires present intent to contract and may be express or implied.

B. The UCC adopts a rule that changes the common law rule that an acceptance must "mirror the terms" of the offer.

Example: Egan Machinery Co. v. Mobil Chemical Co.. This case is an example of application of the UCC "battle of the forms" provision.

C. Acceptance of Unilateral Contract Offers: The offeree must perform the requested act or make the requested promise.

Example: First Texas Savings & Loan Association v. Jergins

D. In general, silence does not constitute acceptance; however, previous dealing by the parties or trade custom may change this rule. *Example:* Fineman v. Citicorp USA, Inc., where the court held that Fineman's failure to respond to the notice to amend a credit agreement constituted acceptance.

E. Who Can Accept the Offer? Generally, only the original offeree

F. What if writing is anticipated: Whether or not an agreement exists prior to a written agreement is based on the intention of the parties. *Example:* Texaco Inc. v. Penzoil Co.

G. Communication of Acceptance: The offeror may stipulate terms of acceptance. *Example:* Reddick v. Globe Life and Accident Insurance Co., where Globe stipulated that it must receive payment by January 20th or insurance coverage lapsed.

H. Authorized Means of Communication

As a general rule, an acceptance is effective when dispatched if dispatched by authorized means. Under modern law, authorized means includes any reasonable means.

Learning Objectives

1. You should understand the significance of an effective acceptance in that an acceptance creates a contract and it is then too late for the offeror to revoke the offer.

2. You should understand that under common law, an acceptance which changed a material term of the offer constituted a counter-offer, which is treated as a new offer.

3. You should note that the UCC "battle of the forms" provision provides that a contract may be created, if the parties intend to contract, even though the terms of the acceptance do not mirror the terms of the offer.

4. You should know the requirements of a valid acceptance.

5. You should know how offers for unilateral contracts are accepted.

6. You should know how offers for bilateral contracts are accepted.

7. You should be aware of the fact that sometimes acceptance is created by the offeree's conduct rather than by his words.

8. You should know that silence is not generally considered to be acceptance; you should also know the exceptions to this rule.

9. You should know the rules about acceptance when the parties anticipate creating a written contract.

10. You should learn the general rules about the time at which acceptances by different means are considered to be communicated and therefore effective.

Learning Hints

1. The significance of an offer is that it creates the power of acceptance. A valid offer may be accepted by the words, "I accept," and therefore an agreement exists.

2. Once an offer has been accepted by an offeree, it is too late for the offeror to revoke his offer.

3. Once an offer has been accepted by an offeree, it is too late for the offeree to change his mind and reject the offer.

4. A counter-offer is a rejection of the terms of the original offer, and thus terminates the power of acceptance. A counter-offer is a new offer, creating the power of acceptance in the other party.

5. An offeree must show a present intent to contract in order to make a valid acceptance. This means that the offeree must show that he is serious and ready to enter into a binding contract on the offeror's terms. Like intent to make an offer, intent to accept an offer is judged by an objective standard. This standard becomes important in certain acceptance situations, such as where the parties have an oral agreement, anticipate that they will later put their agreement in writing, but never do so. In such cases, the court's resolution of the question whether a contract exists without the writing will depend on what the court determines, using the objective standard, about the parties' intent. If the parties act as if they intend to have a contract at the time at which they reach their oral agreement, the court will enforce this oral agreement—even when one of the parties later changes his mind and refuses to sign the written contract.

6. Even though a party's conduct, rather than his words, can constitute acceptance, failure to respond (usually in the form of silence) normally does not constitute acceptance. The general rule is that an offeror cannot unilaterally impose the duty to reply or be bound on an offeree. This means that a contract would not be created in a case where the offeror said, "I offer this to you at $5. If I don't hear from you in two days, we have a contract." There are several exceptions to this rule, however. Situations where a party's silence or failure to act does show acceptance include where the offeree has expressly agreed that his silence will be acceptance (as is the case with most book and record clubs), where the past dealings of the parties or the custom in their business is such that failure to object signals acceptance, or where one person allows another to perform some service without objection, knowing that payment is expected for the service.

7. Remember that the offeror is the "master of the contract," meaning that he may propose whatever contract terms he desires, no matter how unreasonable. To make a valid acceptance, the offeree must accept all of the offeror's terms exactly as they are stated in the offer. In addition, the offeree must satisfy any stipulations the offeror has put in the offer about the method and time of acceptance (as when the offer states "You must respond by registered letter," or "You must accept by noon on September 20").

8. There are three elements in a legally valid acceptance: intent to contract, communication of the acceptance, and agreement to the offeror's terms as set forth in the offer. The question of when an acceptance is communicated and therefore effective is really a separate, and subsequent, issue. You must first show that the acceptance is characterized by the required intent, communication, and agreement to the offeror's terms. Only then do you ask when the acceptance was communicated to the offeror and therefore effective.

9. If the offeree has used a method of communication that was expressly or impliedly authorized by the offeror, the acceptance is communicated and effective when it is sent (in legal terms, "dispatched"), not when it is received by the offeror. An "authorized" means of communication is a method which is either suggested by the offeror, used by the offeror in making the offer, or commonly used in the parties' trade or business. If the offeree uses a method of communication that was not authorized, the effectiveness of his acceptance will be delayed until it is actually received by the offeror.

10. You should be aware of the problems that sometimes arise when the parties deal at a distance or through any means of communication in which there is a time lag between dispatch of the acceptance by the offeree and receipt of the acceptance by the offeror. For instance, sometimes, an attempted revocation and an attempted acceptance cross in the mail. The offeror can protect himself against the chance that he will be bound to a contract before he receives the acceptance by clearly stating in his offer that acceptance is only effective when he actually receives it. The offeror may also wish to require that the acceptance by received by him on or before a certain date to be effective.

True-False

In the blank provided, put "T" if the statement is True or "F" if the statement is False.

_____ 1. In general, a party must have a present intent to contract in order to make a valid acceptance of an offer.

_____ 2. The UCC "battle of the forms" provision adopts the common law rule that an acceptance must mirror the terms of the offer.

_____ 3. To accept an offer to enter into a unilateral contract, the offeree must perform the requested act.

_____ 4. Generally, silence (failure to object) constitutes acceptance of an offer.

_____ 5. The only person with legal power to accept an offer is the original offeree or his/her agent.

_____ 6. As a general rule, acceptance is effective only when received by the offeror if the offeree has used an authorized means of communication.

_____ 7. An attempt to accept by someone other than the offeree is treated as an offer.

_____ 8. If the parties reach a verbal agreement with the understanding that they will later put their agreement into writing, a court may find that the verbal agreement is enforceable even if one of the parties later refuses to sign the writing.

_____ 9. If the offeree does not use the means of acceptance stipulated by the offeror, his acceptance will never be effective.

_____ 10. If the offeree has dispatched inconsistent responses to the offer by sending both a rejection and an acceptance, whichever response reaches the offeror first will determine whether a contract is created.

Multiple Choice

Circle the best answer.

1. Under common law, which of the following is not required for a valid acceptance?
   a. an offer by an offeror;
   b. a present intent to contract by the offeree;
   c. a writing setting forth the terms of the acceptance;
   d. all of the above are required.

2. Larry made an offer to Moe to sell Moe his (Larry's) car for $500. Larry said, "if you do not object within 10 days, we have a contract." Under these circumstances:
   a. Moe must reject the offer within 10 days or a contract is created;
   b. Moe must reject the offer within a reasonable period of time;
   c. Moe is generally under no duty to accept or reject the offer;
   d. Moe may not accept the offer.

3. In general, in order for there to be an enforceable contract, a writing is required:
   a. If the parties intended there would be no agreement unless the agreement was reduced to writing;
   b. If the parties are merchants;
   c. If the parties are non-merchants;
   d. None of the above is correct because a writing is not required.

4. If an offeror stipulates the manner of acceptance:
   a. an offeree may accept in the manner stipulated or may accept by any reasonable means;
   b. the offeree's acceptance is not effective until received regardless of the manner in which he accepts;
   c. the stipulation is only enforceable if reasonable;
   d. the offeree must accept in the manner stipulated in order to create a contract.

5. If an offeree accepts by non-authorized means:
   a. there is no contract;
   b. there is no contract until the acceptance is received;
   c. there is no contract until the acceptance is dispatched;
   d. there is no contract unless the parties are merchants.

6. Farmer Hicks had been selling part of his green bean crop to Frosty King Frozen Foods Co. for five years. Their usual course of dealing was for Hicks to deliver the green beans to Frosty King, which would inspect the beans and notify Hicks within a day or two if it did not want them. Otherwise, Frosty King would send Hicks a check for the beans at the end of the month. One day Hicks delivered green beans to Frosty King as usual. Frosty King kept the beans for a month and said nothing. Four weeks later, Frosty King notified Hicks that it did not want the beans. What result?
   a. Frosty King does not have to pay for the beans because silence is never acceptance.
   b. Because of the parties' prior dealings, Frosty King's failure to respond constituted acceptance, and a legally binding contract resulted.
   c. Frosty King does not have to pay for the beans because Hicks had no legal right to deliver them without Frosty King's prior approval.
   d. Frosty King does have to pay for the beans because silence is always acceptance.

7. Dixie offered to work for Hans as an accountant at a salary of $27,000 per year. Hans told Fred about Dixie's offer. Fred then called Dixie and said that he wanted to hire her to work for him.
   a. Dixie must now work for Fred instead of Hans.
   b. Fred's phone call to Dixie was an acceptance.
   c. Fred's phone call to Dixie was an offer.
   d. Dixie may not revoke her offer to Hans.

8. Seabrook negotiated an oral agreement with Vanderhorst. The two worked out all material terms of their agreement and shook hands on the deal, Vanderhorst stating that she would have her lawyer put the agreement in writing at her earliest opportunity. The next day, Vanderhorst's lawyer drafted a written contract which repeated the terms of the parties' oral agreement. Vanderhorst signed the written contract and sent it to Seabrook, but Seabrook refused to sign it, saying that she had decided to deal with someone else instead. Vanderhorst sues Seabrook for breach of contract. (Assume that this contract was not required by law to be in writing.) What result?
   a. Vanderhorst will win because the parties intended to form a contract at the moment they agreed on material terms and shook hands.
   b. There is no enforceable contract because the writing was never created.
   c. Seabrook will win because an offeror has the right to revoke his offer even after acceptance.
   d. None of the above is a correct statement of the likely result.

9. Nita sent a letter to Amber on November 9 in which she offered Amber a job as a secretary. Amber immediately sent a letter to Nita on November 9 accepting Nita's offer. Meanwhile, Nita had a change of heart and on November 10 sent Amber a letter stating that the job offer was revoked. Amber received Nita's letter on November 10, and Nita received Amber's letter on November 11. What result?
   a. There is no contract because Nita's revocation was sent before Amber's acceptance was received by Nita.
   b. Nita's revocation was ineffective because it was by an unauthorized means of communication.
   c. Since Nita did not stipulate a means of acceptance, Amber's letter was not authorized and no contract was formed.
   d. A contract between Nita and Amber was formed on November 9.

10. A offered to sell B a plot of land. The offer was complete and certain as to all material terms. The offer stated that a telegraphed acceptance was required. Within a reasonable time, B telephoned A to accept. Which of the following is a true statement?
   a. B has not accepted and there is no contract.
   b. B has accepted because a telephone call is a reasonable means of acceptance.
   c. B can use promissory estoppel to enforce a contract here.
   d. B can use quasi-contract to enforce a contract here.

Short Essay

1. Sam's Grocery began a contest eight weeks before Easter in which it promised a free ham if the customer purchased at least $10 worth of groceries each week of the eight week period. The record of purchases was recorded on a card provided by the grocery by a stamp. Three weeks after beginning the contest, Sam's canceled the contest because there were too few people participating to make it worth while. Mildred Fish had three stamps on her card when Sam's grocery canceled the contest. She thinks she's entitled to a canned ham. Is she right? Why or why not?

2. John wrote a letter to Arthur in which John offered to sell his farm to Arthur. John's letter was a legally sufficient offer, and was received by Arthur on October 26. Arthur wrote a letter of acceptance which he was getting ready to mail when he received a telegram from John stating that the offer was withdrawn. Arthur mailed his acceptance on October 26 anyway, and it was received by John on October 28. Is there a contract between John and Arthur?

3. Tom sent Mike a letter offering to sell his house to Mike at a very reasonable price. Mike showed the letter to John. John wrote Tom a letter saying that he, John, would buy the house at the price stated in the letter. Do Tom and John now have a contract? Why or why not?

4. When will an acceptance by the authorized means of communication not be effective on dispatch?
What is the reason for this exception to the general rule?

CHAPTER 10
CONSIDERATION

Outline

I. Consideration in General

  A. Under common law, a promise is generally unenforceable unless it was a bargain—requiring that a person has given up something in exchange for the promise.

  B. Consideration is defined as something of <u>legal value</u>: a promise (or an act) to do something a person has no legal duty to do, or a promise to refrain from doing something one has a legal right to do constitutes legal value.

  C. Generally, courts to do not inquire into the adequacy of consideration.

    Example: <u>Guinn v. Holcombe</u>, where court found lease agreement was supported by consideration, even though the consideration was not given directly to the person making the contractual promise.

II. Rules of Consideration

  A. Preexisting Duty: As a rule, performing or agreeing to perform a preexisting duty is not consideration, because it cannot constitute legal value.

    A promise to perform a preexisting contractual duty cannot support an agreement to modify a contract under traditional common law rule. *Example:* <u>Gross v. Diehl Specialties International</u> (holding that a modification of a contract constitutes the making of a new contract and must be supported by new consideration.)
    Example: <u>Crookham & Vessels v. Larry Moyer Trucking</u>

  B. The Uniform Commercial Code changes the rule and makes a modification of an existing contract for the sale of good enforceable without new consideration. The modification must be <u>commercially reasonable</u> and <u>in good faith</u>.

  C. Promises to Discharge Debts for Part Payment

    1. A promise to discharge a <u>liquidated debt</u> for part payment is generally unenforceable.

    2. A promise to discharge an <u>unliquidated debt</u> constitutes an <u>accord and satisfaction</u> and is enforceable.

  D. Past consideration is not consideration. Forbearance to sue, however, constitutes consideration to support a new agreement, if the promisee in good faith releases a valid claim in exchange for another's promise. *Example:* <u>Dyer v. National By-Products, Inc.</u>

  E. Under the doctrine of <u>promissory estoppel</u>, a promise that is not supported by consideration may be enforceable under the equitable theory that the promise induced <u>reliance</u> by the promisee, and the reliance was reasonable.

    Example: <u>Bower v. AT&T Technologies, Inc.</u>

Learning Objectives

    1. You should understand the rationale for the common law's requirement of consideration.

    2. You should recognize that the requirement of consideration has changed, and that statutory law like the UCC and equitable principles like promissory estoppel may change or eliminate the requirement in certain cases.

    3. You should not that an agreement not supported by consideration is generally unenforceable by either party.

    4. You should be able to give a useful definition of consideration.

    5. You should understand why promises to perform a pre-existing obligation are not consideration.

    6. You should understand why past consideration and illusory promises are not consideration.

    7. You should know when a promise to settle a debt is enforceable, and understand the difference between a liquidated and unliquidated debt.

    8. You should understand how the doctrine of promissory estoppel is sometimes used as a substitute for consideration.

Learning Hints

1. Consideration is defined as something of "legal value." This may be further defined as a promise to do something someone is not legally obligated to do, or to refrain from doing something one is legally entitled to do.
2. Under this definition, a promise to do something one is already obligated to do generally cannot constitute consideration.
3. Likewise, under this definition, a promise not to do something that one is not legally entitled to do cannot constitute consideration.
4. Even though one of the elements of consideration is that something with "legal value" must be given in exchange for the promise, consideration is _not_ required to have economic or monetary value. For example, the making of a promise can be consideration, even though the promise itself has no monetary value.
5. It is very important to remember that promises can be consideration. Many students think that no consideration exists until the promised act is actually performed, but this is _not_ true. When a promise serves as consideration, that consideration arises at the moment the promise is communicated to the promisee.
6. Promissory estoppel is based on the idea of protecting justifiable reliance. Therefore, a promise is sometimes enforced even if it is not supported by consideration if the promise has caused the promisee to act in reliance upon it, and it would be unfair to not enforce the promise.

True-False

In the blank provided, put "T" if the statement is True or "F" if the statement is False.

_____ 1. Under common law, a promise to do something one was already obligated to do could constitute consideration if the promise was made in good faith.

_____ 2. Generally, either an act or a promise can constitute consideration.

_____ 3. Nominal consideration is generally not recognized by courts as consideration unless it was truly bargained for.

_____ 4. The UCC adopts the common law rule that modification of contracts for the sale of goods requires new consideration to be enforceable.

_____ 5. Under the theory of promissory estoppel, a promise not supported by consideration may still be enforceable if the promisee reasonably relied on the promise to his detriment.

_____ 6. If the existence and amount of a debt are certain, the debt is liquidated.

_____ 7. Consideration is not required to have monetary or economic value.

_____ 8. As a general rule, the courts will not inquire into the adequacy of the consideration, just into whether consideration was exchanged.

_____ 9. A binding promise standing alone can be sufficient consideration.

_____ 10. Generally, past consideration cannot constitute consideration for a new promise.

Multiple Choice

Circle the Best Answer

1. John promised to mow Ralph's lawn for $10.00 "if I feel like it." This promise:
   a. Is enforceable so long as the condition is met;
   b. Is enforceable so long as Ralph tenders the $10.00;
   c. Is enforceable so long as $10.00 is reasonable consideration for the promise;
   d. Is unenforceable because John's promise is illusory.

2. Generally, a contract modification is enforceable if:
   a. supported by new consideration;
   b. a contracting party has run into unforeseeable difficulties making his/her performance impossible;
   c. under the UCC, the modification is reasonable and in good faith;
   d. all of the above are correct.

3. An agreement to modify a liquidated debt:
   a. is unenforceable;
   b. is enforceable if made in good faith;
   c. is enforceable if commercially reasonable;
   d. both (b) and (c) are correct.

4. Jane offered Bill $1,000 if Bill would release a legal claim against her which Bill held, and Bill agreed. Under these circumstances:
   a. The agreement is only enforceable if Bill's claim was held in good faith;
   b. The agreement is only enforceable if Bill's claim was reasonable;
   c. The agreement is not enforceable because past consideration cannot constitute consideration for a new agreement.
   d. Both (a) and (b) are correct.

5. The doctrine of promissory estoppel:
   a. Does not apply in cases where a promise is not supported by consideration;
   b. May apply, but only in cases where a promisee actually and reasonably relied on a promise by another;
   c. Only applies if the parties are merchants.
   d. Both (b) and (c) are correct.

6. Cathy went to First Bank and borrowed $2000, repayment due on June 1. A month before the loan was due, Cathy called her banker and offered to pay the loan off in full for $1800 on May 1. The banker agreed, but after receiving her check for $1800, sued her for the $200 balance. What result?
   a. Cathy must pay the $200 balance.
   b. Cathy was under a pre-existing duty to pay the entire $2000, so the banker's promise to accept less was not supported by consideration.
   c. Cathy gave new consideration by paying early, so the banker's promise to accept less is enforceable.
   d. Cathy must pay half the balance, or $100.

7. After Dorothy returned from her adventure in Oz, Auntie Em told her that she would give Dorothy $5000 if Dorothy would refrain from any further travels until her 21st birthday. Dorothy promised to do so, declared that "there's no place like home," removed her ruby slippers, and remained in Kansas until she turned 21. Auntie Em died the next day without having paid Dorothy the money. Dorothy sues her aunt's estate for the $5000. What result, and why?
   a. The estate must pay Dorothy because Auntie Em made an enforceable gift.
   b. The estate must pay Dorothy because Auntie Em's promise was supported by Dorothy's forbearance from travelling.
   c. The estate does not have to pay Dorothy because there was no consideration to support Auntie Em's promise.
   d. The estate does not have to pay Dorothy because her promise was illusory.

8. Which of the following is a true statement about promissory estoppel?
   a. Under the doctrine of promissory estoppel, all gratuitous promises are enforceable.
   b. The promisor must have intended to defraud the promisee before the doctrine of promissory estoppel applies.
   c. The promisee must have acted reasonably in relying on the promise before the doctrine of promissory estoppel applies.
   d. The doctrine of promissory estoppel applies even if the promisee has suffered no detriment from his reliance on the promisor's promise.

9. Which of the following is generally true regarding consideration?
   a. The consideration requirement only applies to bilateral contracts, not unilateral contracts.
   b. The U.C.C. completely abolishes the consideration requirement.
   c. Consideration for a promise involves the idea that there be either benefit given or detriment suffered as a bargained-for exchange for the promise.
   d. Consideration for a promise involves the idea that there be both benefit given and detriment suffered as a bargained-for exchange for the promise.

10. The Wizard of Oz entered an oral contract with Dorothy, the Tin Man, the Scarecrow, and the Cowardly Lion to the effect that he would grant their wishes in exchange for the broom of the Wicked Witch of the West. Dorothy and her friends melted the witch and took her broom to the Wizard, but when they got there the Wizard told them they would have to perform another task before he would grant their wishes. Dorothy and her friends at first agreed, but then refused to do anything more and demanded that the Wizard immediately grant their wishes. Is their promise to perform the second task enforceable?
    a. Yes, because a modification of an existing contract needs no new consideration to be binding.
    b. Yes, because they entered a new contract.
    c. No, because the Wizard had a preexisting duty to grant their wishes in exchange for the witch's broom.
    d. No, because the Wizard's promise was illusory.

11. Father promises to pay son $10,000 if, until son graduates from college, son will refrain from his illegal practice of sneaking into sorority house bathrooms. Which of the following is true?
    a. There is no consideration for Father's promise because Father gets no monetary or economic benefit in exchange for his promise.
    b. There is no consideration for Father's promise because this situation really involves a disguised gift, not a bargain.
    c. There is no consideration for Father's promise because the conduct he has requested from his son involves the performance of a pre-existing legal obligation.
    d. There is consideration for Father's promise.

12. X contracts to do some excavation work for Y, agreeing to dig a hole for the foundation of a building. Y agrees to pay X $20,000. After X finishes, the hole caves in. X then agrees to redo the work if Y will pay him an extra $5000. Y agrees, but after X redoes the work, Y refuses to pay the extra money. What result?
    a. Y's promise to pay the extra $5000 is not supported by consideration, so is not enforceable.
    b. Y's promise to pay the extra $5000 is supported by consideration so is enforceable.
    c. Y's promise to pay the extra $5000 is illusory so is not enforceable.
    d. X's promise to redo the work is not supported by consideration, so is not enforceable.

Short Essay

1. Sidney purchased a new couch from Sears for $900.00. One month later, when Sidney received the bill which was due, he sent Sears a check for $850 and indicated on the check, "payment in full for couch purchased on March 1." Sears cashed the check and sued Sidney for $50.00. Is Sears entitled to the balance of the debt? Why or why not?

2. Assume that Sidney purchased a new couch from Sears for $900.00. After the couch was delivered, Sidney discovered a small stain on the seat of the couch. He called Sears, and he and the manager agreed that Sears would accept $850 for the couch. One month later, when Sidney received the bill which was due, he sent Sears a check for $850 and indicated on the check, "payment in full for couch purchased on March 1." Sears cashed the check and sued Sidney for $50.00. Is Sears entitled to the balance of the debt? Why or why not?

3. Merchants Aarco, Inc. and Smith Brothers, Inc. agree on a contract for the sale of ball bearings, delivery on April 30. Due to a larger number of orders than it expected, Aarco saw that it could not deliver the bearings to Smith until May 15. Aarco asked Smith for an extension to this date, and Smith agreed. When the bearings arrived on May 15, Smith sued Aarco for breach of contract. Who will prevail in the lawsuit, and why?

CHAPTER 11
CAPACITY TO CONTRACT

Outline

I. Minors' Contracts: The minor is given the right to disaffirm (cancel) his/her contracts.

  A. Rationale: The contract is only voidable by the minor, that is, only the minor has the right to disaffirm. The rationale is to protect the minor.

  B. The Minor may disaffirm during minority or within a reasonable time afterward.

    Example: Iverson v. School, Inc. (A minor can disaffirm her endorsement of the check.)

  C. Consequences of Disaffirmance:

    1. Under common law, minors can recover his consideration and must return consideration given in return. In general, the minor who no longer has the consideration does not have to place the adult in statu quo.

    2. If the minor does not disaffirm within a reasonable time after majority he may be held to have ratified the contract.

    3. A growing number of courts have created exceptions to the general rule that minors can disaffirm. *Example:* Dodson v. Shrader, where the court held that the minor could not disaffirm a contract to purchase a truck without putting the seller in statu quo.

  D. Necessaries are those things essential to a minor's welfare. Minors are generally required to pay the reasonable value of necessaries.

II. Contracts of Mentally Impaired and Intoxicated Persons

  A. Test of Incapacity is whether the party, at the time of contracting, could understand the nature and effect of the contract.

    Example: Adams v. Adams (holding that a woman in therapy with a psychologist did not lack the capacity to contract.)

Learning Objectives

1. You should understand the difference between a void and voidable contract.
2. You should understand the right of a minor or one lacking capacity due to mental impairment to disaffirm a contract.
3. You should understand the concept of ratification.
4. You should know why contracts made by minors are voidable, and why these contracts are voidable at the election of the minor, but not at the election of the adult party to the contract.
5. You should understand the time period during which a minor is allowed to disaffirm.
6. You should know the different approaches taken in cases involving the issue of the return of consideration by the disaffirming minor where the consideration has been lost, stolen, destroyed, or dissipated.
7. You should know the various ways in which ratification may be accomplished.
8. You should know what "necessaries" are, the rules governing the minor's liability for them, and the reason that contracts for necessaries are not voidable.
9. You should know the test of incapacity usually applied when a party to a contract is alleged to be mentally impaired or intoxicated.
10. You should know when the contracts of the mentally impaired are treated as void rather than voidable.

Learning Hints

1. A contract made by a minor is voidable by the minor but not by the adult. This means that the minor may elect whether to disaffirm or ratify the contract.
2. In general, an adult contracts with a minor at his own risk. Generally, a minor is not required to place the adult in status quo (that is, in the same position he would have been had the contract not been executed); this rule, however, has been changed in some states.

3. Except for contracts which affect title to real estate, a minor can disaffirm a contract at any time from its making until a reasonable time after reaching the age of majority.

4. Cases in which the consideration received by the minor has been lost, stolen, destroyed, or dissipated have caused much disagreement concerning the minor's ability to disaffirm. A few states allow the minor to rescind in such cases, but require him to pay the adult party to the contract the reasonable value of the consideration he received.

5. Keep in mind that failure to disaffirm within a reasonable time after reaching the age of majority extinguishes the right to disaffirm, and also constitutes ratification.

6. In order to understand the rule making infants liable in quasi-contract for necessaries, suppose that a grocery store sells a minor a loaf of bread for $100. The minor will not be able to avoid paying for the bread, but he will only be liable for its reasonable value. This rule encourages adults to provide necessaries to minors, but prevents them from imposing unconscionable bargains on these minors.

7. The bargains of the mentally impaired are void <u>only</u> when a court has previously determined the person to be mentally incompetent. This ruling is very different from the ruling an ordinary court makes in a case where it is alleged that a contract is voidable on the grounds of mental impairment.

8. The rule that contracts of the mentally impaired or intoxicated can be ratified only after the person has regained mental capacity or sobriety reflects the same policy as the rule allowing minors to ratify their contracts only after attaining the age of majority. In each case, the capacity to contract is a precondition to ratification, for surely the person who lacks capacity to contract also lacks the capacity to ratify.

9. A minor who contracts for necessaries <u>is</u> able to disaffirm when he is furnished necessaries by a parent or guardian. In this situation, disaffirmance is permitted because there is no need to ensure that adults will have an incentive to provide necessaries to the minor.

10. While a contract entered into by an intoxicated party may be voidable if the party failed to understand the nature of the agreement, courts generally do not favor releasing a party from an obligation because he was voluntarily intoxicated. Thus, a court may find that the party has ratified the contract if he does not act promptly in notifying the other party of his election to rescind as a result of intoxication.

True-False

In the blank provided, put "T" if the statement is True or "F" if the statement is False.

_____ 1. Generally, minors contracts are voidable by either party.

_____ 2. In generally, a minor may disaffirm a contract at any time during his minority.

_____ 3. Some contracts, such as a marriage contract, by not be voidable by a minor under state statute.

_____ 4. Under common law, a minor who disaffirmed a contract was not required to place the adult party in <u>statu quo</u> by returning the consideration in the same condition as when he received it.

_____ 5. A contract entered into by a person who has been adjudicated (declared) mentally incompetent by a court is void.

_____ 6. A minor who misrepresents his age to an adult will be estopped from disaffirming his contract with the adult in some states.

_____ 7. A minor who contracts for necessaries must pay the full contract price for necessaries he actually receives.

_____ 8. Contracts made by those who are mentally impaired are void, not voidable.

_____ 9. A minor can ratify a contract at any time after making it.

_____ 10. Like minors, people lacking mental capacity can disaffirm their contracts, and on disaffirmance, must return any consideration they received that they still have.

Multiple Choice

Circle the best answer.

1. A contract entered into by a person who lacked the mental capacity to understand the nature of the contract, but who has not been adjudicated incompetent by a court:
   a. is enforceable;
   b. is voidable;
   c. is void;
   d. is illegal.

2. Generally, a minor may disaffirm a contract unless:
   a. the contract is for "necessaries";
   b. he is emancipated;
   c. he has ratified the contract by failing to disaffirm within a reasonable time after reaching the age of majority;
   d. all of the above are correct.

3. Which of the following would not constitute ratification of a contract by a minor?
   a. performance of the contract by a minor after he reaches the age of majority;
   b. words by a minor after reaching majority that clearly indicate an intent to be bound by the contract;
   c. conduct by the minor after reaching majority clearly indicating an intent to be bound;
   d. all of the above would constitute ratification.

4. "Necessaries" are:
   a. items purchased by a person who is the age of majority;
   b. items purchased by an emancipated minor;
   c. items purchased by a minor which are essential for his welfare;
   d. none of the above is correct.

5. People who lack mental capacity to contract:
   a. are not liable for contracts to purchase necessaries;
   b. are liable for the contract price if they purchase necessaries;
   c. are liable for the reasonable value of necessaries they purchase;
   d. may not disaffirm a contract to purchase necessaries.

6. In which of the following cases is a minor always prohibited from disaffirming before he reaches the age of majority?
   a. Contracts for necessaries
   b. Contracts affecting title to real estate
   c. Contracts in which the minor has misrepresented his age
   d. Contracts in which the consideration received by the minor has been destroyed by the minor

7. Which of the following contracts is void?
   a. A contract made by a minor who is living away from home
   b. A contract made by a minor who has misrepresented his age
   c. A contract made by a person who is intoxicated
   d. A contract made by a person adjudicated to be insane by a court

8. In a state where the age of majority is 19, Tom, a 16-year-old emancipated minor, promised his father that he would repay him at 10% interest for any money he spent putting Tom through college. Father and Tom wrote out and signed this agreement. Tom graduated from college at 21 and got a good job at the accounting firm of Cook D. Books, Inc., at which time Father asked Tom to begin repaying the debt. Tom wrote Father and said he would begin paying on the first of the next month, but Tom never sent Father any money. Father sued Tom to enforce their agreement, and Tom defended by saying that he was a minor when the contract was made and that he now wanted to disaffirm it. Which of the following facts would help Father overcome Tom's defense of incapacity?
   a. The fact that the original contract was in a signed writing
   b. The fact that Tom was emancipated when he entered the contract
   c. The fact that a college education is always a necessary
   d. The fact that Tom ratified the contract

53

9. In October of 1989, the Monroe Circuit Court ruled that Un Luckee, who suffered from schizophrenia, was mentally incompetent and appointed a guardian to manage his affairs. In November of 1989, believing that he was a movie star signing an autograph for a fan, Un Luckee signed a contract agreeing to sell a building he owned to Dave Developer. This contract is:
   a. voidable.
   b. valid if the terms of the contract are fair and Dave had no reason to know that Un Luckee suffered from schizophrenia.
   c. void.
   d. void only if Dave knew that Un Luckee suffered from schizophrenia.

10. Which of the following is a true statement regarding ratification?
   a. The ex-minor's performance or part performance under the contract after he reaches the age of majority can constitute ratification.
   b. A party can disaffirm after ratifying if he does so before the passage of a reasonable time after he reaches the age of majority.
   c. Contracts affecting title to real estate can be ratified before reaching the age of majority.
   d. None of the above is a true statement.

Short Essay

1. Jill, age 16, buys a car from Local Motors and promptly crashes it into a tree. The car is destroyed and Jill, who has paid the full price for the car, tries to disaffirm the contract with Local Motors and recover what she has paid. Under the traditional common law may she do so? Why or why not?

2. What is the reason for requiring minors to pay on a quasi-contract basis for necessaries furnished to them before they disaffirmed the contract for the necessaries?

3. X is a rich kid whose parents supply him with every conceivable necessity of life. One day, X buys a can of peaches at the grocery for $100. X is a minor and decides he wants to disaffirm. Will X be able to do so? Must he pay for the peaches?

CHAPTER 12
VOLUNTARY CONSENT

Outline

I. An agreement must be entered into voluntarily.

    A. Contracts entered into as a result of misrepresentation, fraud, duress, undue influence or mistake are voidable.

    B. A person may ratify an agreement if he waits an unreasonable time after discovery to rescind the contract.

II. Misrepresentation

    A. Misrepresentation of a material fact justifiably relied on to the detriment of the person relying is a basis for contract rescission. Fraud is a misrepresentation made knowingly and with intend to deceive.

    B. Misrepresentation of Fact v. Opinion

        This is a question of fact. See <u>Yuzwak v. Dygert</u>, (whether representations made by a seller are facts or merely sales "puffing" is a matter for the jury.)

    C. Justifiable Reliance. As a general rule, people must act reasonably to protect themselves.

    D. Is failure to disclose to the other party all the material facts misrepresentation? Today, many courts have relaxed the doctrine of <u>caveat emptor</u> and placed such an affirmative duty on sellers if the facts were not discoverable by the buyer.

        Example: <u>Stambovsky v. Ackly</u>, holding that the seller had a duty to disclose to the buyer the fact that the house was haunted.

III. Duress and Undue Influence

    A. Duress is wrongful coercion. Question: When does "hard bargaining" constitute economic duress? Ask whether the act left the other person with no reasonable alternative but to enter the contract.

        Example: <u>Centric Corporation v. Morrison-Knudsen Company</u>

    B. Undue influence is wrongful persuasion, in most cases it involves a special relationship of trust or confidence between the parties.

        Example: <u>United Companies Financial Corporation v. Wyers</u> (A widow with limited abilities who was strongly influenced by a young man may rescind a real estate loan on the grounds of undue influence.)

IV. Mistake

    A. Mistake prevents the "meeting of the minds," and requires proof of an untrue belief about a material fact.

        Example: <u>Wilkin v. 1st Source Bank</u> (holding that an estate can recover art works left in house which was subsequently sold to another.)

    B. Mistake can be mutual or unilateral. It is generally easier to rescind a contract for mutual mistake.

        Example: <u>Lafleur v. C.C. Pierce Co.</u> (where there has been a mistake as to the subject matter of a contract, there is no meeting of the minds.)

Learning Objectives

    1. You should understand the difference between a contract which is voidable and one which is void.

    2. You should be able to define misrepresentation and explain the difference between innocent, negligent, and fraudulent misrepresentation.

    3. You should be able to distinguish undue influence from duress.

    4. You should understand the difference between the traditional definition of duress and the modern approach permitting rescission in cases involving economic duress.

5. You should understand the difference between unilateral and mutual mistake, and to explain why it is generally easier to rescind in cases involving mutual mistake of fact.

6. You must know the remedies available to the injured party (or parties) when a contract is voidable.

7. You must know the elements of misrepresentation, and the two additional elements of fraud.

8. You should understand the different remedies the plaintiff may get in a fraud case which are not available in a misrepresentation case.

9. You should be familiar with the typical situations where undue influence occurs.

10. You should understand the concept of "justifiable reliance" in misrepresentation and mistake cases.

Learning Hints

1. Misrepresentation, mistake, duress and undue influence are legal theories supporting a finding that a contracting party did not, in reality, consent to the terms of an agreement. Generally, if a contracting party can establish the elements of one of these theories, he/she may rescind the contract. However, he is not required to do so, and may choose not to rescind.

2. Generally, courts today are more willing to permit rescission under these theories than in the past, when the doctrine of caveat emptor was a central theme in contract law.

3. Materiality is tested by an objective standard. Material facts are generally those which would induce a reasonable contracting party to enter into the contract. Materiality is determined on a case-by-case basis, and the standard varies with the needs, interests, and expertise of the contracting party.

4. The requirement that there be a causal connection between the misrepresentation and a party's entry into the contract in fraud and misrepresentation cases is not the same thing as the requirement of materiality. The causal connection requirement is concerned with whether or not the party actually relied on the statement, not with whether a reasonable person would have thought the information was important to his or her decision. Often, people entering a contract actually rely on nonmaterial misrepresentations, or fail to rely on clearly material misrepresentations. For fraud or misrepresentation to exist, both materiality of and actual reliance on the misstatement must be present. If one or the other requirement cannot be proved, fraud or misrepresentation does not exist.

5. The "justifiable reliance" element which is required in fraud and misrepresentation cases is not as big a bar to relief as it used to be. Very stringent duties of investigation were once imposed on the relying party, whereas today this is often not the case. Also, the standard varies with the relative expertise of the parties. For example, "justifiable reliance" does not mean the same thing in the sale of a used car to an auto mechanic as it would in the sale of a used car to a novice driver.

6. A newly emerging form of duress is economic duress (sometimes called "business compulsion"). This concept refers to the various forms of economic pressure, such as threats of economic harm, which can be applied in the business context. Generally, the threatened harm must be such that a serious economic loss would occur if the threat were carried out. A distinction is usually made by the courts between situations where the party applying duress takes advantage of the other party's difficult financial condition and situations where the party applying duress actually created the other party's bad financial situation and then took advantage of it. Despite the fact that the conduct sounds unacceptable in both situations, most courts would find economic duress only in the second case.

7. You should notice that fraud and misrepresentation share several elements in common, with fraud including the two additional elements of knowledge and intent to deceive. The distinction between fraud and misrepresentation is important because the victim of fraud has more remedies available to him.

8. Keep in mind that lack of capacity to contract, which will be the subject of the next chapter, is not the same thing as undue influence. Victims of undue influence usually have legal capacity to contract, but their powers of judgment and common sense are overwhelmed by the stronger party to the transaction with whom they are in a confidential relationship.

True-False

In the blank provided, put "T" if the statement is True or "F" if the statement is False.

_____ 1. In order to rescind a contract for misrepresentation, a contracting party must prove that he actually relied on the misrepresentation in making the agreement.

_____ 2. Today, a person who gives another contracting party no reasonable alternative to making a contract may find that the contract is voidable under the doctrine of mistake.

_____ 3. While one can recover damages as well as obtain contract rescission for misrepresentation, the only remedy for undue influence is contract rescission.

_____ 4. One of the basis elements of an action for rescission on the basis of mistake is proof that the mistake involved a material fact.

_____ 5. A person who waits too long after discovering a misrepresentation may not be entitled to rescind a contract, even if the other contracting party is guilty of fraud.

_____ 6. If the injured party to a voidable contract rescinds the contract, he returns what he has received and recovers what he has given under the contract.

_____ 7. In general, predictions about future events cannot serve as a basis of rescission for misrepresentation.

_____ 8. A party must prove that his reliance on a misrepresentation was justifiable in order to have grounds for rescission.

_____ 9. Silence by a seller can never serve as a basis for fraud.

_____ 10. Fraud in the execution makes a contract voidable, not void.

Multiple Choice

Circle the best answer.

1. Mike bought a used car from Flora. Mike and Flora discussed whether the car had ever been involved in an accident, and Flora said it had not. After he bought the car, Mike first learned that Flora had told several people the car had been "totalled" in an accident before she owned it. Mike thinks he's entitled to his money back on the basis of misrepresentation. Is he right?
   a. Yes, Mike should be able to rescind because Flora fraudulently misrepresented the facts;
   b. Yes, Mike should be able to rescind because Flora's failure to disclose the true facts constitutes negligent misrepresentation;
   c. No, Mike cannot rescind because there is no special relationship of trust (no "fiduciary relationship") between Mike and Flora;
   d. No, Mike cannot rescind because Flora did not wrongfully coerce Mike into purchasing the car.

2. A contract which is "voidable" means:
   a. either party may rescind the contract;
   b. only the person who lacked voluntary consent in entering the contract may rescind the contract;
   c. the contract is unenforceable by either party;
   d. none of the above is correct.

3. Which of the following is <u>not</u> an element of fraud?
   a. A false statement of opinion about an important fact;
   b. an intention to deceive;
   c. knowledge that the statement of fact was untrue;
   d. both (b) and (c)

4. Mike sold Bob a horse. It was obvious upon inspection that the horse was lame in one leg. However, Mike assured Bob that the horse could run as well as last year's winner of the Kentucky Derby. If Bob now wants to rescind the sale,
   a. Bob should be entitled to rescind under the doctrine of mistake;
   b. Bob should be entitled to rescind under the doctrine of misrepresentation;
   c. Bob should be entitled to rescind under the doctrine of undue influence;
   d. Bob will not be able to rescind because he did not justifiably rely on the misrepresentation.

5. Undue influence:
   a. requires proof that one party gave the other party no reasonable alternative but to enter into a contract;
   b. requires proof that one party took unfair advantage of another party in persuading him to enter into a contract;
   c. requires proof that one party deliberately misrepresented an important fact in inducing another to enter into a contract;
   d. requires proof that one party failed to disclose a material fact to the other party.

6. X represents that the used car he is selling Y is one "traditionally known for quality." This statement is false, but X will probably not be liable for fraud or misrepresentation. The best reason for X escaping liability is that:
   a. X's statement is not material.
   b. X's statement would not be relied upon by a reasonable person.
   c. X's statement is opinion, not past or present fact.
   d. X's statement is a prediction of the future.

7. Which is a true statement about mistake?
   a. Mistakes about one's ability to perform under a contract are not the type of mistake that will enable one to avoid contractual liability.
   b. Mutual mistake makes a contract void, while unilateral mistake makes a contract voidable.
   c. Mistake includes situations where both parties erroneously believe that some future event will occur and contract on that basis.
   d. Today, mistake of law is never a basis for avoiding contractual liability.

8. A, an antique dealer who should know better, thinks that a chair he has for sale is worth $100, when in fact it is a valuable antique worth $10,000. B, who knows the chair's true value and decides to take advantage of A's stupidity, buys the chair from A for $100. Later A discovers the chair's true value and wants to rescind on the basis of mistake. What result?
   a. A can rescind.
   b. A cannot rescind because this would cause substantial economic harm to B.
   c. A cannot rescind because the mistake was unilateral, not mutual.
   d. A cannot rescind because his mistake was negligent.

Short Essay

1. The Smiths purchased a house owned by Rogers. Rogers knew that the house was infested with termites, but prior to the sale, the Smiths never inquired and Rogers never volunteered that information. Later, after the Smiths moved in and discovered the termites, they sued to rescind the contract. Should they be entitled to rescind? Why or why not?

2. What are the two reasons that justifiable reliance is required for misrepresentation to exist?

3. Larry agreed to sell, and Moe to purchase, ten acres of land in Monroe County, Indiana. Both believed that the land was covered with valuable timber; however, neither knew that at the time they entered into the contract, a fire storm had swept the ten acres and burned all the trees to the ground. Can either or both parties rescind the contract under these facts? Explain.

CHAPTER 13
ILLEGALITY

Outline

I. The Effect of Illegality

  A. Courts generally will not enforce illegal agreements but leaves the parties as it finds them.

    Example: Clouse v. Myers

  B. Sometimes a court will permit recovery if the parties are ignorant of the facts

  C. Parties protected by regulatory statutes may be entitled to enforce the agreement if public policy is served

II. Contracts to commit illegal acts

  A. Contracts illegal by statute

    Example: Kaszuba v. Zientara, where court said agreement between residents of Indiana to purchase lottery tickets in Illinois was not illegal and therefore the agreement was enforceable.

  B. Licensing statutes: Agreements in violation of regulatory licensing statutes are generally unenforceable; however, agreements in violation of a revenue-raising statute are often enforceable.

    Example: Rogers Refrigeration Co. Inc. v. Pulliam's Garage (holding that a service provider's failure to include information required by statute in the service agreement was not substantial enough to deny enforcement of contract for services.)

III. Contracts Which Violate Public Policy

  A. Public policy is determined by a court and reflects acceptable social or economic behavior

    Example: Scott v. Board of Trustees of the Mobile Steamship Ass'n (denial of insurance coverage on the basis of common law marriage violated public policy.)

  B. Exculpatory Clauses

    Example: Milligan v. Big Valley Corporation (upholding exculpatory clause in "general release of claim" signed by person who died while participating in a downhill ski race.)

  C. Contracts in restraint of trade ("non-compete clauses.)

    Example: Nalle Clinic Co. v. Parker (holding that covenant not to compete in an employment contract signed by pediatrician was not unenforceable because not allowing doctor to practice medicine could be harmful to the public.)

  D. Unconscionability: Under this doctrine, a court may refuse to enforce a contract or contract clause it finds to be "unconscionable."

    1. Generally requires finding that parties lacked equal bargaining power and contract contains substantively unfair provision.

    2. UCC 2-302 is the UCC provision on unconscionability; the Restatement has adopted a similar approach.

Learning Objectives

  1. You should understand the concept of public policy, which may be determined by a court.

  2. You should understand that a court will generally refuse to enforce an agreement it finds to violate public policy; further, the general rule is "hands off" illegal contracts, so that the court will leave the parties as it finds them.

  3. You should know when ignorance of the facts making a contract illegal will enable a party to recover damages or consideration.

  4. You should know the situations in which a party is permitted to rescind an illegal contract and obtain relief.

  5. You should know when a court will enforce the legal portions of a contract which also contains an illegal term.

  6. You should know and understand the difference between an illegal wager and a legal risk-shifting contract or speculative bargain.

7. You should know and understand the difference between licensing statutes which are intended to raise revenue and those which are intended to protect the public, and you should know the significance of this distinction in situations where the party violating the licensing statute is seeking relief under a contract.

8. You should understand that the concept of unconscionability is a powerful concept because courts may use this concept to invalidate agreements.

Learning Hints

1. Generally speaking, the courts will not enforce illegal bargains at all, and will leave the parties to such an agreement in the position in which it finds them. This is what is meant by the phrase "hands off illegal agreements" in the textbook. The courts will usually deny even a quasi-contract recovery in the case of an illegal bargain. The reason for this "hands off" policy is to reinforce the public policies making such agreements illegal in the first place, mainly by deterring parties from entering into such agreements.

2. In some situations, however, a party to an illegal agreement is given some relief when this can be done without seriously undermining the public policies making the agreement illegal. In other situations, parties are felt to be deserving of relief despite these public policies.

3. It is not a simple matter to determine public policy, because this concept reflects current social, economic, and political realities. For example, some courts have invalidated "surrogate motherhood" contracts on the theory that such contracts violate general public policy, and also violate public policy which underlies adoption statutes.

4. In addition to being illegal, exculpatory clauses can often be attacked on the grounds that they were not the product of voluntary consent, or that they are unconscionable.

5. The materials you have already studied concerning duress, undue influence, and capacity are relevant to the general issue of shockingly unequal bargains.

6. Today most unconscionability problems arise in the context of contracts for the sale of goods so are usually treated under the Uniform Commercial Code. However, unconscionability also exists as a common law concept and is often applied in the context of contracts which do not involve the sale of goods.

7. Unconscionability is a concept which cannot be defined very specifically. Courts give this concept content by injecting their notions of fairness and sound public policy into the decisions in which unconscionability is an issue. The courts often distinguish between substantive unconscionability, which involves unfairness in the terms of the contract itself, and procedural unconscionability, which involves the way in which the agreement was reached, including things like terms in fine print, contract language which is not understandable by the ordinary person, high-pressure sales tactics, and one party's ignorance, limited education, or lack of fluency in the language. Some courts hold that both procedural and substantive unconscionability must be present for a contract to be illegal on the grounds of unconscionability.

8. "Covenants not to compete" are agreements in restraint of trade; in other words, a party to an employment contract may agree that he/she will not compete with the other party in the event the employment relationship is terminated. Such agreements are enforceable only if reasonable both to geographic location and to time.

True-False

In the blank provided, put "T" if the statement is True or "F" if the statement is False.

_____ 1. Generally, if a court finds that a contract is illegal, the contract is unenforceable by either party.

_____ 2. If a contract is divisible (that is, the legal parts can be separated from the illegal parts), the contract is unenforceable by either party.

_____ 3. An agreement in violation of a licensing statute, such as a statute pertaining to the licensing of real estate brokers, is enforceable if the statute is regulatory.

_____ 4. Usury laws are statutes prohibiting the performance of certain work on certain days of the week.

_____ 5. An exculpatory clause purporting to relieve a party of liability for negligence may be enforceable if the parties have freely and knowingly agreed to the clause, and the activity is not an essential public activity.

_____ 6. When a contract is illegal, courts usually will not allow even a quasi-contractual recovery.

_____ 7. In some cases, a party who rescinds a contract before any illegal act has been performed will be allowed to recover the consideration he has given to the other party pursuant to the contract.

_____ 8. Exculpatory clauses seeking to relieve a party from liability for fraud or willful misconduct are always illegal.

_____ 9. Any agreement which restricts competition is an illegal bargain.

_____ 10. Despite the "hands off" rule, in cases where a person whom a statute seeks to protect enters into an agreement in violation of the statute, the protected person is permitted to enforce the agreement.

Multiple Choice

Circle the best answer.

1. The concept of "unconscionability":
   a. Is not defined in the UCC;
   b. Is not defined in the Restatement;
   c. Requires a finding of procedural unconscionability (lack of equal bargaining power);
   d. All of the above are correct.

2. Covenants not to compete:
   a. Must be limited to a reasonable time;
   b. Must be limited to reasonable geographic location;
   c. Must be reasonable both as to time and place;
   d. Violate public policy and are unenforceable.

3. A contract of adhesion:
   a. Is a standardized form contract where the parties lack equal bargaining power;
   b. Is a contract in restraint of trade;
   c. Is an illegal contract;
   d. Both (b) and (c) are correct.

4. Which of the following statements is not correct?
   a. Even if the parties to an agreement have met all the requirements for a valid contract, the agreement is unenforceable if it calls for performance contrary to the public interest;
   b. When determining the legality of an agreement, courts presume the parties intended a legal result;
   c. An agreement may be illegal even if it does not violate a statute if it violates public policy as determined by a court;
   d. A party to an illegal agreement who cannot recover damages for breach is generally entitled to recover in quasi-contract for benefits conferred on the other party.

5. If a party cancels an illegal agreement before any illegal act has been performed:
   a. the party can not recover consideration already given;
   b. the party can not recover consideration already given, but may be entitled to recover damages under a quasi-contract theory;
   c. the party can generally recover consideration because this encourages parties to cancel illegal agreements;
   d. the party is entitled to enforce the contract to the extent necessary for him to recover the reasonable value of services or consideration given to the other party.

7. Where one or both parties are unaware of facts making their agreement illegal:
   a. courts will always enforce the agreement.
   b. courts may grant recovery for performance rendered before a party learned of the illegality.
   c. the contract will be voidable rather than void.
   d. no recovery of any sort will be permitted.

8. If two parties bet that a certain stock will rise 30 points in a week:
   a. their agreement is illegal.
   b. their agreement is illegal only if one party had inside information about the stock.
   c. their agreement is unconscionable.
   d. their agreement is a legal securities transaction.

9. Sam Singer signs an employment contract with Ron Restauranteur which provides that if and when he leaves Ron's employ, he will not sing in any other restaurant or supper club for one year. Is this clause illegal?
   a. The clause is illegal and unenforceable because it is not limited geographically.
   b. The clause is illegal because all agreements in restraint of trade are illegal.
   c. The clause is legal because it is for the purpose of protecting interests created by the contract and is no greater than is necessary to protect those interests.
   d. The clause is legal because it is ancillary to the contract.

10. Which of the following is most likely to be enforced by a court?
    a. A contract in violation of a revenue-raising licensing law
    b. A contract for the assassination of the President
    c. A contract in which two competitors agree to stop competing with each other
    d. An exculpatory clause that seeks to relieve one of the parties from liability for willful fraud

11. A state statute requires that salesmen be licensed, but it establishes no qualifications for the license other than the payment of $10 to the county clerk. The license is automatically issued to anyone who pays the $10. If a person entered a contract to buy goods from a salesman who had not obtained this license:
    a. the contract would be valid and enforceable.
    b. the contract would be voidable.
    c. the contract would be void.
    d. the contract would be unenforceable.

Short Essay

1. Miles and Standish enter a contract for the purchase of a machine gun. Sales of such guns are illegal, and both parties know this. Miles pays Standish but Standish never delivers the machine gun. Miles sues Standish for breach of contract. What result?

2. Vito Finger's new supper club bears a sign on its wall which reads, "Vito's Place will not be responsible to patrons for any loss or damage incurred here in excess of $200." Patti Patron slips and falls on a meatball dropped on the floor by one of Vito's waiters, and incurs $1000 in medical bills and $1200 in damage to her designer evening gown. What is Patti's best legal position?

3. Are restrictive covenants in restraint of trade ever enforceable? If so, in what circumstances?

CHAPTER 14
THE FORM AND MEANING OF CONTRACTS

Outline

I. STATUES OF FRAUDS: All states have statutes requiring certain kinds of contracts to be evidenced by a writing.

    A. Classes include contracts executors of estates to be personally liable, collateral contracts, transfers of interest in real property, and contracts incapable of being performed within one year.

    B. Effect is to make oral contracts <u>unenforceable</u>, not void or voidable.

    C. In some states, doctrine of <u>promissory estoppel</u> will permit a plaintiff to recover reliance damages even though oral contract would otherwise be unenforceable.

    Example: <u>Olson v. Ronhovde</u>, holding that person who relied on an oral promise to lease property could enforce the lease.

II. Particular Contracts Covered by the Statute of Frauds

    A. Contracts to Answer for the Debt of Another (Collateral contracts)

    Exception: The "leading object" doctrine is an exception to this rule. Under this doctrine, if a person promising to secure the debt of another, is motivated by personal benefit, the oral promise is enforceable.

    B. Contracts transferring interest in land

    Exception: "Part performance" of a contract for sale of land. This requires that the buyer has taken some affirmative act of ownership toward the property and paid part of the purchase price.
    Example: <u>Unitas v. Temple</u>

    C. Bilateral Contracts that cannot be performed within one year. This test is <u>narrowly construed</u> by courts. Thus, if there is any way the oral agreement could be performed within one year, it is not unenforceable under this test.

    Example: <u>Tomson v. Stephan</u>, holding that an agreement never to reveal terms of a settlement agreement could be performed within one year, and thus is not within the statute of frauds.

III. What kind of writing is required?

    A. Generally, most states required only a memorandum of the agreement, signed by the party to be charged.
    Example: <u>Lee v. Voyles</u>

IV. Interpreting Contracts:

    A. Rules of construction: Courts try to determine the "principal objective" of the parties.

    B. Parol Evidence Rule: If a written contract is the "final and complete expression of agreement" between the parties, evidence of additional or different terms are not admissible.

        1. Exceptions arise; for example, if the parties lacked consent or the contract is ambiguous or incomplete, the rule does not apply.
        Example: <u>MacFarlane v. Rich</u>. The court said, "Where the language of the agreement is perfectly clair, that language cannot be contradicted by parol evidence."

Learning Objectives

    1. You should understand that many oral contracts are enforceable. Only those contracts prohibited by the statute of frauds are unenforceable.

    2. You should understand the difference between an unenforceable and a void or voidable contract. An oral contract which is fully executed (fully performed) cannot be rescinded because it was not in writing.

    3. You should understand the "parol evidence rule," which prohibits introduction of evidence that contradicts the terms of a written agreement.

    4. You must know the types of contracts which are required by the statute of frauds to be evidenced by a writing.

5. You must know the legal status of a contract that falls within the requirements of the statute of frauds but fails to comply with those requirements.

6. You should be aware of the role that promissory estoppel sometimes plays in making enforceable oral contracts which would otherwise be unenforceable under the statute of frauds.

7. You should know the difference between an original contract and a collateral or guaranty contract, and the practical significance of this distinction under the statute of frauds.

8. You should know when part performance of an oral contract for the sale of an interest in land exists, and the effect this has under the statute of frauds.

9. You should know the rules governing what matters must be included in the written memorandum required by the statute of frauds.

10. You should know the general rules the courts use in interpreting written contracts.

Learning Hints

1. The statute of frauds lists several different kinds of contracts which must be in writing to be enforceable. These include contracts in contemplation of <u>marriage</u>, contracts which cannot be performed within one <u>year</u>, contracts for the sale of <u>land</u>, contracts by <u>executors</u>, <u>guarantor</u>/ee (collateral) contracts, and, under the UCC, contracts for the <u>sale</u> of goods for $500 or more. A good way to remember these categories is to remember "MYLEGS."

2. Not all oral contracts are unenforceable. Only those required to be in writing by the statute of frauds must be in writing to be enforceable.

3. The "writing" required by the statute of frauds is something less than a formally written contract signed by all parties. Generally, to satisfy the statute of frauds, there must be a written memorandum, containing all material terms of the agreement, signed by the party to be charged (that is, the party relying on the statute of frauds as a defense.)

4. Three features of seventeenth century English law caused the original statute of frauds to be enacted: oral contracts were enforceable, the parties to the contract could not testify at trial, and there were few legal devices for correcting unfair jury verdicts. Therefore, it often occurred that parties "proved" the existence of an oral contract through paid, perjured testimony. As a result, Parliament required those contracts in which the potential for fraud was great, or the consequences of fraud were especially serious, to be evidenced by a writing to be enforceable.

5. An oral contract is still valid if it has already been performed or if neither party objects to its enforcement, and for other legal purposes.

6. Technically, the first type of contract covered by the statute of frauds—a contract in which an executor or administrator promises to be personally responsible for the decedent's debts—is also a collateral or guaranty contract.

7. Be sure you notice that the situations in which part performance of an oral contract for the sale of land takes the contract outside the statute of frauds are very similar to the situations in which promissory estoppel takes a contract outside the statute of frauds.

8. Remember that the statute of frauds rule covering contracts which cannot be performed within one year after their formation <u>applies only to executory bilateral contracts</u>. This means that if the contract has been completely executed (performed), the statute does not apply to it.

9. The "party to be bound" or the "party to be charged" whose signature must appear on the writing is the party <u>who is trying to use the statute to escape the contract</u>. This is typically a party who refuses to perform, who is sued as a result, and who argues that the contract is unenforceable under the statute of frauds. The other party's signature need not appear in order for the reluctant party to be bound.

10. As the textbook makes clear, the "exceptions" to the parol evidence rule are not really exceptions at all, because they all involve situations in which a party is not trying to contradict the terms of the writing, but is trying to challenge the underlying validity or explain the meaning of the writing.

True-False

In the blank provided, put "T" if the statement is True or "F" if the statement is False.

_____ 1. Because a contract to employ a person "for life" cannot be performed within one year, it must be in writing to be enforceable.

_____ 2. Contracts for transfer of interest in real property, including long term leases, must be in writing under the statute of frauds.

_____ 3. In order for "part performance" to take an oral contract for purchase of land out of the statute of frauds, a person must have both paid some consideration toward the purchase, and taken some action indicating ownership of the property.

_____ 4. The parol evidence rule prohibits introduction of misrepresentation, fraud, or duress, in the making of written contracts.

_____ 5. The "leading object" exception to the statute of frauds arises in cases where a person enters into an oral contract for the purchase of land.

_____ 6. An oral contract which has been fully performed by both parties is not required to be evidenced by a writing.

_____ 7. Promissory estoppel will sometimes make enforceable an oral promise which would otherwise be unenforceable because of the statute of frauds.

_____ 8. The parol evidence rule does not apply to oral contracts.

_____ 9. The memorandum required by the statute of frauds may be made up of several documents as long as they clearly relate to the same agreement and to each other.

_____ 10. If one of the parties drafted the contract, and it is ambiguous, these ambiguities are resolved against the drafter.

Multiple Choice

Circle the best answer.

1. If an oral contract is declared unenforceable under the statute of frauds, and one of the parties has performed under the contract, that party:
   a. may enforce the contract
   b. may not recover the value of his consideration;
   c. may recover the reasonable value of consideration under "quasi-contract" theory;
   d. may recover damages under promissory estoppel.

2. Jack and Jill entered into an oral contract wherein Jack agreed to sell, and Jill to purchase, 10 acres of land. Jill paid $500 down and moved into the house on the property and began redecorating the kitchen and bath. Subsequently, Jack decided to sell the property to another at a higher price and attempted to evict Jill. Jill wants to enforce their agreement, but Jack says the agreement is unenforceable because it is not in writing. Under these facts:
   a. The contract is unenforceable;
   b. The contract is unenforceable, but Jill is entitled to recover the money she has already paid and value of redecorating done to date;
   c. The contract is unenforceable, but Jill may recover damages under "promissory estoppel" theory;
   d. The contract is enforceable under the "part performance" exception to the statute of frauds.

3. The parol evidence rule does <u>not</u> apply in cases involving evidence of:
   a. lack of reality of consent by the contracting parties as a result of misrepresentation or mistake.
   b. evidence to clarify an ambiguous term in the agreement;
   c. subsequent oral agreements between the parties;
   d. All of the above.

4. John hired Mary to be his executive vice-president "for life." If this is an oral agreement:
   a. It is unenforceable as a collateral contract under the statute of frauds;
   b. It is unenforceable under the parol evidence rule;
   c. It is unenforceable because it cannot be performed within one year;
   d. It is enforceable.

5. What kind of writing is required by the statute of frauds?
   a. A formal written contract containing all the terms of the parties and signed by all parties;
   b. A memorandum signed by all parties;
   c. A memorandum signed by the "party to be charged";
   d. A memorandum, not necessarily signed by the parties.

6. A contract that fails to comply with the statute of frauds is:
   a. void.
   b. voidable.
   c. fully enforceable by either party.
   d. unenforceable.

7. Which of the following is not a recognized rule of contract interpretation?
   a. Printed terms will control handwritten terms in case of a conflict between them.
   b. Ambiguities will be resolved against the party who drafted the contract.
   c. All terms of the contract will be read in terms of the contract's principal objective.
   d. Trade usage can be employed to help resolve the meaning of ambiguous contract terms.

8. Jim's Haberdashery has been buying its neckties from Broadhurst Neckware for many years and has always received a 10% discount whenever it paid at the time of delivery. Generally, however, such discounts are not granted by neckware manufacturers to retailers. On February 1, Jim's issued a purchase order to Broadhurst for 300 neckties at $6.00 each, which Broadhurst acknowledged on its own form as an order for "300 neckties @ $6.00." Broadhurst shipped the merchandise, and upon delivery Jim's tendered a check for $1620 ($1800 less 10%). Broadhurst claims Jim's still owes it $180 and sues, but Jim's seeks to introduce evidence explaining that it does not owe the money. What result?
   a. Jim's evidence will be excluded because it tends to alter, vary, or contradict a written contract.
   b. Jim's evidence will be admitted because it merely fills gaps in an incomplete written contract.
   c. Jim's evidence will be admitted because parol evidence is always admissible to prove that a writing contradicts an earlier oral agreement of the parties.
   d. Jim's evidence will be admitted to prove trade usage.

9. Two parties entered a written contract which provided that payment would be based on "seller's cost," a term which was not defined in the contract. The parties disagreed as to the meaning of the term, and at trial one party offered oral evidence as to which definition of "seller's cost" the parties meant. How will the court rule on the admissibility of this evidence?
   a. Once a written document has been created, no parol evidence is admissible.
   b. Although parol is admissible under certain circumstances, the party in this case is offering evidence which contradicts the writing, and it is therefore inadmissible.
   c. Because the evidence is offered to prove duress, it is admissible.
   d. If the court finds that the term "seller's cost" is ambiguous, it will admit parol evidence to help clear up the ambiguity.

Short Essay

1. Jack Jones was the principal creditor of "Magical Mystery Tours," ("Tours") a travel agency. "Tours" needed to finance expansion of its business and attempted to borrow money from Bank Two. Bank Two refused to finance the expansion unless Jones would guarantee payment. Jones orally promised to guarantee payment, but never signed any written agreement to repay in the event "Tours" defaulted on the loan. "Tours" got the loan, and subsequently defaulted. Jones relies on the statute of frauds as a defense. Can Bank Two enforce Jones' promise? Why or why not?

2. Greetings, Inc. made an oral contract with Oz Manufacturing for 1000 t-shirts saying "Surrender Dorothy." The contract price was $2 per shirt. Greetings made an initial payment of $1000 for the shirts, and Oz accepted and cashed the check, but then refused to deliver any shirts to Greetings. Greetings sues Oz, but Oz claims it does not have to perform because their contract violated the statute of frauds. What result, and why?

3. How does the statute of frauds involve the possibility of injustice? What legal doctrine is increasingly used to protect against this possibility?

CHAPTER 15
THIRD PARTIES' CONTRACT RIGHTS

Outline

I. Assignment and Delegation in General

A. A contract consists of rights and duties. A transfer of rights is called an <u>assignment</u>; a transfer of duties is <u>delegation</u>.

B. Most, but not all, contracts are assignable. If the assignment would materially alter the duties of the promisor it is unenforceable.

Example: <u>Cooper v. Gidden</u> (A covenant not to compete is assignment as a part of the sale of a business.)

II. Consequences of Assignment

A. An original promisor may assert defenses against the assignee that he could assert against the assignor (that is, the original contracting party.)

B. An assignee can assert the original rights of the assignor against the promisor.

Example: <u>Decatur North Associates, Ltd. v. Builders Glass, Inc.</u>, holding that an assignee could enforce warranty rights against the original promisor.

C. Assignor must notify the promisor of the assignment.

Example: <u>Mid-States Sales Co. v. Mountain Empire Dairymen's Ass'n</u>

D. Assignors who are paid for making an assignment are held to make certain implied guaranties about the assignment.

III. Consequences of Delegation

A. Like assignment, not all duties are delegable.

Example: <u>In re Lashelle</u> (ex-husband's duty to make mortgage payments was not delegable because such payments were in lieu of child support.)

B. Generally, an assignment of rights includes a delegation of duty under both the UCC and Restatement.

IV. Third-Party Beneficiary Contracts

A. There are two types of third-party beneficiaries under a contract: Intended and Incidental.

1. An Intended beneficiary is either a <u>donee</u> or <u>creditor</u> beneficiary, and acquires rights to enforce the original contract depending on which category of beneficiary he/she is.

2. An Incidental beneficiary acquires no contract rights.

B. A Donee Beneficiary is a beneficiary of a contract where the promisee's primary purpose was to make a gift to the third party. A donee beneficiary can enforce the contract against the original promisor, but not promisee.

Example: <u>Warren v. Monahan Beaches Jewelry Center, Inc.</u> (Fiancee of purchaser could sue jewelry store for selling purchaser a fake diamond ring intended as a gift to plaintiff.)

C. Creditor Beneficiaries: If the promisor's performance will satisfy a legal duty that the promisee owes a third party, the third party is a creditor beneficiary and may enforce the contract against both the promisee and promisor.

Learning Objectives

1. You should understand the difference between contract rights and duties and an assignment and delegation;

2. You should understand the difference between contract rights and duties which are assignable/delegable and those which are not;

3. You should understand the difference between creditor and donee beneficiaries, and incidental beneficiaries.

4. You should understand who the assignor, assignee, and promisor are in the context of an assignment, and what the rights and duties of each are after the assignment occurs.

5. You should understand exactly what a delegation of duties involves and what the rights and duties of the parties involved are after the delegation occurs.

6. You should know why the assignee should give notice of the assignment to the promisor.

7. You should know what implied warranties are given by an assignor who is paid for the assignment to the assignee.

Learning Hints

1. In every bilateral contract situation there is a promisor and promisee, and each party has corresponding rights and duties. Thus either party (or both) may generally assign rights and transfer duties to a third party, who then acquires certain rights and duties under the contract.

2. A delegate of a duty under a contract must consent to that delegation and assume the duty under the contract in order to be obligated to the promisee.

3. An assignment of rights generally includes a delegation of duty under the UCC and the Restatement.

4. Public policy favors assignment, and anti-assignment clauses are strictly construed and may be unenforceable in some cases for public policy reasons.

5. A third-party beneficiary will only acquire contract rights if he/she is an intended beneficiary. An example of an intended beneficiary is the beneficiary under an insurance contract.

6. Remember that an assignment does not require formalities, a writing, or consideration to be valid.

7. Assignments are not permitted in situations where the assignment would materially change the promisor's duty or the promisor's risk. This means that an assignment of an insurance contract by the party who is both the insured and the beneficiary to another who becomes both insured and beneficiary would be invalid.

8. An example of a situation in which a delegation of duties would be invalid because it is a delegation of duties which depend on personal skill, character, or judgment would be a situation in which B, who is an artist, assigns his contract to paint A's portrait to C, who is not an artist.

9. Remember that the assignee must give notice of the assignment to the promisor or the promisor is not bound to render performance to the assignee. This means that if the promisor renders performance to the assignor because he has not been notified of the assignment, the promisor is discharged and the assignee would be forced to sue the assignor to obtain the assigned benefit.

10. If a duty is properly delegated but the assignee fails to render performance to the promisor, the assignor is still liable to the promisor, and will therefore be legally required to render performance himself. Then the assignor would be forced to sue the assignee to obtain reimbursement for his performance of the delegated duties.

True-False

In the blank provided, put "T" if the statement is True or "F" if the statement is False.

_____ 1. An assignment of rights generally includes a @X = delegation of duty.

_____ 2. An assignor who assigns rights under a contract only impliedly warrants that the claim is valid if the assignment was paid for by the assignee.

_____ 3. An incidental beneficiary to a contract acquires contract rights and may enforce the contract against either party.

_____ 4. An assignment of rights generally does not extinguish the contract rights of the assignor.

_____ 5. A delegation of contract duties generally does not extinguish the contract obligations of the delegating party.

_____ 6. A valid assignment does not require that the assignee give consideration.

_____ 7. Contract clauses forbidding assignment are always enforced.

_____ 8. If the promisor was a minor at the time the contract was made and it is later assigned, he will have the same defense of lack of capacity against the assignee as he would have had against the assignor.

_____ 9. A donee beneficiary is the recipient of a contractual gift.

_____ 10. Both assignors who are paid for making an assignment and those who give assignments away are potentially liable to their assignees for certain implied guarantees.

Multiple Choice

Circle the best answer.

1. Bob contracted with "Flowers R Us" to send a dozen roses to his girlfriend Shirley. If the florist fails to send the flowers, who can enforce the contract?
   a. Only Bob, who was the original contracting party;
   b. Only Shirley, who was the beneficiary of the contract;
   c. Both Bob and Shirley, because Bob is a party to the original contract and Shirley is a donee beneficiary;
   d. Neither party because an assignment extinguishes the original contract rights.

2. Jack rented an apartment to Jill, who signed a written lease. Jack assigned the rental agreement to XYZ corporation, which purchased the apartment building. Which of the following did Jack warrant when he assigned the lease to XYZ?
   a. That Jill was an adult with the capacity to contract;
   b. That Jack had not assigned the rental agreement to anyone else;
   c. That Jill had the money to pay the claim;
   d. Both (a) and (b).

3. Jack rented an apartment to Jill, who signed a written lease. Jack assigned the rental agreement to XYZ corporation, which purchased the apartment building. If Jill defaults on the rental payments, who may sue her for the rent payment and why?
   a. Only Jack may sue Jill because he was the original contracting party;
   b. Only XYZ may sue Jill because an assignment extinguished Jack's rights under the contract;
   c. Either party may sue Jill because Jack is an original contracting party and XYZ is a creditor beneficiary of the contract;
   d. Neither party because this contract is not assignable.

4. Jack rented an apartment to Jill, who signed a written lease. Jack assigned the rental agreement to XYZ corporation, which purchased the apartment building. If Jill discovers that her apartment is infested with termites, which is a breach of the implied warranty of habitability in the lease, who may she sue for damages?
   a. Jill may only sue Landlord because he was the original contracting party;
   b. Jill may only sue XYZ because it is the assignee of the contract;
   c. Jill may sue either Landlord or XYZ corporation;
   d. Jill may sue Landlord but may only sue XYZ if she consented to the assignment.

5. Which of the following third-parties acquires no contract rights?
   a. An assignee;
   b. A donee beneficiary;
   c. A creditor beneficiary;
   d. An incidental beneficiary.

6. In which of the following cases might an assignment of contract rights be invalid?
   a. Where a right to receive money is assigned
   b. Where a right to receive goods is assigned
   c. Where the assignor's promise not to compete with the buyer of a business is assigned along with the sale of the business
   d. Where a right to have one's requirements of coal met is assigned

7. The assignee on a valid assignment:
   a. takes free of all defenses the promisor has against the assignor.
   b. is usually subject to an implied delegation of the assignor's duties.
   c. is entitled to the promisor's performance even if he does not give notice of the assignment to the promisor.
   d. is a donee beneficiary of the original contract.

8. X, an artist, contracts to paint a portrait for Y, then X assigns the contract to Z, who has no artistic skills. Which is a true statement?
   a. X's contract rights cannot be assigned because this would materially change Y's obligation.
   b. X's contract duties cannot be delegated to Z because this would materially impair Y's rights under the contract.
   c. After the assignment, X will no longer be liable to Y.
   d. None of the above

9. A hires B to build a building which, unbeknownst to either A or B, will cause C's property values to go up. If B fails to perform,
   a. C can sue as a donee beneficiary.
   b. C can sue as a creditor beneficiary.
   c. C can sue as an intended beneficiary.
   d. C cannot sue as he is an incidental beneficiary.

10. Which of the following is a true statement about assignments?
    a. A valid assignment requires consideration.
    b. To be valid, an assignment must be in writing.
    c. Contract rights can be given away as well as sold.
    d. Once a valid assignment occurs, the delegation of the assignor's contractual duties is always automatic.

Short Essay

1. Mr. Landlord and Judy entered into a lease agreement @T2 = wherein Judy agreed to lease an apartment for one year and to pay Landlord $500/month in rent. Three months later, Judy assigned her lease to Sally. If Sally defaults on the rent payment, what are Mr. Landlord's rights under the agreement?

2. Mr. Landlord and Judy entered into a lease agreement wherein Judy agreed to lease an apartment for one year and to pay Landlord $500/month in rent. Three months later, Landlord sold the apartment building to XYZ corporation, and assigned his rights to the lease agreement to XYZ. Discuss three implied warranties made by Mr. Landlord to XYZ in this assignment.

3. After an assignment, to what defenses is the assignee subject?

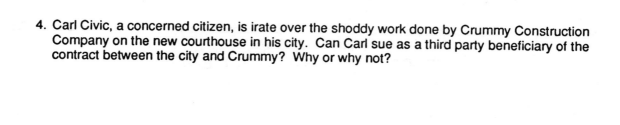

4. Carl Civic, a concerned citizen, is irate over the shoddy work done by Crummy Construction Company on the new courthouse in his city. Can Carl sue as a third party beneficiary of the contract between the city and Crummy? Why or why not?

CHAPTER 16
PERFORMANCE AND REMEDIES

Outline

I. Duty to Perform under a Contract

   A. May be qualified by a condition

      1. Types of conditions include precedent, subsequent, and concurrent
      Example: Standefer v. Thompson, holding that express language of condition is not necessary to create a condition in a contract.

   B. Standards of Performance

      1. Substantial performance: standard which falls short of complete performance but does not constitute material breach
      Example: Weiss v. Nurse Midwifery Associates (applying a substantial performance standard in promise to provide prenatal and postnatal care.)

      2. Anticipatory repudiation occurs when a promisor, prior to time for performance, indicates an intent not to perform his or her duties under the contract
      Example: Cobabe v. Stanger

   C. Special Problems

      1. A "personal satisfaction" clause arises when the promisor agrees to perform to the promisee's personal satisfaction.

      2. "Time is of the essence" creates a "strict performance" standard so that failure to perform as required by the contract results in a material breach.
      Example: Miceli v. Dierberg (Failure to close sale of real property at 10:00 a.m. as required by the contract results in a material breach of contract.)

II. Excuses for Non-Performance

   A. Impossibility (includes "commercial impracticability or commercial frustration.")

   B. Examples include death of promisor, intervening illegality, destruction of subject matter.
   Example: Arabian Score v. Lasma Arabian Ltd. (Fact that horse died within one year of sale does not relieve contracting party from obligation of performance.)

III. Discharge

   A. Release of contractual obligations occurs through performance, agreement, waiver, or intentional alteration of the instrument.

   B. All states also discharge obligation through statutes of limitations.
   Example: Tahan v. Garrick, Inc. (Discharge by mutual agreement of contract to purchase condominiums.)

IV. Remedies (Damages or remedies for Breach of Contract.)

   A. Damages must be proved with reasonable certainty.
   Example: Tristar Cosmetics, Ltd. v. Westinghouse Broadcasting (lost profits are not too speculative to be recovered as damages.)

   B. Kinds of damages recoverable include compensatory, consequential, nominal, liquidated, and punitive.
   Example: Redgrave v. Boston Symphony Orchestra, Inc. (lost opportunities may be compensated as consequential damages)

   C. Plaintiffs have a duty to mitigate (avoid or minimize) damages
   Example: National Football League Players Ass'n v. National Football League Management Council

   D. Equitable remedies may be ordered when damages at law (money damages) are inadequate. Most common equitable remedies are specific performance and injunctions.

Learning Objectives

1. You should understand that the topic of performance and remedies are really separate topics.

2. You should understand that performance issues arise in determining whether there has, in fact, been a breach. These issues include the question of whether performance was due (or whether there are conditions to performance), the standard of performance, and excuses for performance.

3. You should note that a court will always award damages at law (money damages) rather than impose equitable remedies (such as an injunction or specific performance) in a breach of contract case, so long as the non-breaching party can be adequately compensated by money damages.

4. You must understand what a condition is, what conditions precedent, subsequent, and concurrent are, and how each type of condition affects the duty to perform under a contract.

5. You must know the difference between complete performance, substantial performance, and material breach, and the effects of each on the rights and duties of the parties to the contract.

6. You should know the rules governing contracts to perform to personal satisfaction.

7. You should know the rules about the time for performance.

8. You should know all of the different ways in which the doctrine of impossibility can excuse the duty to perform.

9. You must know all of the different ways in which a party can be discharged from the duty to perform.

10. You must know what compensatory, consequential, nominal, liquidated, and punitive damages are and when each type is available in a contract case.

Learning Hints

1. Performance conditions may be express, implied in fact, or implied by law. An example of a condition implied by law is the condition that performance obligations should occur simultaneously. This means that a person must be ready, willing, and able to tender his performance in order to successfully sue the other party for breach if the other party fails to perform as promised.

2. There are two standards of performance; courts generally adopt a substantial performance standard in contract cases where it is very difficult to perform perfectly. For example, construction contracts generally impose a substantial performance standard on the parties.

3. Just because a court imposes a substantial performance standard does not mean that a party may not sue the other party for breach. However, in the event the breach is non-material, the non-breaching party will still be obligated to perform (for example, to pay the contract price for construction), but he may be entitled to subtract from that contract price the loss caused by the breach.

4. Keep in mind that conditions precedent and subsequent have the same practical result: both make the duty to perform conditional upon the occurrence of some future event.

5. In contracts to perform to the personal satisfaction of the other party, the standard of performance is a subjective one (whether the other party is honestly dissatisfied) when the contract involves matters of personal taste, comfort, or judgment, and objective (whether the other party's dissatisfaction is reasonable) when the contract involves matters of mechanical fitness, utility, or marketability. An example of a contract involving matters of personal taste, comfort, or judgment would be a contract for the painting of a portrait, and an example of a contract involving matters of mechanical fitness, utility, or marketability would be a contract for the installation of a furnace.

6. In order for impossibility to excuse the duty to perform, the contract must be for a personal service and the promisor must die or fall victim to an incapacitating illness. If the promisor's duty to perform could be carried out by someone else, performance will not be excused.

7. If the contract is executory, compensatory damages can be computed by subtracting the plaintiff's cost of performance from the value of the promised performance. If A is to sell B a bike for $100, B's recovery (if any) when A breaches would be the reasonable value of the promised bike minus $100. If the contract is executed and the performance is defective, compensatory damages are computed by subtracting the value of the defective performance from the value of the promised performance. In the above example, if A sells B a defective bike, B could recover the reasonable value of the bike as promised minus the actual value of the defective bike he received.

8. It is hard to give a general definition of consequential damages, but examples of consequential damages are easy to name. They include personal injury, damage to property that is not the subject of the contract, lost profits, and lost business good will.

9. The general test of whether an equitable remedy is appropriate is whether there is an adequate legal remedy available to the plaintiff. This usually means that the types of money damages discussed in the textbook are inadequate.

10. Keep two things in mind about liquidated damages provisions: the reasonableness of the stipulated figure is determined from what the parties knew or should have known <u>at the time the contract was entered</u>, <u>not</u> from the plaintiff's actual damages; and once the two tests for the enforcement of a liquidated damages provision are met, the court will enforce the provision even if the plaintiff's actual damages are higher or lower than that figure.

True-False

In the blank provided, put "T" if the statement is True or "F" if the statement is False.

_____ 1. A condition qualifies a party's duty to perform under a contract.

_____ 2. A condition precedent is a condition which must occur before a party's duty to perform arises.

_____ 3. "Time is of the essence" is an example of a substantial performance standard.

_____ 4. Under the doctrine of anticipatory repudiation, a contracting party must wait until the time for performance is due in order to sue for breach.

_____ 5. Under the doctrine of impossibility, a contracting party may be excused from performance if the subject matter of the contract is destroyed through no fault of the promisor.

_____ 6. A contractual condition must be expressly stated in the contract.

_____ 7. Anticipatory repudiation cannot be inferred from the promisor's conduct.

_____ 8. The object of compensatory contract damages is to put the plaintiff in the position he would have been in had the contract been performed as promised.

_____ 9. The defendant is liable for all consequential damages that result from his breach of contract.

_____ 10. A promisor who materially breaches the contract has no right of action under the contract and is liable to the promisee for damages resulting from the breach, but he may be able to recover in quasi contract for benefits he has conferred on the promisee.

Multiple Choice

Circle the best answer.

1. Yves is an interior decorator. Thomas enters a contract with Yves whereby Yves agrees to prepare a design for the redecoration of Thomas's home. Thomas agrees to pay Yves a sum of money for this design on condition that he (Thomas) is personally satisfied with the design. Which of the following statements concerning this "personal satisfaction" clause is most nearly correct?
   a. Thomas must pay for the design even if he is honestly dissatisfied with it, so long as Yves can prove that a reasonable person would have been satisfied with the design;
   b. If Yves completes the design, Thomas will have to pay the reasonable value of the design under the doctrine of substantial performance;
   c. Thomas will not have to pay Yves if he is dissatisfied with the design, even if he (Thomas) acts in bad faith;

d. Thomas will not have to pay Yves if he honestly is dissatisfied with the design, even if a reasonable person would have been satisfied with the design.

2. L contracted to build a house for M. After the job was completed, M refused to pay L the balance he owed him under the contract, claiming that L had done some of the work in an unsatisfactory manner, and that M was also entitled to damages because of delay in completion of the construction. If L sues M for the balance of the contract price, and M counterclaims for damages for breach, which of the following performance standards will the court most likely employ in this case?
    a. strict performance;
    b. substantial performance;
    c. time is of the essence;
    d. UCC 2-508, which permits the seller the opportunity to "cure" the beach if time for performance has not expired.

3. L contracted to build a house for M. After the job was completed, M refused to pay L the balance he owed him under the contract, claiming that L had done some of the work in an unsatisfactory manner, and that M was also entitled to damages because of delay in completion of the construction. If M can prove that L willfully and intentionally breached the contract by using substandard plumbing fixtures in the home, which of the following performance standards will the court most likely employ?
    a. strict performance;
    b. substantial performance;
    c. time is of the essence;
    d. UCC 2-508, which permits the seller the opportunity to "cure" the breach if time for performance has not expired.

4. Injuries to a person or to his/her property as a foreseeable result of breach of a sales contract are recoverable as:
    a. consequential damages;
    b. liquidated damages;
    c. incidental damages;
    d. punitive damages.

5. Which of the following statements concerning contract performance under the UCC is not correct?
    a. The UCC recognizes the doctrine of anticipatory repudiation, and permits a contracting party to sue for breach in cases where a party repudiates the contract before performance is due;
    b. The UCC recognizes the doctrine of commercial impracticability, a doctrine which excuses performance in cases where performance is made impossible or impracticable by the occurrence of a contingency, the non-occurrence of which was a basic assumption on which the contract was made;
    c. The UCC generally protects a party's expectation interest in a contract, but permits recovery of incidental and consequential damages in appropriate cases;
    d. The UCC permits contracting parties to limit remedies for breach by agreement, and expressly permits parties to limit consequential damages for personal injuries in the case of consumer goods.

6. Which of the following will excuse performance of a contractual obligation?
    a. The death of the promisor in a contract to sell goods
    b. The breakdown of the promisor's truck in a contract to deliver goods
    c. The passage of a law after the contract is created which makes performance 50% more expensive for the promisor
    d. The promisee's failure to cooperate in the performance of the contract

7. Which of the following events would never discharge or excuse the duty to perform one's contract obligations?
    a. Incapacitating illness or death of the promisor on a personal service contract
    b. Commercial impracticability if the contract is for the sale of goods
    c. The happening of a condition precedent
    d. Material breach by the other party to the contract

8. Specific performance is <u>least</u> likely to be ordered when:
   a. the contract is for the sale of land.
   b. the contract is for the sale of antiques or works of art.
   c. compensatory damages are an adequate remedy.
   d. punitive damages are awarded.

9. Which is <u>most</u> likely to be a material breach of contract?
   a. The installation of a furnace with which the buyer is personally dissatisfied where the contract promises performance to the buyer's personal satisfaction
   b. The failure to install a furnace because the house in which it was to be installed burns down
   c. The installation of a furnace on November 2 where the contract says installation is to be on November 1 and that time is of the essence
   d. The failure to install a furnace because, after the contract is entered, furnaces of that type are declared illegal by statute

10. Equitable remedies in a contract case:
    a. include specific performance and injunctions.
    b. are available even when money damages would be an adequate remedy.
    c. are available whenever the plaintiff asks for them.
    d. are never awarded.

Short Essay

1. X contracts with Y to provide Y with ball bearings to use in Y's plant. The contract price was $800. X knew nothing about Y or his business and mistakenly delivered ball bearings of inferior quality. As a result, Y suffered $10,000 in lost profits. The value of the defective ball bearings which X delivered to Y was $500. The parties' contract provided for liquidated damages of $500,000 if X failed to properly perform. What damages is Y entitled to recover?

2. When is failure to perform on time a material breach of the contract? When is it substantial performance?

3. A contracted to install irrigation ditches on Y's farm. Shortly after A and Y entered the contract, a flash flood devastated Y's land, making A's job much more difficult and expensive, though not impossible. What is the traditional attitude of the common law to A's claim that he should be excused from performance due to impossibility? What relatively new doctrine might A use to get himself excused from performance?

4. On January 1, Bob and John entered into a contract where in Bob agreed to sell John 10 acres of land. The closing was set for April 15. On March 15, John learned that Bob had sold the property to someone else. John wants to sue Bob for breach of contract immediately. Can he, or must he wait until April 15? Explain.

CHAPTER 17
FORMATION AND TERMS OF SALES CONTRACTS

Outline

I. Application of the Uniform Commercial Code

   A.   Article 2 applies to all contracts <u>for the sale of goods.</u>

   B.   Some contracts are "mixed" (include both sale of goods and provision of services.) In this case, the test is which "predominates?"

      Example: <u>Abelman v. Velsicol Chemical Corp.</u>(Contract to obtain termite tretament is a service contract, not a contract for the sale of goods.)

   C.   UCC Article 2 differs from traditional contract law because it is more <u>flexible</u> and based on concepts of <u>reasonableness</u> and <u>good faith.</u>

      1. Some UCC sections apply a different standard to contracts between merchants.

II. Formation of Sales Contracts

   A.   Parties may enter into a contract under the UCC by their behavior or conduct.

   B.   The Code changes the common law rule that an offeror can revoke the offer at any time prior to acceptance. A "Firm offer" by a merchant in a signed writing under UCC 2-205 is not revocable for the time stated (but in no case longer than 3 months).

      Example: <u>Lowenstern v. Stop & Shop Companies, Inc.</u> (Enforcing a store's "rainchecks" as a firm offer under the UCC.)

   C.   The UCC changes the common law rule of acceptance in two ways:

      1. A timely expression of acceptance creates a contract even it contains different or additional terms from the offer (UCC 2-207)

        Example: <u>Middletown Engineering Co. v. Climate Conditioning Co., Inc.</u>

      2. An acceptance is effective under the UCC if made by reasonable means. This changes the common law "mailbox rule" in some cases by expanding the concept of reasonable manner of acceptance.

III. Consideration and the Code

   A.   The UCC provides that a good modification of a sales contract needs no consideration to be binding.

   B.   However, an unconscionable contract (which contains unfair terms and is the product of unequal bargaining power) is not enforceable under UCC 2-302.

      Example: <u>Sho-Pro of Indiana v. Brown</u> (holding that the court has the authority to refuse to enforce a contract it finds to be unconscionable at the time it was made, and defining the factors to be used in making that determination.)

IV. Writing and the UCC

   A.   The UCC Statute of Frauds provision is UCC 2-201, and requires contracts for the sale of goods for $500 or more to be in writing to be enforceable.

   B.   The Code also contains alternative methods of satisfying this section. These include the "specially manufactured goods" exception.

      Example: <u>Smith-Scharff Paper Company v. P.N. Hirsch & Co. Stores, Inc.</u>
      Other exceptions include the "merchant's memo exception", partial performance, and admission in court pleadings.

V. Terms of Sales Contracts

   A.   The UCC provides for "gap filling" provisions, including price, quantity, delivery, and time terms.

   B.   The UCC also changes rules of title and rights of third parties.

      Example: <u>Russell v. Transamerica Insurance Co.</u>

C. Under the UCC, a seller who has voidable title can pass good title to a good faith purchaser for value:

Example: <u>Charles Evans BMW, INc. v. Williams</u> (purchaser acquired good title to a car when it purchased it from a person who had obtained title through criminal fraud.)

D. Under the UCC, the party who bears the risk of loss of goods is not necessarily the person who has title.

E. Under the UCC, risk of loss and title may differ in "Sales on Trial.

Example: <u>In Re Auclair McGregor v. Jackson</u> (Firearms delivered to consignee were subject to the claims of consignee's creditors.)

Learning Objectives

1. You should understand that common law rules have been changed in some cases in contracts for the sale of goods because all states but Louisiana have adopted the Uniform Commercial Code.

2. You should know what the Uniform Commercial Code (U.C.C.) is, and to what kinds of contracts it applies.

3. You should know how the UCC defines "merchant" and what provisions treat merchants differently from non-merchants.

4. You should know how the U.C.C. rules about creation of contracts differ from contract law rules about creation of contracts.

5. You should know what a firm offer is and how it differs from the contract law rule about revocation of offers.

6. You should know the U.C.C. rules about acceptance (especially regarding the battle of the forms and the manner and medium of acceptance) and how they differ from those of contract law.

7. You should know the instances in which the U.C.C. rules about consideration for promises not to revoke and for contract modifications differ from contract law rules.

8. You should know what the term "unconscionability" means and what remedies the Code allows the courts to fashion when a contract is unconscionable.

9. You should know when the U.C.C.'s statute of frauds (Section 2-201) applies, and what is required to satisfy the Code's writing requirement.

10. You should know how the U.C.C. "fills gaps" when a contract does not specify price, time, delivery, or quantity.

11. You should know the U.C.C. rules about when title passes from seller to buyer.

12. You should know the three situations in which the U.C.C. protects a purchaser's title in goods against the rights of third parties.

Learning Hints

1. Article 2 of the UCC applies to contracts for the sale of goods. The Code does not apply to other kinds of contracts, for example, service contracts, employment contracts, and contracts for the sale of goods. However, other statutes may apply in special cases. For example, many states have contracts regulating the provision of insurance.

2. It is not always easy to tell whether a contract is governed by the UCC. Some contracts are "mixed" because they provide both for the sale of goods and provision of services. In such cases, courts look to see which "predominates."

3. The UCC changes the common law rules in certain instances. However, if a specific code provision does not address an issue, the courts apply common law rules. Examples of common law rules which apply in sales cases are the rules governing rescission for lack of capacity and lack of reality of consent (e.g., misrepresentation, fraud, and duress.)

4. Generally, the UCC adopts a more flexible approach to contract law, and contracts may be formed by the conduct of the parties. It is still necessary, however, to find that parties <u>intended</u> to contract in order to find an enforceable contract under the UCC.

5. Sometimes the U.C.C. has special, tougher rules for "merchants." (A merchant is a person who is in the business of selling goods of the particular type involved in the case. For example, J.C. Penney is a merchant of clothing. But if you sell your used coat to your roommate, you are not a merchant). However, don't get mixed up and think that the U.C.C. only applies to merchants. The U.C.C. applies any time there is a sale of goods. It will be helpful to go back through the chapter and make a list of the rules that apply only to merchants.

6. The term "firm offer" has a specific meaning under the U.C.C. which is different from the term's meaning in common English usage. Many students get confused because they think a firm offer is any specific, definite offer. This is wrong. A firm offer under the U.C.C. is an offer that cannot be revoked for a period of time. When you think "firm offer," think "irrevocability." Look back through the chapter and list the three things that must exist before an offer is considered to be a firm offer under the U.C.C. Now review your reading to determine how long a firm offer is considered to be irrevocable.

7. Consideration is required for sales of goods contracts, just as it is for other types of contracts. The U.C.C. has relaxed contract law consideration doctrines in two ways, however: (1) no consideration is needed when the parties voluntarily agree to change a term in an existing contract and (2) no consideration is needed for a firm offer.

8. Under contract law, the offeror was the "master of the contract" in all regards. If the offeree wanted to accept an offer, he had to accept it totally and not add anything new to it. That rule has been modified under the U.C.C. Under the Code, a court would look at how the parties acted and what they said to determine if there was an agreement between the two. It doesn't matter if the offeree has added some new terms in his acceptance, so long as the acceptance was timely and definite. If, however, an offeree said something to the effect that "I am only accepting if you agree to my new terms," that would not be a valid acceptance, even under the U.C.C.

9. If a court determines that there was a valid acceptance, the next question is whether the terms added by the offeree are part of the contract. If both of the parties are merchants, the new term can become part of the contract even if the offeror does not expressly agree to it. Look at the textbook to review the circumstances under which an added term might become part of the contract.

10. The U.C.C. requires some independent evidence of contracts for the sale of goods for $500 or more. One way to provide this evidence would be for the parties to have indicated the existence of the contract in a writing signed by the party who is denying the existence of the contract (the "party to be charged"). Another way is to have a confirmatory memorandum sent by one merchant to another merchant. The memo should be signed, indicate that a contract has been made, and state the quantity. If the other merchant receives it and has reason to know its contents and does not object to it in writing in 10 days, the memo provides evidence that a contract existed sufficient to satisfy the Code's statute of frauds. A third situation in which there is independent evidence of the existence of the contract is where the "party to be charged" (see above) admits the existence of the contract under oath or in court documents. That would be enough evidence of a contract to satisfy the statute of frauds, at least up to the quantity of goods that he admits. A fourth situation in which there is independent evidence of the existence of the contract is if one of the parties has accepted part payment or part delivery from the other. If so, the contract is enforceable up to the quantity performed. A fifth situation in which there is independent evidence of the existence of a contract is where one party has ordered specially manufactured goods from the other. If the other has started production and can't resell the goods, the oral contract is enforceable. Remember, these rules apply only if the contract is for $500 or more.

11. You will learn that the U.C.C. permits parties to have a contract even though they have left some terms open. To provide a means of resolving disputes that arise over open terms, the U.C.C "gap-filling" provisions supply presumptions that are to be applied when the parties have failed to agree upon one or more terms. Notice that these presumptions draw upon prevailing practices in the particular market or industry involved (for example, if a price term is left open, the U.C.C. presumes that the price is to be a "reasonable price" at the time and place for delivery).

12. "Title" means ownership, "risk of loss" means financial responsibility for the consequences of any disastrous occurrence (such as theft or destruction) that may befall goods, and "insurable interest" means the right to take out insurance on the goods.

13. There are a lot of rules to remember about title and risk of loss. You will probably find it helpful to make up a chart showing the point at which title and risk of loss pass to the buyer. Think of the process of selling goods as a continuum in time, beginning with the moment the contract is created and ending with the delivery of goods to the buyer. In between these two points there is a lot of variation. In some contracts, shipment of the goods across great distances is required; in others, the buyer must pick the goods up from a warehouse or at the seller's place of business. Draw out these possibilities along a "time line" and mark the point at which title and risk of loss would pass. Notice that title will generally pass when the seller has completed his obligations concerning physical delivery of the goods. Notice that risk of loss generally passes at the point at which the buyer has the right to control the goods (and is likely to have insurance to cover their loss).

14. In some sales, there is the express possibility that the buyer may send the goods back to the seller (sale or return, sale on approval, and consignment sales). There are special rules about title, risk of loss, and creditors' interests for these situations which you should add to your chart.

True-False

In the blank provided, put "T" if the statement is True or "F" if the statement is False

_____ 1. Goods are "identified" to a contract when it is clear that certain goods are the specific ones to which the contract refers.

_____ 2. The UCC treats merchants and non-merchants the same in determining whether there was a "firm offer" which is not revocable for the time stated in the offer.

_____ 3. Risk of loss is determined by who has title to goods under the UCC.

_____ 4. A "good faith purchaser for value" may take better title to goods under the UCC than the seller.

_____ 5. A court may refuse to enforce a contract under the UCC if it finds it was "unconscionable" at the time of formation.

_____ 6. A "firm offer" can be made orally.

_____ 7. Under the U.C.C., an acceptance is invalid if it adds any terms that were not stated in the offer.

_____ 8. Consideration is required to modify an existing contract for the sale of goods.

_____ 9. Article 2 of the U.C.C. does not apply to service contracts, or to contracts in which service is the predominant element.

_____ 10. Under the U.C.C., a valid contract may exist even if the parties have not expressly agreed upon the price of the goods to be sold.

_____ 11. A fixed price is essential to the creation of a binding contract for the sale of goods under both the common law and the Code.

_____ 12. If a contract of sale is silent about the time for delivery, the Code presumes that the goods are to be tendered within a reasonable time.

_____ 13. It is impossible for anyone who buys goods from a seller with voidable title to obtain good title to the goods.

_____ 14. Under the Code, buyers may have an insurable interest in goods before they actually obtain title to the goods.

_____ 15. An FOB term can be either a destination or a shipment term.

_____ 16. In "output" or "requirements" contracts, the Code limits quantity to such actual output or requirements as may occur in good faith.

_____ 17. Generally, title never passes to the buyer before the buyer has actually received the goods.

_____ 18. Under the U.C.C., even an innocent buyer can never receive better title to the goods than the seller has.

_____ 19. If the buyer rejects tender of the goods, title automatically revests in the seller.

_____ 20. If none of the special rules regarding risk of loss applies, the risk of loss generally passes to the buyer from a merchant seller only when the buyer actually receives the goods.

Multiple Choice

Circle the best answer.

1. Under the U.C.C., if an offeror does not stipulate a particular means of acceptance:
   a. the offeree may respond by any reasonable means, and the acceptance will be effective upon dispatch.
   b. the offeree may respond by any reasonable means, but the acceptance will not be effective until receipt;
   c. the offeree's response will be treated as a counter-offer which the original offeror is free to accept or reject;
   d. the offeree's response will be an effective acceptance, even if the offeree does not intend to enter into a contract.

2. Article 2 of the Uniform Commercial Code:
   a. Applies to all contracts;
   b. Applies to all contracts for the sale of goods;
   c. Applies to all contracts for the sale of goods valued at $500 or more;
   d. Applies only to contracts for the sale of goods between merchants.

3. In order to make a "firm offer" under the UCC:
   a. It must have been made in a signed writing;
   b. The offeror must have been a merchant;
   c. The offer must have been made in an advertisement;
   d. Both (a) and (b) are correct.

4. An agreement modifying an existing contract under the UCC:
   a. Requires new consideration to be binding
   b. Only requires new consideration to be binding if the seller is a merchant;
   c. Only requires new consideration to be binding if both parties are merchants;
   d. Requires no new consideration to be binding but must be in good faith.

5. Under the UCC, which of the following is an exception to the rule that contracts for the sale of goods of $500 or more must be in writing to be enforceable?
   a. the "merchant's memo" exception;
   b. part performance by the parties;
   c. the "specially manufactured goods" exception;
   d. All of the above are exceptions.

6. Excon, Inc. (a merchant) placed an order for air magnet valves with Cheatum, Inc. (a merchant). Excon's offer stipulated that no variations or additions could be made in its terms. Cheatum sent a definite and timely acceptance form, which contained several additional terms. Which of the following is most nearly correct?
   a. Cheatum's inclusion of additional terms was a counteroffer which terminated Excon's offer.
   b. Excon will be bound by the additional terms stated in the acceptance.
   c. Excon and Cheatum have a contract, but the contract does not include the additional terms stated in Cheatum's acceptance.
   d. There is no contract because Cheatum acted unreasonably.

7. Falcon Imports sent a telegram to Harry Hotdog, offering to sell Harry a rare painting. In its offer, Falcon specified that "your written acceptance must be sent by certified mail." Harry wrote a letter of acceptance and sent it by regular first class mail. Harry's letter was sent on May 1 and delivered to Falcon on May 3. On May 2, Falcon sold the painting to someone else. Harry sues Falcon for breach of contract. What result?
   a. Under the U.C.C., acceptance by any reasonable means is effective when dispatched. Thus, a contract was formed on May 1.
   b. The U.C.C. would not apply to this case unless both Harry and Falcon are merchants.
   c. A contract was formed on May 3, when Falcon received Harry's acceptance.
   d. Under the U.C.C., an offeror may still stipulate a specific manner of acceptance. No contract was formed because Harry did not use the stipulated method for communicating his acceptance.

8. McGraw owned a clothing store. One day, when Taggart was shopping in the store, McGraw approached him and told Taggart that he had a Harris tweed suit in Taggart's size that he would sell to him at 30% off the suggested retail price. Taggart stated that he needed several days to make up his mind, and McGraw replied orally that he would keep the offer open for one week. Five days later, Taggart returned to the store. Before Taggart could say a word, McGraw told him that the offer was revoked. What result?
   a. A valid and enforceable contract was formed when Taggart told McGraw that he wanted to buy the suit.
   b. McGraw made a firm offer that could not be revoked for three months.
   c. McGraw did not make a firm offer because the offer was not in writing. Therefore, he was free to revoke it before acceptance.
   d. Two of the above are correct.

9. A writes B, "I will sell you one carload of widgets for $5000." B writes back, "I accept. You are to pay the freight to my place of business, and I will pay the $5000 thirty days after delivery." A and B are merchants, and these shipment and payment terms are standard in their industry. What result?
   a. Under common law contract rules, B has accepted.
   b. A contract exists under the U.C.C.
   c. B's additional statements will be construed as a material alteration.
   d. No contract was formed unless A called B and agreed to the new terms.

10. Axelrod agreed over the telephone to sell 1,000 scissors to Berry at $1.00 each. Berry sent Axelrod a check for $500, which Axelrod indorsed and cashed. Two days later, Axelrod sent Berry a letter, saying "Deal's off. Enclosed is my check for the return of your $500." Berry sues Axelrod for breach of contract. What result, and why?
   a. The contract is completely unenforceable because it violates the U.C.C.'s statute of frauds.
   b. Part of the contract is enforceable because Axelrod accepted part payment.
   c. The entire contract is enforceable because Axelrod accepted part payment.
   d. No part of the contract is enforceable because the scissors were not specially manufactured goods.

11. Buyer owns a retail store in Baltimore. Seller is a manufacturer in Los Angeles. Buyer orders goods from Seller to be shipped by a carrier "F.O.B. Los Angeles." In this contract, risk of loss would pass to Buyer:
   a. when Seller delivers the goods to the carrier.
   b. when the goods are identified to the contract.
   c. when the contract was made.
   d. when the goods are delivered to their destination.

12. Clayton signed a contract on April 1 to purchase a new car off the lot from French Auto Sales. French's salesman told Clayton that he would need 24 hours to clean the car up and service it before Clayton picked it up. That night (the evening of April 1) a thief stole the car off the lot.
   a. The risk of loss was on French until Clayton actually received the car.
   b. The risk of loss was on Clayton as soon as he signed the contract.
   c. Neither party bears the risk of loss, since the car was stolen without fault of either party.
   d. The risk of loss passed to Clayton as soon as the goods were identified to the contract.

13. Maris, a retailer in New Orleans, ordered goods from Wix Corporation, a manufacturer in Philadelphia. The contract called for the goods to be shipped by a carrier "F.O.B. New Orleans." Assuming that neither party breaches the contract, the risk of loss will pass to Maris, the buyer:
   a. when the goods are loaded with the carrier in Philadelphia.
   b. when the goods are delivered in New Orleans.
   c. when the contract is signed.
   d. when the goods are identified to the contract.

14. Which of the following is a false statement?
   a. The term "F.O.B." at a named place marks the point to which the seller has the duty to deliver and, in the absence of an agreement otherwise, the place the risk of loss passes to the buyer.
   b. The term "C & F" is a standardized shipping term which indicates that the seller is obligated to insure the goods.

85

c. The term "C.I.F." means that the price of the goods includes the cost of shipping and insuring them.

d. The term "no arrival, no sale" means that the seller must ship the goods, but he is not in breach of the contract if they do not arrive.

15. H.G. Gloom, Inc. agreed to sell widgets to Bill Bonnie. No special provision as to when the price was to be paid was included in the contract, and there is no established industry custom. Which of the following is correct?

a. No contract resulted because of indefiniteness.

b. The price will be due within a reasonable time after delivery of the widgets.

c. The price will be due when the seller accepts the buyer's order for the goods.

d. The price will be due when the seller tenders delivery of the goods.

Short Essay

1. In May, Farmer agreed in writing to sell his entire crop of artichokes to Canner for $1.75 per bushel. In June, the price of fertilizer rose dramatically, and Farmer told Canner in good faith that he'd have to get $2.00 per bushel for the crop. Canner agreed and the price amendment was put in writing and signed by both parties. Farmer delivered the artichokes, but Canner refused to pay more than $1.75 per bushel for them. Farmer sues Canner for breach of contract. What result under traditional common law? How has the UCC changed your answer?

2. Larry owned a motorbike which he sold to Moe for $500. Moe paid for the bike with a "bad check" which later bounced for insufficient funds. Moe in turn sold the bike for $50 to Curly. Does Curly have good title to the bike? Explain.

3. X and Y made a contract of sale whereby X, the seller, was to ship the goods F.O.B. seller's place of business via Fly-by-Night Trucking Co. On May 1, X delivered the goods to Fly-by-Night. On May 6, the goods arrived in Y's city. On May 8, Y picked up the goods. At what point did title to the goods pass to Y?

4. Buyer, a grocer, wrote Seller, a retailer of canned goods, "Please ship me 150 cases of Wormy Creamed Corn via Speedy Trucklines as soon as possible for $10 per case, and bill me in 30 days. /Signed/Buyer." Seller received the order the next day. He wrote Buyer, "Am accepting your order and am shipping your Wormy Creamed Corn tomorrow via Speedy Trucklines. Will bill you 30 days after date of shipment. Interest rate of 10 percent on overdue invoices, beginning 45 days after date of invoice. /Signed/Seller." Buyer received this acknowledgement, but made no response to it. Buyer paid the original price on the invoice 60 days after shipment, but refused to pay the interest. Seller sues Buyer. Must Buyer pay the interest? Why or why not?

5. Ann, a homemaker, wrote a letter to Quilting Bee, a retail store, offering to sell it one of her quilts for $500. Was this a firm offer? Why or why not?

6. What is the difference between a "sale or return" and a "sale on approval" with regard to when the risk of loss passes to the buyer? What is the reason for this difference?

CHAPTER 18
WARRANTIES AND PRODUCT LIABILITY

Outline

I. Warranty Theory: Product Liability is based on one or more of the following legal theories: Warranty; negligence, or strict liability.

A. Express Warranties

    1. Express warranties arise when a seller makes a statement of fact or promise concerning the goods which becomes the basis of the bargain between the parties.
Example: Cipollone v. Liggett Group, Inc., holding that advertisements can create an express warranty, but they must be proven to have been part of the "basis of the bargain" on which purchaser purchased the product.

B. Implied Warranties are imposed under the UCC: the implied warranty of merchantability and the implied warranty of fitness for a particular purpose.

    1. The implied warranty of merchantability requires that goods be fit for their ordinary purpose.
Example: Virgil v. "Kash N' Karry" Service Corp. (finding breach of warranty occurred when thermos bottle purchased at defendant's store imploded.)
Example: Mexicali Rose v. Superior Court (Chicken bone in chicken enchilada did not constitute breach of implied warranty of merchantability under the "foreign-natural" test of merchantability of food.

    2. The implied warranty of fitness for a particular purpose arises when the sellers knows the particular purpose for which buyer is purchasing the goods and knows that the buyer is relying on the seller in making the purchase.
Example: Klein v. Sears & Co. (Seller found liable for breach of warranty of fitness in sale of riding lawnmower.)

    3. The implied warranty of title protects the buyer's ownership of goods purchased from seller.
Example: Brokke v. Williams (pawnbroker liable for breach of warranty of title when goods sold to purchaser were later discovered to have been stolen.)

II. Exclusion of Modification of Warranties

A. The UCC (2-316) permits exclusion of limitation of warranties. It is difficult, if not impossible, to make an express warranty and limit or disclaim it at the same time.

B. Disclaimer of Implied Warranties

    1. The UCC permits a seller to exclude the implied warranty of merchantatibility. The seller must mention the word merchantability and the disclaimer must be conspicuous.

    2. The implied warranty of fitness for a particular purpose may be disclaimed in writing, and must be conspicuous.

    3. However, a disclaimer which meets these requirements may be unenforceable because it is unconscionable under the UCC.

    4. A seller may also limit its liability for breach of warranty; a limitation of liability which is unconscionable or fails of its essential purpose is unenforceable.
Example: Wright v. T&B Auto Sales, Inc.

C. Beneficiaries of Contract Warranties

    1. Under the UCC (2-318), a person who is not in privity with the seller (that is, who did not purchase the goods directly from the seller) may be unable to recover damages under a warranty theory. However, the consumer may still recover damages under a negligence or strict liability theory.
Example: In Re Air Crash Disaster at Sioux City Iowa on July 19, 1989 Banks v. United Airlines, Inc.

    2. Under the Magnuson-Moss Warranty Act of 1975, if a seller of a consumer product that costs more than $5 gives the consumer a written warranty, certain requirements apply, and there are different provisions for a full or limited warranty.

III.Negligence: Breach of a duty of care by a seller resulting in a foreseeable injury to the purchaser may constitute negligence.

    A.   Examples include inadequate inspection, negligent manufacturing processes, negligent product design, and negligent failure to warn.

       Example: <u>Daniell v. Ford Motor Co., Inc.</u> (Ford Motor Company not liable under a negligent failure to warn or negligent design theory to consumer who was unable to escape from the trunk of an automobile after locking herself in. The court said the seller cannot be liable where a product is used in a manner that could not reasonably be anticipated.)

    B.   Privity and disclaimers generally do not apply.

IV.Strict Liability: Under the Restatement 402A, a plaintiff may recover under this theory if the following elements are proven:

    A.   Elements: Product sold by a <u>merchant-like seller</u> in a <u>defective condition</u> <u>unreasonably dangerous</u> to the <u>ultimate user or consumer</u> who sustains <u>physical harm or property damage</u> as a result of the defect.

       Example: <u>Wheeler v. Andrew Jergens Company</u> (even though shampoo had been tampered with, seller of shampoo which caused consumer's hair to fall out could be liable under this theory.)

    B.   Issues arise in determining whether a product is <u>unreasonably dangerous</u> or <u>defectively designed</u>. Courts generally look to the "state of the art" at the time of manufacture.

    C.   Defenses include misuse of the product and assumption of the risk.

    D.   "Industry-wide" liability is an outgrowth of strict product liability. Under this theory, a large number of people who were injured by defective products (for example, asbestos), may sue multiple manufacturers engaged in making that product.

       Example: <u>McElhaney v. Eli Lilly & Co.</u> (Plaintiff may sue several manufacturers of DES, even though she cannot identify the manufacturer of the drug that injured her.

Learning Objectives

    1. You should note that the general topic of "products liability" includes application of several different legal theories used by persons injured by defective products.

    2. Each different theory, whether negligence, warranty, or strict liability, have different requirements and, in some cases, different defenses apply.

    3. The evolution of product liability law has not been orderly and planned, but rather courts have recognized and permitted the expansion of different theories as applied in products liability actions.

    4. You should understand that frequently, a plaintiff will maintain an action based on several different theories, but will not be entitled to recover multiple damages if the seller/manufacturer is found liable under more than one theory.

    5. You should know what an express warranty is and how an express warranty may be created.

    6. You should know what the implied warranty of merchantability guarantees, as well as when that warranty arises.

    7. You should know what the implied warranty of fitness for a particular purpose guarantees, as well as when that warranty arises.

    8. You should know what the implied warranty of title is, as well as how it differs from the other warranties discussed in Chapter 18.

    9. You should know how the various warranties can be excluded or disclaimed by the seller.

  10. You should become familiar with the kinds of circumstances in which attempted disclaimers of warranties may be found unconscionable, and should know the standards provided by the Uniform Commercial Code for determining whether a limitation of warranty liability should be enforced.

  11. You should know which persons, in addition to the purchaser of the product, may be allowed to benefit from a warranty.

  12. You should become familiar with the major provisions of the Magnuson-Moss Warranty Act.

13. You should know the kinds of circumstances in which a seller may be held liable in a negligence-based product liability action.

14. You should know the basic elements of strict liability, as well as how strict liability is different from liability for negligence and liability for breach of warranty.

15. You should know what defenses are available in a strict liability action.

16. You should know what the industrywide liability doctrine is and when it applies.

Learning Hints

1. Keep in mind that different legal theories may apply in different cases. Breach of warranty actions are most like contract actions, and the remedies generally include contract-like damages. For example, a person who proves breach of express or implied warranty against the seller should be able to recover "expectation damages" or "basis of the bargain damages," which generally is the difference between the value of the product, as warranted, and its actual value as a result of the defect.

2. In breach of warranty cases, however, the consumer may also recover other contract damages. These may include "consequential damages," which are damages that are foreseeable as a result of the breach. In some cases, a consumer who is injured by a defective product may recover damages for personal injury as "consequential" damages under a breach of warranty theory.

3. Most consumers who suffer physical injury as a result of a defective product will sue under a "strict liability" or "negligence" theory. Under this theory, the consumer does not have to establish privity of contract (which may be required in some states under a warranty theory), and disclaimers of liability by sellers are unenforceable under this theory.

4. A strict liability theory dispenses with the requirement that the consumer prove the seller was negligent in manufacturing, designing, packaging or distributing the product. All the purchaser must prove is that the product was "defective" and "unreasonably dangerous," and that this resulted in physical injury or property damage to the purchaser.

5. Product misuse and assumption of the risk are defenses to an action under strict liability; these defenses, as well as contributory or comparative negligence, would be permitted in negligence actions as well. However, product misuse which is <u>foreseeable</u> may not relieve a seller of liability.

6. No formal language or written guarantee is necessary for a seller to make an express warranty. If the seller describes the goods, makes a statement of purported fact or a promise concerning the goods, or displays a sample or model of the goods to the buyer, an express warranty may be created. Where an express warranty is created, the goods must measure up to the description, statement of purported fact, promise, sample, or model. If the goods do not measure up, there is a breach of warranty. Be aware, however, that a seller's mere commendation of the goods or a seller's generalized opinion concerning value of the goods does not ordinarily rise to the level of an express warranty. Instead, such statements are considered to be only "sales talk" or "puffing."

7. Remember that even if a statement or other act by the seller appears at first glance to be an express warranty, there is actually no express warranty (and hence no liability for breach of express warranty) unless the seller's statement or other act became <u>part of the bargain</u>. This generally means that what the seller said or did must at least have been a contributing factor in the buyer's decision to purchase the goods. Obviously, the <u>part of the bargain</u> test cannot be satisfied in a situation in which the buyer did not know about the seller's statement or other act until after the buyer had purchased the goods.

8. Express warranties may be made through the seller's advertising material.

9. It is exceedingly difficult, if not virtually impossible, for a seller to make a fully effective disclaimer of liability for an express warranty once the seller has made an express warranty. Sellers can, however, limit their liability for breach of express warranty by putting a clause in the contract that provides for an exclusive or limited remedy in the event of a breach of warranty. For example, such a clause could provide that the remedy for breach of warranty is limited to repair or replacement of the defective goods. These clauses are usually upheld unless they are found to be unconscionable.

10. The implied warranty of merchantability is an automatic guarantee of reasonable quality in sales of goods made by merchants, unless, of course, the warranty has been disclaimed properly by the merchant. A generally reliable rule of thumb is that a merchant is one who is in the business of selling a particular type of goods. Do not forget that the implied warranty of merchantability arises only if the seller is a merchant <u>as to the particular goods being sold</u>. For example, the implied warranty of merchantability is not created when a seller who is in the business of selling automobiles sells his neighbor a refrigerator he (the seller) had in his basement.

11. The implied warranty of fitness for a particular purpose is based on the seller's knowing or having reason to know: (a) the special, individual, or particular purpose for which the buyer wants the goods; and (b) that the buyer is relying on the seller to select goods suitable for fulfillment of that purpose. Note that if the basic elements of an implied warranty of fitness for a particular purpose are present, even a seller who is not a merchant may be found to have made this implied warranty. As with the implied warranty of merchantability, however, the seller may disclaim liability for breach of the implied warranty of fitness for a particular purpose.

12. Remember that the implied warranty of merchantability guarantees that the goods will be fit for the <u>ordinary</u> purposes to which such goods customarily are put, and that the implied warranty of fitness guarantees that the goods will be fit for the <u>particular</u>, individual purpose of the buyer. This means that in some cases, goods which are adequate enough to pass the merchantability test may fail the fitness for particular purpose test. In other cases, however, the goods may be such that both the implied warranty of merchantability and the implied warranty of fitness for a particular purpose are breached.

13. The implied warranties of merchantability and fitness for a particular purpose are fairly easy for sellers to exclude or disclaim, provided that the seller follows the disclaimer rules set out in the UCC. Look closely at the disclaimer rules set out in your text and note that the rules differ somewhat, depending upon which implied warranty the seller is attempting to exclude.

14. Negligence law focuses on whether the seller failed to use reasonable care in connection with the designing, manufacturing, or marketing of its product. In other words, negligence is a fault-based legal theory in which the conduct of the seller plays the central role. Strict liability, on the other hand, is a legal theory in which the focus is on the condition of the product itself, rather than on the conduct of the seller. Strict liability is liability imposed without regard for whether the seller was somehow at fault in its conduct. This means that under strict liability, it is possible that a seller could be found liable for injuries caused by a defective, unreasonably dangerous product, even if the seller used all due care to prevent injuries. In a negligence suit, the seller would not be held liable if the seller exercised reasonable care, even though injuries nevertheless resulted.

15. Among the requirements for strict liability is that the product must be in a defective condition that makes the product unreasonably dangerous. This is really two requirements in one. First, the product must be defective. Second, the product must be unreasonably dangerous because of its defective condition. It is not enough that the product is merely defective. For example, a dishwasher that does not run properly is defective, but it is not unreasonably dangerous. However, if a defect in the dishwasher causes the machine not only to fail to run properly but also to explode violently, the dishwasher is both defective and unreasonably dangerous.

True-False

In the blank provided, put "T" if the statement is True or "F" if the statement is False.

_____ 1. A sample or picture of a product may create an express warranty.

_____ 2. It is very difficult, if not impossible, to disclaim an express warranty.

_____ 3. The UCC does not permit a seller to disclaim an implied warranty of merchantability or fitness for a particular purpose.

_____ 4. Under a strict liability theory, a plaintiff still must establish that a seller failed to use reasonable care (that is, breached a duty to the plaintiff) in the manufacture or sale of a product.

_____ 5. Assumption of the risk is not a defense to an action under strict liability.

_____ 6. If the plaintiff brings her product liability suit on a strict liability theory but she was not in privity with the defendant, she will lose her suit on that basis.

_____ 7. If a seller is not a merchant with respect to the goods of the kind being sold, that seller cannot be held, under the Uniform Commercial Code, to have made or breached the implied warranty of fitness for a particular purpose.

_____ 8. As a general rule, a seller of goods is held to have impliedly warranted that he had the right to sell the goods and that the goods are free of any claims or liens about which the buyer has not been made aware before the sale.

_____ 9. If a college professor sells his 1985 Volvo automobile without warning the buyer of a serious defect in the car's brakes, and if the buyer experiences severe injuries in an accident caused by the defective brakes, the buyer should be able to win a strict liability suit against the professor.

_____ 10. The Magnuson-Moss Warranty Act does not require sellers of consumer products to make written warranties.

_____ 11. If the court allows the plaintiff to rely on an industrywide liability theory, the plaintiff will be required to prove which particular manufacturer produced the harm-causing product.

_____ 12. A statement by the seller of an automobile that "this car is a steal of a deal" is likely to be classified by a court as an express warranty.

Multiple Choice

Circle the best answer.

1. Jill accidentally cut off her ring finger on her left hand while using an electric knife to carve her Thanksgiving turkey. The accident occurred when she placed her left hand on the turkey to steady it. Jill sued the manufacturer of the knife, alleging she is entitled to recover damages under a strict liability theory (Restatement of Torts Section 402A). In her action under a strict liability theory, which of the following is Jill not required to prove?
   a. That the manufacturer was regularly engaged in the business of selling electric knives;
   b. That the knife was defective and unreasonably dangerous;
   c. That the manufacturer was negligent either in designing the knife or failing to properly inspect the knife for defects before sale;
   d. That Jill suffered physical injury or property damage as a result of using the product.

2. Jill accidentally cut off her ring finger on her left hand while using an electric knife to carve her Thanksgiving turkey. The accident occurred when she placed her left hand on the turkey to steady it. Jill sued the manufacturer of the knife, alleging she is entitled to recover damages under a strict liability theory (Restatement of Torts Section 402A). Which of the following is not defense to Jill's action for damages based on strict liability of the manufacturer?
   a. That Jill assumed the risk of such injury when she used the knife;
   b. That the product was not unreasonably dangerous because the utility of the product outweighs the magnitude of danger inherent in using it;
   c. That Jill misused the product;
   d. All of the above are defenses to an action for strict liability.

3. A seller who makes an affirmation of fact about a product which becomes the basis for the bargain can be liable to a consumer under which of the following theories?
   a. express warranty;
   b. implied warranty of merchantability;
   c. implied warranty of fitness;
   d. strict liability.

4. n order for a seller to disclaim the implied warranty of merchantability, the disclaimer must:
   a. be in writing;
   b. be signed by the merchant;
   c. use the word "merchantability";
   d. all of the above.

5. Pittman ordered a chicken sandwich from a restaurant. While eating, he was injured by a chicken bone that lodged in his throat. Pittman sued the restaurant for breach of the implied warranty of merchantability. Under which of the following tests will Pittman have the best chance of recovering damages?
   a. "foreign/natural" test;
   b. consumer's "reasonable expectations" test;
   c. strict liability for ultra hazardous activities;
   d. Pittman probably cannot recover for breach of the implied warranty of merchantability because a chicken dinner is not considered "foods" under the UCC.

6. Under which of the following theories is a disclaimer most likely to be effective?
   a. A disclaimer of strict liability in the sale of a new car;
   b. A disclaimer of negligence in the sale of a bicycle;
   c. A disclaimer of implied warranty (meeting the UCC requirements for disclaimer) in the sale of a typewriter;
   d. All of the above disclaimers are enforceable so long as the disclaimers are conspicuous.

7. Which of the following is true of express warranties?
   a. They can only be made by a merchant.
   b. Liability for breach of them is easily disclaimed.
   c. They can only be made in writing.
   d. None of the above.

8. Oma Gosch purchased a vacuum cleaner (manufactured by PDQ Co.) at the local X-Mart Discount Store. The day after Gosch made the purchase, her live-in companion, Bart Suave, was properly using the vacuum cleaner at the apartment he and Gosch shared. A serious defect in the vacuum cleaner caused it to catch fire while Suave was using it. Suave sustained severe burns as a result. Suave has now sued X-Mart. Which of the following is a true statement about Suave's suit?
   a. Suave should be able to rely successfully on a breach of implied warranty of merchantability theory even though he did not purchase the vacuum cleaner from X-Mart.
   b. The fact that the vacuum cleaner was seriously defective necessarily means that X-Mart was negligent; therefore, Suave would prevail on a negligence theory.
   c. Suave cannot win a product liability suit against X-Mart because X-Mart did not manufacture the vacuum cleaner it sold to Gosch.
   d. None of the above.

9. Elvis Greaseley purchased a new 100% polyester sequined jumpsuit at Doubleknit Fashions, a popular clothing store. Before the purchase arrangements were completed and before Greaseley paid the purchase price, a Doubleknit Fashions saleperson verbally informed Greaseley that "we hereby disclaim liability for breach of any and all implied warranties of whatever nature." Assume that the implied warranty of merchantability and the implied warranty of fitness for a particular purpose would apply to the transaction, unless these warranties were disclaimed or excluded effectively. On these facts, Doubleknit Fashions
   a. has made an effective disclaimer of the implied warranties of merchantability and fitness for a particular purpose.
   b. has made an effective disclaimer of the implied warranty of merchantability, but not the implied warranty of fitness for a particular purpose.
   c. has made an effective disclaimer of the implied warranty of fitness for a particular purpose, but not the implied warranty of merchantability.
   d. has made an effective disclaimer of neither the implied warranty of merchantability nor the implied warranty of fitness for a particular purpose.

10. Bambi LaFawn owned and operated a pet shop. She purchased a roll of carpet (which contained ten square yards) with the intention of having it installed in her pet shop. LaFawn later decided to sell the carpet to someone else after realizing that the carpet's color was not what she wanted in her shop. She sold the roll of carpet to Chip Munque, using a sample piece of the carpet to induce Munque to buy. Which of the following is an accurate statement?
   a. If LaFawn did not expressly guarantee the quality of the carpet, Munque cannot credibly claim that an express warranty was made.
   b. The implied warranty of merchantability was part of the parties' transaction.

c. LaFawn made an express warranty that the full ten square yards of carpet would conform to the sample shown by her.

d. Even if LaFawn knew that Munque had a particular purpose in mind for the carpet and that Munque was relying on her for the selection of goods suitable for that purpose, the implied warranty of fitness for particular purpose could not have been part of the parties' transaction.

11. Under the Magnuson-Moss Warranty Act,

a. a seller who fails to give a written warranty concerning consumer products sold by her is subject to certain federally imposed penalties.

b. sellers of certain consumer products must make certain disclosures to consumers if they (the sellers) issue a written warranty concerning those products.

c. sellers of certain consumer products impliedly warrant that the products will be fit for the particular purposes of the consumers who purchase the products.

d. the giving of a limited (as opposed to full) warranty concerning a consumer product is prohibited.

Short Essay

1. Jane wanted to purchase a new "EZ" brand vacuum cleaner but the particular vacuum cleaner she wanted was not in stock. The seller showed Jane pictures of several different vacuum cleaners in a catalog and she selected a green vacuum cleaner. The seller ordered the vacuum cleaner but when it arrived, the vacuum cleaner was blue instead of green. Which, if any, warranties did the seller breach under these circumstances?

2. Jane wanted to purchase a new "EZ" brand vacuum cleaner but the particular vacuum cleaner she wanted was not in stock. The seller showed Jane pictures of several different vacuum cleaners in a catalog and she selected a green vacuum cleaner. The seller ordered the vacuum cleaner and when it arrived, it was exactly as shown in the picture. Jane took the vacuum cleaner home but it failed to clean properly. Further, when she tried to check under it, she cut he finger on a piece of sharp metal protruding from the side of the vacuum. Under these circumstances, which warranties, if any, did the seller breach? May Jane recover damages for personal injury under a breach of warranty theory?

3. How are the product liability theories of <u>negligence</u> and <u>strict liability</u> different from each other? In what respects are they similar?

4. Orville Dull, an accountant, took a break for lunch and went to the Griese Grill, a fast food restaurant. Remembering a recent Griese advertisement which stated that "our pork tenderloins are made from nothing but the highest grade of pork available," Dull ordered a pork tenderloin as part of his lunch. After popping the first bite of it into his mouth, Dull began to choke and gasp for air. An alert Griese employee rushed Dull to the local hospital's emergency room, where a physician extracted from Dull's throat a large rubber band that had two paper clips fastened to it. Still attached to and partially covering the rubber band and paper clips was some of the crunchy coating used by Griese on its tenderloins. Dull, who was hospitalized for three days, experienced significant pain and suffering while his throat was healing. On what warranty-based legal theories would Dull have an excellent chance of prevailing in a suit against Griese? State the reasons for your answer.

CHAPTER 19
PERFORMANCE OF SALES CONTRACTS

Outline

I. Performance of Sales Contracts is Governed by Article II of the Uniform Commercial Code

   A. General provisions apply, such as the requirement of "good faith", and the fact that courts may interpret sales contracts by relying on past course of dealing and customs and practices of the trade, unless there is a conflict between those considerations and the express terms of the contract.

   Example: Weisz Graphics Division of the Fred B. Johnson Co., Inc. v. Peck Industries, Inc. (holding that a time limitation of 12 months on releases was standard in the industry and became part of the parties' agreement).

   B. Under the UCC, a party may <u>waive</u> the right to cancel a contract if he or she fails to object to breach; there is also a presumption favoring assignment and delegation of duties under the UCC.

II. Basic obligations as to delivery

   A. The basic duty of the seller is to deliver the goods, and the buyer is to accept and pay for the goods. Unless the parties agree otherwise, the place of delivery is the <u>seller's place of business</u>. (Ucc 2-308).

   B. If the seller is required to ship the goods, the seller must make a reasonable contract with a carrier and notify the buyer that the goods are shipped.

   C. The buyer has the right to inspect the goods; an exception is <u>cash on delivery (COD)</u>, which means the buyer must pay for the goods before inspection.

III. Acceptance, Revocation and Rejection

   A. Acceptance occurs if a buyer fails to reject the goods within a reasonable time; To reject, the buyer must <u>notify</u> the seller and <u>specify</u> the defect. Acceptance of part of a commercial unit is acceptance of the whole.

   Example: Shelton v. Farkas (holding that buyer had not accepted a violin because two days was a reasonable period of time within which to inspect and reject the violin.)

   B. A buyer may <u>revoke acceptance</u> of nonconforming goods where the nonconformity <u>substantially impairs the value of the goods</u> and (2) the buyer accepted them <u>without knowledge of the nonconformity</u> or because of <u>assurances</u> by the seller that the nonconformity would be cured. Revocation must be invoked prior to <u>substantial change in the goods</u>.

   Example: North River Homes, Inc. v. Bosarge (holding that the purchasers effectively revoked acceptance of a mobile home.)

   C. To reject, buyer must act within reasonable time and give notice.

   Example: Tai Wah Radio Manufactory Ltd. v. Ambassador Imports Ltd. (Failure to timely reject a shipment of goods constitutes acceptance.)

   D. The Seller has the right to cure breach by reshipping conforming goods, so long as performance can be completed within time for original performance.

   E. After Rejection, Buyer's duties depend on whether the buyer is a merchant or non-merchant:

   1. A non-merchant, must hold the goods with reasonable care, but is not obligated to ship them back to the seller.

   2. A merchant must follow reasonable instructions of the seller, and, absent other instructions, must try to resell the goods if they are perishable.
   Example: Lykins Oil Company v. Fekkos (Farmer who purchased a tractor which he rejected was not liable for the purchase price when it was stolen while awaiting pickup by the seller.)

IV. Assurance, Repudiation, and Excuse

   A. A party may demand assurance if there is a reasonable basis for believing the other party may not be able to perform.

B. The UCC recognizes the doctrine of <u>anticipatory repudiation</u> and the doctrine of <u>commercial impracticability</u>, which excuses performance for unforeseen events making it difficult or impossible to perform.

Example: <u>Alimenta (U.S.A.) Inc. v. Gibbs, Nathaniel (Canada), Ltd.</u> (A 1980 drought and its effect on the peanut crop were not reasonably foreseeable when a contract to purchase peanuts was entered into, and the doctrine of commercial impracticability excused seller from full performance of its contract obligations.)

Learning Objectives

1. You should understand the importance of the doctrine of "good faith" under the UCC, which imposes on every contract for the sale of goods a duty of good faith in its performance. The concept of "good faith" is defined as "honesty in fact," and cannot be disclaimed by the parties. Thus a court may consider "good faith" in determining whether a breach of contract has occurred, and if so, an appropriate remedy.

2. You should note that the UCC places great importance on past dealings between contracting parties and on custom and trade practice in interpreting sales contracts. Absent express contract language to the contrary, a court will consider these factors in determining whether breach has occurred and appropriate remedies.

3. You should know the basic obligations of the seller with regard to delivery.

4. You should be able to describe the buyer's right of inspection and know how the buyer's right of inspection differs in a C.O.D. sale.

5. You should know the legal effect of acceptance of goods and what conduct on the part of the buyer indicates acceptance.

6. You should be able to describe the buyer's rights upon improper delivery and should know what is necessary for a valid rejection.

7. You should know what actions a seller can take when the buyer rejects the goods. You should also be able to describe the buyer's duties concerning rejected goods.

8. You should know the meaning of the term "revocation of acceptance" and what is necessary to make a valid revocation.

9. You should know what a party's rights are when it has justifiable concern about the other party's ability to perform the contract.

10. You should know when a party to a contract is excused from performing his obligations.

Learning Hints

1. The UCC applies to contracts for the sale of goods. In sales contracts, the Code adopts a "strict performance" standard. This standard, however, is softened by Code provisions giving a seller an "opportunity to cure" non-conformity, and a provision requiring prompt rejection and notice by the purchaser.

2. The UCC permits a buyer to "revoke his/her acceptance" under certain circumstances. This provision has been used by consumers in "lemon car" cases, and similar cases, to reject goods which are non-conforming, but the seller continues, unsuccessfully, to attempt to "cure" the defects.

3. Buyers normally have the right to inspect <u>before</u> they pay. However, in a C.O.D. (cash on delivery) sale, the buyer must pay before inspection unless there is some glaring defect in the goods that the buyer can perceive without an inspection. The fact that C.O.D. buyers must pay before inspection does <u>not</u> mean that they lose their right to reject, revoke, or bring suit for breach of contract. It simply means that the other party has their money while they are doing these things.

4. Don't get the terms "acceptance," "rejection," and "revocation" as used in this chapter mixed up with the same terms as they are used in the chapters dealing with <u>creation</u> of contracts. In this chapter, we're talking about a buyer's acceptance or rejection or revocation of acceptance of the seller's performance of his contractual obligation to deliver goods, whereas in the earlier chapters we were talking about acceptance, rejection, or revocation of offers to determine whether a contract was ever created in the first place.

5. When goods are delivered to the buyer, he has a reasonable time to inspect them. If the buyer wants to reject the goods, he must act quickly. He must give the seller notice of rejection in which he describes the defects in the goods. He must be careful not to do anything that would contradict the seller's ownership of the goods (such as continuing to use them after a reasonable period for inspection has elapsed), or he will be considered to have accepted the goods.

6. Note that when there has been a rejection of goods, the seller has a certain amount of time in which he has the right to cure the defect or deliver conforming goods. Therefore, even if the buyer wants out of the contract once he has received defective goods, the seller still has another chance to get it right.

7. A buyer accepts the seller's performance when he indicates that the goods are satisfactory, or when he treats the goods in a way that shows ownership of them (such as using them after a defect is discovered or taking them on vacation with him), or when he merely fails to make a proper rejection. In other words, if the buyer fails to do any of the things required for a valid rejection, he is considered to have accepted. For example, if goods were delivered to you in a defective condition that made them totally worthless and you put them in your basement and did not use them but delayed notifying the seller for a period of time that would be considered unreasonable, you are considered to have accepted the goods.

8. Once the buyer has accepted the goods, he's normally stuck with them. He may still have remedies against the seller for breach of contract, but he no longer has the right to send the goods back unless the circumstances are such that he can revoke his acceptance of the goods.

9. Once the buyer has accepted the seller's performance, he must have a very good reason for revoking or undoing his acceptance of the goods. For one thing, he must be able to show that the defect was serious enough to constitute a substantial impairment of the value of the goods. Second, he must be able to show that he had a good reason for not rejecting the goods in the first place, such as the fact that the defect was difficult to discover earlier or the seller gave assurances that the defect would be cured. Third, the buyer must go through the same steps to make a valid revocation that were necessary for a valid rejection; i.e., notice within a reasonable time. Finally, the condition of the goods must be such that there has not been a substantial change in their condition.

10. Remember: rejection is done instead of acceptance. Revocation is done after acceptance.

11. A buyer's responsibilities toward goods rightfully rejected depends on whether the buyer is a merchant or not. Generally, a non-merchant buyer only has the duty to exercise reasonable care toward the goods and is not required to ship them back to the seller. A merchant buyer, however, must follow the seller's reasonable instructions regarding the goods, and must, in the case of perishable goods, attempt to sell them for the seller absent contrary instructions.

True-False

In the blank provided, put "T" if the statement is True or "F" if the statement is False.

_____ 1. The Uniform Commercial Code adopts a "strict performance" rather than a "substantial performance" standard with regard to sales contracts.

_____ 2. A buyer who rightfully rejects goods under the UCC is not required to give notice to the seller of the rejection unless the goods are perishable.

_____ 3. A seller may "cure" a non-conformity by re-shipping conforming goods, even if time for performance under the original contract has expired.

_____ 4. The basic obligation of a seller is to deliver conforming goods called for by the contract.

_____ 5. Absent agreement as to the place of delivery, the goods are to be delivered to the buyer at the buyer's place of business.

_____ 6. Usages of trade and the course of dealing between the parties are used to supplement or explain a contract of sale.

_____ 7. A party's failure to object to late deliveries can be a waiver of the right to cancel the contract if other deliveries are late.

_____ 8. A buyer may accept any part of a commercial unit without accepting the rest of the unit.

_____ 9. Normally, the buyer has the right to inspect the goods before he accepts or pays for them.

_____ 10. If the contract requires the seller to put the goods into the possession of a carrier, the seller must make a reasonable contract with the carrier to take the goods to the buyer.

Multiple Choice

Circle the best answer.

1. A-1 Skates is a company located in Wilmington, Delaware, that manufactures roller skates. B is a retail sporting goods store called "Skates R Us" in Bloomington, Indiana. B places an order to purchase 100 pairs of roller skates in various sizes from A-1 Skates. Absent agreement, where are the skates to be delivered?
   a. The seller's place of business in Wilmington, Delaware,
   b. The buyer's place of business in Bloomington, Indiana
   c. The railway station or truck loading dock of the shipper in Wilmington, Delaware, carrying the goods;
   d. The railway station or truck loading dock in Bloomington, Indiana, where the goods arrive.

2. A-1 Skates is a company located in Wilmington, Delaware, that manufactures roller skates. B is a retail sporting goods store called "Skates R Us" in Bloomington, Indiana. B places an order to purchase 100 pairs of roller skates in various sizes from A-1 Skates. Assume that A-1 shipped the wrong style of skates to B. In order to reject, B must:
   a. Reject within a reasonable time after shipment;
   b. Notify A-1 of its rejection;
   c. Return the skates to A-1;
   d. Both (a) and (b) are correct.

3. A-1 Skates is a company located in Wilmington, Delaware, that manufactures roller skates. B is a retail sporting goods store called "Skates R Us" in Bloomington, Indiana. B places an order to purchase 100 pairs of roller skates in various sizes from A-1 Skates. Assume that A-1 shipped the wrong style of skates to B and B properly rejects them. What are B's obligations as to the skates?
   a. B must ship them back to A-1;
   b. B must re-sell them for A-1;
   c. B must follow A-1's reasonable instructions;
   d. B is not required to do anything except hold the skates with reasonable care for the seller.

4. A-1 Skates is a company located in Wilmington, Delaware, that manufactures roller skates. B is a retail sporting goods store called "Skates R Us" in Bloomington, Indiana. B places an order to purchase 100 pairs of roller skates in various sizes from A-1 Skates. If the order is "COD":
   a. Buyer must inspect the goods before payment;
   b. Buyer may inspect the goods before payment;
   c. Buyer cannot inspect the goods before payment;
   d. Buyer must pay, even if it can tell without inspection that the goods are non-conforming.

5. In order to revoke acceptance of goods:
   a. The goods must be non-conforming;
   b. The non-conformity must not have been apparent at time of acceptance, or acceptance must have been a result of seller's assurances that the non-conformity would be cured;
   c. The revocation must occur within the time for performance of the original contract.
   d. Both (a) and (b) are required.

6. Betty's Boutique ordered several lines of women's dresses from Trendy Co.. Trendy accepted. The contract provided that Trendy would select an assortment of sizes in the various lines that Betty's had ordered. Because Betty's was a relatively small customer, Trendy selected dresses in only sizes 4 (very small) and 42 (very large). Must Betty's accept all of these dresses?
   a. Yes, because Betty's gave Trendy the right to select the sizes.
   b. Yes, because Betty's has waived its rights under the contract.
   c. No, because Trendy has not acted in good faith.
   d. No, because the parties do not have a contract.

7. Bart buys a new stereo on credit from Sounds, Inc. Bart takes the stereo home that day and tries it out. He finds that the turntable does not work. He immediately takes the stereo back to Sounds, Inc. He tells the salesman that he does not want the stereo because it is defective, and he describes the defects. He follows this conversation with a letter repeating what he told the salesman. Sounds, Inc. sues Bart when Bart refuses to pay for the stereo. Which of the following is true?
   a. Bart has properly rejected the stereo.
   b. Since Bart used the stereo, he cannot reject it.
   c. If Bart had kept the stereo for a year without notifying Sounds, Inc. that there was anything wrong with the stereo, he could still reject it.
   d. Bart had no right to inspect the stereo before paying for it.

8. Lelia's Furniture Co. entered into a written contract to sell two expensive sofas to Pipp, delivery to be made in November. In September, Lelia's learned from Pipp's attorney that Pipp was planning to file bankruptcy. Lelia wrote to Pipp and demanded assurances that Pipp would pay for the sofas. Pipp made no reply. Which of the following is true?
   a. Pipp has no duty to reply.
   b. If Lelia's does not deliver the sofas to Pipp on time, Lelia's will be in breach of contract.
   c. If Pipp does not reply in 30 days, he is considered to have repudiated the contract.
   d. Two of the above are true.

9. Reed Co. made a contract with Glomco to manufacture certain goods for Glomco and deliver them by June 1, 1983. Soon after the creation of the contract, Reed's workers went on strike and the plant shut down. Because Reed was able to hire only a few nonunion workers, he was forced to shut down the plant. Glomco sues Reed for breach of contract. What result?
   a. If Reed can prove that the strike was unforeseen and that performance has become commercially impracticable, Reed will be excused from performance.
   b. Reed will not be excused from performance unless a court finds that performance was literally impossible.
   c. Glomco will win the suit even if the court finds that Reed's performance was commercially impracticable and that the strike was unforeseen, since Glomco is not at fault.
   d. Glomco will win, because once a contract is made, a person can never be excused from his duties under the contract.

10. Which of the following would constitute acceptance of goods?
   a. The buyer treats the goods as if he owns them.
   b. The buyer fails to make a valid rejection of the goods.
   c. The buyer indicates that he will keep the goods.
   d. All of the above would constitute acceptance of the goods.

Short Essay

1. Farmer Fred contracted with Jimmy's Grocery to sell 500 pounds of apples, which were to be delivered on September 15. On September 1, Fred notified Jimmy's that he would be unable to deliver the apples due to an unusual and unexpected flood of his orchard which destroyed his crop. Jimmy sued Fred for breach of contract. What result and why?

2. Farmer Fred contracted with Jimmy's Grocery to sell 500 pounds of apples, which were to be delivered on September 15. Fred and Jimmy had contracted numerous times in the past, and Fred always delivered the apples to Jimmy's grocery on the date agreed. On September 15, Fred failed to deliver the apples, and Jimmy subsequently sued for breach of contract. One of Fred's defenses to breach was the fact that Jimmy had the responsibility under the UCC for picking up the apples at Fred's place of business. Is Fred correct? Explain.

3. Betty buys a clock radio on credit from Radio Hut. When she gets the radio home, she finds that there is a small nick in the case of the radio. Since it works properly, Betty uses the radio and says nothing to Radio Hut. A year later, Betty takes the radio back to Radio Hut and tells the salesman that she is revoking her acceptance of the radio. Is this a valid revocation? Why or why not?

4. Reginald orders goods from Novelty Supply Co. When the goods arrive, they are defective. What must Reginald do to make a valid rejection of the goods?

CHAPTER 20
REMEDIES FOR BREACH OF SALES CONTRACTS

Outline

I. Remedies in General

A. The Object is to put the injured party in the same position he/she would have been had the contract been performed.

B. Liquidated damages are damages the parties agreed on in the contract as the amount that will be paid in the event of breach.

Example: Baker v. International Record Syndicate, Inc. (holding that liquidated damages provision in contract was enforceable under UCC 2-718).

C. Consequential damages are damages, such as injury to persons or his property, that were a foreseeable result of breach.

  1. Consequential damages may be excluded or limited in commercial (not consumer) contracts, so long as that exclusion or limitation is not unconscionable.
  Example: Lobianco v. Property Protection, Inc.

D. The UCC statute of limitations provides that an action for breach of sales contracts must be filed within four years after the breach.

Example: Ronyak v. General Motors Corp. (holding lawsuit for breach of warranty in purchase of automobile and jack was barred by UCC statute of limitations.)

II. Seller's Remedies

A. In general, a seller has number of remedies against a breaching buyer under the UCC.

  1. The seller may cancel the contract; if in the process of manufacturing, the seller should choose an alternative under 2-704(2) which will minimize or mitigate loss.
  Example: Madsen v. Murrey & Sons Co., Inc. (Seller should have mitigated damages after breach of contract by buyer; Seller should have finished completing construction of pool tables and not dismantled the tables, using materials for salvage and firewood.)

B. The seller may resell the goods and recover damages, including incidental damages;

C. In some cases, seller is entitled to purchase price. If, for example, goods are specially manufactured goods and not suitable for resale, seller may be entitled to purchase price.

D. If buyer wrongfully rejects or repudiates the goods, the seller is entitled to the difference between the contract price and the market price of the goods, and lost profit (UCC 2-708).

Example: Islamic Republic of Iran v. Boeing Co. (Boeing was entitled to the difference between the contract price and resale price of the 747 aircraft.)

E. If buyer is insolvent, seller may withhold delivery, and has the right to require the return of any goods obtained within the previous 10 days.

III. Buyer's Remedies

A. A buyer has a number of remedies under the UCC. Upon rightful rejection or revocation of acceptance, the buyer may cancel, recover the purchase price paid to seller, and recover damages.

B. Buyer can cover, which means he/she can purchase substitute goods. If so he is entitled to recover incidental and consequential damages.

Example: Migerobe, Inc. v. Certina USA, Inc. (Lost profits are recoverable as consequential damages caused by breach of contract.)

C. As an alternative to cover, buyer can recover damages based on the difference between contract price of the goods and market price at the time of breach.

Example: Kneale v. Jay Ben, Inc.

D. Damages for defective goods are determined by the difference between the value of goods received and their value had they been as warranted. *Example:* Barr v. S-2 Yachts, Inc.

E. If the goods are unique, Buyer may have equitable remedies, such as specific performance.

Learning Objectives

1. You should understand that the UCC provides several remedies to sellers and buyers in breach of sales contract cases.
2. You should note that upon a seller's breach, a buyer is entitled to cover (that is, to purchase other goods to minimize damages) but it not required to do so under the UCC.
3. Likewise, a seller may resell goods in the event of breach by the buyer, but is not required to do so.
4. You should understand that the seller or buyer, in statements (2) and (3) above must, however, mitigate damages in order to recover incidental or consequential damages for breach of sales contract.
5. Underlying the notion of freedom of contract is the notion that parties should be able to break contracts (and pay damages) as well as make contracts. Consequently, courts are reluctant to award punitive damages for breach of sales contracts, especially in the case of commercial contracts rather than consumer contracts.
6. You must know what liquidated damages provisions are and the tests for deciding when such provisions will be enforceable.
7. You must know what consequential damages are, the various types of consequential damages, and when they will be recoverable.
8. You must know the UCC statute of limitations and the various times from which it will run.
9. You should be able to list the five general remedies available to the seller when the buyer breaches a sales contract.
10. You should know the conditions under which the seller can resell the goods after the buyer's breach, and the damages the seller can recover after he resells.
11. You should know the two possible measures of the recovery available to the seller when the buyer fails to accept the goods or repudiates the contract and the seller elects not to resell.
12. You should be able to list the four general remedies available to the buyer when the seller breaches a contract for the sale of goods.
13. You should know the general test for determining the buyer's recovery when the seller fails to deliver the goods.
14. You should know the general test for determining the buyer's recovery when the seller delivers defective goods.
15. You should know the general test for determining the buyer's recovery when the seller fails to deliver and the buyer covers.

Learning Hints

1. The UCC adopts a "strict performance" standard, which means that a material breach of contract occurs when there is a failure to deliver conforming goods under a contract. In the event of seller's breach, however, the buyer is required to give notice to the seller of the breach, and the seller is given the opportunity to cure the breach.
2. If the seller breaches the contract, the buyer is entitled to certain remedies. In general, the buyer is not required to "cover" (that is, to obtain the goods elsewhere), but his/her failure to do so will limit the buyer's ability to recover consequential damages, such as lost profits, as a result of the breach.
3. In some cases, the buyer may be entitled to specific performance, which means that the buyer may enforce the contract and obtain the goods. This remedy is limited to cases where the goods are unique, and thus damages at law (money damages for breach) are inadequate.
4. The UCC provides that a seller who has already begun manufacturing the goods, upon breach of contract by the buyer, must minimize damages by acting in a commercially reasonable manner. In some cases, this requires the seller to complete manufacture and attempt to resell the goods to another buyer.

5. You will notice that, after some introductory material, the chapter is organized around the different seller and buyer remedies the UCC makes available. In studying the chapter, keep this organization in mind. You might want to outline the chapter, treating each remedy individually under these general headings.

6. Remember that the term "consequential damages" is a broad one. It includes personal injury, property damage (meaning damage to property other than the goods sold), and things like lost profits, lost business, and the like.

7. In product liability cases, where consumers sue for defective goods, some courts use the tort statute of limitations even in cases brought under the UCC. This statute of limitations usually begins to run when the plaintiff actually suffered injury or discovered or should have discovered a defect in the goods. The point of using the tort statute of limitations in these cases is to give additional protection to the buyer.

8. As the text tells you, the seller is entitled to the purchase price of goods lost or damaged after the buyer assumed the risk of their loss.

9. Section 2-702(2) of the UCC, which gives the seller the right to reclaim goods received on credit by the buyer while insolvent, is basically the UCC's version of the common law remedy of rescission for fraud. The "fraud" here is the buyer's receipt of the goods in a situation where it is unlikely that he will be able to pay for them. The seller must demand the return of the goods within ten days of their receipt, and must actually know about the buyer's insolvency. However, this ten day requirement does not apply when the buyer has made a written misrepresentation of solvency within three months before delivery.

10. Section 2-715(2)(b) of the UCC says that the buyer can recover for personal injury or property damage resulting from a defect in goods sold when these damages are "proximate" results of the defect. Just what "proximate" means in this context is unclear, but the intent of the Code's drafters was to limit the seller's liability for certain unforseeable losses.

True-False

In the blank provided,put "T" if the statement is True or "F" if the statement is False.

_____ 1. A buyer must give the seller notice of rejection or revocation of acceptance within a reasonable time in order to reject non-conforming goods under the UCC.

_____ 2. The UCC requires a seller to attempt to re-sell goods in the event of breach by the buyer.

_____ 3. The UCC requires a buyer to attempt to "cover" by obtaining goods elsewhere in the event of breach by a seller.

_____ 4. A buyer is entitled to specific performance only in cases where money damages are inadequate.

_____ 5. In some cases, a buyer may be entitled to "lost profits" as consequential damages from a breaching seller.

_____ 6. If the parties to a contract for the sale of goods agree on the amount of damages to be paid in case of breach, this is always enforceable what because it represents the will of the parties.

_____ 7. Under the UCC, a plaintiff must always sue within four years of the time the defect is discovered.

_____ 8. After the buyer's breach, a seller who resells goods intended for the buyer can recover the difference between the resale price and the price the buyer agreed to pay.

_____ 9. A seller who successfully sues the buyer for the contract price of the goods must then turn the goods over to the buyer.

_____ 10. If the seller breaches the contract and the buyer elects not to cover, the buyer can still recover the difference between the contract price and the market price at the time the buyer learns of the seller's breach.

Multiple Choice

Circle the best answer.

1. Bob and Tom entered into an agreement where Bob would develop and print 100 commercial photographs for Tom. In their written contract, the parties stipulated that in the event of loss or destruction of the photographs, Bob would pay to Tom the sum of $1,000 each. All the photographs were destroyed in Bob's photo lab in a fire during the developing process. If Tom sues Bob for damages, which of the following is most correct?
   a. Tom can recover $100,000 under the liquidated damage clause in the contract if the court determines that amount is reasonable;
   b. Tom can recover damages based on the reasonable value of the photographs if the court finds the amount of damages stipulated in the contract is unreasonable.
   c. Both (a) and (b) are correct.
   d. Liquidated damages clauses in sales contracts violate public policy and therefore are never enforceable.

2. Buyer in Bloomington, IN, ordered 500 barbie dolls from seller, in Chicago. The dolls were to be delivered on or before December 1. On December 1, Buyer received 500 ken dolls. Under these circumstances:
   a. There is a breach of contract and buyer may reject the goods;
   b. There is a breach of contract and buyer must "cover" (attempt to purchase 500 barbie dolls from another seller) in order to recover damages for breach;
   c. Buyer is not required to notify buyer of breach under these circumstances because the seller no longer has time to "cure" his non-performance.
   d. All of the above are correct.

3. Buyer in Bloomington, IN, ordered 500 barbie dolls from seller, in Chicago. The dolls were to be delivered on or before December 1. On December 1, Buyer received 500 ken dolls. To what damages for breach may buyer be entitled under the UCC?
   a. Buyer may recover damages based on the difference between the value of the goods to be delivered under the contract and the value of the goods as were upon delivery;
   b. Buyer may recover damages for lost profits in the event buyer attempts to cover by purchasing other goods;
   c. Buyer is entitled to "specific performance," that is, to an order mandating performance of the contract by the seller;
   d. Both (a) and (b) are correct.

4. Limitation of consequential damages in the sale of consumer goods:
   a. Is "unconscionable per se" under the UCC;
   b. Is permitted so long as the parties intended to exclude such damages;
   c. Is permitted so long as reasonable;
   d. Is unconstitutional.

5. The statute of limitations in actions for breach of contract under the UCC is:
   a. Two years;
   b. Four years;
   c. Six years;
   d. Ten years.

6. Which of the following is not one of the remedies available to the seller when the buyer breaches a contract for the sale of goods?
   a. Cancellation of the contract
   b. Cover
   c. An action for the price of the goods
   d. Recovery of the seller's lost profit on the deal

7. Incidental damages include:
   a. the costs of storing defective goods.
   b. lost profits.
   c. personal injury.
   d. the difference between the value of the goods as warranted and as received.

8. If the buyer receives defective goods from the seller:.
    a. he can cover.
    b. he must give the seller notice of the defect within a reasonable time after discovering the defect.
    c. he can rescind the contract at once.
    d. he can obtain specific performance at his option.

9. A buys some machinery from B. In the contract of sale, B warrants that the machinery will be free of defects for five years, and the parties agree to make the statute of limitations for the sale five years. Due to a hidden defect in the machinery which was present when it was delivered to A, it fails four and one-half years after delivery. A immediately sues B. This suit:
    a. is barred by the statute of limitations.
    b. is not barred by the statute of limitations because of the provision in the contract extending the statute to five years.
    c. is not barred by the statute of limitations because the warranty covered the future performance of the machinery.
    d. Two of the above.

10. Seller and Buyer enter a contract. Buyer refuses to accept the goods when they are delivered and Seller keeps them. In this case, Seller's least likely remedy is to:
    a. recover the price of the goods.
    b. resell the goods and recover the difference between the contract price and the resale price.
    c. recover the difference between the contract price and the reasonable market price of the goods.
    d. recover the lost profits he would have made on the deal.

Short Essay

1. A orders ball bearings from B for his manufacturing operation, telling B that he needs them for machinery used to fulfill a contract with another party, and that if B does not perform A will not have time to obtain substitute goods. The reasonable value of ball bearings of this sort is $10,000. B ships A some defective ball bearings worth $2,000. As a result, A cannot fulfill his other contract and loses $25,000 in the process. A also incurs $300 in costs for storing the defective bearings. A sues B. What damages can A recover?

2. X contracts to sell Y a piece of machinery for $1 million. The machinery is to be used in Y's new business venture, which is an untried and unpatented manufacturing process. The parties put in their contract a clause stating that if X breaches the contract, he must pay Y $500. Why might this clause be unenforceable? Could Y perhaps recover more than $500 if X breaches their contract? Why or why not?

3. A agrees to sell his used car to B for $5000, but then B repudiates the contract. After being forced to wait one month and spending $50 in storage costs for the car, A sells it to C for $4500. What is A required to do before he can recover from B damages based on the resale? Assuming A does this, what amount can he recover from B?

CHAPTER 21
THE AGENCY RELATIONSHIP—CREATION, DUTIES, AND TERMINATION

Outline

I. Agency relationships arise when one person (agent) acts for the benefit of and under the direction of another (principal.)

    A. Agency relationships may arise from agreement or may be implied from the circumstances.

    Example: Lang v. Consumers Insurance Service (An agency need not be express but may be implied from the facts of a particular situation.)

    B. Generally, the capacity of the principal determines the agency's capacity to contract on behalf of the principal.

II. An agent owes certain duties to the principal

    A. An agent is a fiduciary and owes a duty of loyalty to the principal.

    Example: Radio TV Reports v. Ingersoll (Ingersoll breached a duty of loyalty to his employer when he remained in the employment relationship and bid on a contract in competition with employer.)

    B. Usually, a dual agency is a breach of duty of loyalty; however, an exception arises when the dual agent is merely a middleman (as in real estate contracts.)

    C. An agent breaches the duty of loyalty if he disclosed confidential information obtained in the agency relationship.

    Example: Prudential Insurance Company v. Van Matre (Prudential was unable to prove breach because it could not prove that employee acquired confidential information.)

    D. An agent must obey instructions, exercise care and skill, and has a duty to communicate information to principal.

    Example: Levin v. Kasmir World Travel (Travel agent had a duty to notify customers of a visa requirement.)

    E. An agent has a duty to account for funds and property, and to keep funds separate from his/her own.

III. Duties of Principals to Agents

    A. A principal must compensate the agent. Under the procuring cause rule, if an agent was the primary factor in a purchase or sale, he/she may be entitled to the commission regardless of who eventually completes the sale.

    Example: Willis v. Champlain Cable Corp. (Contract between principal and agent was clear and unambiguous regarding payment of commissions, and thus the express contract language overrides the procuring cause rule.)

    B. Special Rules:

        1. Duration of employment is reasonable one (absent express agreement);

        2. A real estate broker is generally entitled to commission when he/she procures a "ready, willing, and able" buyer.

        3. It is customary for a company to pay an insurance agent a commission on all premiums paid on the insurance contract sold.

IV. Termination of Agent's Powers

    A. By agreement

    B. An agency based on mutual consent may be terminated at any time by either party.

        1. An agency coupled with an interest arises when the power of agency is given as security; such an agency is irrevocable without the consent of the agent.

        2. Termination of an agency may be prohibited under federal and state law (as, for example, in cases of illegal discrimination based on race, color, sex, etc..)

        3. Termination by operation of law, including death or insanity or bankruptcy of either party.

C. An agent may still be liable to <u>third persons</u> after termination of the agency unless the principal gives <u>actual notice</u> or the third party has <u>constructive notice</u> of the termination.

Learning Objectives

1. You should understand that an agency is a relationship that may arise through express agreement, or may be implied from circumstances.

2. Generally, an implied agency only arises when the principal acts in such a way as to imply that an agency exists.

3. You should know what a principal is and what an agent is, and should begin to understand how the agency relationship may facilitate the completion of business transactions.

4. You should recognize the numerous ways in which the agent's duty of loyalty can arise, and should be aware of the potential problems that accompany any self-dealing by the agent.

5. You should be aware of the agent's general duty to obey instructions, but be able to recognize the special circumstances in which the agent will be excused for violating instructions.

6. You should become familiar with the agent's general duty to exercise care and skill, as well as the agent's duty to communicate, to the principal, agency-related information that comes to the attention of the agent.

7. You should be aware of the risks an agent faces when she commingles personal property with agency property, or when she uses the principal's money or property for her (the agent's) own personal purposes.

8. You should be aware of the general nature of the duties the law will impute to the principal in the absence of contractual provisions to the contrary.

9. You should understand the general rights of the agent to compensation, including the rights an agent may have to receive contingent compensation, such as commissions, upon termination of the agency.

10. You should recognize the general situations in which the principal has a duty to reimburse or indemnify the agent.

Learning Hints

1. An agency relationship is an important legal concept because it facilitates commercial enterprise. Utilizing an agency relationship, a principal may do business with many more individuals of corporate entities than he/she would be able to do individually.

2. An agency relationship may arise as a result of an express agreement. Certain kinds of agency agreements, for example real estate agency agreements between a principal and agent must be in writing in order to be enforceable in many states.

3. There are many kinds of agency relationships. One of the most common is the employee/employer relationship.

4. An agency relationship may also arise as a result of circumstances. In some cases, for example, a court may find that a principal has created the <u>implied authority</u> for an agent to act on his/her behalf. This relationship may even arise in cases where the parties do not believe such an agency to exist.

5. The agent's duty of loyalty lies at the very heart of the agent's responsibilities to the principal and governs all of the agent's activities. Any time an agent engages in self-dealing or appears to be engaging in an improper act, the agent is in violation of this duty unless the principal approves of the activity. Accordingly, the agent must fully and openly disclose all conflicts and potential conflicts to the principal.

6. If an agent's activities could lead to any appearance of impropriety, the agent must make a full disclosure to the principal. Therefore, an agent's purchases from the principal or an agent's sales to the principal fall into the category of activities that must be disclosed to the principal, in order that the principal is not taken advantage of by the agent. Further, if the agent is serving two principals (making the agent a dual agent), the agent possesses dual loyalties and must disclose the situation to both principals.

7. Because the agent is acting on behalf of the principal, it follows that the agent has a duty to follow the principal's instructions. However, in certain situations, the agent may have implied authority to deviate from the principal's instructions. These situations usually occur when the principal cannot be reached immediately and some emergency threatens to damage or destroy agency property. As the agent has been hired to further some goal in connection with the principal's property, it would not be in the best interests of either the agent or the principal if the property were damaged. Accordingly, the agent may possess special authority to supersede the principal's instructions.

8. Because the agent is considered to be one with the principal, the principal is entitled to any gifts the agent receives from third parties in connection with the agency. This follows from the agent's duty of loyalty. Any of these gifts might encourage an agent to pursue self-interest over the interests of the principal. Therefore, the gifts will belong to the principal unless the principal consents to the agent's keeping them, after a full and open disclosure by the agent.

9. The agent's duty of loyalty clearly is violated if the agent discloses the principal's confidential information to others without the principal's consent, or uses the confidential information to benefit himself. The agent's duty not to make such uses of the principal's confidential information continues even after the agency has terminated. After termination of the agency, the former agent may use the general knowledge and skills he gained while working for the principal, however. Therefore, it is important that a distinction be made between general knowledge or skills on the one hand, and confidential information or trade secrets on the other. In order for information to be considered a trade secret, the principal must have taken significant steps to keep the information substantially secret, and must generally have allowed only a limited number of persons to have access to it, on strictly a confidential basis.

10. If an agent uses agency property for personal purposes or commingles agency and personal property, the agent may be subjected to liability. These practices, being inconsistent with the best interests of the principal, smack of a conflict of interest. In order to discourage these practices, the principal may, where the agent has engaged in such a practice, choose to take the benefit of any contract the agent enters into—because the agent in theory was to have been acting for the principal. Alternatively, where the agent has engaged in such a practice, the principal may choose to disavow any responsibility for transactions that were not profitable and/or sue the agent for conversion.

11. The agent's ability to recover from the principal for expenses incurred is of the same general nature as a quasi-contract remedy. It would be unduly harsh not to require the principal to pay for the benefits that an agent in good faith has bestowed upon the principal. Similarly, fairness demands that the principal indemnify the agent for loss experienced by the agent while acting on behalf of the principal. Of course, the principal is not held liable to the agent for the amounts of the agent's expenses if the expenses were unauthorized. For similar reasons, the principal has no obligation to indemnify the agent for a loss experienced by the agent if the loss resulted from some fault on the part of the agent.

12. The agent's entitlement to commissions—even after termination of the agency—is based on reasoning akin to what is set forth in #7, above. The agent should recover the commission when his or her activities were the procuring cause of a completed transaction. Otherwise, the principal or a subsequent agent will be receiving a windfall at the expense of the original agent.

True-False

In the blank provided, put "T" if the statement is True or "F" if the statement is False.

_____ 1. An agency agreement must be in writing to be enforceable.

_____ 2. Absent express agreement, an agent owes no special duties to the principal.

_____ 3. An agent may be liable for embezzlement or conversion if he commingles funds of the principal with his own.

_____ 4. Under the duty of loyalty, an agent must avoid even the appearance of impropriety.

_____ 5. Death of the principal automatically terminates an agency relationship.

_____ 6. A person who lacks capacity to contract cannot be an agent.

_____ 7. The agent's duty of loyalty requires that gifts received from third parties should be presented by the agent to the principal, if the gifts pertained to the subject matter of the agency.

_____ 8. Marriage does not automatically make each spouse the agent of the other.

_____ 9. Generally, either party to an agency relationship has the power to terminate the agency at any time, because the relationship is based on mutual consent.

_____ 10. When agency goods are commingled with the private goods of the agent, the agent bears the risk of any loss to the principal in the event that the commingled goods cannot be separated.

Multiple Choice

Circle the best answer.

1. Which of the following is <u>not</u> a duty of a principal to an agent:
   a. the duty to compensate the agent;
   b. the duty to reimburse and indemnify;
   c. the duty to keep accounts;
   d. all of the above are duties a principle owes an agent.

2. In an agency relationship where the agency is coupled with an interest:
   a. only the principal may terminate the agency;
   b. the agent must consent in order for the principal to terminate the agency;
   c. neither party may terminate the agency;
   d. none of the above is correct.

3. John was hired as an agent for "Best Foods" on January 1, his agency relationship to expire on November 1. On February 1, Best Foods filed bankruptcy. On March 1, John first learned of the bankruptcy. When did the agency terminate?
   a. On February 1, when Best Foods filed bankruptcy;
   b. On March 1, when John learned of the bankruptcy;
   c. Within a reasonable time of when John learned (or should have learned) of the bankruptcy;
   d. November 1.

4. A "fiduciary relationship" means:
   a. That the principal owes a duty of loyalty to the agent;
   b. That the agent owes a duty of loyalty to the principal;
   c. That both parties owe a duty of loyalty to each other;
   d. That neither party owes a duty of loyalty to the other.

5. An agent has implied authority if:
   a. The principal has ratified past actions, leading third persons to believe authority exists;
   b. the principal fails to notify past customers that the agency has been terminated;
   c. an emergency necessitates prompt action by the agent to safeguard the interests of the principal
   d. all of the above create an agency by implied authority.

6. In the absence of an agreed upon rate of compensation,
   a. the agent will be presumed to be a gratuitous agent.
   b. the principal and agent will share the profits, but the principal will assume all ordinary losses.
   c. the reasonable value of the work will generally be the amount of compensation to which the agent is entitled.
   d. the principal and agent will share all profits and losses.

7. If the principal wishes to guard against continued liability for the actions of a former sales agent, the principal, upon termination of the agency, should
   a. never deal with any of the former customers with whom the agent had dealt.
   b. give individual written notice of the agency termination to former customers whose identities are known to the principal.
   c. give notice of the termination in a newspaper of general circulation.
   d. give the notices contemplated in answers b and c.

111

8. As an employee at Woody's Grocery Store, Earl learned from Woody how to recognize truly fresh produce when farmers brought their produce to the store. After he ceased being Woody's employee, Earl opened his own grocery store and put his knowledge about recognizing fresh produce to good use. Earl's store became well known for its fine produce. Soon, Woody's former customers began buying their produce and other groceries at Earl's store instead of at Woody's. Woody then sued Earl for the damages allegedly resulting to him because of the loss of customers. Woody will
   a. win the suit because Earl, in operating a business that competed with Woody's, used confidential information belonging to Woody.
   b. lose the suit, because Earl was merely making permissible use of general knowledge he had gained while working for Woody.
   c. win the suit, because an agent's duty of loyalty always prohibits him from going into competition with the principal even after the agency relationship has ended.
   d. lose the suit even though Earl used confidential information, because nothing in the facts indicates that Earl had agreed in writing not to use such information.

9. Ruth is a loan officer employed by Legbreaker Finance Co. Her employer has given her authority to receive loan applications and approve the making of loans. Which of the following statements is/are accurate?
   a. Ruth must take reasonable care to investigate the credit standing of prospective borrowers before approving loans.
   b. Ruth is an insurer of the collectibility of loans she approves.
   c. If she is a good credit risk, Ruth may approve a loan of company funds to herself without first obtaining the approval of company officials.
   d. All of the above.

10. An agent serving both parties to a transaction
   a. is not entitled to compensation from either party regardless of the circumstances.
   b. must reveal the dual role only to the second party she begins representing.
   c. is entitled to compensation from both parties if either party has consented to the dual role.
   d. is within the law if both parties to the transaction give their approval following the agent's disclosure of the dual role.

Short Essay

1. Bob stole a coat from "Mac's Cleaners" and, wearing the coat, went into a local department store and purchased $500 worth of cleaning supplied, posing as an employee of "Mac's." Later, when the department store sent Mac's a bill for the supplies, Mac's refused to pay. The store says an implied agency arose and Mac's is liable for Bob's purchase. Is it right? Explain. Would your answer change if Bob had worked for "Mac's Cleaners," but purchased the supplies without "Mac's" express consent?

2. Wanda was retained by Otto to sell an original painting that he owned. Although various potential buyers informed Wanda of their possible interest in purchasing the painting, none of them actually purchased it. Believing that another buyer could not be found, Wanda then made arrangements to sell the painting to her father, Jerome, for a price that was $600 less than what Otto had originally said he wanted to receive for the painting. Wanda did not tell Otto that Jerome was her father. Otto approved the sale at the lesser amount. After the sale had taken place, Otto learned for the first time of the family relationship between Wanda and Jerome. Otto then claimed that Wanda had breached her duty as an agent. Was Otto correct? Why or why not?

3. Irv, assistant manager of the P-Mart Discount Store, locked up the store shortly after closing time and headed toward the First Local Bank. In a manila envelope he was carrying, Irv had mixed together $1,200 in P-Mart cash and $400 of his own funds. His intent was to separate the P-Mart and personal funds upon reaching the bank's lobby, and to then make appropriate deposits at the bank's night depository. Before Irv reached the bank, however, an unidentified person attacked him, seized the manila envelope, and ran away. In the process, $600 of the funds dropped from the envelope to the ground. That amount was recovered, but the rest was not. The thief was never apprehended. As between Irv and P-Mart, how should the $600 that was recovered be allocated? Explain your reasoning.

CHAPTER 22
LIABILITY OF PRINCIPALS AND AGENTS TO THIRD PERSONS

Outline

I. Agent's Authority to Bind the Principal

A. The agent's authority is either <u>actual</u> or <u>apparent</u>. It may also arise as a result of <u>ratification</u> of the agent's actions by the principal.

B. Actual Authority is either express or implied.

　　1. Express authority arises from express language in an agency agreement—for example, a power of attorney is an express agency agreement.

　　2. Implied authority arises because an agent possess the implied authority to do whatever is reasonably necessary to accomplish the objectives of the agency. The test is the "justifiable belief of the agent."

C. Apparent authority is based on conduct by the principal which causes a third person to reasonably believe an agency exists. The test is the "justifiable belief of the third party."

　　Example: <u>Barton v. Snellson</u> (Finding attorney lacked express or implied authority to accept settlement agreement on behalf of his clients.)

D. Ratification occurs when a principal authorizes an act of an agent after the act was done. Test is the "intention of the principal."

　　1. Requires proof that the agent acted on behalf of the principal and principal had capacity to act.

III. Related Liability Issues: Liability of Principal

A. Principal is generally bound by agent's representations if the agent had express, implied, or apparent authority to make such statements. The principal is generally liable for misrepresentations made by the agent under these theories.

　　Example: <u>Arbour v. Hazelton</u> (Buyer entitled to rescind contract for sale of business based on misrepresentation of selling agent.)

　　1. A principal may give notice of lack of agent's authority through an <u>exculpatory clause</u>. However, many courts permit a third party to rescind a contract for misrepresentation even though the contract contains such a clause.

B. Payments to the agent discharge debt to the principal; the principal is not bound if the agent colludes with the third party to withhold such payments from the principal.

C. Principal's Liability for Acts of Subagents: A subagent is an agent of the agent. Both the principal and agent may be bound by the authorized acts of the subagent.

　　Example: <u>Equilease Corporation v. Neff Towing Service</u> (A subagent had authority to bind the principal to a towing and storage contract.)

IV. Contract Liability of the Agent

A. Generally, the agent is not liable for the contracts made on behalf of the principal. Exceptions include: unauthorized actions by the agent, nonexistent or incompetent principals, agreements by the agent to assume liability, undisclosed or partially disclosed principal.

B. Liability is imposed on an agent who has exceeded his authority based on an <u>implied warranty of authority</u>.

C. If the principal is not in existence or is incompetent, the agent is liable. In addition, an agent may become a party to a contract along with the principal, thus assuming liability.

D. If the principal is <u>disclosed</u>, the contract is between the principal and third party.

E. If the principal is <u>undisclosed</u>, the agent is liable (but the agent may be entitled to indemnification from the principal.)

　　Example: <u>You'll See Seafoods v. Gravois</u> (Because third party was unaware of an agency relationship between agent and corporation, agent was liable as an agent.)

F. A principal is <u>partially disclosed</u> when the third person knows he is dealing with an agent but does not know the identity of the principal. The agent is liable on contracts on behalf of a partially disclosed principal.

V. Liability for Torts

A. Principals are liable for the Torts of their Agents under three theories:

1. Direct liability (Principal was directly liable, for example, in negligently hiring or supervising the agent.)

2. Respondeat Superior: Principals (generally employers of tort-feasing employees) may be liable to third persons injured by the torts of their agents under this theory of imputed liability. Requires determination whether the agent was an <u>independent contractor</u> for which no liability arises under this theory, or <u>employee</u>. Liability for negligence of agents is common, but courts are less likely to impose liability on principals for their agents' intentional torts.
Example: J. v. Victory Tabernacle Baptist Church (Church was liable under a direct liability theory for negligently hiring a rapist.)

3. Agent generally cannot avoid liability for his own torts.

Learning Objectives

1. You should understand the difference between duties and liabilities of an agent vis a vis a principal, and that of an agent and principal to third parties.

2. You should understand the different legal implications of an express, implied, and apparent agency.

3. You should understand the concept of <u>respondeat superior</u> and the difference between and employee and independent contractor.

4. You should understand the circumstances under which a principal may be directly liable for the torts of his/her agent.

5. You should know how apparent authority may arise, and should recognize that where the agent possessed apparent authority, the principal's liability to third persons is the same as if there had been actual authority.

6. You should understand how ratification of an unauthorized act may occur, and what the effect of ratification is.

7. You should be able to distinguish among agencies involving disclosed, undisclosed, and partially disclosed principals. It is also important that you be familiar with the liability the principal and the agent may face in each of these three agency situations.

8. You should understand the liability of the agent to third persons when the agent has committed unauthorized acts, and should know why the agent is obligated to indemnify the principal when the principal is held liable to the third party in cases involving apparent authority.

9. You should become familiar with the rules governing when a principal is held accountable for the representations of an agent. You should also understand how a properly constructed exculpatory clause may minimize, for principals, problems of this nature.

10. You should know how to determine whether information given to an agent is considered notice to the principal.

Learning Hints

1. Whether a principal will be bound to a third party on contracts made by an agent depends on the agent's authority to act for the principal. That authority may be either express, implied, or apparent.

2. A principal may also be bound on contracts if he/she ratifies the acts of the agent.

3. Generally, a principal will be liable for representations made by the agent, if those representations were made with authority.

4. Whether an agent is personally bound on contracts made on behalf of a principal depends on whether the principal was disclosed to the third party.

5. A principal may be liable for the torts of his/her agent under the theory of direct liability, or respondeat superior.

6. Remember that an agent may have authority to bind the principal even though the principal has not specifically authorized the agent to do the particular act done by the agent. The doctrines of implied authority and apparent authority, if made applicable by the facts of a given case, may lead to the kind of result described in the preceding sentence.

7. The legal effect of the agent's authorized actions is, in most circumstances, that the principal is bound to the same degree the principal would have been bound if the principal had done the act personally.

8. The principal is the source of actual authority and apparent authority. Both actual authority (which may be express or implied) and apparent authority depend upon some action or inaction by the principal.

9. It will be easier for you to distinguish between implied authority (which is a form of actual authority) and apparent authority if you learn the respective tests for each. The test for implied authority is the justifiable belief of the agent, whereas the test for apparent authority is the justifiable belief of the third person with whom the supposed agent dealt. In either situation, however, the justifiable belief must stem from something the principal has said or done, or has failed to say or do. It is in that sense that the principal is the source of all authority.

10. The agent assumes certain risks when she is part of an undisclosed or partially disclosed agency. The foremost risk is that the agent may be held liable if the principal fails to perform. There is some consolation for the agent in that if the agent acted with authority, the agent has a right to be indemnified by the principal in the event that the agent is held liable to the third person. This will be small consolation, however, if the principal's reason for failing to perform the principal's obligation to the third person was the principal's weak financial position or, worse yet, the principal's bankruptcy. In those situations, the agent's right to be indemnified by the principal may become virtually meaningless.

11. When an agent performs unauthorized acts or makes unauthorized representations, the agent, rather than the principal, is the party who is liable to the third person with whom the agent dealt. The principal cannot be held liable to the third person where the principal has done nothing to create actual authority or provide the basis for apparent authority. If the agent had no actual authority but did possess apparent authority, the principal will be liable to the third person, but the agent, in turn, will have an obligation to indemnify the principal.

12. When the agent "represents" a nonexistent or incompetent principal, the agent clearly is the party who will be liable to the third person with whom the agent dealt. In such an instance, there is no principal with legal capacity to be bound by any contract.

13. Be certain to remember that notice given to an agent is considered as notice to the principal only if the information relates to the business of the agency. Therefore, in determining whether a third person's giving of notice to an agent constitutes notice to the principal, one ordinarily must do more than merely inquire as to whether the party receiving the notice was an agent of the principal. It is usually necessary to make a further inquiry concerning whether the information given to the agent by the third person pertained to the business of that particular agent's relationship with the principal.

14. It is logical that a principal is not bound by an agent's action where the agent was involved in a conflict of interest situation of which the third person was aware. The agent has a conflict of interest when he is acting to serve his own interests or those of the third party, rather than those of the principal. As you have already learned, an agent is to subordinate his own interests to those of the principal. If the third person with whom the agent dealt is aware of the conflict or is an active participant in it, the agent's action cannot be said to have been taken with apparent authority, because the third person could not have had a justifiable belief that the agent was authorized to take such an action.

15. The difference between direct liability and liability under respondeat superior is that with direct liability, the principal really is being held accountable for her own tort or wrongdoing, not necessarily for that of the agent. Perhaps the agent did commit a tort (for which the agent himself will be liable), but the principal may have committed a separate tort by being negligent in supervising the agent or by being involved in the agent's wrongdoing—such as by directing the agent to commit the tortious act. Imposing direct liability on the principal would be appropriate in such instances. Of course, the agent would also be liable for his tort. Holding a principal lia-

ble on the basis of respondeat superior is something different. Under respondeat superior, the principal is held liable for the torts of her employees, if the torts were committed in the scope of employment. No active fault or wrongdoing on the part of the principal is required. Respondeat superior is grounded on the public policy of giving injured third persons another, presumably financially responsible, party to look to besides the employee for payment of the injured parties' damages. Once again, even if the principal is held liable under respondeat superior, the employee who actually committed the tort is held liable in his own right.

True-False

In the blank provided, put "T" if the statement is True or "F" if the statement is False.

_____ 1. A principal is bound on any contracts entered into by her agent, even if the agent acted without express, implied, or apparent authority.

_____ 2. An agent has the implied authority to do whatever is reasonably necessary to accomplish the purposes of the agency.

_____ 3. Apparent authority is a concept imposed by law to protect the principal from liability for unauthorized acts of an agent.

_____ 4. An independent contractor is liable for the torts committed by his principal.

_____ 5. Under the principle of direct liability, a principal may be liable for negligently hiring an agent who commits a tort against a third party.

_____ 6. An agent may still be able to bind the principal after the principal informs the agent of the termination of the agent's authority.

_____ 7. If an agent represents an unincorporated association, the agent will be personally liable to the third person with whom the agent dealt in the event that the association fails to perform.

_____ 8. It is possible that one may be liable for the acts of someone posing as her agent, even though no actual authority had been given to the person who posed as the agent.

_____ 9. An agent acting within the scope of his authority will usually be immune from liability for torts he commits.

_____ 10. In an agency involving a disclosed principal, the third person may, at his option, hold either the principal or the agent legally responsible for performing the obligation owed to him.

Multiple Choice

Circle the best answer.

1. Jane was hired as a janitor for a local cleaning service. While cleaning a client's home, she negligently left a bucket of water in front of the front door. When the client came home from work, she slipped and fell over the bucket. Who may the client sue, if any?
   a. Only the agent (Jane) is liable for her own torts;
   b. Only the principal (the cleaning service) is liable for the negligent acts of its agents;
   c. Both Jane and the cleaning service may be liable;
   d. Neither is liable, because a principal and agent are only liable for intentional, not negligent torts.

2. An employer may be liable under respondeat superior:
   a. only if the tort of the employee was committed within the scope of employment;
   b. only if the employer knew or should have known that the employee would likely commit the tort;
   c. even if the employee was acting to achieve a personal objective rather than for the benefit of the employer;
   d. all of the above are correct.

3. Marie was a contestant for the title of Miss USA/Hawaii. The contestant was run by Mr. Richard, a franchisee of the Miss Universe Pageant, Inc.. After she finished first runner-up, Marie sued Miss Universe, Inc., arguing that its agent Mr. Richard had acted improperly and prevented her from winning the title. Under which of the following circumstances is Mr. Richard an agent of Miss Universe, Inc., for purposes of this action?
   a. If the express contract between the parties (Richard and Miss Universe) provided that Richard was an agent for purposes of the pageant;

b. If Richard's authority to run the pageant on behalf of Miss Universe was implied from his franchise agreement;

c. If Richard had apparent authority to run the pageant based on the reasonable perception of a third party like Marie;

d. In all of the above circumstances, Richard is an agent of Miss Universe.

4. Marie was a contestant for the title of Miss USA/Hawaii. The contestant was run by Mr. Richard, a franchisee of the Miss Universe Pageant, Inc.. After she finished first runner-up, Marie sued Miss Universe, Inc., arguing that its agent Mr. Richard had acted improperly and prevented her from winning the title. If Richard establishes that he is an <u>independent contractor</u>, rather than an employee of Miss Universe:

a. Marie may still recover damages from Miss Universe under the theory of <u>respondeat superior</u>;

b. Marie is not entitled to recover damages from Miss Universe under the theory of <u>respondeat superior</u>;

c. Marie may still recover damages from Richard, assuming she can prove her case;

d. Both (b) and (c) are correct.

5. If an agent enters into a contract with a third party on behalf of a principal who is incompetent:

a. Both the agent and the principal are liable on the contract;

b. Just the agent is liable on the contract;

c. Just the principal is liable on the contract;

d. Neither the principal or agent is liable on the contract.

6. The source of apparent authority is

a. the principal.

b. the agent.

c. the third party with whom the agent dealt.

d. an express contract between the agent and principal, under which contract the agent is given authority to do the act in question.

7. Butch Wingnut worked as parts manager for Marginal Appliances, Inc., a business that sold and serviced a broad range of appliances. He frequently signed company checks to cover purchases he made for the corporation. The checks had the name "Marginal Appliances" printed on them, without "Inc." or any other designation indicating that Marginal was incorporated. Wingnut always signed the checks in this manner: "Marginal Appliances" on one line, followed by "Butch Wingnut" on the next line. Marginal experienced serious financial setbacks and went out of business without being able to cover the amounts of several checks signed in the above manner by Wingnut. One was a $4,000.00 check made out to Shorty's Parts Supply Co. Shorty's has now sued Wingnut for the $4000.00. Which of the following statement provides the best analysis of the facts?

a. Wingnut cannot be held liable to Shorty's because Wingnut was acting only as an agent for Marginal.

b. Wingnut could be held liable to Shorty's because he failed to indicate his agent's capacity on the checks and because the checks did not make it clear that Marginal was a corporation.

c. Wingnut will be held liable to Shorty's for the reasons stated in answer b, regardless of whether Shorty's knew that Marginal was a corporation and that Wingnut was acting as an agent.

d. The determining factor in whether Wingnut is held liable to Shorty's is Wingnut's intent: if he intended to act only as an agent in signing the check, he will not be liable.

8. The things a reasonable agent justifiably believes are customary for agents such as himself to perform would be categorized as part of the agent's

a. apparent authority.

b. express authority

c. actual authority.

d. illusory authority.

9. Claudine was the owner and operator of a sporting goods store. Before leaving on a three-week vacation, Claudine informed one of her sales clerks, Roy, that she would like him to serve as acting manager of the store during her absence. Claudine told Roy to do the standard types of things a manager would need to do in order to keep the business operating, but specifically told him that he was not to hire any new employees, under any circumstances, while she was away. Assume, however, that in the area in which the store was located, it was customary for persons acting as managers to have authority to hire and fire employees as necessary. While Claudine was away on her vacation, another of the sales clerks quit his job. Roy then hired a new sales clerk to replace the one who had quit. This action by Roy
   a. could be binding on Claudine even though Roy had no actual authority to take the action he took.
   b. was expressly authorized, because Claudine had given him broad authority to do the things a manager would need to do in order to keep the business operating.
   c. was impliedly authorized, because it was customary for managers to have the authority to hire and fire.
   d. cannot be binding on Claudine even if Roy possessed apparent authority, because he acted in a manner contrary to instructions given by Claudine.

10. A principal's ratification
   a. cannot be of an act of someone who had not been appointed as an agent at all.
   b. may be of an act of an agent who has exceeded the authority given to him.
   c. may be of the beneficial parts of an agent's unauthorized act, without an assumption of the burdensome parts thereof.
   d. cannot be found to have taken place unless the principal expressly states that she wishes to ratify the unauthorized act.

11. Dewey Cheatem, owner of Dewey Cheatem Used Car Sales, employed several salespersons to assist in selling cars. Cheatem ran numerous television ads in which he stated that because he and his salespeople were dedicated to selling customers a used car, they would "not be undersold, no way, no how." In this month's sales meeting, Cheatem informed his salespersons that they were authorized to sell any car on the lot for any amount they could negotiate with the customer, so long as the salespersons did not reduce the sticker price by more than 20 percent. He also told the salespersons that only he (Cheatem) could make deals involving a sticker price reduction of more than 20 percent. After a particularly slow week for business, Les Scruem (a Dewey Cheatem salesperson) sold a car for 30 percent less than the sticker price to an ordinary consumer, E.Z. Mark. Upon learning what had occurred, Cheatem informed Mark that he (Mark) must either return the car or pay Cheatem the extra 10 percent Mark had saved, because Scruem had not been authorized to reduce the sticker price by more than 20 percent. Which of the following is the strongest legal argument against the validity of the demand made by Cheatem upon Mark?
   a. That in light of the slow week the business had experienced, Scruem had a justifiable belief that his sale of the car to Mark at 30 percent off the sticker price was what Cheatem would have wanted him to do.
   b. That Scruem was acting within the scope of his employment when he made the sale to Mark, and that under prevailing tort law, the action taken by Scruem is binding on Cheatem.
   c. That because Mark knew that Scruem was one of Cheatem's employees, the terms of the sale negotiated by Scruem are binding on Cheatem.
   d. That regardless of the instructions given by Cheatem to Scruem and the other salespersons, the facts justify a conclusion that Scruem possessed apparent authority.

12. Alf enjoyed fixing up old cars and selling them at a profit. Soon Alf's reputation was so well-established that he had problems making purchases of used cars at reasonable prices. Many persons in the area where Alf lived knew of his operation, so they tended to hold out for higher prices before selling their old cars to Alf. Accordingly, Alf retained several persons to make purchases of used cars for him. Bertha, one of the agents Alf retained for this purpose, contracted to purchase a car from Clyde without disclosing that she was making the purchase for Alf. When Clyde later discovered the actual nature of the transaction, he (Clyde) refused to comply with the contract of sale. On these facts, Clyde

a. is in breach of contract, with either Alf or Bertha being entitled to file suit to enforce the contract.

b. is justified in refusing to perform the contract, because Bertha did not disclose that she was acting on behalf of Alf.

c. is in breach of contract, with only Bertha being entitled to file suit to enforce the contract.

d. has a valid fraud claim against Bertha.

Short Essay

1. Parker hired Aikens as general manager of his local tobacco store. The store is a sole proprietorship and for years Parker had employed various people as general manager. Parker always gave the general manager the authority to purchase tobacco from Thirkill. However, without informing Thirkill of this fact, Parker explicitly told Aikens <u>not</u> to purchase tobacco without Parker's express instructions. Aikens purchased a shipment of tobacco from Thirkill. When Parker discovered what Aiekns had done, he refused to pay Thirkill for the shipment. Is Parker liable to Thirkill? Explain.

2. What is the difference between an "independent contractor" and an "employee?" What is the significance of this distinction?

3. Powers owned nine apartment buildings, each of which needed a new roof. Therefore, she retained Able, whose business was to do roofing work and miscellaneous construction projects. Able did the re-roofing on all nine buildings over a four-month period, during which time he was so busy doing work for Powers that he did no work for others. Powers had some expertise concerning roofing matters. As to each of the buildings, she gave Able a detailed set of directions that she wanted him to follow with regard to how the work should be done. Powers also insisted that Able use tools and equipment supplied by her, and that he work from 8:00 a.m. to 5:00 p.m., Monday through Friday, until he had finished putting a new roof on each of the nine buildings. Powers did not withhold income tax or social security contributions from her payments to Able, because she considered him an independent contractor rather than an employee. In the locality where Powers and Able lived, roofing work was generally done by independent contractors. One day, while Able was on the roof of one of Powers's buildings and was in the course of performing his roofing duties, he negligently tossed a hammer toward the ground. Unfortunately, the hammer struck Hapless, who was walking on the sidewalk near the building. The seriously injured Hapless brought suit against Powers. Is Powers liable for Able's negligence? State the reasons for your answer.

4. Gil Groovy, an unemployed business school graduate, decided that he would like to work as a salesperson at a local stereo store. Unable to obtain an interview with the store's owner, Hiram "Hi" Fye, Groovy devised a scheme to catch Fye's attention and demonstrate his considerable marketing skills at the same time. For several weeks, Groovy regularly held parties in his home. During these parties, Groovy always played his stereo and extolled its virtues to his listening audience. At the conclusion of each of these affairs, he would offer to sell the same type of stereo system and personally install it, for no additional charge, in the buyer's home. Groovy eventually informed Fye that he had secured orders for 13 stereo systems. He also informed Fye of what he had told the prospective buyers at his parties. An overjoyed Fye agreed to the sales and allowed Groovy to install the systems in the buyers' homes. Later, Fye billed each of the buyers for installation charges, because it was not the usual practice, in his business, to provide installation services at no charge. Is Fye entitled to recover the installation charges from the buyers? State the reasons for your answer.

CHAPTER 23
EMPLOYMENT LAWS

Outline

I. Health and Safety Legislation

A. Workers' Compensation

1. In the 19th century, an employee injured on the job was often barred from recovering damages under the defenses of contributory negligence and assumption of the risk; under the fellow-servant rule, an employer avoided liability if the negligence of another worker caused the harm.

2. Most states today have adopted workers' compensation laws. These eliminate fault as a basis of liability; in return, the amount the employer must pay is limited.

3. An employee can only recover if within the class of employees covered by the law; further, the injury must be work-related.
Example: Gayler v. North American Van Lines (An accident arises out of employment when there is a causal connection between injury and performance of duties by the employee.)

B. OSHA (Occupational Safety and Health Act of 1970) applies to all businesses that affect interstate commerce.

1. Imposes duty on employers to prevent workplace hazards and authorizes labor department to issue health and safety standards.

II. Wages and Pensions

A. Fair Labor Standards Act mandates a minimum hourly wage and overtime wage, and prohibits oppressive child labor.

B. Most states have laws protecting workers by limiting the amount of wages which can be garnished.

C. Employment Retirement Income Security Act (ERISA) adopted in 1974, regulates the management and vesting of established retirement plans.

D. Collective Bargaining and Union Activities

1. The Norris-LaGuardia Act was the first act prohibiting the enforcement of yellow-dog contracts.

2. The National Labor Relations Act recognizes the right of workers to organize and bargain collectively.

3. The Labor-Management Relations Act was passed in 1947 to limit what was seen to be excessive power of unions. This act declares certain union and employer practices to be unfair labor practices.
Example: General Teamsters Local No. 162 v. N.L.R.B. (holding that firing of striking employees who engage in picket line misconduct is not an unfair labor practice.)

4. The Labor-Management Reporting and Disclosure Act further checks unions by promoting honesty and democracy in running the union's internal affairs.

III. Employment Discrimination

A. The Equal Pay Act of 1963 prohibits sex discrimination in pay.
Example: Blocker v. A T & T Technology Systems (AT & T did not violate the Equal Pay Act by paying employee less than male accountants because male senior auditors had seniority which was reflected in their pay.)

B. Title VII of the Civil Rights Act of 1964 prohibits discrimination on the basis of race, color, religion, sex, or national origin and applies to employers in interstate commerce with at least 15 employees.

1. Discrimination includes not only intentional discrimination but acts that have a discriminatory impact. It encompasses sexual harassment as a form of discrimination.
Example: Meritor Savings Bank v. Vinson

2. Discrimination is permitted if a characteristic is a bona fide occupational qualification, but not BFOQ exception is permitted with respect to discrimination based on race or color.

C. The Civil Rights Act of 1991 overturned several Supreme Court decisions in discrimination cases and will likely increase successful discrimination suits in the future.

D. ADEA (Age Discrimination i Employment Act) prohibits employers of 20 or more from discriminating against employees based on age.

Example: Mahoney v. RFE/RL Inc. (Mandatory retirementage was prohibited under the ADEA)

E. The Americans with Disability Act (ADA) protects qualified individuals with a disability from discrimination. A qualified individual is one who can perform the essential functions of a job with or without reasonable accommodation of the disability.

Example: Overton v. Reilly ("reasonable accommodation" under the ADA includes job restructuring for employee who could not adequately communicate with the public.)

IV. Employment at Will

A. This doctrine permits employers to fire an employee who was hired "at-will" (without a specific term.)

B. Court-created exceptions include cases striking down the at-will doctrine on grounds of (1) public policy (2) implied terms of the employment contract and (3) the implied covenant of good faith.

Example: Paralegal v. Lawyer (Employer's firing of an at-will employee who was a whistleblower violated public policy.)

V. Employee Privacy

A. The Employee Polygraph Protection Act prohibits private employers from using such tests to screen applicants and in other instances.

B. Some courts have held that drug tests violate the employee's right to privacy, but there are exceptions.

Example: National Treasury Employees Union v. Von Raab (Drug tests of U.S. Customs employees do not violate Fourth Amendment.)

Learning Objectives

1. You should understand how the changes in society have affected the court's and legislature's attitude toward common law employment doctrines, such as the at-will doctrine, and how contemporary realities of the workplace have led to increased legislation whose goals are worker-protection.

2. You should note that anti-discrimination laws are a continuous source of litigation and that the opinions of the courts clearly shape and define the boundaries of protections under these laws.

3. You should understand the application of the Occupational Safety and Health Act (OSHA). You should know not only the general reach of the Act, but also the procedures which must be followed in the enforcement of its provisions.

4. It is important to be aware of the impact that the workers' compensation laws have had on the legal treatment of injuries in the employment setting. This requires an understanding of how the statutory scheme has transformed the traditional tort recoveries in the workplace.

5. You should understand the Fair Labor Standards Act (FLSA) and its exemptions.

6. You should be able to identify and distinguish the various labor laws that grew out of the Depression. Understand how each supplements the others, and be able to recognize their general theme of insuring a balance between labor and management.

7. In the context of the various labor laws, understand what constitutes unfair labor practices for labor and management. Know why each practice is considered unfair.

8. Recognize the types of discrimination prohibited by the Civil Rights Act. You should understand the BFOQ exception. You should also understand how the Act is administered.

9. Compare and contrast the Equal Pay Act with the Civil Rights Act. You should also understand the Age Discrimination Act and be able to see how these three acts complement each other.

10. You should be familiar with the Employment Retirement and Income Security Act, and understand its general purpose. Be aware of the standards that ERISA imposes on new and existing pension plans.

11. You should be familiar with the employment at will doctrine, the judicially created exceptions to the doctrine, and the reasons these exceptions have been created.

12. You should be familiar with recent legislation, such as the Americans with Disabilities Act, protecting disabled workers, and with legislation, such as the Age Discrimination in Employment Act protecting workers from age discrimination.

Learning Hints

1. Common law doctrine, like the employment at will doctrine, may be limited by court decision or by legislative action. For example, some courts have prohibited firing an employee at-will for "whistleblowing," because permitting such firing violates public policy.

2. Most states today have adopted workers' compensation laws protecting workers injured on the job. The structure of these laws is generally to establish an administrative framework within which determination of injury and payment is made. While abolishing contributory negligence and other employer defenses to protect workers, the legislatures also have limited, in some cases substantially, the awards available to injured workers.

3. Note how OSHA differs in its approach from the approach that underlies tort law. In tort law, the courts generally allow private employers great discretion in how the workplace is maintained. However, if injuries occur, the employer will usually be liable to the injured party. OSHA, on the other hand, represents a more centralized approach to job safety. Under its coverage, health and safety standards take on the force of law.

4. Under OSHA the states are able to enforce their own health and safety programs as long as they are as stringent as the federal program. Labor leaders have complained that the states are not enforcing the law and that the Reagan Administration does not decertify the states which fail to live up to federal standards.

5. Workers' compensation is a continuation of recent trends in tort law which are making property owners more and more responsible for injuries which occur on their property and which they may be in the best position to avoid or minimize. Without access to the common law tort defenses, the employer will almost always have to pay for job related injuries, notwithstanding the negligence of the injured employee. The recoveries under workers' compensation, however, are generally quite low. This persuades plaintiffs with strong cases to sometimes sue in tort where jury awards can be quite large. However, in such a tort action, the defendant will have available to him the traditional defenses of contributory negligence and strict liability.

6. You might notice that most of the laws discussed in this chapter only reach businesses that are engaged in interstate commerce. This is because they are federal laws which draw their authority from the Commerce Clause. However, the courts have construed the concept of "interstate commerce" quite broadly, allowing laws enacted pursuant to the Commerce Clause to reach almost all commercial behavior.

7. Note that the labor laws are premised on the notion that competition will not function in the labor market. They assume that workers will almost always be unable to individually bargain with employers. Therefore, these laws give labor a limited exemption from the antitrust laws to the extent that the union is bargaining for legitimate benefits . The labor laws represent the government replacing its bias toward a market approach with a notion of countervailing power as a means of protecting private interests.

8. The other laws in this chapter represent other methods of protecting private interests. Rather than pursuing the market or countervailing power (as in labor relations), they illustrate the third approach to restraining private power—strict government regulation.

9. The antidiscrimination laws raise a number of problems. The debate ranges from the legality of reverse discrimination to the definition of substantially equal work. Throughout this debate, one common question arises: is the purpose of the antidiscrimination laws to achieve equal opportunity or equal results?

10. Recent legislative acts have protected workers from discrimination based on age or disability. The scope and effect of these recent laws, such as the ADA and ADEA, will likely continue to be defined by court decisions well into the future.

True-False

In the blank provided, put "T" if the statement is True or "F" if the statement is False.

_____ 1. An employer may discriminate based on sex if it proves that sex is a bona fide occupational qualification under Title VII.

_____ 2. Sexual harassment is a form of discrimination prohibited under Title VII.

_____ 3. Title VII covers U.S. citizens working for U.S. companies overseas.

_____ 4. Under workman's compensation laws, a worker can recover for any injuries sustained during the time he is employed, even if those injuries are not work-related.

_____ 5. The "fellow-servant" rule is a defense used by employers in Title VII cases.

_____ 6. An injured employee must give up his right to sue the employer in tort in exchange for a recovery under the workers' compensation laws.

_____ 7. The courts originally found organized activities by workers to be criminal restraints of trade.

_____ 8. The Occupational Safety and Health Act (OSHA) seeks to make the workplace safer, unlike workers' compensation laws, which are designed to compensate employees for workplace injuries which have already occurred.

_____ 9. While a BFOQ exception exists for race discrimination, it is not available for religious discrimination.

_____ 10. Voluntary affirmative action plans have been made illegal by the Supreme Court because they involve reverse discrimination.

Multiple Choice

Circle the best answer.

1. Which of the following federal laws prohibits oppressive child labor?
   a. OSHA;
   b. Workman's compensation laws;
   c. Fair Labor Standards Act;
   d. None of the above.

2. The Employment Retirement Income Security Act (ERISA):
   a. Mandates federal employers to establish pension plans for employees;
   b. Regulates both employer and union sponsored pension plans;
   c. Only applies to federal employee benefit plans;
   d. All of the above are correct.

3. A "yellow dog contract":
   a. Is a contract requiring a worker who takes a job to promise not to join a union;
   b. Is illegal under federal law;
   c. Is a contract which violates OSHA health and safety requirements;
   d. Both (a) and (b) are correct.

4. Which of the following laws protects the right of workers to organize and bargain collectively?
   a. OSHA;
   b. Worker's compensation laws;
   c. National Labor Relations Act;
   d. ERISA

5. If an employer pays a female employee less than a male employee for a job that requires equal skill, effort, and responsibility:
   a. The employer violates the Equal Pay Act unless it can prove the different rates are a result of a factor other than sex;
   b. The employer violates the 14th amendment's due process clause as interpreted by the courts;
   c. The employer violates the National Labor Relations Act;
   d. The employer violates all of the above.

6. Numerous states have passed laws regulating garnishment of wages which:
   a. make the wages of debtors subject to the claims of creditors.
   b. prohibit the firing of employees whose wages are subject to garnishment.
   c. Both a and b
   d. Neither a nor b

7. Organized activity by workers in the United States:
   a. was initially held to be criminal by the courts.
   b. initially met little opposition from employers.
   c. met with great success in the early 19th century.
   d. Both b and c.

8. Exemptions from the workers' compensation statutes frequently include:
   a. employers with three or fewer employees.
   b. farmers.
   c. household services employees.
   d. All of the above

9. The Equal Pay Act of 1963 reaches discrimination based on:
   a. sex.
   b. race.
   c. religion.
   d. All of the above

10. A bona fide occupational qualification (BFOQ) exception is available:
    a. with respect to discrimination based on race.
    b. for sex discrimination but not for discrimination based on age.
    c. for discrimination based on national origin.
    d. None of the above

11. The employment at will doctrine will not shield employers from liability for firings which:
    a. are against public policy.
    b. are in violation of implied terms of the employment contract.
    c. violate an implied covenant of good faith and fair dealing.
    d. All of the above

Short Essay

1. Sue works for Fine Furniture Company delivering furniture. She has just finished a delivery in the company truck when she remembers it is her son's birthday. She decides to get him a present before she makes her next delivery and is on his way to the store when she is hit by a semitrailer truck. Sue seeks to recover damages under her state's workman's compensation laws. Will she be successful? Explain.

2. Explain the difference between quid pro quo sexual harassment and a sexually harassing environment.

3. Simmons, an employee of Midwest Steel, was injured while working on the assembly line at the company's only plant. At the time of his injury he was not wearing the safety goggles which were required of employees at the plant. On several occasions on the day that Simmons was injured, the shift foreman ordered him to wear the goggles. As soon as the foreman was out of sight, Simmons would take the goggles off. His injury arose when he was struck in the eye by a screw which fell from the screw gun operated by another employee working on the line. Is the employer liable to Simmons under the workers' compensation laws? Explain.

4. Perles was injured when the assembly line on which he was standing was inadvertently turned on by a fellow employee. The line was never operated during the normal course of the work-day; instead, the furnaces which were manufactured on the line were manually moved down the line. Several weeks earlier the OSHA inspector had informed the plant manager that the line needed to have a sign which warned employees of the danger of standing too close to the end of the line. The inspector also told the plant manager to repair the switch for the line since it was easily engaged by even the slightest contact. None of these corrections were made prior to Perles' injury. Immediately after the injury, a fellow employee contacted the inspector and informed him of the accident. That same day the inspector and an employee representing the union visited the plant manager and told him that they wanted to visit the scene of the accident immediately. The manager informed the employee that if he did not return to work immediately he would be fired. The manager told the inspector that he was too busy to allow him on the premises at that time, refusing his request to inspect the factory. Has the manager violated the law? Explain fully.

CHAPTER 24
WHICH FORM OF BUSINESS ORGANIZATION?

Outline

I.Different types of Business Organizations Include:

A. Sole Proprietorship (Business operated by person as his own personal property.)

B. Partnerships (voluntary associations designed to carry on business for profit.)

1. In a general partnership, each partner shares in the profits and losses of the business.

2. In a limited partnership, limited partners may share in the profits without becoming personally liable on the debts of the business.

C. A Corporation is a separate legal entity; Shareholders of a corporation are not personally liable for its debts.

D. Other forms include the Business Trust and real estate investment trust, and joint-stock association.

II.Factors in Choosing a Form of Business Organization:

A. Limited Liability

1. Liability of limited partners and shareholders in a corporation is limited to their investment; general partners and sole proprietors have the risk of unlimited personal liabilities.

B. Taxation: Different advantages accrue to partnerships and corporations.

1. An S Corporation is taxed like a partnership.

2. There are different advantages of corporate taxation and of sole proprietorship and partnership taxation.

C. Formalities

1. Formalities required for creation of a corporation or a limited partnership, such as filing with government officials, are not required for individual proprietorships or general partnerships.

D. There are also Financing and Management advantages and disadvantages relating to different business organizations.

E. Legally, a corporation continues after the death or insolvency of a shareholder, but a partnership is dissolved on the death of a partner.

F. It is easier to sell one's investment in a publicly held corporation; a partner is generally not entitled to force the partnership business to be liquidated.

III.Franchising

A. Franchising is a contractual relationship, and typically the franchisor is a corporation and the franchisee forms a corporation to operate the franchised business.

B. Some complaints associated with franchising include the fact that the contracts are typically "contracts of adhesion" with terms favoring the franchisor.

C. As a result of franchising problems, both the federal and state governments now generally regulate the franchise relationship.

Learning Objectives

1. You should be able to identify different factors one should consider in determining which business organization will best achieve an organizer's goals.

2. You should be able to explain the difference between a partnership, sole proprietorship, and corporation.

3. You should be able to identify tax implications of various forms of business organization.

4. You should be able to identify management and formation differences between the various forms of business organizations.

5. You should know which business organizations are entities separate from their owners, as well as the purposes for which they are considered to be separate from their owners.

6. You should know the basic differences between general and limited partnerships.

7. You should understand the limited liability advantage of the corporation.

8. You should be able to recognize the different types of corporations.

9. You should know what a franchise is and why business persons choose to buy franchises, as well as the major legal problems that may accompany the use of franchises.

10. You should be able to identify federal and state legislation which may impact upon the franchise agreement.

Learning Hints

1. One significant advantage of a corporation is that it limits liability of the shareholders to their investment in the corporation. However, in smaller Subchapter S corporations, most lending institutions will require personal as well as corporate liability as a condition to lending money to the business.

2. One significant advantage of a corporation is the fact that it continues on after the death of its stockholder(s); in the case of a partnership, a partnership will terminate by law upon the death of a general partner.

3. A determination of the appropriate organization form for a business must be made on a case-by-case basis. The owners of each business have objectives that may make one business form superior to another in the context of their respective situations. That one business organization form works well for one particular business does not necessarily mean that the same form will work well for a different business.

4. A sole proprietorship is the easiest business organization to create. A person merely establishes a business, and the sole proprietorship is created automatically.

5. The sole proprietor has unlimited liability for the obligations of the business operated as a sole proprietorship. Unlimited liability means that the sole proprietor's individual assets (her house, her car, etc.) can be attached by creditors of the business if the assets of the business are insufficient to pay the creditors' claim against the business.

6. It is extremely easy to create a partnership. Many partnerships are created by persons who do not know they are creating a partnership. Even though persons may say they are not partners, they often have created a partnership anyway if they share profits and otherwise act as if they are partners.

7. Note that the shared ownership requirement in the definition of a partnership refers to shared ownership of the business, not necessarily shared ownership of the assets. The two most important factors tending to indicate shared ownership of the business are the sharing of profits and the sharing of the management of the business. Remember that two persons may perform different management functions and still be partners. For example, one partner might solely be in charge of hiring employees and the other partner might solely be in charge of purchasing inventory. In addition, it is important to remember that the shared ownership need not be an equal sharing of ownership. Different partners may contribute different amounts of capital to the partnership and still be partners. Certain partners may receive a larger share of the profits than other partners do. There is still a partnership in such situations.

8. Limited partners are not held personally liable for partnership debts beyond the limited partner's investment in the partnership. Do not forget, however, that a limited partner is entitled to such a limit on his personal liability only if he refrains from participating in the management of the partnership. If one who started out as a limited partner becomes involved in management of the partnership, he thereby becomes a general partner and, in the process, loses the benefit of the restrictions on liability otherwise extended to limited partners.

9. Unlike the sole proprietorship or the partnership, a corporation is an entity separate from its owners in all respects. In fact, managers of the corporation need not be shareholders in the corporation.

10. The corporate form of business may not be used improperly, however. If it is used in such a manner, the court may "pierce the corporate veil." When this occurs, shareholders may be held personally liable. Although courts do not routinely pierce the corporate veil, they will do so where those who formed the corporation provided it with a grossly inadequate amount of capital. In such situations, a fraud on creditors is likely, and the corporate entity must be disre-

garded and access to shareholder assets must be allowed in order to enable legitimate claims of creditors to be satisfied. Similarly, courts will pierce the corporate veil and subject shareholders to personal liability where it is proved that shareholders merely treat the corporation as an extension of themselves, such as by having the corporation pay their personal expenses. In instances of this sort, the corporation is merely the alter ego of the shareholders and not really a separate entity anyway. Shareholders must deal with the corporation at arms' length, just as unrelated persons would do in a business setting. The subject of piercing the corporate veil is dealt with in more depth in Chapter 27 of your text.

11. A franchise is not really a form of business organization. Instead, it is a form of business opportunity. A franchise may be operated as a sole proprietorship, partnership, or corporation, or in any other form of business organization.

12. The chief legal problems in franchising result from an inherent aspect of franchising: the franchisor's desire to control the quality of the franchisees' products and services. Contracts of adhesion, unreasonable franchise terminations, and antitrust violations may result from the franchisor's intent to dominate the franchisor-franchisee relation and thereby maintain quality control.

True-False

In the blank provided, put "T" if the statement is True or "F" if the statement is False.

_____ 1. No express agreement is necessary to create a general partnership.

_____ 2. The principal reason to incorporate a business is to limit liability of the owners/shareholders of the corporation.

_____ 3. A real estate investment trust is taxed as a regular corporation.

_____ 4. An S corporation or Subchapter S corporation @X = is taxed like a corporation rather than a partnership.

_____ 5. One tax advantage of a corporation is that if shares of a corporation are exchanged for shares of another corporation, the transaction is tax-free.

_____ 6. A partner's liability for partnership debts is not limited to the amount of her contribution of capital to the partnership.

_____ 7. A major disadvantage of the partnership form of business is that partnerships are entities on which income tax is imposed.

_____ 8. A close corporation is not treated by the law as an entity separate from its owners.

_____ 9. A joint stock association is a corporation that has most of the characteristics of a partnership.

_____ 10. General partners in a limited partnership may face unlimited liability for partnership debts.

Multiple Choice

Circle the best answer.

1. Which of the following is required in order to establish a Subchapter S corporation?
   a. There can be no more than 35 shareholders;
   b. The shareholders must all be individuals or estates;
   c. The shareholders must consent to having the corporation taxed as a partnership.
   d. All of the above are necessary to establish an S corporation.

2. Which of the following is <u>not</u> true of a corporation?
   a. legally, a corporation is not affected by the death or insolvency of a shareholder.
   b. The corporate form makes financing easier than that of a sole proprietorship;
   c. Today, federal law protects minority shareholders from being "frozen out" by the majority;
   d. Generally, it is easier to preserve goodwill in a corporation as owners change than in a partnership or sole proprietorship.

3. Which of the following is <u>not</u> an advantage of franchising to the franchisee?
   a. The franchisee generally has the right to use a trademark owned by the franchisor;
   b. The franchisee often has access to a standardized and tested method of conducting the business;

    c.   In some instances, a franchisor will build and equip the place of business and lease it to the franchisee;

    d.   Termination clauses in franchise agreements generally favor the franchisee.

4. In which of the following ways have state and federal governments regulated franchises?
   a. The Federal Trade Commission requires by rule that franchisors disclose certain information to prospective franchisees;
   b. All states have enacted uniform franchising laws designed to protect franchisees;
   c. Many states prevent deceptive advertising of franchise opportunities through their deceptive trade practices or consumer protection legislation;
   d. Both (a) and (c) are correct.

5. A "close corporation":
   a. Is a limited partnership;
   b. Is a publicly held corporation selling shares to investors;
   c. Is a corporation in which stock is held by family members;
   d. None of the above is correct.

6. Of the following statements concerning sole proprietorships, which is inaccurate?
   a. The liability the sole proprietor has for debts of the business operated as a sole proprietorship is limited to the amount of capital she has put into the business.
   b. A sole proprietorship may be established without filing, in a government office, written documents evidencing such an intent.
   c. A sole proprietor is not required to use her name as the name of the business.
   d. The wages paid by a sole proprietor to her employees may be deductible items on the sole proprietor's tax return.

7. Of the following statements concerning business organizations, which is/are accurate?
   a. Federal income tax is imposed on corporations and partnerships.
   b. General partners are not subject to personal liability for partnership debts.
   c. Shareholders of a corporation ordinarily are not held personally liable for corporate debts.
   d. All of the above.

8. Biff and Maxine agreed to operate a auto parts store together and to split the profits from the store. They never signed a formal partnership agreement. Biff and Maxine
   a. cannot be partners because they did not have an agreement in writing.
   b. have created a limited partnership.
   c. probably are partners despite the lack of a written agreement.
   d. have created a dual proprietorship.

9. Earl Overbearing is in charge of nearly all of the management duties for a real estate sales business. Which of the following is an accurate statement about the relationship between Overbearing and the business?
   a. If the business is operated as a limited partnership, Overbearing cannot be a limited partner.
   b. If the business is operated as a close corporation, Overbearing must be a shareholder.
   c. If the business is operated as a corporation (close or otherwise), Overbearing will be personally liable for the debts of the corporation.
   d. None of the above.

10. The limited partnership
    a. may consist entirely of limited partners if the parties forming it so choose.
    b. automatically becomes a general partnership if any general partners become involved in the business.
    c. allows investors who do not participate in management to share in the profits of the business without becoming personally liable for partnership debts.
    d. is treated as a corporation for taxation purposes.

Short Essay

Short-Answer

1. Briefly list and discuss five factors one should consider in choosing which form of business organization to select.

2. There are a number of important attributes of various forms of business organizations. These include whether the form limits liability of the owners, taxation consequences, necessary formalities for forming the organization, cost of filing and maintaining necessary documents, and formalities for termination, financing implications, questions of management, and liquidity of the owner's investment in the business.

3. Arthur King is the chief executive officer of Camelot, Inc., a close corporation. He is also the majority shareholder in the corporation. King knows that two lawsuits are about to be filed against Camelot. One pertains to an alleged breach of a contract to which Camelot was a party. King had been actively involved in the negotiation of the terms of the contract. The other lawsuit that will be filed against Camelot pertains to an automobile accident allegedly caused by the negligence of Lance Allot, a Camelot employee. Allot was acting within the scope of his employment when the accident occurred. King is concerned that he could face personal liability for damages that may be awarded in these suits, if Camelot's assets prove insufficient to satisfy the damage awards. Should he be concerned? Why or why not?

4. Tinker was a limited partner in Evers & Chance Limited Partnership. Evers and Chance were the firm's general partners. Tinker had invested $50,000 in the limited partnership. Evers and Chance had each invested $10,000. Originally, Evers and Chance had done all of the managing of the partnership business. As time went on, however, Tinker became involved, along with Evers and Chance, in management of the firm's business activities. After this change in responsibility for management had taken place, Evers (while in the course of partnership business) negligently caused crippling physical injury to Cobb. Assume that Cobb's tort claim is a valid one worth at least $500,000, an amount easily in excess of not only the initial contributions to the partnership but also the value of all partnership property and assets. What is the extent of liability (if any) that Tinker, Evers, and Chance, respectively, may have to Cobb?

5. Bart, Toni, and Skip have decided to begin a retail sales business. Each has substantial income from sources other than the planned business. The three expect the business to be unprofitable for a few years before it becomes successful. They will be the only owners and managers. What form of business organization would be a logical one for them to choose? State the reasons for your answer.

CHAPTER 25
FORMATION AND OPERATION OF PARTNERSHIPS

Outline

I. Creation of a Partnership

  A. No express agreement is necessary, and one who receives a share of profits from a business may be treated as a partner.

    1. A partnership is an association of two or more persons carrying on a business for profit as co-owners.

    2. An individual, partnership, or corporation may qualify as a person that can form a partnership.

    3. One who shares in the management of the business as well as in the profits is more likely to be considered a partner.
    Example: <u>Bass v. Bass</u> (holding that parties carried on a business as co-owners for profit and thus were business partners.)

  B. A partnership can also arise through <u>estoppel</u>. A person may hold another liable as a partner if she proves that she relied on the holding out of the partnership or consent of the partner. This is a device to protect creditors who rely on a party's purported status as a partner.

II. Nature of the Partnership

  A. The partnership is a separate entity from the partners for some purposes, and an aggregate of the individual partners in other instances.

  B. It is highly desirable to have written articles of partnership even though this is not necessary.

III. Management and Authority of Partners

  A. Each partner normally has an equal voice in managing the business.

  B. Authority to act for a partnership may be express, implied, or apparent.

  Example: <u>FTC Securities v. Norwest Bank</u> (Partner in aircraft leasing business had authority as a partner to endorse and negotiate checks in carrying on the usual business of the partnership.)

  C. Even if a partner lacked authority to contract for the partnership, ratification by the other partners makes the contract enforceable against the partnership.

IV. What is Partnership Property?

  A. All property originally contributed to the partnership as well as that purchased later is partnership property.

  B. Real property may be conveyed by any partner with authority to do so. Property is held by the partners as tenants in partnership.

  Example: <u>Cromer v. Cromer</u> (Insurance proceeds were partnership property.)

V. Other Issues

  A. Compensation of Partners

    1. Compensation is presumed to be the partner's share of profits. Absent agreement, profits are shared equally.

  B. Duties of Partners

    1. The duties of partners are substantially the same as those of agents to principals.
    Example: <u>Levy v. Disharoon</u> (A partner owes a duty of loyalty to other partners.)

  C. Enforcement of Partnership Rights and Liabilities

    1. Partners become jointly liable on debts of the partnership; under the doctrine of <u>respondeat superior</u>, a partner is liable for torts committed by other partners.
    Example: <u>Martinez v. Koelling</u> (Partnership liability in tort extends to any partner.)

    2. Moe and Curly were partners in a massage parlor. Moe negligently injured Renata when he bent her arm backwards during a massage. Moe has disappeared so Renata sued Curly for damages. Curly wasn't even in the building when the tort occurred. Is Curly liable for Moe's negligence?

3. Yes. A partner is generally liable for the torts of his co-partner committed within the scope of employment under the doctrine of mutual agency. Liability is joint and several.

Learning Objectives

1. You should understand how a partnership is created.
2. You should understand the implications of agency law for partners within a partnership;
3. You should be able to articulate the duties which a partner owes other partners.
4. You should distinguish between a partner's express, implied, and apparent authority to act on behalf of the partnership.
5. You should know the kinds of provisions customarily contained in articles of partnership.
6. You should understand how the concept of estoppel may be used to hold someone liable as if he were a partner, even though he may not actually have been a partner.
7. You should know when an individual partner can bind the partnership, when a majority vote of partners is required, and when unanimous agreement of the partners is necessary.
8. You should be able to distinguish between trading and nontrading partnerships and should know the importance of distinguishing between the two.
9. You should be able to distinguish partnership property from a partner's individual property, and should know the rights of partners in partnership property.
10. You should understand charging orders and assignments of partnership interests.
11. You should become familiar with the purposes for which a partnership is regarded as an entity separate from the partners comprising it.
12. You should know the duties a partner owes to the partnership and the other partners, as well as the rights a partner possesses in a partnership.

Learning Hints

1. Parties may form a partnership without express agreement. In fact, a partnership may arise even though the parties did not actually intend to create a partnership.
2. A partnership creates certain rights and duties in the partners. One right is the right to share equally in the profits of the partnership even if the partners have not contributed equally to the partnership.
3. A partnership may arise when creditors allege the existence of a partnership. In some cases creditors argue partnership by estoppel based on their reasonable reliance of a partnership.
4. A partner may have express, implied, or apparent authority to act for the partnership. These concepts are similar to the agency concept of authority.
5. At common law, any partner is liable for the entire debt of the partnership if the other partners are judgment proof.
6. The partnership agreement (often called the articles of partnership) is the basic governing document of the partnership. It usually defines the most basic rights and obligations of the partners. Remember, however, that a valid partnership may exist even though the parties do not have a written partnership agreement.
7. When partnership by estoppel applies, the persons represented to be partners are treated as partners only for the purpose of holding them liable to a creditor, and not for any other purpose. Hence, the persons held liable under this doctrine do not acquire any of the rights associated with being partners.
8. The best way to understand the distinction between trading and nontrading partnerships is to understand that trading partnerships require substantial working capital. In other words, there is an ordinary business need to borrow money. For example, manufacturing firms are trading partnerships because they need to borrow significant amounts of money to finance their purchases of raw materials. They need to borrow money because a substantial period of time elapses between their purchase of raw materials and their sale of the finished product. If one understands this, it is easy to see why a partner in a trading partnership has implied authority or apparent authority to borrow money in the partnership's name.

9. Remember that unless the partners have agreed otherwise, the partners will share the profits equally among themselves. This is true even though initial contributions of capital by the various partners may not have been equal. It is quite common, however, for partnership agreements to provide that certain partners will receive a greater share of the profits than other partners will receive.

10. Similarly, unless the partnership agreement states otherwise, partners share partnership losses in the same manner in which they share profits, regardless of the respective amounts the individual partners contributed as capital. Of course, the various partners are free to agree that certain partners will bear a greater share of losses than will other partners.

11. The business judgment rule protects a partner from liability to the partnership for "judgment calls" that turn out to be unfortunate decisions. If the partner undertakes a reasonable investigation before making a business decision and acts honestly when making the business decision, a court will not hold the partner liable for the negative consequences the partnership experienced as a result of the incorrect decision. The rationale for the rule is that a court is not equipped to make business judgments.

12. The same principles regarding tort and criminal liability that exist in agency law exist in partnership law also. You should review the discussion of those concepts in the agency law materials if you have difficulty with them in connection with partnership law.

True-False

In the blank provided, put "T" if the statement is True or "F" if the statement is False.

_____ 1. The Uniform Partnership Act has been adopted @X = by a majority of states in the United States.

_____ 2. A corporation may qualify as a person for purposes of forming a partnership.

_____ 3. A minor lacks the capacity to become a partner in a partnership.

_____ 4. A partnership must adopt a firm name.

_____ 5. Absent express agreement to the contrary, any partner may sell, mortgage, or devise partnership property.

_____ 6. If parties have demonstrated a clear intent not to share losses, that demonstration of intent tends to indicate that the parties are not partners.

_____ 7. If partner A's implied authority to take a particular action has been eliminated by vote of partners B, C, and D, partner A necessarily will not have apparent authority to take that action.

_____ 8. Although the partnership will face liability for a tort committed by a partner while acting within the scope of partnership business, the other partners who did not commit the tort cannot be held liable.

_____ 9. Partnership property must be titled in the partnership's name.

_____ 10. Partners are prohibited from selling to or buying from the partnership.

Multiple Choice

Circle the best answer.

1. Which of the following is not a requirement of a partnership?
   a. An express agreement;
   b. An association of at least two people;
   c. Intent to carry on a business for profit;
   d. Intent to carry on the business as co-owners.

2. A partnership by estoppel:
   a. Arises by express agreement of the parties;
   b. Arises by implied agreement of the parties;
   c. Arises when a third party, such as a creditor, reasonably relies on the purported status of a partner, even though no partnership in fact exists;
   d. Is prohibited by federal and most state laws.

3. Jack and John entered into a partnership to purchase real estate. Jack was a real estate broker who had bought and sold property in the past. John was a finance major who managed the books for the partnership. They had no formal written partnership agreement. Sometime after forming the partnership, John entered into an agreement with a financial accounting firm to regularly audit the company's books. Jack objected, saying John did not have the authority to bind the partnership on the contract. Under these circumstances:
   a. John had the express authority to enter into the contract;
   b. As managing partner, John had the implied authority to enter into the contract;
   c. As managing partner, John had the apparent authority to enter into the contract;
   d. Both (b) and (c) are correct.

4. A "trading partnership":
   a. Is a business such as commercial farming, general contracting, or manufacturing business engaged in the buying and selling of merchandise for profit;
   b. Is a business which generally needs to borrow funds to finance its inventory;
   c. Is a partnership in which partners generally have implied and apparent authority to borrow for the business.
   d. All of the above are correct.

5. Bob, Caryl, Ted, and Alice formed a partnership to operate a restaurant called "Our Town." They each contributed funds and/or equipment for use in the restaurant, and Ted contributed a used van he already owned. Several months later, Ted "borrowed" the van to take it on vacation. Under these circumstances:
   a. Ted has the right to use partnership property so long as it is for the benefit of at least one partner;
   b. Ted may use partnership property for personal use if it is property which he contributed to the partnership;
   c. Ted has no right to take possession of the firm's property for personal use;
   d. Because Ted used the van for his vacation, this is permitted as a "partnership use."

6. Partnership property
   a. includes property originally contributed to the partnership, but not property purchased later for the use of the partnership.
   b. includes all property used in the business, regardless of who owns it.
   c. must be titled only in the firm name.
   d. includes all property purchased with partnership funds, unless the partners have shown a contrary intent.

7. Steppen and Wolf have been partners in a used motorcycle sales business for several years. Last year, Steppen bought 20 used cars on his own time with his own money, and then sold them. He made profits of $4,500 on the sales. Wolf recently discovered that Steppen had made these sales. On these facts,
   a. Wolf is not entitled to a share of the profits made by Steppen on resale of the motorcycles, because Steppen purchased the motorcycles with his own funds and on his own time.
   b. Steppen did not breach his duty of loyalty by profiting on the sales of the motorcycles, so long as he continued to devote his usual number of hours to the partnership business.
   c. Wolf is entitled to half of the $4,500 in profits received by Steppen, or to whatever Wolf's usual share of profits is (if the parties have agreed to share profits on some basis other than equally).
   d. Wolf is entitled to terminate the partnership but has no claim to any portion of the profits made by Steppen on the sales of the 20 motorcycles.

8. Chloe is a partner in a retail sales business that has assets of $300,000. The partnership frequently borrowed to meet operating requirements. Needing money to pay personal debts, she recently borrowed $15,000 from a bank and signed the name of the partnership on the loan contract. Chloe told the bank that the money was for the firm, but she actually used the money for herself only. Chloe is now unable to repay the loan. The partnership
   a. is not liable to the bank on the loan, because Chloe was acting outside the scope of her authority.
   b. is liable to the bank on the loan, because the partnership is a trading partnership.

c. is not liable to the bank on the loan, because Chloe committed a fraud upon the bank and upon the partnership.

d. is liable to the bank on the loan, because Chloe was negligent in failing to tell the bank the real purpose for obtaining the loan, and because the negligence of a partner is imputed to the partnership.

9. A partner has implied authority to bind the partnership
   a. whenever third persons justifiably believe the partner has authority to enter into a contract with them on behalf of the partnership.
   b. only on those contracts that he, according to the terms of the partnership agreement, is expressly authorized to make.
   c. only if the partnership agreement specifically states that he will have implied authority of that nature.
   d. on contracts that are usually appropriate to the business in which the partnership is engaged.

10. Kyle, Tara, and Maggie formed a partnership to operate an obedience school for dogs. Kyle and Tara each contributed capital of $20,000. Maggie contributed $10,000. The three partners agreed that Kyle and Tara would each assume 45 percent of any losses of the business, and that Maggie would assume the remaining 10 percent of the losses. Their agreement contained no express provision concerning how profits were to be divided. During the first year of operation, the business made $60,000 in profits. What is Maggie's share of the profits?
   a. $12,000
   b. $6,000
   c. $20,000
   d. $10,000

Short Essay

1. Walton, Sr., the sole owner of a small retailing business, was attempting to purchase some goods on credit from a manufacturer with whom he had not done business previously. In talking in person with the manufacturer's representative, Walton pointed to his daughter, Waltona (a nationally known retailer who was also visiting for a few days). Walton then stated that "my partners and I have always paid our bills on time." Waltona heard and saw what her father had said and done, but she made no comment in the presence of the manufacturer's representative. The manufacturer's representative knew, however, that Waltona was neither her father's partner nor otherwise involved in business with him. The manufacturer thereafter sold Mr. Walton goods on credit, and Walton failed to pay for them when payment was due. If the partnership has no assets, and the manufacturer sues Waltona and Walton under these facts, against whom (if anyone) will it be successful?

2. Millie and Mary decided to open a bakery together. Millie contributed equipment and Mary made the first three months' lease payment. They worked together in the bakery for three months when Millie stormed out and said she wanted no more part in the business. Neither party ever signed any written partnership agreement. Are they partners? Why or why not?

3. Tammy, Jim, Jimmy, and Jerry were partners in a lucrative business enterprise. While performing partnership business, Jimmy negligently caused injury to Trixie, an innocent member of the public. Trixie recently filed suit against <u>Jerry</u> in an attempt to hold him responsible for Jimmy's negligence. Is Jerry liable to Trixie? Why or why not?

4. Perry Dry is a partner in an accounting firm known as Dull, Dry & Boring. Dry performed extensive accounting services for a client of the firm. The client was quite appreciative because the work performed by Dry enabled her to obtain a large income tax refund. Dull, Dry & Boring billed the client $2,000 for the work. Besides promptly paying the bill, the client sent (to Dry's home) a separate check in the amount of $1,000, made payable to the order of Dry. Along with the $1,000 check, the client sent Dry a note stating that she was grateful for Dry's fine work and that the $1,000 check was meant for him personally, as further compensation for his accounting services. May Dry keep the $1,000 for himself, or must he turn it over to the firm? State the reasons for your answer.

CHAPTER 26
DISSOLUTION OF PARTNERSHIPS

Outline

I. Dissolution in General

A. A partner's demand for dissolution does not automatically terminate the partnership. Dissolution occurs when a partner ceases to be associated in carrying on the business (wrongfully or non-wrongfully), by law, or by court decree.

B. Nonwrongful termination occurs upon dissolution without violation of the partnership agreement.

   1. For example, a partnership may terminate at a certain time by agreement; absent agreement, any partner may dissolve a partnership at will.

   2. Each nonwrongful partner may demand the partnership be wound up and liquidated.

C. A partner who wrongfully dissolves the partnership loses the right to demand a winding up and liquidation. The partner breaching the agreement is paid the value of his interest less damages for breach.

   Example: <u>Beck v. Clarkson</u> (Wrongful dissolution of partnership).

D. Dissolution by Operation of Law may occur upon death or bankruptcy of any partner, and a court may dissolve a partnership by judicial decree.

II. Winding Up: Purpose is to liquidate the assets at their highest value and bring the business affairs of the partnership promptly to an end.

A. Normally the partners themselves wind up. If dissolution is by court order, the court usually appoints a <u>receiver</u> to wind up.

B. Powers during Winding Up

   1. Note: Except for actions necessary to wind up the partnership, dissolution terminates the actual authority of the partners. They may retain apparent authority, however.

   2. Partners should give <u>notice</u> to creditors of the former partnership.

   3. The partners who wind up are not entitled to compensation except following the death of a partner.

   Example: <u>Thomas v. Schmelzer</u>

III. Continuation

A. Parties may agree that there is no automatic dissolution of the partnership on the withdrawal or death of a partner.

   1. Many agreements contain "Buyout" provisions which permit continuation of the partnership.

B. The continuing partnership becomes liable for the debts incurred by the original partnership; however, the parties may agree to a <u>novation</u> which relieves the withdrawing partners of liability on the debts of the old partnership (but does not bind to creditors).

   Example: <u>Sunbelt Federal Bank v. Butel & Dutel</u> (In order for a partner who has withdrawn from a partnership to relieve himself from responsibility for debts contracted after his withdrawal, he should give notice to creditors.)

C. If a partner wrongfully withdraws from the partnership, the other partners may continue the partnership but must either pay the breaching party his interest or continue the business only for the agreed on term and then settle with all partners.

   Example: <u>Oliker v. Gershunoff</u>

IV. Termination: Distribution of Assets

A. Solvent Partnerships: Each partner receives his/her original contribution play an equal share of the profits, regardless of their original contribution, absent an agreement to the contrary.

B. Insolvent Partnerships: Partnership creditors have first claim, with creditors of individual partners having first claim on the assets of individual partners.

Learning Objectives

1. You should understand how a dissolution of a partnership occurs.
2. You should understand the effect of a partnership dissolution;
3. You should be able to identify the partners' rights and obligations upon dissolution and winding up.
4. You should understand the differences in the respective meanings of dissolution, winding up, and termination.
5. You should know what events cause a dissolution of the partnership.
6. You should know what a partnership at will is.
7. You should know when a dissolution is wrongful and when it is nonwrongful, as well as what the consequences of a wrongful dissolution are.
8. You should know which parties have the right to wind up a partnership, and should be familiar with the implied authority a partner possesses during winding up.
9. You should know the importance of giving firm creditors notice of the dissolution of the partnership, as well as the possible consequences of failing to give proper notice.
10. You should be familiar with the circumstances under which the remaining partners may elect to continue the partnership when one partner ceases being a partner.

Learning Hints

1. A partner's demand for dissolution does not automatically terminate the partnership; however, in absence of an agreement to the contrary, the UPA gives any partner a right to insist on liquidation of the partnership assets on dissolution.
2. Dissolution occurs when any partner ceases to be associated in the carrying on the business; it can occur through violation of the partnership agreement, without violation of the agreement, by law, or by court decree.
3. A nonwrongful partner may demand the business of the partnership be wound up and liquidated.
4. A wrongful partner loses the right to demand a winding up and liquidation.
5. Death or bankruptcy of any partner automatically dissolves the partnership.
6. You must be careful not to confuse dissolution, winding up, and termination. Dissolution may be viewed as the beginning of a process of severing the ties among partners. The severing is not complete until the next two steps in the process (winding up and termination) have also taken place. Remember, however, that under certain circumstances, continuation of the partnership by the remaining partners may be an option in lieu of winding up and termination.
7. Winding up involves liquidating the assets of the business at their highest value and distributing the proceeds to the firm creditors and partners. Remember that in winding up partnership affairs, the partners conducting the winding up may choose to complete unperformed contracts that had been entered into by the partnership prior to dissolution, if doing so would help create a greater amount of assets for distribution. Similarly, the partners conducting the winding up may choose to assign unperformed partnership contracts to other parties, if doing so would produce a suitable amount of assets and facilitate a proper conclusion of partnership affairs.
8. Winding up may not always be required following a dissolution, however. Instead of winding up, continuation of the business may be chosen by all the nonwrongful partners where the partnership was wrongfully dissolved by the act of a partner. Continuation may also be chosen by all the partners where a dissolution of the partnership was a proper, nonwrongful dissolution. In such circumstances, the business may be continued by means of a new partnership, a sole proprietorship, corporation, or any other business form after the old partnership is dissolved.
9. Termination means that the partnership has ended in all respects. It must follow at the end of winding up.
10. A partnership at will exists at the will of the partners. It may be dissolved by any partner at any time. Such a dissolution is nonwrongful.

11. Although a partner has the power to dissolve a partnership at any time, the partner who wrongfully dissolves the partnership faces liability to the other partners. He cannot seek a winding up or perform the winding up. He is not entitled to a share of the partnership's goodwill. Although he still is entitled to receive the value of his partnership interest, there may be deducted, from that amount, the damages sustained by the other partners as a result of his wrongful dissolution of the partnership.

12. A partner's assignment of her partnership interest does not by itself cause a dissolution. It does, however, permit the other partners to agree unanimously to dissolve the partnership, which dissolution is nonwrongful. The reason for permitting the nonassigning partners to dissolve the partnership is that the assigning partner's personal financial difficulty (almost always the reason a partner assigns a partnership interest) makes it unlikely she will be able to bear her share of partnership liabilities. The same rule applies if a creditor has obtained a charging order against a partner's interest in the partnership.

13. Just as proper notice of the termination of an agent must be given, so must proper notice of a dissolution be given to partnership creditors and certain other parties. If proper notice is not given, a partner will retain the apparent authority to do whatever he did before the dissolution. Hence, the partner could make the other partners liable on contracts that the partner had no express or implied authority to make.

14. Note that an outgoing partner will continue to have liability on past obligations of the partnership, unless a novation occurs. Do not forget that a novation can only take place with the agreement of the other partners and the creditors. Besides the liability for past obligations of the partnership, the outgoing partner will have liability on future obligations of the partnership, unless proper notice is given of the partner's leaving the partnership.

15. Note that an incoming (new) partner has limited liability for partnership obligations arising prior to his entering the partnership (liability for such obligations is limited to partnership assets) and full liability for obligations arising after he became a partner.

16. Distributing partnership assets to firm creditors and partners is easy when the partnership has been profitable. It is more difficult when the partnership has suffered a loss, especially if the partners have contributed different amounts of capital to the partnership. You should read carefully the examples appearing at the end of Chapter 26 of your text. You will find some of them easier to understand if you remember that the partners share the losses, not merely the amount still owed to creditors.

True-False

In the blank provided, put "T" if the statement is True or "F" if the statement is False.

_____ 1. A partner who dissolves a partnership at will without agreement of the other partners wrongfully dissolves the partnership.

_____ 2. Any nonwrongful partner may demand that the business of the partnership be wound up and liquidated.

_____ 3. After dissolution, the partners lack actual authority to act on behalf of the partnership;

_____ 4. After dissolution, the partners lack apparent authority to act on behalf of he partnership.

_____ 5. When a party dies, the surviving partner or partners can pass title to partnership property.

_____ 6. Dissolution is the process of settling partnership affairs.

_____ 7. A partnership at will must exist for at least six months but may be dissolved by any partner after the expiration of that period of that time.

_____ 8. A novation eliminates a withdrawing partner's liability for past debts of the partnership.

_____ 9. During winding up, the partners are not permitted to complete unperformed partnership contracts that were entered into before the dissolution of the partnership.

_____ 10. The partners who wind up the partnership's business are entitled to special compensation for that work.

Multiple Choice

Circle the best answer.

1. In which of the following situations is a partner not entitled to a winding up and liquidation of partnership?
   a. Death of partner;
   b. Bankruptcy of partner;
   c. wrongful termination of partnership agreement;
   d. non-wrongful termination of partnership agreement.

2. In which of the following situations does a court normally appoint a receiver to wind up partnership business upon dissolution?
   a. Death of partner;
   b. Bankruptcy;
   c. Court order;
   d. All of the above.

3. Which of the following statements concerning "continuation" of a partnership is not correct?
   a. The continuing partnership becomes liable for the debts incurred by the original partnership;
   b. Partnership agreements declaring that there will be no dissolution upon death or withdrawal of a partner are unenforceable because they violate public policy;
   c. A novation in which continuing partners agree to relieve the withdrawing partners of liability are not binding on creditors unless they have joined in the novation;
   d. A novation may be inferred by courts from the conduct of the creditor.

4. C, A, and R are parents in a laundry business. C retired when he reached age 45 in 1993, but the partnership agreement stipulates that the partnership will exist until 2000. Under these circumstances:
   a. The partnership is dissolved unless a new partner purchases C's interest;
   b. A and R may wind up the business;
   c. C may wind up the business;
   d. If A and R wind up the business, they have the same implied authority to enter into contracts they had before winding up.

5. Eric, Mike, and Arlen, as partners, operate a janitorial service. The partnership is dissolved if:
   a. the business is moved to another state;
   b. the partners convert it to an video-rental business;
   c. Eric withdraws from the partnership and Mike and Arlen continue to operate the business;
   d. None of the above dissolves the partnership.

6. Walt, Yvette, and Zeke were partners in WYZ Partnership, a dissolved partnership. WYZ's business—manufacturing and selling paint—is being wound up. Zeke is performing the winding up. He discovered a WYZ contract to deliver 10,000 gallons of white paint to X-Mart Department Stores by Feb. 15, 1992. The performance of the contract has not yet begun. WYZ has 50,000 gallons of white paint in its inventory. It owns a 100,000 square foot manufacturing plant. For which of the following does Zeke possess express or implied authority during winding up?
   a. Painting the manufacturing plant in preparation for its sale.
   b. Selling the 10,000 gallons of white paint to X-Mart pursuant to the contract.
   c. Selling the manufacturing plant.
   d. All of the above.

7. The liability of an incoming partner for obligations of the partnership arising after he became a partner
   a. is limited to the extent of his capital contribution to the partnership.
   b. exists when notice of his joining the partnership is given.
   c. is unlimited.
   d. is limited to the extent of partnership assets.

8. Oliver and Eb have been partners in farming for 15 years. The last three years, Oliver and Eb have argued bitterly over the choice of crops to plant. Oliver wants beans. Eb wants corn. Because of their conflict, they have not raised any crops for three years. Oliver has tried to convince Eb that they should dissolve the partnership. Eb has always refused, pointing out that the partnership agreement calls for a 20-year term for the partnership. Oliver has decided to seek a court-ordered dissolution of the partnership. Will the court dissolve the partnership?
   a. No, because the 20-year term specified in the partnership agreement is five years away from expiring.
   b. No, because a risk that parties take when they form a partnership is that they will disagree over business matters.
   c. Yes, because the conflict between Oliver and Eb is apparently irreconcilable and so serious that the partnership cannot make a profit.
   d. Yes, because from the standpoint of Oliver, he and Eb have a partnership at will.

9. Susan, Karen, and Ned are partners in SKN Investments. Susan contributed $50,000, and Karen and Ned contributed $20,000 each when the partnership was formed. They agreed that Susan would receive 50 percent of the profits and that Karen and Ned would receive 25 percent each. No provision was made for the division of losses. SKN became insolvent and still owed creditors $24,000 after all the partnership assets had been used. Among Susan, Karen, and Ned, what amount represents Susan's proper share of the $24,000 still owed to creditors?
   a. $12,000
   b. $6,000
   c. $8,500
   d. $7,000

10. In winding up the affairs of a partnership, the partners doing the winding up
   a. may be allowed to complete unperformed partnership contracts entered into by the partnership before the partnership's dissolution, even if money must be borrowed in order to allow performance of the contracts.
   b. may be allowed to complete unperformed partnership contracts entered into by the partnership before the partnership's dissolution, but only if money does not have to be borrowed in order to allow performance of the contracts.
   c. cannot complete unperformed partnership contracts.
   d. may enter into contracts for wholly new business, if it is not necessary to borrow money in order to perform the new obligation.

Short Essay

1. Cliff, Diane, and Norm formed a partnership to purchase and operate a local tavern. The partnership agreement had no termination date. Two years after forming the partnership, Cliff and Diane agreed to purchase Norm's interest and to take on an additional partner, Woody. They continued to do business with their supplier Mr. Bud, who was aware of the new partnership arrangement. One year later, the partnership dissolved when the partnership filed bankruptcy. Mr. Bud sues Norm for debts to him the partnership incurred while Norm was a partner. Norm says he's no longer responsible for the debt. Is Norm correct?

2. Mona contributed $20,000 in capital when she, Alvin, and Gwen formed their partnership. Alvin and Gwen each contributed capital $10,000. The partnership agreement was silent on how profits and losses were to be divided. The partnership became insolvent. Creditors' claims of $29,000 now remain after all partnership assets have been exhausted. Among Mona, Alvin, and Gwen, what are their respective shares of the amount still owed to creditors? Explain your reasoning.

3. Prentice, Daphne, and Quentin were the partners in PDQ Enterprises, which is now dissolved. At the time the partnership was formed, each of the three contributed $25,000 in capital. During the first year of the partnership's existence, Quentin loaned it $15,000. A liquidation of the firm's assets raised $91,000. Creditors of the partnership have legitimate claims totaling $82,000. According to the provisions of the UPA, how should the $91,000 be distributed?

CHAPTER 27
FORMATION AND TERMINATION OF CORPORATIONS

Outline

I. Nature of a Corporation

    A. A Corporation is a separate legal entity

    B. Three principal types of corporations are governmental/municipal corporations, nonprofit corporations, and for-profit corporations.

    C. The For-profit corporation is either a close corporation or publicly held corporation.

II. The Preincorporation process

    A. Promoters bring the corporation into being and owe a fiduciary duty to the corporation.

        1. Promoters are liable on contracts they make on behalf of corporations under agency law. If the promoter, corporation, and third parties agree to substitute the corporation for the promotor, this is a novation and releases the promotor from liability.
        Example: Aloe Limited, Inc. v. Koch (Holding a novation released promotor from liability.)

    B. Liability of Corporation: corporation may pay promoters for their services. If board acts to adopt the contract after incorporation, or accepts the benefits of the contract, the corporation is liable (except in Massachusetts).

    C. A corporation must prepare articles of incorporation complying with state's incorporation statute. Many corporations "shop around" for the state that offers most benefits to the enterprise.

    D. There a mandatory and optional contents of the articles of incorporation.

    E. The corporate bylaws establish rules for the conduct of the internal affairs of the corporation.

    F. Under the ultra vires doctrine, a transaction beyond the corporation' power may be unenforceable, but courts have taken different positions on this issue.
    Example: Bryant Construction Company v. Cook Construction Company

    G. Problems of Defective Incorporation: Under the revised MBCA, the filing of the articles of incorporation is conclusive proof of incorporation. Historically, in a de jure corporation, the promoters substantially complied with all mandatory provision; the de factor corporation exists when there is an honest attempt to comply with the mandatory provisions of the statutes.

    H. Piercing the Corporate Veil

        1. In some cases a shareholder may be held personally liable on a corporate debt. Undercapitalization, or cases where a corporation is the alter ego of the shareholder may create such a situation.
        Example: Scott v. AZL Resources, Inc. (Court refused to pierce the corporate veil.)

III. State Regulation of Corporations

    A. A corporation is a domestic corporation in the state where it is incorporated, and a foreign corporation in all other states.

    B. Foreign corporations may be sued in state courts if it has minimum contacts with the state.
    Example: Rostad v. On-Deck, Inc. (Nationwide distribution program gave corporation sufficient contacts with state to support jurisdiction.)

IV. Termination of Corporation

    A. A corporation may terminate by agreement, or be dissolved by judgment of a court.

Learning Objectives

    1. You should understand the obligations and liabilities of a corporate promoter.

    2. You should understand the problems of a defectively formed corporation;

    3. You should understand the formalities required to incorporate and circumstances under which a court will "pierce the corporate veil."

    4. You should be able to recognize the various types of corporations.

5. You should know the legal principles governing the promoter's and the corporation's liability on pre-incorporation contracts, including what must be done to relieve a promoter of liability on a preincorporation contract and what must take place before the corporation itself is held liable on such a contract.

6. You should understand the respective functions of the articles of incorporation and the bylaws.

7. You should understand how the term doing business may mean different things, depending upon whether the issue to be resolved pertains to jurisdiction over a foreign corporation, or instead to taxation of a corporation, or instead to the need for a foreign corporation to qualify to do business in another state.

8. You should know how a corporation may be dissolved, and should understand that it is more difficult to dissolve a corporation than it is to dissolve a partnership.

Learning Hints

1. A corporation is a separate legal entity. One of the principal advantages of incorporation is that the liability of shareholders are limited to the value of the shares in the corporation. An exception arises, however, in cases where courts have permitted a creditor to "pierce the corporate veil" in order to hold shareholders personally liable for the debts of the corporation.

2. Legal issues may arise as a result of the preincorporation process.
Generally, promoters are personally liable for contracts they make on behalf of the corporation; however, a corporation generally ratifies the contracts of the promoters so that it becomes liable for such contracts.

3. In order to incorporate, incorporators file articles of incorporation in a state where it desires to be incorporated. This may be any state, if the corporation is engaged in the interstate commerce.

4. A corporation is largely a creature of statute. It is not possible to create a corporation "accidentally." To incorporate a business, a person must at least substantially comply with the formalities required by the applicable state incorporation law.

5. Note that a corporation is an entity separate and distinct from its shareholders and managers for all purposes, including, for instance, domicile, liability, existence, and taxation.

6. The promoter performs an important economic function in our society by bringing together people who have business ideas but not necessarily much money, and people who have money but not necessarily any business ideas. For performing this function, the promoter generally is compensated. The usual rule, however, is that the corporation is not required to compensate the promoter. The reason for this rule is that the services were performed before the corporation existed. Therefore, technically speaking, nothing was done for the corporation. Remember, however, that promoters have fiduciary duties to the corporation despite its nonexistence at the time of the promotional activities.

7. Do not confuse the terms articles of incorporation and certificate of incorporation. The articles are the basic governing document of the corporation. They state many of the rights and responsibilities of shareholders and managers of the corporation. The certificate of incorporation is a document issued by the secretary of state to certify that a particular corporation exists in the eyes of the law.

8. As stated above, the articles of incorporation serve as the basic governing document of the corporation. In that sense, the articles are analogous to a constitution. The bylaws of the corporation are analogous to statutes. Just as statutes cannot be inconsistent with the governing constitution, bylaws cannot be inconsistent with the governing articles of incorporation. The bylaws contain important matters, but not matters as fundamental as those in the articles. This distinction in the importance of the respective provisions in the articles and the bylaws helps explain why ordinarily the articles may be amended only by a vote of the shareholders, whereas the bylaws may be amended by a vote of the board of directors. Note, however, that the articles of incorporation and the bylaws cannot contain anything contrary to the state incorporation statute.

9. Another variation on the piercing the corporate veil theme is the accepted doctrine that courts will hold a parent corporation liable for the obligations of its subsidiary corporation if the parent dominates the subsidiary and the domination results in some improper purpose. These cases may involve, for instance, a parent corporation that creates a subsidiary corporation, gives it very few assets, and then directs most of the subsidiary's actions and uses the subsidiary as its instrument for incurring debt the parent otherwise would incur. In such situations, there is a great potential for creditors to be defrauded, because the subsidiary would not have the financial ability to pay many of its debts. Allowing the creditor to hold the parent liable for the debts prevents misuse of the corporate form.

10. Note that when a foreign corporation does business in another state, it need not incorporate in that state. It must merely qualify to do business there.

True-False

In the blank provided, put "T" if the statement is True or "F" if the statement is False.

_____ 1. Promoters are not personally liable for debts made on behalf of a corporation.

_____ 2. In almost all states, if a corporation board accepts the benefits of a contract entered into by a promotor, the corporation is legally bound on the contract.

_____ 3. The articles of incorporation are the basic documents of the corporation and major source of its powers.

_____ 4. The by-laws are a restatement of the articles of incorporation filed with the secretary of state of the state of incorporation.

_____ 5. Under the revised MBCA, the filing of the articles of incorporation is conclusive proof of incorporation.

_____ 6. A court will pierce the corporate veil and impose liability on a shareholder for a corporate debt whenever that person is the corporation's majority shareholder.

_____ 7. Once a corporation is actually incorporated, it automatically becomes liable on pre-incorporation contracts made by a promoter on behalf of the corporation.

_____ 8. If a foreign corporation sends a delivery truck driven by an employee into a state and the employee's negligence while operating the truck there causes an accident in which another party is injured, the corporation will be subject to a suit by the injured party in that state's courts.

_____ 9. The revised Model Business Corporation Act prohibits corporations from issuing shares of stock to promoters in exchange for their preincorporation efforts.

_____ 10. A publicly held corporation is a corporation owned and operated by the federal government or a state or local government.

Multiple Choice

Circle the Best Answer.

1. In order to form a corporation, the promoters must:
   a. enter into a written agreement setting out duties and responsibilities of the incorporators;
   b. file articles of incorporation with the appropriate state official;
   c. file necessary documents with the state and federal taxing agencies;
   d. all of the above are necessary to form a corporation.

2. In determining which state within which to incorporate, a corporation engaged in instate commerce:
   a. must incorporate in the state of its principal place of business;
   b. must incorporate in the state where its principal stockholders reside;
   c. may incorporate in a any state which offers the most benefits to the business;
   d. may incorporate in as many states as it chooses.

3. Which of the following statements concerning the ultra vires doctrine is correct?
   a. Traditionally, courts have given effect to acts of corporations which exceeded the corporation's power under its articles of incorporation, if such acts were reasonable;
   b. The MBCA takes the position that an act which is ultra vires is null and void and of no effect;

c. Courts have not all agreed in handling the question of enforcement of corporate acts which are <u>ultra vires</u>;

d. All of the above statements are correct.

4. Historically, a <u>de facto</u> corporation:

a. Existed when there was an honest attempt to comply with the mandatory provisions of the corporate statute but failed to meet statutory requirements in a material respect;

b. arose when the promoters substantially complied with all mandatory provisions of the law;

c. arose when persons held themselves out as representing a corporation when no real attempt to incorporate had been made.

d. All of the above resulted in a <u>de facto</u> corporation.

5. In order for a creditor to "pierce the corporate veil":

a. There must be domination of the corporation by one or more of its shareholders;

b. A shareholder must dominate the corporation for an improper purpose;

c. The corporation must agree to indemnify shareholders in the event of their personal liability;

d. Both (a) and (b) are correct.

6. A corporation's bylaws

a. provide the basic source from which the corporation's powers come.

b. often supplement the articles of incorporation by more precisely defining rights and responsibilities of parties involved in the corporate structure.

c. are controlling when they conflict with the articles of incorporation, in keeping with the legal principle that specific provisions control general provisions where the two appear to be inconsistent.

d. are more difficult to amend than are the articles of incorporation.

7. AWOL Co. was the name chosen by Alice, Wally, Otto, and Lulu for a corporation they intended to form. Not all of the incorporation requirements were met, so incorporation did not take place officially before the parties' business (a hardware store) went into operation. Alice, a purported shareholder who had been the promoter of the business and had taken primary responsibility for taking care of the incorporation requirements, actively participated in management and policy decisions for the business. She knew that not all of the incorporation requirements had been met. Wally and Otto, who were also purported shareholders, participated in management and policy decisions for the business, but they did not know of the defective incorporation. Lulu, the other purported shareholder, neither participated in management and policy decisions for the business nor knew of the defective incorporation. Butch's Hardware Supply, Inc. extended credit to the AWOL business. When the large debt went unpaid, Butch's did some checking on AWOL and learned that because of the defective incorporation, AWOL Co. had no legal existence. Butch's then filed suit against Alice, Wally, Otto, and Lulu, seeking to hold them personally liable for the debt. Of the following statements concerning the suit filed by Butch's, which is accurate?

a. If the old MBCA governs this case, Alice, Wally, and Otto will be liable, and Lulu may be liable.

b. If the revised MBCA governs this case, Alice, Wally, and Otto will be liable, but Lulu will not be liable.

c. Neither a nor b.

d. Both a and b.

8. Which of the following constitute(s) "doing business," for purposes of whether a foreign corporation must qualify to do business in a state?

a. Taking orders and filling them from outside the state.

b. Taking orders and filling them from outside the state, if the salesperson resides within the state.

c. Maintaining, within a state, a stock of goods from which to fill orders.

d. Both b and c.

9. Under the MBCA, the articles of incorporation must include

a. a listing of the names of each shareholder.

b. a statement of the number of shares of capital stock the corporation shall have authority to issue.

c. a statement setting forth the respective amounts of each shareholder's capital contributions.

d. a disclosure of the debt structure of the corporation.

10. Which of the following acts of a foreign corporation is sufficient contact with a state to require the corporation to become qualified to do business in the state?

a. Making a single contract in the state

b. Driving a truck through the state

c. Maintaining a sales office in the state

d. None of the above

Short Essay

1. A, B, and C are the only shareholders and directors of ABC, Inc. A owns 90 percent of the shares. A year ago, A, B, and C had a severe argument and have not agreed with each other on any issue since. The board meetings always end up in shouting matches. C refuses to participate in management of the corporation, and the corporation's profits have dipped and threaten to become losses. B wants to dissolve the corporation. May she?

2. Pete, the corporate promoter of XYZ Corporation, sold a patent to the corporation for $10,000. It cost him only $2,000 to buy the patent from its owner. Pete disclosed the cost to the board and it approved the purchase, but the shareholders were not told. When the shareholders discovered Pete's profit on the sale of the patent, they sued him. Must Pete return the $8,000 profit to the corporation?

3. Husker Co., a Nebraska corporation, has received orders from customers in North Dakota. It plans to ship the goods by its own trucks from Nebraska to North Dakota. To get to their destination, the Husker trucks must proceed across roads in South Dakota. Must Husker qualify to do business in South Dakota before it may ship the goods to North Dakota in the manner just described? Why or why not?

4. Buck LaRue was the sole proprietor of Buck's Bucket, a tavern. Buck decided to incorporate the business. He proceeded to form Bucket, Inc., a corporation of which he was the president and the majority stockholder. All shares of stock not owned by Buck were owned by his wife, Mitzi. Buck and Mitzi did not keep Bucket, Inc.'s bank accounts separate from their own personal accounts. Reasoning that they were the only shareholders in the corporation, Buck and Mitzi drew freely from the combined bank accounts. They also routinely drove, for personal purposes, an automobile titled in the name of the corporation. They did not pay the corporation anything for the use of the vehicle. During the first five years the corporation was in existence, no shareholders' and directors' meetings were held, with the exception of initial meetings the first year. The corporation always made a timely filing of its corporate income tax return. Discuss the remedies a creditor of Bucket, Inc. would have, on the basis of the facts just described, in the event that the debt is unpaid and corporate assets are insufficient to satisfy the creditor's claim.

CHAPTER 28
MANAGEMENT OF THE CORPORATE BUSINESS

Outline

I. The Board of Directors

    A. Directors have authority to manage the business of the corporation. In large corporations, directors tend to ratify management decisions by officers

    B. General powers of the board include declaring a dividend, setting the price of stock, electing officers and filling vacancies on the board.

    C. Some actions require Board Initiative, such as amendment of the articles of incorporation, merger or sale of corporate assets, or voluntary dissolution, with stockholder approval.

    D. State statutes generally establish requirements for number of directors and their qualifications. Directors are elected by shareholders and normally hold office until the next annual meeting.

    Example: Aprahamian v. HBO & Co. (Board of directors enjoined from delaying annual meeting and board elections.)

    E. Procedure to fill Vacancies, Removal of Directors and Frequency of meetings may be determined by state statute, articles of incorporation, or the bylaws.

II. Duties of Directors and Officers

    A. The power of officers to bind the corporation is the same as that of any agent.

    B. The officers and directors owe the corporation a fiduciary duty.

        1. The "prudent person standard" and "business judgment rule" applies in cases where directors and officers are charged with failing to act with due care and diligence in corporate affairs.
        Example: Smith v. Van Gorkom (Business judgment rule does not apply in a case where the directors did not reach an informed judgment.)

        2. Some states have enacted legislation designed to limit directors' liability for breach of the duty of care.

    C. Directors and officers are not prohibited from entering into transactions with the corporation so long as they make full disclosure; they may not usurp corporate opportunity.

    Example: Cannon Oil & Gas Well Service v. Evertson

    D. Federal securities laws prohibit insiders from buyer or selling its stock.

III. Liability for Torts and Crimes

    A. The corporation is liable for all torts committed by its employees within the scope of their employment under the agency concept of respondeat superior. Courts today may also impose criminal liability on the corporation for the acts of its directors, officers, or managers.

    Example: State v. Smokey's Steakhouse, Inc.

    B. Officers and directors have been held personally liable or criminally liable for the illegal behavior of a subordinate if she knew or should have known of the illegal conduct and failed to take reasonable measures to prevent it. Corporations often indemnify officers and directors for the costs of defending and/or settling such suits.

    Example: McClean v. International Harvester Co.

Learning Objectives

    1. You should understand the responsibilities of directors and officers to the corporation.

    2. You should understand the circumstances under which a director or officer may be liable for torts and crimes committed by the corporation.

    3. You should understand the circumstances under which the corporation itself may be subject to criminal prosecution as a result of the acts or breach of duty of its employees, directors, or officers.

    4. You should understand the roles of the shareholders and the board of directors in the corporation.

5. You should know the rights and powers of the board of directors and the rights and powers of individual directors.

6. You should know how vacancies in the board of directors may be filled, as well as the bases upon which a director may be removed from the board.

7. You should understand how boards of directors use subcommittees.

8. You should know the inherent powers possessed by the officers of a corporation.

9. You should master the business judgment rule and its application, and should be aware of recent legislative responses to increased director liability.

10. You should know when a corporation must and may indemnify an officer or director.

Learning Hints

1. The shareholders do not make management decisions; their power to influence management is to replace directors who then will replace the officers.

2. The business of the corporation is managed by the board of directors. However, in large corporations, the directors tend to ratify management decisions of top executives.

3. The Board has some general powers; other actions, such as amending the articles of incorporation, requires approval of the shareholders following Board initiative.

4. Directors are not agents for the corporation. However, agency law principles apply in questions involving the power of an officer to bind the corporation.

5. No director by himself has any inherent power to act for the corporation, although the board of directors might grant him such power.

6. The business judgment rule is one of the most important legal rules in all of corporation law. The rule states that absent bad faith, fraud, or breach of a fiduciary duty, the judgment of the board of directors is conclusive. Restated, the rule means that if the board acts honestly without any personal interest in the business decision and makes a reasonable investigation before making the business decision, the board will have no liability to the corporation, even though the decision ends up having a harmful effect on the corporation. The reason for the rule is that business managers, not courts, are best able to make business decisions. Therefore, a court will not substitute its judgment for that of the board, unless the board members failed to make a reasonable investigation, acted dishonestly, intended to defraud the corporation, or personally profited from the business decision.

7. Some examples may assist you in determining whether the business judgment rule would apply to a particular decision. The business judgment rule would not apply to a decision of the board to buy land if all the directors owned the land that the corporation buys, because the directors personally profited from the transaction. Similarly, the rule would not apply to a decision of the directors to issue common stock to themselves. The rule would apply, however, to a board decision to open a new manufacturing plant, if the board made a reasonable investigation prior to making the decision.

8. The basis for making usurpation of a corporate opportunity improper is that the officer or director is stealing something (an opportunity) that belongs to the corporation.

9. As an employer, a corporation is liable for the torts of its employees, when the torts are committed within the scope of employment. This is the case because of the doctrine of respondeat superior, which you studied earlier in connection with agency law.

10. A corporation is not generally liable for the crimes of an employee, because most crimes require criminal intent. As the corporation is not a natural person, it has no mental capacity and cannot form any intent to commit a wrong. However, if a high-level manager with discretionary authority has criminal intent while acting for the corporation, the manager's criminal intent will be imputed to the corporation, making the corporation liable for the crime.

True-False

In the blank provided, put "T" if the statement is True or "F" if the statement is False.

_____ 1. Majority stockholders have the power to manage the affairs of the corporation if they determine that the directors have failed to perform that function in a reasonable manner.

_____ 2. The MCBA permits directors to act without a meeting if all of the directors consent in writing to the action taken.

_____ 3. Actions taken by a board are ineffective unless a quorum is present, which means that all directors of the corporation must be present to take a particular action.

_____ 4. Both directors and officers are agents of the corporation.

_____ 5. A corporation may not ratify an unauthorized @X = acts by its officers or other agents.

_____ 6. <u>Board initiative</u> means that the power to conduct the day-to-day operations of the corporation initiates with the board of directors.

_____ 7. The MBCA allows directors to fix their own compensation unless this is prohibited by the articles of incorporation.

_____ 8. In the modern corporation, the board of directors does not make most of the day-to-day management decisions.

_____ 9. Directors of a corporation are elected by the shareholders.

_____ 10. Under the MBCA, the remaining members of the board of directors may fill vacancies on the board.

Multiple Choice

Circle the best answer.

1. Which of the following does <u>not</u> require intiative by the Board of Directors and approval of the stockholders?
   a. filling vacancies on the board of directors;
   b. amending the articles of incorporation;
   c. sale of all of the corporation's assets;
   d. voluntary dissolution of the corporation.

2. Which of the following is <u>not</u> a typical committee of the board of directors of a publicly held corporation?
   a. Executive committee;
   b. Audit committee;
   c. Nominating committee;
   d. Treasury committee.

3. If a corporate officer exceeds his/her authority under the articles or bylaws:
   a. The officer is liable if the corporation is damaged by an act exceeding her authority under the by-laws.
   b. The officer is not liable in damages unless she knew that the act was outside the scope of her authority;
   c. If the transaction is <u>ultra vires</u>, and the director justifiably believed it to be within the scope of the corporation's business, she is not liable.
   d. Both (a) and (c) are correct.

4. The "business judgment rule":
   a. Protects officers from liability for mistakes in judgment;
   b. May apply in conflict of interest cases;
   c. Must be an informed decision with a rational basis. decision
   d. Both (a) and (c) are correct.

5. The fiduciary duty a corporate officer and director owes the corporation:
   a. Does not prohibit them from entering into transactions with the corporation so long as those transactions are reasonable;
   b. Does not prohibit them from entering into transactions with the corporation so long as the directors fully disclose their interest in the transaction;
   c. Prohibits any self-dealing with the corporation;
   d. None of the above is correct.

6. Monique, a director of Marginal Corp., owns real estate that Marginal wishes to purchase for expansion purposes. Monique paid $140,000 for the property ten years ago. She agreed to sell the land to Marginal for $230,000—the property's fair market value—after informing the other four directors what her cost was. The other four directors gave their approval. When a

Marginal shareholder discovered Monique's profit, he sued her on behalf of Marginal to recover the profit she made through self-dealing. Is Monique liable?

    a. Yes, because directors are barred from doing business with the corporations for which they serve as directors.

    b. No, unless selling the property to Marginal was Monique's idea originally.

    c. Yes, unless the shareholders other than the one who brought suit all approved of the transaction.

    d. No, because she disclosed the profit she would make, a disinterested board approved, and the transaction called for a fair price.

7. If a corporation ratifies its officer's unauthorized act,

    a. the act binds the corporation just as if the act had been authorized, and the officer is released from liability to the corporation.

    b. the ratification is effective only if the board of directors adopted a resolution expressly ratifying the act.

    c. the act binds the corporation to perform the obligation to third parties contemplated by the act, but the corporation remains free to impose liability on its officer for having taken the unauthorized act.

    d. both b and c are correct.

8. Of the following statements concerning corporate directors, which is accurate?

    a. Individual directors do not have the authority to bind the corporation by actions that are independent of the board's actions.

    b. If an action of the board of directors is in violation of the directors' duties to the corporation, even a director who specifically dissented from the decision to take the action will be liable to the corporation.

    c. Because directors are not employees of the corporation, they are not considered "insiders" for purposes of the legal rules governing insider trading of securities.

    d. Directors are generally liable for torts committed by officers they have appointed.

9. While at his office, Merle, the vice president of acquisitions for Normal, Inc., was called by a Solid Corp. attorney, who asked whether Normal would be interested in purchasing approximately 25 percent of the outstanding shares of Solid. Various things about Solid may have made the tentative proposal an attractive, not to mention financially feasible, prospect for Normal. Merle responded by telling the attorney what he (Merle) genuinely believed to be true: he (Merle) did not think that Normal would be interested. Merle (who is independently wealthy) said that he was willing to buy the shares personally, however. He purchased the shares for $10,000,000. A year later, he sold the shares to some private investors for $17,000,000. When the Normal directors discovered Merle's purchase and subsequent sale of the Solid shares, they sued him on behalf of the corporation. In view of the facts just stated, which of the following is accurate?

    a. Merle is not liable to Normal because he had no intent to defraud.

    b. Merle is liable to Normal for usurping a corporate opportunity.

    c. Merle exceeded his authority to act for Normal.

    d. Merle engaged in impermissible self-dealing with Solid.

10. A corporation has committed a crime if

    a. its salesman coerces a customer into buying the corporation's products.

    b. its assembly line worker intentionally mismanufactures a product to make it dangerous to users.

    c. its vice-president for sales agrees with competitors to fix prices in violation of the antitrust laws.

    d. any of the above occurs.

Short Essay

1. The directors of XYZ Corporation appointed officers and key executives and thereafter left all management decision in the hands of the officers. The directors held yearly meetings in Washington, but made no detailed inquiries into the operation of the corporate business. The corporation suffered heavy losses for three years, until it was discovered that the officers in charge of daily management were diverting substantial portions of corporate assets for their person use. If the stockholders sue the <u>directors</u> for their loss, are the directors liable?

2. Flushes R Us, Inc. (FRU) is a corporation whose principal business is the manufacturing and sale of toilets. Gert is the manager in charge of the employees in FRU's product delivery division. Eddie is one of the employees in that division. One day, while Eddie was en route to a retail customer's place of business (where he was to make a delivery of a large quantity of FRU toilets), Eddie negligently operated the truck he was driving and caused injury to a pedestrian. In doing so, Eddie was violating a specific corporate directive that employees were not to be negligent. The injured pedestrian filed suit against Eddie, Gert, and FRU in an effort to obtain money damages for her injuries. Who is liable? Why?

3. If corporate directors have made a decision that produced negative consequences for the corporation, and if the directors wish to avoid liability to the corporation by relying upon the shield provided by the business judgment rule, what requirements must have been satisfied in the decision-making process?

CHAPTER 29
FINANCING THE CORPORATION AND THE ROLE OF SHAREHOLDERS

Outline

I. Financing the Corporation

A. Equity securities arises from the sale of ownership interests in the business; debt securities is typified by bonds and other obligations.

B. Common stock:

1. If the corporation only has one class of stock, it is common stock; if more than one class, the common shareholders usually bear the major risks and benefits of the business.

2. Preferred stock gives shareholders a preference as to dividends and distribution of assets. Rights of preferred shareholders may vary.

C. The stockholders must provide consideration for their shares (money, property, or services already performed.)

D. Shares may be assigned a value, called par value, in the articles of incorporation or a stated value at the time of issuance.

E. Capital Surplus arises when shares sell for more than their part or stated value.

1. Directors may issue options to purchase shares of the corporation; options represented by certificates are known as warrants.

II. Debt Securities

A. Corporations may borrow money by issuing debt securities. These include notes, debentures, and bonds.

B. A debenture is a long-term unsecured debt instrument; a long-term secured debt security is a bond. A convertible bond or debenture may be exchanged for an equity security.

III. The Shareholder

A. Shareholders have few functions—their principal function is the election of the directors.

B. A shareholder usually acquires stock by purchase.

C. Annual Shareholder's meetings are required in all states but Delaware. The main purpose of the meeting is the election of directors. Notice is required before the meeting, but shareholders may waive notice.

D. The MBCA requires a written document appoint a proxy as an agent to vote for a shareholder, and the SEC (Securities and Exchange Commission) regulates proxy statements.

Example: Carey v. Pennsylvania Enterprises (Invalidating shareholder election because only shareholders of record are entitled to vote.)

E. The bylaws govern procedures of the meeting, and a quorum must be present before any voting. Many corporations permit shareholders to cumulate their votes.

F. Right of Inspection and Preemptive Right.

Example: Advance Concrete Form v. Accuform (Corporation is not required to grant an inspection right to shareholder if it would be adverse to the best interests of the corporation.)

G. Dividends: Declaration of dividends is subject to the business judgment of the board of directors.

Example: Conduti v. Hellwig

1. Types of dividends include cash and stock dividends. A preferred shareholder usually has preference in dividends.

IV. Other Shareholder Rights

A. Amendment of the articles of incorporation must be approved by the shareholders; merger or consolidation also requires approval. Most states deny the right of appraisal if the shares are traded on a securities exchange.

Example: Morely Brothers v. Clark (Appraisal appropriate in case where stock was not publicly traded and there was no ready market for the shares.)

157

B. Lawsuits by Shareholders may be based on breach of contract; in some cases a class action may be brought. A shareholder may bring a derivative action on behalf of the corporation in unusual cases.

   Example: Kamen v. Kemper Financial Services

C. A Shareholder is liable to the corporation in very limited circumstances, as when he purchases "watered stock."

Learning Objectives

1. You should understand the considerations in a court decision to uphold the board's defensive tactics.

2. You should understand the difference between common and preferred stock.

3. You should understand the rights and obligations of the holders of various types of stock.

4. You should know what types of consideration a corporation may receive in exchange for its shares.

5. You should know when a corporation may redeem its shares and when it may purchase its shares on the open market.

6. You should be able to recognize the many debt instruments a corporation may issue.

7. You should understand the role of the shareholders in a corporation's governance.

9. You should know how shareholder meetings (particularly special meetings) are called, what the notice requirements are for shareholder meetings, and what sorts of actions are taken at shareholder meetings.

10. You should understand what a proxy is.

11. You should know what cumulative voting is and how it enables minority shareholders to elect directors.

12. You should understand what preemptive rights are and what the right of appraisal is.

Learning Hints

1. There are two major sources of corporate financing: equity securities, which arises through the sale of ownership interests in the business, and debt securities, typified by bonds and other obligations of the business.

2. Common stock shareholders usually bear the major risks of the business and benefit most from its success.

3. Preferred stock gives the owner a preference as to dividends and distribution of assets.

4. The par value of shares may be established in the articles of incorporation; par value and stated value reflect the minimum amount of consideration for which the shares can be issued. In many cases, the shares are worth more than part or stated value and the directors have a duty to receive the fair value of the stock.

5. If the directors issue shares to such purchasers for less than the par or stated value of the shares, such a situation presents a "watered stock" problem. Watered stock is an easy problem to detect. For example, corporate directors issue one dollar par shares for 75 cents per share. The "water" is 25 cents per share. (The term derives from the practice of dishonest cattlemen who took their cattle to the river to drink water before taking them to the stockyards. By doing so, the cattlemen caused their cattle to weigh more. The added weight was misleading, however, in that it was attributable to water rather than beef.)

6. Proxies serve as a useful tool for management to control a corporation without management's necessarily owning many shares itself. Most shareholders tend to sign and return proxies submitted to them by management, leading to the typical situation that what management wants to happen at a shareholders' meeting generally will happen. Of course, groups of shareholders may also seek the proxies of other shareholders, but such groups rarely have the success management ordinarily has in soliciting proxies.

7. Where cumulative voting is required by statute, as in a number of states, or is allowed by the corporation even though state law does not require it, a group of minority shareholders has an enhanced opportunity to elect a director of that group's choice. Your text sets forth the formula

used, under cumulative voting, to determine the number of shares necessary to elect one director. As an illustration of how the formula works, assume that 1000 shares are being voted at the shareholders' meeting, and that four directors are to be elected. Applying the formula, one would divide 1000 (the number of shares being voted) by five (the number of directors to be elected, plus one). The resulting figure of 200 is then increased by one, meaning that 201 shares are needed to elect one director.

8. Some corporate transactions fundamentally change the character of the shareholders' investment. For this reason, the law requires shareholder approval before the fundamental change may occur. For example, a merger significantly increases the assets and liabilities of the corporation the shareholder owns and increases the number of shareholders who own the corporation. Also, an amendment of the articles of incorporation changes the basic governing document of the corporation. Hence, a shareholder vote must approve these transactions. By contrast, the sale of inventory in the ordinary course of business is a minor matter that does not require shareholder approval.

9. Note that before a corporation may pay any dividend to common shareholders, it must pay the preferred shareholders' dividend preference. If there is an arrearage on cumulative preferred shares, the entire arrearage must be paid before any dividend may be paid to common shareholders.

10. The existence of the right of appraisal recognizes that a shareholder needs a remedy when she votes against a merger, consolidation, or sale of substantially all the assets of the corporation that the shareholders as a whole approve. In such transactions, the shareholder's investment is being substantially changed against her will. The right of appraisal allows the shareholder to receive the value of her shares as of the moment before the transaction was effected. Hence, if the shareholder believes the transaction reduced the value of her investment, she may obtain the value of the investment prior to the transaction by enforcing her right of appraisal.

True-False

In the blank provided, put "T" if the statement is True or "F" if the statement is False.

_____ 1. If there is only class of stock in a corporation, it is preferred stock.

_____ 2. If an arbitrary value is assigned to shares of stock in the articles of incorporation, this is called a "fair market value."

_____ 3. A warrant is a certificate representing an option to purchase shares in a corporation.

_____ 4. An indenture is a short-term debt instrument.

_____ 5. Under the MBCA, a shareholder may waive notice of the annual stockholder's meeting.

_____ 6. Corporate directors cannot issue shares of stock at a value greater than par value.

_____ 7. In most large public corporations, shareholders exercise great influence over the corporation's affairs.

_____ 8. Although a corporation must issue common stock, it need not issue preferred stock.

_____ 9. Although preferred shareholders usually have a dividend preference over common shareholders, preferred shareholders often do not have the same rights to vote that common shareholders possess.

_____ 10. Through the use of proxies, management is generally able to control the corporation without necessarily owning many shares itself.

Multiple Choice

Circle the best answer.

1. Which of the following is a characteristic of common rather than preferred stock?
    a. the holder has a preference as to dividends;
    b. the holder has a preference as to distribution of assets when the corporation is dissolved;
    c. the holder will benefit most from the success of the corporation, but will also bear the major risks of the business.
    d. all of the above are characteristics of common stock.

2. Long-term secured debt securities are called:
   a. stock;
   b. notes;
   c. debentures
   d. bonds.

3. The principal duty of a stockholder is to:
   a. Elect the directors of the corporation;
   b. Elect the officers of the corporation;
   c. Determine the par value of the stock of the corporation;
   d. None of the above.

4. A shareholder may vote at a shareholders' meeting:
   a. if the incorporation statute or articles and bylaws of the corporation must so permit;
   b. if the person has legal title to the stock;
   c. if there is a quorum at the meeting;
   d. all of the above are correct.

5. Which of the following statements concerning lawsuits by shareholders is not correct?
   a. Shareholders may sue the corporation for a breach of their shareholder contract;
   b. Class actions by common stock shareholders are not permitted under present securities laws;
   c. Because a corporation is a legal entity separate from the shareholder, a shareholder is usually not able to sue to enforce a right of the corporation;
   d. In some cases, a shareholder may bring a derivative action as a representative of the corporation if the directors refuse to bring some action or have a conflict of interest.

6. Cargo Corporation issues 100,000 shares of its $1 par value common shares for a total consideration of $50,000 cash, the fair market value of the shares. Is there anything wrong with this issuance?
   a. No, because they were issued for fair market value.
   b. No, because cash is a proper type of consideration for shares.
   c. Yes, because the fair market value must have been more than $50,000.
   d. Yes, because the shares were issued for less than their par value.

7. Shareholder approval is usually required for
   a. mergers.
   b. consolidations.
   c. sales of substantially all the assets of the corporation.
   d. all of the above.

8. Cumulative voting is a procedural device
   a. whose use is barred by the revised MBCA.
   b. that is designed to assist majority shareholders in maintaining positions of influence within the corporate structure.
   c. designed to give minority shareholders a chance to elect a director of their choice.
   d. that can be employed only where directors have been divided into classes, for election purposes.

9. On September 15, 1990, Whitman signed a preincorporation subscription to buy 1,000 common shares of Slim Corp., a proposed corporation that was to be incorporated in a state that has adopted the Model Business Corporation Act. Slim was incorporated in Oct. 1, 1990 in such a state. Before Slim's board of directors took action to accept Whitman's preincorporation subscription, Whitman informed the board (on Oct. 2, 1990) that he was revoking the subscription. Shortly thereafter, the board voted to accept Whitman's subscription. When Slim attempted to force Whitman to buy the shares, he refused. Slim then sued Whitman. Is Whitman bound by his subscription?
   a. No, because he revoked it before the board accepted it.
   b. Yes, because less than six months elapsed between Whitman's signing of the subscription and the board's acceptance of it.
   c. No, because the corporation was not in existence at the time Whitman signed the subscription.

d. Yes, because ordinary principles of contract law indicate that an offer cannot be revoked before it has been accepted.

10. Which of the following is/are true of a corporation's ability to repurchase shares of stock it previously issued?

    a. A corporation may purchase its shares from any willing shareholder regardless of whether the articles of incorporation specify that the corporation may do so.

    b. Once a corporation repurchases any of its shares, the corporation may vote the repurchased shares in elections.

    c. A corporation cannot force an unwilling shareholder to sell her shares back to the corporation, regardless of whether the corporation's articles of incorporation purport to give the corporation such a power.

    d. All of the above.

Short Essay

1. The board of ABC Corp. negotiates a merger with the board of L&G, Inc. The exchange ratio is one share of ABC common shares for one share of L&G common shares. ABC shares are traded on the New York Stock Exchange. L&G's shares are traded in the over-the-counter market. Both corporations' shareholders approved the merger by a three-to-one margin. Ed, a shareholder of ABC, thinks the exchange rate is too favorable for L&G shareholders. Delbert, a shareholder of L&G, believes that the deal is bad for L&G shareholders. Both voted against the merger and notified their respective corporations of their intents to seek appraisal of their shares. Under the law applied in most states, are Ed and Delbert eligible to enforce the right of appraisal?

2. Huge Corp. was incorporated in a state whose law requires that shareholders be permitted to cumulate their votes for directors. At an upcoming annual meeting, four Huge directors will be elected. There will be 600 shares voting. A group of minority shareholders wishes to elect a director of its choice. What is the number of shares required to elect one director under cumulative voting? Explain your reasoning.

3. Roland Astute, a shareholder of Steamroller Corporation, uncovered evidence that, in his opinion, showed that the corporation's treasurer was embezzling corporate funds. Uncertain of whether the corporation's board of directors would agree with his assessment of what the evidence showed, Astute did not discuss the matter with the board or with other shareholders. After conferring with his attorney, Astute filed a derivative suit against the treasurer, in an attempt to recover for the losses the treasurer's actions had caused the corporation to experience. Under the circumstances, is Astute's derivative suit properly before the court? Explain.

4. Hapless, Inc.'s directors have requested that shareholders approve a proposed merger involving Hapless and another corporation. One class of previously issued Hapless stock is a nonvoting class. The corporation itself holds certain shares that had been sold to shareholders and then reacquired by the corporation. At the shareholders' meeting, the holders of the nonvoting shares claim a right to vote on the proposed merger. The corporation, through its directors and officers, claims a right to vote the treasury shares on the merger question also. The MBCA is in effect in the state of incorporation. Do the holders of the nonvoting shares have a right to vote on the proposed merger? Does the corporation have the right to vote the reacquired shares on the merger question? Why or why not?

CHAPTER 30
CLOSE CORPORATIONS AND LIMITED PARTNERSHIPS

Outline

I. Nature of the Close Corporation

  A. Most incorporation are close corporations: Characteristics include few shareholders who are active in the business and know each other.

  B. A close corporation differs from a sole proprietorship or partnership because the corporation is a separate legal entity; however, confusion sometimes arises.

    Example: United States v. Cusack (Corporate officer was in fact the corporation and an employer.)

II. Modern Regulation: Most states have adopted statutes regulating the close corporation. These may restrict number of shareholders

  A. Problems with Free Transferability of Shares: Usually shares in the close corporation are not intended for sale to the public.

  B. Under the right of refusal, either the corporation or the shareholders are given first right to buy shares in the corporation offered for sale.

    Example: Swanson v. Shockley

  C. Buy-and-Sell Agreements usually require a shareholder's estate to sell the shares to the corporation at an agreed price.

  D. Consent Restraints requires a seller to gain permission from the board or shareholders to sell shares to outsiders.

III. Governance Issues

  A. There are several devices which minimize the threat of domination by majority shareholders. These include different classes of stock, voting trusts, supermajority voting, restrictions on directors' discretion, and reduction in formalities.

  B. Shareholder agreements providing for arbitration to resolve disputes in corporate governance are more likely to be enforced today than in the past.

IV. Limited Partnerships: The purpose is to permit partnership investors to have limited liability.

  A. Under the RULPA, a limited partnership certificate must be filed with the secretary of state.

  B. Under traditional law, a limited partnership failing to file the necessary certificate is treated as a general partnership. This rule is relaxed under the ULPA and RULPA.

    Example: 8 Brookwood Fund v. Sloate

  C. A limited partner acquires certain partnership rights.

    Example: Allright Missouri v. Billeter (Limited partner may bring a derivative suit on behalf of the partnership.)

  D. Dissolution of a Limited Partnership result in a different payout than that of an ordinary partnership.

Learning Objectives

    1. You should be able to explain the circumstances under which a corporate officer or director is compelled to turn over corporate records.

    2. You should be able to explain how close corporations differ from publicly held corporations.

    3. You should be able to identify traits with close corporations and limited partnerships have in common.

    4. You should be able to explain how a limited partnership is terminated.

    5. You should develop a familiarity with the management and control problems that owners of a close corporation face, as well as with how these problems may be minimized.

    6. You should understand why shareholders of a close corporation may wish to place restrictions on transferability of shares, as well as how the transferability of shares may be restricted lawfully.

7. You should understand why there often is virtually no market for the shares of a close corporation and should know what devices are used to guarantee a shareholder a market for her shares.

8. You should become familiar with the devices available to close corporations to minimize the danger of complete domination of minority shareholders by majority shareholders.

9. You should know what special statutes and the Model Business Corporation Act have done to reduce the problems inherent in the close corporation.

10. You should know why limited partnerships are used.

11. You should know what formalities must be satisfied in order for a limited partnership to be created, and should know the consequences of a defective attempt to create a limited partnership.

12. You should know the similarities and differences between the rights and responsibilities of a partner in a limited partnership and those of a partner in a general partnership.

Learning Hints

1. Close corporations differ from public corporations because there are few shareholders who are usually active in the management of the business.

2. Unlike public corporations, there is not established market for the stock of a close corporation.

3. Most states today have enacted laws recognizing the close corporation and the special problems associated with it.

4. Shareholders in close corporations frequently restrict the transferability of shares to maintain the private nature of the business.

5. Transferability of shares is a double-edged sword in a close corporation. First, it is possible that a shareholder may sell his shares to someone the other shareholders do not want as a shareholder. Second, there is often such a thin market for the shares that a shareholder is unlikely to find a buyer at a satisfactory price when he wants to sell the shares. Therefore, as a matter of proper planning, nearly every close corporation should have an agreement among shareholders that restricts the transferability of shares but also guarantees the shareholders a market for their shares.

6. Restrictions on the transferability of shares traditionally have been disfavored, because the law does not like to interfere with a person's right to sell his property. Courts, however, have begun to recognize the special need for such restrictions in the close corporation context. So now, generally speaking, rights of first refusal are permissible, as are agreements that require the shareholder to offer the shares to the corporation or other shareholders at a stipulated price. Consent restraints (requiring board or shareholder approval of the sale of shares) are not regarded as favorably by courts as are rights of first refusal because they (consent restraints) grant the board or shareholders the power to prohibit the transfer of the shares. The board and/or other shareholders do not acquire that power with a right of first refusal or an agreement to offer the shares to the corporation or other shareholders before offering them to outsiders, because in those situations, if the corporation or shareholders refuse to buy the shares, the selling shareholder then is free to sell to an outsider. Nevertheless, outright consent restraints are being enforced with greater regularity by courts today than they once were.

7. Of course, in reality there are few people willing to buy shares of a close corporation. The most obvious potential buyers are the other shareholders. However, if, for example, one shareholder retires from the business and decides to sell her shares, there is no assurance that the other shareholders will want to or be able to purchase the retired shareholder's shares. A buy-out agreement is a common device to ensure a shareholder of a market for her shares. The buy-out requirement should be triggered only by proper reasons for a sale of shares, such as death, disability, or retirement of the shareholder at an appropriate age. Where death is a triggering event in a buy-sell agreement, there ordinarily is life insurance in force to fund the purchase.

8. Control is a special problem in a close corporation, because majority votes of directors or of shareholders are enough to approve most corporate transactions. It is easy, therefore, for the majority shareholders to exclude the minority shareholders from effective control of the corporation. For example, three of five shareholders may elect themselves as directors and appoint themselves as officers, while refusing to elect the other shareholders as directors or appoint them as officers. To reduce conflicts in the control of a close corporation, supermajority (or even unanimous) voting requirements sometimes are used, but these can lead to deadlock. Voting trusts may help avoid deadlock, but one must find a trustworthy, competent trustee. Generally speaking, eliminating a control problem introduces another one. The shareholders must make a decision concerning which problem they want.

9. The fiduciary duty courts have imposed upon majority shareholders in a close corporation is nothing more than a requirement that the majority shareholders deal fairly with the minority shareholders. In other words, a majority shareholder should not use the corporate power she possesses to harm the interests of the minority shareholders.

10. Note that a limited partnership is a creature of statute. A limited partnership cannot exist unless a state statute permits the creation of one. A limited partnership, unlike an ordinary partnership, cannot be created inadvertently. It can be created only by strict compliance with the state statute. Note that if these requirements are not met, a limited partnership is not formed. Where there has not been strict compliance with the requirements, the relation is treated as a partnership. In that event, all the partners have unlimited liability, unless appropriate action is taken to limit liability.

11. Note that many, but by no means all, of the rules that apply to general partnerships also apply to limited partnerships. For example, the general partners' authority to act and fiduciary duties are the same in both forms of business. Also, in a general partnership and in a limited partnership formed in a state where the ULPA is in force, all partners share profits equally, absent a contrary agreement. However, where the limited partnership was formed in a state where the RULPA is in force, profits are distributed on the basis of each partner's contribution, unless there is an agreement to the contrary. Among the essential differences between general partnerships and limited partnerships is the notion that a limited partner has no managerial authority, whereas all partners in a general partnership have such authority. Another of the most significant differences between general partnerships and limited partnerships can be seen in an examination of the respective rules governing distribution of assets upon liquidation.

12. It is easy to understand why a limited partner risks losing her limited liability when she engages in control of the business. She has limited liability only because she is a passive investor whose decisions do not affect the profitability of the business. It would be unfair to impose unlimited liability upon a person who has no real control over the operation of the business. On the other hand, if a person exercises control (and thereby contributes to the level of profitability of the enterprise), it makes good sense to impose unlimited liability on that person. Of course, even though a limited partner is not to exercise control over the day-to-day operation of the business, the limited partner always has the right to enforce the terms of the limited partnership agreement and the related right to bring a derivative suit against general partners who have harmed the limited partnership.

True-False

In the blank provided, put "T" if the statement is True or "F" if the statement is False.

_____ 1. Very few states regulate close corporations by statute.

_____ 2. Legally, a close corporation is a separate legal entity from its officers or directors.

_____ 3. Close corporation shares are generally not intended to be sold to the public at large.

_____ 4. The voting trust is a device that is sometimes used to protect minority stockholders.

_____ 5. The purpose of a limited partnership is to permit partners to take advantage of taxation rules for partnerships but to limit their liability as partners.

_____ 6. Close corporations may experience problems largely because the corporate form of business is sometimes too inflexible for the close corporation.

_____ 7. The withdrawal of a limited partner automatically dissolves the limited partnership.

165

_____ 8. The right of first refusal is designed to guard against the possibility that shares may fall into the "wrong hands."

_____ 9. A limited partner is a creditor of the limited partnership and may get his capital contribution back at any time.

_____ 10. In order to maintain the essentially private nature of the business, shareholders of a close corporation may agree to place reasonable restrictions on shareholders' sales of their shares.

Multiple Choice

Circle the best answer.

1. The MBCA limits the number of shareholders that a close corporation may have to:
   a. 5
   b. 15
   c. 50
   d. 500.

2. Which of the following statements concerning right of refusal is not correct?
   a. Under the right of first refusal, the corporation but not the shareholder may purchase shares offered for sale, at a price below that which would apply to an outsider.
   b. Under the right of first refusal, the corporation or shareholder may purchase shares offered for sale, but must pay the price offered by an outsider willing to purchase them.
   c. The right of first refusal is void and unenforceable under most state statutes;
   d. Modern courts usually uphold these restrictions on stock transferability, even if the restrictions are unreasonable.

3. If a shareholder of a close corporation dies, and her estate is required by agreement to sell her shares to the corporation at an agreed price:
   a. The agreement is called a "buy-sell" agreement and is generally enforceable;
   b. The agreement is called a "consent restraint" and is generally enforceable;
   c. The agreement is called a "right of refusal" and is generally enforceable;
   d. The agreement is not enforceable.

4. Which of the following statements concerning corporate governance issues is correct?
   a. Shareholder agreements providing for arbitration are more likely enforceable today than in the past;
   b. Today, shareholders frequently enter into agreements overriding the discretion normally left to directors;
   c. In some states, a court may appoint a provisional or temporary director to provide a tiebreaker in cases where the shareholders of a close corporation are deadlocked;
   d. All of the above are correct statements.

5. A limited partner acquires which of the following liabilities?
   a. Liability to the partnership for any part of the capital contribution stated in the certificate;
   b. Liabilities for any amounts paid to him that should not have been paid;
   c. Liabilities for the general debts of the partnership, even if those exceed the capital contribution stated in the certificate;
   d. Both (a) and (b) are correct.

6. Of the following statements concerning post-dissolution distribution of limited partnership assets under the RULPA, which is correct?
   a. The rules governing the order in which limited partnership assets are distributed following dissolution are the same as the rules governing distribution of general partnership assets following dissolution.
   b. In a post-dissolution distribution of assets, limited partners are entitled to be paid their shares of profits and their capital contributions before general partners receive their share of profits.
   c. In a post-dissolution distribution of assets, limited partners and general partners are to be paid their respective shares of profits before limited partners are paid their capital contributions.

166

d. In a post-dissolution distribution of assets, nonpartner creditors of the firm are given a higher priority, for asset distribution purposes, than are limited partners and general partners who have extended loans to the firm.

7. The transferability of shares of a close corportation can be reduced by means of
   a. voting trusts.
   b. buy-sell agreements.
   c. consent restraints.
   d. supermajority voting provisions.

8. Which of the following should a limited partner refrain from doing in order to avoid risking the loss of her limited liability?
   a. Engaging in day-to-day management of the limited partnership' business.
   b. Enforcing the limited partnership agreement against other partners.
   c. Inspecting the limited partnership's books and records.
   d. All of the above.

9. Pleasant Valley Limited Partnership has 10 general partners and 10 limited partners. Each of the general partners contributed $1000 to the capital of the firm. Each of the limited partners contributed $3000 to the capital of the firm. Pleasant Valley has a profit of $100,000 to be disbursed among the general and limited partners. Under the ULPA's rule on sharing of profits, what is each general partner's share of the profits?
   a. $1000
   b. $2000
   c. $2500
   d. $5000

10. Consent restraints
    a. may assist in keeping unwanted persons out of the close corporation structure.
    b. are less likely to be enforced by a reviewing court than are rights of first refusal.
    c. are accurately discussed in neither a nor b.
    d. are accurately discussed in both a and b.

Short Essay

1. Briefly describe three devices used in close corporations to place restrictions on the transferability of shares.

2. Alf, Biff, Chloe, and Darcy are planning a business that will be a close corporation. They want to agree to the right of first refusal and have a buy-sell agreement, but they do not know what events should trigger the applicability of each. What advice do you give them?

3. Bob and Carol are general partners and Ted and Alice are limited partners in a limited partnership known as BC Limited Partnership. The partnership agreement states that earnings realized by the limited partnership are to be divided equally among the four partners. The firm has assets of $100,000 and liabilities to creditors of $60,000. It realized net earnings of $50,000 during a recently-completed business year. If a distribution of earnings is made, how much should each of the four partners receive? State the basis for your answer.

4. Zeke, Yvette, and Woody owned a service station as partners in accordance with the applicable limited partnership statute. Woody was the only limited partner. After the firm became unprofitable, Zeke and Yvette asked Woody to help pump gas, order parts and supplies, and negotiate for loans. Woody did this for several months until he resigned from the limited partnership. Elroy loaned the limited partnership money because of Woody's negotiating efforts. The loan has not been repaid and is now past-due. The limited partnership does not have enough assets to allow full payment of the loan. Elroy recently sued Zeke, Yvette, and Woody in an effort to impose personal liability on them. Of the three defendants, which ones are liable to Elroy? Why those defendants?

CHAPTER 31
SECURITIES REGULATION

Outline

I. Federal Legislation

A. There are several federal acts regulating securities. These include the Securities Act of 1933, The Securities Exchange Act of 1934 and creation of the SEC (Securities and Exchange Commission) in 1934.

B. Definition of security is very broad.

Example: Reves v. Ernst & Young (demand note is a security.)

1. Securities includes investment contracts.

C. The Securities Act of 1933 contains registration and anti-fraud provisions and restricts the issuer's ability to communicate with prospective purchasers of securities.

1. There are some exemptions to the 1933 Act: Two types of exemptions are government issued or guaranteed securities, and short-term notes and drafts.

2. There are also certain transaction exemptions.

D. Anti-fraud Provisions: violation may result in both criminal and civil penalties.

II. Securities Exchange Act of 1934: This act is chiefly concerned with disclosing material information to investors and requires periodic disclosure by issuers of publicly held equity securities.

A. Regulation of Proxy Solicitations

1. SEC rules regulate proxy solicitation by regulating contents of the statement, ensuring proxy statements are not misleading, and facilitating proxy contests.

B. Liability Provisions provide remedies to victims of fraudulent, deceptive, or manipulative practices.

1. Litigation must be commenced within one year after discovery of a violation and no more than three years after the violation has occurred.
Example: Lampf v. Gilbertson

2. Many cases involve the failure to disclose nonpublic, corporation information known to an insider.
Example: United States v. Chestman

C. RICO (Racketeer Influenced and Corrupt Organizations Act) also applies to fraud in the sale of securities.

III. Other Issues

A. The Williams Act in 1968 amended the 1934 Act to provide investors with more information to make tender offer decisions; most state have also enacted statutes regulating tender offers.

Example: CTS Corporation v. Dynamics Corporation

Learning Objectives

1. You should be able to define a security;

2. You should understand the liabilities that federal securities laws impose on those who deal in securities.

3. You should know what insider trading is, and what limits are placed on those with inside information.

4. You should become familiar with the registration requirements imposed by the Securities Act of 1933.

5. You should know the securities and transactions in securities that are exempt from the registration requirements of the 1933 Act.

6. You should understand the provision in Section 11 of the 1933 Act concerning liability for misleading or false information in a registration statement, and should understand, with regard to a Section 11 case, the defendant's burden of proving due diligence if he wishes to escape liability.

7. You should become familiar with the 1933 Act's other antifraud provisions besides Section 11.

8. You should understand the periodic disclosure requirements imposed by the Securities Exchange Act of 1934.

9. You should know how and why the SEC regulates solicitations of proxies.

10. You should be familiar with Rule 10b-5's broad prohibition of misstatements and omissions of material fact in connection with the sale or purchase of securities, as well as with the basic elements of a Rule 10b-5 claim by a purchaser or seller of securities.

11. You should understand how Rule 10b-5 applies to a purchaser's or seller's failure to make continuing disclosures of material facts, and should understand how Rule 10b-5 operates to prohibit insider trading on the basis of material information not generally available to the investing public.

12. You should be familiar with the SEC's regulation of tender offers, and with why such regulatory action is required by law.

Learning Hints

1. The federal and state securities laws define the term "securities" very broadly.

2. There are different securities acts which regulate securities. The Securities Act of 1933 is concerned primarily with public distributions of securities and is chiefly a one-time disclosure statute. The Securities Act of 1934 requires periodic disclosures from issuers of securities. The 1934 Act also created the Securities and Exchange Commission, which has authority to issue rules and regulations and bring enforcement actions against violators.

3. Transactions in securities are subjected to extensive regulation because of their inherent nature: they are intangible assets whose values are not apparent merely from an examination of a security certificate. Instead, an investor needs to be given information about the business issuing the security in order to make an informed investment decision. Because historically too little information has been voluntarily disclosed by issuers of securities, the securities laws require that issuers disclose the information an investor needs to make an informed investment decision.

4. A security is defined so as to include investment contracts. When one is investing in another person's business, one is not familiar with the business. One needs to be given information to determine whether to invest in the business.

5. With regard to the registration requirement imposed by the Securities Act of 1933, you should always remain mindful of the rule that every transaction in securities must be registered or be exempt from registration. Where registration of a securities offering is required, the prospective issuer must be very careful not to allow impermissible publicity concerning the proposed offering during the prefiling and waiting periods, and must also refrain from engaging in prohibited transactions during those periods.

6. When an exemption removes the need to register an offering with the SEC, the exemption may be either a securities exemption or a transaction exemption. The basic exemptions are explained well in your text. Do not forget, however, that a transaction exemption offers more narrow relief from the registration requirements than does a securities exemption. The transaction exemption is more narrow, because it applies only to a particular sale of a certain security, not to subsequent sales of the same security. Even if a transaction exemption applies to a particular sale, subsequent sales would be subject to the registration requirement, unless, of course, another transaction exemption would apply.

7. Section 11 of the 1933 Act is an important liability provision dealing with errors in and omissions from registration statements. It is an unusual provision, in that purchasers need not show they relied on the error of omission or that they purchased the securities from the defendant. Neither must the plaintiff prove negligence or an intentional misstatement or omission on the part of the defendant. Instead, the defendant must prove due diligence if he wishes to escape liability.

8. In order to be entitled to the protection of the due diligence defense, the defendant in a Section 11 case must prove that he was not negligent in ascertaining the truthfulness of the registration statement. That is, the defendant must prove that he acted as a reasonable person would have acted under the same circumstances. This requires that most defendants make a reasonable investigation into the accuracy of the registration statement. It also shifts the burden of establishing the mental culpability of the defendant from the plaintiff to the defendant.

9. The Securities Exchange Act of 1934's provisions dealing with short-swing trading by insiders rest on the logical presumption that a statutory would not be buying and selling shares within such a short period if time if he were not using insider information. Remember, however, that the issuer of securities may recover profits made by a statutory on prohibited short-swing trading, without having to prove that the insider actually was relying on improper information in when he bought and sold the shares.

10. The SEC was given regulatory control over proxy solicitations and shareholder proposals because of the abuses that had arisen in large, public corporations. Because of widely-dispersed bodies of small shareholders, these corporations were managed by self-perpetuating boards of directors who could ignore the demands of shareholders. The SEC proxy rules make it easier for shareholder democracy to be realized.

11. SEC Rule 10b-5, promulgated pursuant to the Securities Exchange Act of 1934, is an exceedingly important liability provision that prohibits a broad range of false statements, as well as failures to state material facts, in connection with the sale or purchase of securities. A considerable amount of litigation has stemmed from conduct that either the SEC or a private plaintiff claims was in violation of Rule 10b-5's broad proscription. Be certain to remember that in a Rule 10b-5 case, the plaintiff must prove that the defendant acted with scienter (an intent to deceive or defraud) and that the plaintiff, in purchasing or selling the securities, relied upon the defendant's false statement of a material fact. In a case involving an omission to state a material fact, reliance is not necessarily required.

12. Insider trading is swept within the Rule 10b-5 umbrella. The essential concept to be remembered concerning insider trading is that one who has inside information concerning certain securities and matters that may affect their value must either disclose the information or refrain from trading. It is a violation of Rule 10b-5 to buy or sell either on an exchange or in a direct transaction when one is privy to material information that is not generally available to the investing public. Remember, too, that the rule just stated applies to virtually anyone who obtains "inside" information, regardless of whether that person is an officer or director or other typical insider. Potentially disastrous financial consequences may be experienced by a defendant who has violated Rule 10b-5.

True-False

In the blank provided, put "T" if the statement is True or "F" if the statement is False.

_____ 1. The term security is broadly defined in federal and state law.

_____ 2. An investment contract not evidenced by a certificate is not a security for purposes of securities laws.

_____ 3. During the prefiling period, an issuers may publish a notice about a prospective offering.

_____ 4. EDGAR is an enforcement wing of the Securities and Exchange Commission.

_____ 5. The 1933 Act exempts certain transactions from registration provisions; however, other provisions of the 1933 act continue to apply to exempt transactions.

_____ 6. Under Section 11 of the Securities Act of 1933, a purchaser of securities may obtain damages because of an untrue statement in the registration statement for those securities, even if the purchaser had not read the registration statement before purchasing the securities.

_____ 7. Sales of limited partnership interests may be considered sales of securities, for purposes of the federal securities laws.

_____ 8. Purchasers of securities sold pursuant to the private offering exemption from registration must hold their securities for at least six months before reselling them.

_____ 9. The Securities Act of 1933 has the effect of requiring that every transaction in securities be registered with the SEC or be exempt from registration.

_____ 10. During the waiting period following the filing of a registration statement with the SEC, the issuer of the security may neither offer nor sell the security.

_____ 11. Once the SEC has declared a registration statement effective, the issuer is free to sell the securities if it provides the purchaser with either the preliminary prospectus or the final prospectus.

_____ 12. Under SEC rules, shareholder sometimes may be able to compel the corporation to include shareholder proposals in the corporation's proxy statement.

Multiple Choice

Circle the best answer.

1. Under the Securities Act of 1933, the issuer of securities:
   a. must file a registration statements with the Securities and Exchange Commission;
   b. must make a prospectus available to prospective purchases;
   c. must do both of the above;
   d. is required to do neither of the above.

2. A "red herring prospectus"
   a. is a preliminary prospectus permitted by the 1933 Securities Act;
   b. is a type of general advertisement of prospectus during the waiting period;
   c. is illegal;
   d. none of the above is correct.

3. Which of the following is not exempt from the registration requirements of the 1933 Securities Act?
   a. government issued securities;
   b. government guaranteed securities;
   c. short-term notes;
   d. all of the above are exempt securities.

4. Which of the following statements concerning proxy solicitations is not correct?
   a. The primary purpose of the SEC's proxy rules to inform shareholders in voting for directors or management resolutions;
   b. If misleading statements are made in a proxy statement, a court may enjoin the holding of the shareholder meeting;
   c. A shareholder may not solicit proxies in competition with management;
   d. Under SEC rules, a corporation must include a shareholder's proposal in its proxy statement if the shareholder owns at least 1 percent of the securities to be voted at the meeting.

5. Which of the following elements are required to prove fraud, a violation of Rule 10b-5 of the 1934 Act?
   a. Misstatement or omission of material fact;
   b. Scienter (knowledge) by the defendant;
   c. Reliance by the purchaser;
   d. All of the above are elements of a 10b-5 fraud violation.

6. The following statements pertain to either the Securities Act of 1933 or the Securities Exchange Act of 1934 (and rules based thereon). Which statement is accurate?
   a. The 1934 Act is primarily a one-time disclosure provision.
   b. Rule 10b-5 (promulgated under Section 10(b) of the 1934 Act) is violated if a seller of securities negligently fails to reveal, before selling the securities, material facts that would be likely to influence the value of the securities in the eyes of a prospective buyer.
   c. A purchaser of securities may win a suit under Section 11 of the 1933 Act even if she was not in privity with the party on whom she seeks to impose liability for a material omission in a registration statement.
   d. The 1933 Act imposes continuing duties of periodic disclosure upon issuers of certain securities.

7. Which of the following actions by a corporate director would violate SEC Rule 10b-5?
   a. Usurping a corporate opportunity.
   b. Buying or selling corporate shares in reliance on inside information.
   c. Using corporate funds for personal purposes.
   d. All of the above.

8. Which of the following is/are prohibited by the Securities Exchange Act of 1934?
   a. A corporate insider's profiting on a sale and purchaser of that corporation's stock within a six-month period.
   b. The public sale of securities without an SEC registration.
   c. Omissions of material fact in a registration statement.
   d. All of the above.

9. Under current securities law,
   a. Rule 10b-5 may be invoked by a party who was deterred from purchasing stock because of another person's materially false statements concerning that stock.
   b. a "tippee" who receives confidential information from a corporate insider is not prohibited from trading, on the basis of that information, in the securities of the corporation as to which the "tipper" is an insider; the insider, however, is barred from trading on the basis of that information.
   c. the fact that securities are being issued and sold does not necessarily mean that the securities and the issuers must satisfy the registration requirements of federal law.
   d. all of the above are true.

10. Ursula and Walt are developing condominium sites in Arkansas. There are 100 condominiums in the complex. Most purchasers intend to use their condominiums only two weeks a year. To entice more people (from various states) to purchase the condominiums, Ursula and Walt offer to be rental agents for the condominiums. In other words, Ursual and Walt will seek out renters. All rental income from all the condominiums is combined. Each purchaser receives a share of the income according to the number of days his condominium is available to be rented, not according to how many days it is actually rented. Are Ursula and Walt selling securities for purposes of the Securities Act of 1933?
    a. No, because nothing in the facts indicates that Ursula and Walt have formed a corporation.
    b. Yes, because the buyers are investors in a common enterprise, with the expected profits to come primarily from the efforts of Ursula and Walt.
    c. No, because the buyers are attempting to profit from the efforts of Ursula and Walt rather than from their own efforts.
    d. Yes, because Ursula and Walt are seeking investors on an interstate basis rather than in one solitary state.

Short Essay

1. Bud owns a large ostrich farm. The farm is losing money, so he decides to sell the ostriches. He advertises the ostriches for sale, at the same time offering to keep the ostriches on his farm and to feed them for an annual fee. Each purchaser who opts to have Bud feed her ostrich will share pro rata the expenses of feeding the ostriches and the profits from their sale. Is Bud selling a security?

2. Griede Corp. intends to issue $1,300,000 in securities during a six-month period. The potential investors are likely be from various states in the western half of the United States. Some of the investors probably will be highly sophisticated investors, but others are expected to be first-time investors with limited knowledge concerning investment-related matters. Must Griede register this transaction in securities according the provisions of the Securities Act of 1933? Explain your reasoning.

3. Revolutionary Medical Devices, Inc. (RMD) has nearly completed perfecting a diagnostic machine that will revolutionize the ways in which numerous serious ailments are currently diagnosed. All previous means of diagnosing these serious ailments will effectively become obsolete. Rumors about some sort of breakthrough by RMD have been circulating in the business community, but RMD says nothing, deciding instead to sit on the news until the machine is perfected. RMD stock is selling for $500 per share. Is RMD risking a violation of SEC Rule 10b-5 by not commenting on the rumored invention? Explain the basis for your answer.

4. Irv, a custodian at Gargantuan Corp., was dusting a corporate executive's desk one evening when he discovered and read an interesting document containing information that was not available to the investing public. The information was such that if it were available to the investing public, the price and value of Gargantuan stock would soar. Irv informed his friend, Simone, of what he had read in the document. Simone then purchased 100 shares of Gargantuan stock from Cletus, without telling Cletus the information given to her by Irv. When this information finally was made available to the investing public, the value of Gargantuan stock indeed soared. Simone resold, at a substantial profit, the 100 shares she had purchased from Cletus. Cletus thereafter sued Simone in an attempt to recover the profit Simone had made. Simone denied any liability to Cletus, claiming that because she was not an officer, director, or employee of Gargantuan, she had done nothing wrong. Is Simone liable to Cletus? Why or why not?

CHAPTER 32
LEGAL LIABILITY OF ACCOUNTANTS

Outline

I. Common Law Liability to the client

A. Contractual liability. Ordinarily, an accountant may not delegate her responsibilities without the consent of the client.

B. Tort liability. Failure to comply with reasonable standards of care may result in liability under a <u>negligence</u> theory.

II. Common Law Liability to third persons

A. Historically, third parties not in privity (direct contractual relationship) with the accountant were unable to recover damages under a contract theory (except in third party beneficiary cases.)

B. Today, many courts refuse to apply the privity doctrine.

C. The Ultramares Approach (No liability absent privity).

Example: <u>Bily v. Arthur Young & Co.</u> (Mere presence of a foreseeable risk of injury to third person is not sufficient to impose liability for negligent conduct.)

D. "Near Privity Approach" holds accountants liable in some cases; Restatement is liable to those third parties who are "specifically foreseeable."

Example: <u>First Florida Bank v. Max Mitchell & Co.</u>

E. Other approaches are the "reasonably foreseeable users" approach and the "Balancing Approach."

III. Statutory Liability of Accountants:

A. Civil Actions under the 1933 Act include liability for misstatements or omissions of material facts in the registration statements required by the Act.

B. Under the 1934 Act, liability is imposed for misstatement or omission of a material fact in connect with the purchase or sale of any security.

C. Both Acts have criminal provisions which may apply against accountants.

D. State licensing boards also regulate ethical conduct of accountants. Limitation of accountant's advertising may be unenforceable if overbroad.

Example: <u>Fane v. Edenfield</u>
Example: <u>Moore v. California State Board of Accountancy</u>

E. Liability may differ depending on whether there is a qualified opinion, unqualified opinion, or enforceable disclaimer.

Learning Objectives

1. You should understand the difference between an action by a client and a third party for damages against an accountant.

2. You should understand the difference between an action in contract or tort against an accountant.

3. You should consider the ethical implications of accountants who voluntarily disclose improprieties of their clients to government officials.

4. You should understand the nature and extent of the accountant-client privilege.

5. You should understand the role of GAAP and GAAS in determining the liability of accountants.

6. You should understand the historical and present role of privity in the principles governing the legal liability of accountants.

7. You should know and understand the bases of an accountant's civil liability to a client for fraud, as well as liability based on the securities laws.

8. You should be able to recognize whether a specific act of an accountant creates potential liability and to whom the accountant may be liable.

9. You should know the sources of an accountant's criminal liability, including federal and state securities laws and tax laws.

10. You should know what protection is accorded to the work papers of an accountant, as well as who owns the work papers and who hold rights in them. You should know whether communications between an accountant and his clients are privileged, and if so, the extent of protection given to such communications.

Learning Hints

1. The law may apply different rules in an accountant liability case depending on whether the plaintiff suing the accountant is a client or a third party. Generally, a plaintiff who is a client may recover under contract or tort theory. Historically, however, third parties were often unable to recover under these theories because they were not in privity with (contractual relationship with) the accountant.

2. Many courts today have refused to apply the privity doctrine to third-party negligence suits against accountants, and there are at least five different approaches for handling such suits.

3. Federal and state securities laws also give injured persons a right to sue in negligence or fraud; in addition, both laws contain criminal penalties.

4. The working papers of the accountant generally belongs to the accountant, but the accountant generally must get the client's permission to transfer them to another accountant. Communications between accountants and their clients may be protected under state confidentiality statutes, but these are not always enforceable in federal courts.

5. As is the case with most professionals, the law nearly always permits accountants to set the standard by which they are judged. If an accountant has acted as the reasonably prudent accountant would have acted under same circumstances, the law will rarely impose liability upon the accountant. This explains why compliance with GAAP and GAAS will generally protect the accountant from liability. The only instance in which compliance with GAAP and GAAS may not relieve the accountant of liability is when the accountant has nevertheless provided a misleading financial picture. Note that the standard is objective, rather than subjective. It is not enough that the accountant do her best. She must do what the reasonably prudent accountant would have done.

6. Note the varying levels of importance given to privity when you are studying the different bases of accountants' liability. For example, privity generally is required for contract claims and often, but now not always, required even for negligence claims against accountants. Privity is not required, however, for fraud claims, Securities Act Section 11(a) claims, or Securities Exchange Act Rule lOb-5 claims.

7. Remember, as was pointed out in Chapter 31, that the purpose of the federal securities acts is to provide investors with information adequate to enable them to make informed investment decisions. Truth in securities transactions is valued highly, so it should not be surprising that the federal securities acts are structured in such a manner that accountants are subject to their provisions. Note the difference between Section 11(a) liability and Rule lOb-5 liability. Section 11(a) has a negligence standard, but Rule lOb-5 has a scienter standard. Under Section 11(a) the <u>defendant</u> must disprove his negligence. Under Rule lOb-5 the plaintiff must prove the defendant acted with scienter. Section 11(a) applies only to misstatements or omissions in registration statements under the Securities Act while Rule lOb-5 has a broader sweep, prohibiting misstatements or omissions of material fact in connection with any securities transaction in interstate commerce.

8. Note that an accountant may have criminal liability for actions for which he also has civil liability. In other words, the same action by an accountant may have both civil and criminal consequences. Criminal proceedings against an accountant do not bar civil proceedings based on the same wrongful activity, and vice versa.

True-False

In the blank provided, put "T" if the statement is True or "F" if the statement is False.

_____ 1. Under the "no delegation rule," an accountant may not delegate her duties to another even if the client consents.

_____ 2. The Securities Act of 1933 explicitly imposes liability on accountants for omissions of material facts in the information furnished for registration statements.

_____ 3. An attorney who violates a state or federal statute may be liable to injured clients under a negligence per se theory.

_____ 4. Issuing an unaudited statement creates a disclaimer as to the financial statement's accuracy.

_____ 5. A fraud claim against an accountant cannot succeed unless the party bringing the fraud claim was in privity with the accountant.

_____ 6. A number of courts today will hold an accountant liable to nonclients in a negligence action, if the accountant knew that a client would be furnishing a copy of the accountant's work to the nonclients.

_____ 7. In order to establish that an accountant committed fraud, proof that the accountant merely failed to comply with GAAP and GAAS will normally be insufficient.

_____ 8. Accountants are usually criminally liable for negligently preparing tax returns.

_____ 9. The current trend in the law is to make accountants liable to fewer persons who use financial statements prepared by accountants.

_____ 10. Accountants are held liable under the Securities Act of 1933 for false or misleading information they furnish for a securities registration statement, only if the plaintiff proves that the accountants failed to exercise due diligence.

Multiple Choice

Circle the Best Answer

1. Which of the following approaches holds that the accountant is liable only to those third parties who are "specifically foreseeable?"
   a. _Ultramares_ approach;
   b. _Restatement_ approach;
   c. Balancing approach;
   d. None of the above.

2. In order to be liable for fraud, an accountant must:
   a. have intended to deceive;
   b. have known of the falsity of her statement;
   c. have injured a foreseeable user of her work product;
   d. all of the above are required for liability under fraud.

3. If an accountant deliberately misstates a material fact in a registration statement:
   a. she may be criminally liable under federal securities law;
   b. she may be subject to punitive damages for fraud;
   c. she is only liable to those with whom she is in privity;
   d. both (a) and (b) are correct.

4. Which of the following statements concerning an accountant's working papers is _not_ correct?
   a. The working papers that an accountant prepares in making an audit are the property of the client;
   b. The accountant must get the client's permission in order to transfer working papers to another accountant;
   c. Some states have adopted statutes providing that communication between accountants and their clients are privileged and protected from discovery procedures in a lawsuit;
   d. Federal courts do not always recognize state statutes protecting accountants' working papers.

5. Which of the following is an accurate statement concerning an accountant's potential criminal liability?
   a. An accountant cannot be held criminally liable under the Securities Act of 1933 and the Securities Exchange Act of 1934 because those Acts provide only for civil liability.
   b. An accountant's negligent preparation of a client's income tax return may subject the accountant to criminal liability.
   c. An accountant's failure to use reasonable care will subject him to criminal liability, if that failure takes the form of neglecting to comply with GAAP and GAAS.
   d. None of the above.

6. First Bank has loaned money to Postrex Corporation, in reliance upon financial statements prepared for First Bank by Armand Yount & Co., CPA's. First Bank had hired Armand Yount to prepare the statements. Armand Yount did the work negligently, and as a result, Postrex Corporation's financial condition was indicated to be much stronger than it was. Postrex Corporation became bankrupt and First Bank was unable to collect on the loan. Which of the following is correct?
   a. First Bank may recover from Armand Yount if it brings suit under SEC Rule IOb-5.
   b. Under the approach taken in many states today, First Bank is likely to prevail against Armand Yount if it brings suit on a tort theory.
   c. Both of the above.
   d. Neither A nor B.

7. Dullard & Denson, a CPA firm, negligently certified a balance sheet of Shaky Corp. This balance sheet—which made Shaky look far more financially stable than it really was—served as the major factor in Insolvent Savings & Loan's decision to make a substantial loan to Shaky. Shaky later defaulted on the loan and filed for bankruptcy, making the loan effectively uncollectible. Insolvent has sued Dullard & Denson for negligence. Applicable state law adheres to the Ultramares approach. Who will win the suit?
   a. Insolvent, because Dullard & Denson's negligence caused it to make a loan it would not have made had it known the truth about Shaky.
   b. Dullard & Denson, because the Ultramares approach allows only fraud as a basis of liability of an accountant to any party.
   c. Dullard & Denson, because it and Insolvent were not in privity.
   d. Insolvent, because Dullard & Denson is responsible for the fraud of Shaky.

8. Of the following statements concerning SEC Rule IOb-5 and/or Securities Act Section 11, which is incorrect?
   a. Only an accountant's clients may successfully sue under Rule IOb-5.
   b. The defendant must prove due diligence under Section 11.
   c. The plaintiff must prove scienter under Rule IOb-5.
   d. Both liability provisions apply only to securities transactions.

9. Incomp & Inepped (I&I), a CPA firm, negligently certified the balance sheet of Schlemiel Corp. The balance sheet made Schlemiel look quite solid financially even though it was not. I&I did not know that Schlemiel's officers would be showing the balance sheet to Local National Bank in an effort to obtain a loan, but I&I did know that Schlemiel had frequent borrowing needs. After relying heavily on what the balance sheet appeared to indicate, Local National made a loan to Schlemiel. Schlemiel later went "belly-up," without repaying the loan. Local National has sued I&I for negligence. Local National
   a. should win the suit if applicable state law follows the Ultramares approach.
   b. could win the suit if applicable state law follows the reasonably foreseeable users approach.
   c. should win the suit if applicable state law follows the Restatement approach.
   d. could win the suit if applicable state law adheres to any one of the approaches referred to in answers a, b, and c.

10. Whitney, a certified public accountant, agreed to perform certain accounting work for a client. The work was expected to take several days once Whitney began performing it. Whitney promised to complete the work by November 1, 1990. After beginning the work, Whitney realized she would need certain records that were in the possession of the client. She therefore notified the client, on September 15, 1990, of her immediate need for the records. When the client still had not delivered the records by October 1, 1990, Whitney reminded the client. She did so again on October 15, 1990, because she still had not received the records. The client delivered the records to Whitney on October 30, 1990. Because of the press of other business, Whitney did not begin the work for the client until October 31, 1990. She completed the work on November 4, 1990. Claiming to have missed a fabulous business opportunity because Whitney had not completed the accounting work by November 1, 1990, the client sued Whitney for breach of contract. Who will prevail in the suit?
   a. The client, because Whitney's failure to meet the agreed deadline caused the client to experience a loss.

b. The client, because Whitney was negligent in failing to finish the work by the agreed deadline.

c. Whitney, because the client's tardiness in furnishing the needed records provides Whitney with a defense.

d. Whitney, because she was not negligent and did not commit fraud.

Short Essay

1. Jerry hired Two and Two Accounting Firm to prepare a financial statement for his business. Six months later, Two and Two Accounting Firm dissolved and was sold to Bob, a certified public accountant. Two and Two assigned its contract with Jerry to Bob, and delegated its (Two and Two's) duty to prepare the financial statement. Jerry doesn't want Bob to prepare the statement. Is the assignment and delegation of the contract by Two and Two to Bob enforceable? Explain.

2. Briefly discuss three major judicial approaches refusing to apply the privity doctrine to third-party negligence suits against accountants.

3. Dewey, Cheatem & Howe (DCH), a CPA firm, was hired by Dolt Corp. to audit financial statements that will be included in a Securities Act registration statement. DCH failed to discover that year-end inventory for 1989 was overstated by 85 percent. As a result, earnings for 1989 were overstated by 62 percent. DCH failed to discover the overstated inventory and earnings, because it never did a physical check of the inventory. Instead, it accepted as truthful whatever employees of Dolt stated. Horace bought preferred shares issued pursuant to the defective registration statement. Dolt went bankrupt within three months. Horace has sued DCH for damages under Securities Act Section 11. Will Horace win? State the basis for your answer.

CHAPTER 33
PERSONAL PROPERTY

Outline

I. Nature of Property

    A. Ownership in property may be defined as a bundle of legal rights in relationship to property. Property is either _real_ or _personal_.

    B. Personal property includes all objects other than the earth's crust and things firmly attached to it.

        1. Tangible property has a physical existence;

        2. Intangible property has no such existence. For example, a patent right is intangible.

II. Acquiring Ownership of Personal Property

    A. Ownership of unowned property results from taking possession of it.

        Example: Michael v. First Chicago Corporation (Bank had not intended to abandoned CDs.)

    B. A finder of lost property must return it to the owner if he knows who the owner is. All states have statutes of limitations protecting finders of lost or unclaimed property.

        Example: In the Matter of Unknown Silver Coins

    C. If property is mislaid, this results in a bailment.

    D. A gift requires proof that the donor intended to make the gift, made delivery of the gift, and the donee accepted the gift.

        1. A gift _causa mortis_ is a gift made in contemplation of death, and is a conditional gift.
        Example: Succession of Young (No effective inter-vivos gift because no delivery.)

        2. A conditional gift may be revoked before the donee complies.
        Example: Fierro v. Hoel (A ring given in contemplation of marriage is a conditional gift which must be returned if the marriage does not take place.)

    E. Uniform Gifts to Minors Act provides a method for making gifts to minors.

    F. Confusion results in each person owning a proportionate share of the entire quantity of personal property; title to personal property can also be obtained by accession.

        Example: Ochoa v. Rogers (Original owner was not entitled to recover possession of property substantially improved by improver.)

III. Co-Ownership includes joint tenancy, tenancy in common, tenancy by the entirety, and community property.

    A. Tenancy in common entitles a o-tenant to divide the property.

        Example: Hufnagel v. Burns (discussing rights of a tenant in common.)

Learning Objectives

    1. You should understand the difference between personal and real property.

    2. You should understand the ways in which a person acquires ownership of personal property.

    3. You should understand the meaning of the terms "property," and "ownership."

    4. You should understand the difference between lost, mislaid, and abandoned property.

    5. You should understand the requirements for making a valid gift.

    6. You should be familiar with the various kinds of personal property.

    7. You should know the circumstances under which a person can become the owner of personal property by possession of the property.

    8. You should know what differences there are between a gift _inter vivos_ and a gift _causa mortis_.

    9. You should know the legal status of a conditional gift.

    10. You should be able to describe the major features of the Uniform Gifts to Minors Act.

    11. You should be able to describe the distinguishing features of the four forms of co-ownership of personal property: tenancy in common; joint tenancy; tenancy by the entirety; and community property.

Learning Hints

1. Ownership is defined as a "bundle of rights" in personal or real property. Sometimes, a person may have less than all the sticks in that bundle. For example, a tenant acquires certain rights of possession in real property, but the lessor retains the right of ownership.

2. The law treats ownership rights differently in cases of abandoned, lost, and mislaid property. Generally, if a person finds lost property, he has an obligation to return it to the true owner, and to notify the owner if he knows who the owner is.

3. In order to make an effective gift, a person must complete delivery of the gift. This means that a gift is generally revocable at any time prior to delivery. Some courts have created exceptions in cases where a donee justifiably relies on the promise to make a gift, and suffers loss as a result of that reliance.

4. A person may obtain ownership of personal property by mere possession, but only where the property is unowned because it is wild or has been abandoned by its previous owner.

5. If A makes a gift to B, B becomes the owner of the property and has better rights in that property than anyone in the world—even better than the original owner. A has no right to demand the property back.

6. Gifts inter vivos ("during life") cannot be revoked once the donor has satisfied the three requirements of a gift stated above. Gifts causa mortis (in contemplation of death) are gifts made conditional on the donor's death. Unlike the inter vivos gift, the gift causa mortis can be revoked by the donor after delivery.

7. Confusion occurs when property belonging to two or more owners is mixed in a way that makes it difficult to separate the property. In cases of good faith confusion, courts give each person his or her proportionate share. Accession means increasing the value of property by adding materials or labor. It is similar to confusion in that both involve the combination of property originally belonging to two different owners. However, accession involves a supplementation of the original property with new and different parts or labor, whereas confusion involves a mixing up of two or more kinds of indistinguishable property. Where there has been bad faith accession, the original owner gets to keep the improved property without reimbursing the person who improved it. Where the accession has been done in good faith, however, the person who improved the property will have some right to reimbursement or rights in the property.

8. The distinction between lost property and mislaid property is that with lost property, the owner did not intend to put the property in the place where it is found, whereas with mislaid property, the owner intentionally put the property in a certain place and then forgot about it. The distinction between lost and mislaid property and abandoned property is that the former owner of abandoned property intentionally placed the property somewhere and does not want it back, whereas the owners of lost and mislaid property want the property back.

True-False

In the blank provided, put "T" if the statement is True or "F" if the statement is False.

_____ 1. Trees growing on land are considered tangible personal property.

_____ 2. When abandoned property is embedded in the soil, it belongs to the person who first finds it.

_____ 3. Generally, a donor may be revoked by the donor before the donee has begun compliance with the conditions.

_____ 4. Accession occurs when the value of personal property increases without adding materials and/or labor.

_____ 5. The distinguishing feature of a joint tenancy is that on the death of one of the owners, her interest passes to her heirs or the persons specified by will and not the other tenant(s).

_____ 6. Patent rights constitute tangible property.

_____ 7. A gift causa mortis can be revoked by the donor before he dies.

_____ 8. If the owner's property is improved through the efforts of another party, the owner will have an obligation to pay for the improvement, regardless of the circumstances under which the improvement took place.

_____ 9. In a community property state, neither spouse owns anything that the law considers to be separate property.

_____ 10. Gifts <u>inter vivos</u> and gifts <u>causa mortis</u> are conditional in that both kinds of gifts may be revoked, after delivery, if the donor so desires.

Multiple Choice

Circle the best answer.

1. Dave put out several old bookcases to be picked up and hauled away by trashhaulers. Jill saw the bookcases and took them home with her. Dave subsequently sued Jill to recover the bookcases. Under these circumstances:
   a. Dave is entitled to the bookcases because he owned the bookcases until such time as they were picked up by the trash haulers.
   b. Dave is entitled to the bookcases because the property was mislaid property;
   c. Jill is entitled to the property because it was abandoned.
   d. Neither are entitled to the property because it belonged to the trashhaulers.

2. Vicky went to a local department store to purchase a new purse. She laid her old one on the counter and, forgetting it was there, left the store. The old purse is:
   a. mislaid property;
   b. abandoned property;
   c. lost property;
   d. all of the above.

3. Aunt Sally promised little Lucy her diamond ring when Lucy reached the age of 16. Sally put the ring in her bank deposit box with a note "for Lucy." Only Sally had the key to the box. If Sally dies before Lucy reaches the age of 16, is the gift effective?
   a. Yes, because Sally intended to make the gift;
   b. Yes, because Sally put the ring in the bank deposit box, intending to deliver it to Lucy on her 16th birthday;
   c. Both (a) and (b) are necessary to prove a gift;
   d. There is no effective gift, because Sally failed to relinquish control of the ring and thus there was no delivery.

4. If property is mistakenly improved in good faith by someone who believes that he is its owner:
   a. The original owner is entitled to the property and to the improvement;
   b. The improver is entitled to the property and to the improvement;
   c. The person who improved the property is entitled to recover the cost of the improvement made to it, or to pay the original owner the value of the property at the time that he obtained it.
   d. None of the above is correct.

5. A tenancy by the entirety most resembles:
   a. a tenancy in common;
   b. a joint tenancy;
   c. a tenancy in partnership;
   d. a corporation.

6. Edgar told his nephew, Alvin, that he planned to give Alvin his pearl cufflinks. Several months later, Edgar gave the cufflinks to Alvin's cousin, Mort. Edgar died the next week. Edgar's estate is seeking the return of the cufflinks. Alvin claims ownership of the ring. Which of the following statements is accurate?
   a. Alvin is the true owner of the cufflinks because Edgar promised to give them to him first.
   b. Edgar did not make a gift of the cufflinks to Alvin because Edgar did not deliver them to Alvin.
   c. Edgar's gift of the cufflinks to Mort was a gift <u>causa mortis</u>, which is legally invalid.
   d. Even if Edgar did make a valid gift of the cufflinks to Mort Edgar's estate has the right to get the cufflinks back.

7. Ned was in a car accident and was badly injured. As he lay in the intensive care ward of the local hospital, certain that he would soon die, he stated the following to his friend and longtime physician, Dr. Mal Practice: "I want you to have my gold watch." Ned then gave the watch to Practice, who thanked Ned for it. Miraculously, Ned later recovered. He asked Practice to return the watch to him, but Practice refused. Which of the following statements is accurate?
    a. Because Ned did not specify that his gift was conditional, he cannot get the watch back.
    b. Ned cannot get the watch back because all of the elements of a valid gift (intent, delivery and acceptance) were present here.
    c. Ned can get the watch back, because a gift causa mortis is not effective if the donor recovers from the peril.
    d. Because Ned was alive when he made this gift, it was an inter vivos gift.

8. Of the following statements concerning confusion of goods, which is/are correct?
    a. When two persons' property becomes mixed and cannot be separated, each person then owns her proportionate share of the mixed goods, assuming that the mixing occurred by accident and without negligence on the part of either person.
    b. When two persons' property becomes mixed and cannot be separated, then each person owns her proportionate share of the mixed goods even if the mixing occurred through the negligence of one of the persons, but not if the mixing occurred as the result of intentional and wrongful action by one of the persons.
    c. The legal rules governing confusion of goods deal only with rights of possession of personal property, because title to personal property cannot be obtained through confusion of goods.
    d. a and c.

8. Alberta and Bridget owned a yacht as tenants in common prior to Alberta's death. Clyde is the sole beneficiary under Alberta's will. Which of the following is true?
    a. Clyde can own part of the boat only if he pays Bridget for her share.
    b. Alberta's interest in the sailboat will pass under the terms of her will to Clyde.
    c. Alberta's interest in the yacht automatically passed to Bridget upon Alberta's death.
    d. It would be impossible for Alberta and Bridget to own the sailboat as tenants in common because they were not a married couple.

9. Of the following statements concerning conditional gifts, which is/are correct?
    a. If the donor delivers possession of the property to the donee before the donee has fulfilled the conditions attached to the gift, the donor loses the right he otherwise would have to revoke the gift before the conditions had been satisfied.
    b. If the donee has partially completed the conditions attached to the making of the gift, the donor cannot withdraw the gift without giving the donee a reasonable opportunity to comply fully with the conditions.
    c. Under the majority rule across the country, gifts of engagement rings are considered conditional gifts, with the donor being entitled to recover possession of the ring if the engagement is broken, regardless of the reason for the breakup.
    d. All of the above.

Short Essay

1. Abe, Bill, Carl, and Dave, owned property as joint tenants. Abe died, leaving his wife Shirley as his sole heir. Bill died one week later, leaving no heirs. Who owns the property and in what proportion?

2. Alice lost her wedding ring at the local mall. Jack found it on the floor, and read Alice's name and wedding date on the inside of the ring. What duties, if any, does Jack have to Alice?

3. A thief stole Zelda's motorcycle. The thief later abandoned the motorcycle—still in the same condition it was in at the time of the theft—in a heavily wooded area. The next day, while hiking through the woods, Elroy found the motorcycle. Not having any idea whose it was, Elroy took it home. After having the motorcycle in his possession for six months (during which time no one claimed it) Elroy put a new engine in the motorcycle and installed a new seat to replace the somewhat worn seat the motorcycle had at the time Elroy found it. Shortly thereafter, Zelda learned that Elroy had found the motorcycle, so she contacted Elroy and claimed it. Elroy agreed to return the motorcycle to Zelda but demanded that she pay him the reasonable value of the improvements he had made to the motorcycle. Zelda balked at Elroy's demand. Is Elroy entitled to be compensated for the reasonable value of the improvements? State the reasons for your answer.

4. Farley purchased a rocking chair at a garage sale for $20. When his next-door neighbor, Daphne, said that she liked the rocking chair, Farley told her to "consider it yours." He then carried the rocking chair to Daphne's house and placed it in her living room. Daphne later had an antique dealer appraise the rocking chair. The dealer placed a $1,300 value on it. Farley later learned of this appraisal. He then demanded that Daphne return the rocking chair so that he could give it to his daughter. Daphne refused. May Farley recover possession and ownership of the rocking chair? Why or why not?

CHAPTER 34
BAILMENTS

Outline

I. Nature of a Bailment

A. The delivery of personal property by a bailor to another person (bailee), who accepts it and is required to return it, is a bailment.

B. A bailment is created by express or implied contract.

Example: Jones v. Hanna (no bailment where the defendant exercised not control over the property and did not have actual possession of it.)

Example: York v. Jones

II. Rights and Duties of Bailor/Bailee

A. The Bailee has a duty to take reasonable care of the property and return it at the termination of the bailment.

1. The duty of care may depend on who benefits from the bailment.

Example: Mr. Transmission, Inc. v. Thompson (Mr. Transmission was liable to Thompson for the acts taken with respect to Thompson's transmission.)

B. The bailee must return the goods to the bailor in an undamaged condition; failure to do so results in the presumption (rebuttable) of negligence.

Example: Simon v. Maloney (Bailee liable for the loss of coins entrusted to him.)

C. Disclaimers of liability are often unenforceable because they violate public policy.

Example: Magee v. Walbro, Inc. (Limitation of liability for lost fur jacket was not enforceable.)

D. A bailee has the right to compensation; further, a bailor makes an implied warranty that there are no hidden defects in the property making it unsafe for use.

Example: Hartmann v. Black & Decker Mfg. Co. (Bailor in mutual benefit bailment had duty to use reasonable care to ensure bailed property was reasonably safe for use.)

III. Special Bailment Situations

A. Common carriers are held to a higher level of responsibility than private carriers.

B. Hotelkeepers are protected under the laws of most states

Example: Gooden v. Day's Inn

Learning Objectives

1. You should understand the rights and duties of a bailor and bailee as a result of a bailment.

2. You should understand the effectiveness of disclaimers of liability in a bailment situation;

3. You should know what a bailment is and what its essential elements are.

4. You should be able to describe the distinguishing features of the three different types of bailments.

5. You should know the factors that will be considered in determining the bailee's duty of care toward the bailed goods.

6. You should know how the bailee's duty of care toward the goods differs according to the type of bailment involved.

7. You should be able to discuss the bailor's liability for defects in the bailed property, and should know how this liability differs according to the type of bailment involved.

8. You should be able to describe the respective liabilities of special bailees such as common carriers, hotelkeepers, and banks that rent safety deposit boxes.

Learning Hints

1. In order to determine the rights and duties of a bailor and bailee, you need to know whether a bailment exists and the kind of bailment created. A bailment involves the division of ownership and possession of personal property between two people, with the person who is in possession of the property having the obligation to return the property to the owner.

185

2. In analyzing a case in which one person's property was lost or damaged while in the possession of another, the first step is to determine whether a bailment existed. To have a bailment, all of the following must normally exist: (1) the bailor owns the property or otherwise has the right to possess it; (2) the bailor surrenders the possession of the property to the bailee; and (3) the bailee has the duty to return the goods.

3. A bailment need not be created by express contract, but it can arise as a result of an implied contract. Behavior between two parties may result in the creation of a bailment even though no express agreement was entered. For example, parking your car in a garage with an attendant who takes your keys probably results in a bailment.

4. Special bailment situations exist. For example, if the bailee is a common carrier, it is generally held to a higher standard of care than a non-public carrier.

5. State statutes may apply in certain bailment situations. For example, many states have statutes protecting hotel and innkeepers from liability or limiting their liability for lost or stolen property in certain circumstances.

6. The bailee's legal responsibility toward the bailed property depends on what he is getting out of the bailment. If the bailment is purely for the benefit of the bailor, the bailee's duty of care toward the property is minimal. As the benefit to the bailee increases, the bailee's duty toward the property rises. The standard is not one of strict or absolute liability, however, except for common carriers. Most bailees are held to a standard of reasonable care.

7. By the same token, the bailor's responsibility for injury caused by defects in the bailed property differs according to what he was getting out of the deal. Notice how the standard of care increases as the benefit to the bailor rises.

True-False

In the blank provided, put "T" if the statement is True or "F" if the statement is False.

_____ 1. A bailment must be created by express contract.

_____ 2. Bailments for the benefit of the bailor arise when both parties benefit from the bailment.

_____ 3. Generally, a bailee can not limit or disclaim liability for intentional torts.

_____ 4. When personal property is rented or loaned, the bailor makes an implied warranty that there are no hidden defects in the property making it unsafe for use.

_____ 5. Most courts hold that the renter of a safety deposit at a bank creates a bailment.

_____ 6. Common carriers may avoid liability for damage to goods in their possession if they can show that the damage resulted from the inherent nature of the goods.

_____ 7. A bailee is allowed by law to limit his liability for damage caused to bailed goods by his intentionally wrongful conduct.

_____ 8. In some instances, the bailee may have a lien on the bailed property to secure payment of the reasonable value of the bailee's services.

_____ 9. In some states, certain bailors have been held strictly liable for injuries caused to bailees by defective goods.

_____ 10. In a bailment for the sole benefit of the bailor, the bailee has a slightly higher duty of care than in a bailment for mutual benefit.

Multiple Choice

Circle the Best Answer.

1. Richie Rich rented storage space from XYZ warehouse. Rich locked his antique motorcycle in a storage compartment and kept the key. When his property was destroyed by fire, he sued for damages. Under these circumstances:
   a. XYZ is liable as a bailee of the property;
   b. XYZ is not a bailee, but it may be liable under a simple negligence theory;
   c. XYZ is not liable as a bailee, and is not liable for negligence even if it breached a duty of reasonable care in protecting the property from fire;
   d. In a negligence action, Rich's contributory negligence would not be admissible as a defense.

2. A bailee will owe the greatest duty of care to protect personal property in her possession in which of the following situations?
   a. a bailment for the benefit of the bailor;
   b. a bailment for the benefit of the bailee;
   c. a bailment for mutual benefit;
   d. the bailee owes the greatest duty of care in all of these circumstances.

3. Which of the following statements concerning disclaimers of liability by bailees is not correct?
   a. A bailee may not disclaim liability for intentional wrongful acts against the property;
   b. A bailee may be liable for the negligence of its employees as to bailed property;
   c. A disclaimer of liability must be communicated to the bailor in order to be effective.
   d. All of the above statements are correct.

4. Bob rented an electric saw from "Ralph's Rental Rodeo." If Bob is injured as a result of a hidden defect in the saw, which of the following statements is correct?
   a. States do not impose strict liability in such cases because the property was rented rather than purchased;
   b. Because the bailment is a mutual benefit bailment, the bailor is only liable for disclosing defects which it knew existed;
   c. Because the bailment is a mutual benefit bailment, the bailor is probably liable for breach of a duty to exercise reasonable care;
   d. The fact that the bailor is a commercial lessor does not result in imposition of a higher standard of legal responsibility in this case.

5. Following a violent tornado, Bernie discovered his neighbor's lawnmower had landed in Bernie's living room. In these circumstances:
   a. Bernie is an involuntary bailee of the lawnmower;
   b. Bernie owes no duty of care toward the lawnmower;
   c. Bernie may use the lawnmower if he needs to;
   d. All of the above are correct.

6. Which of the following is least likely to create a bailment?
   a. You lend your lawnmower to your next-door neighbor so that he can mow his lawn.
   b. The university borrows an artist's painting to display in the college union building for one month.
   c. You park your car in the parking lot of a shopping mall, keep the keys, and have the freedom to drive the car out whenever you wish.
   d. You check your hat and coat with an attendant in a checkroom at a restaurant.

7. In order to play a practical joke on a neighbor, Herb Sly removed a dehumidifier from the neighbor's garage. With the consent of his friend, Hugh Mongous, Herb stored the dehumidifier at Hugh's home. The dehumidifier was damaged beyond repair when Hugh, who weighed 298 pounds, negligently used the dehumidifier to stand on while he was painting the ceiling of his living room. On these facts,
   a. there was no bailment relationship between Herb and Hugh, because Herb had neither title to, nor a right to possess, the dehumidifier.
   b. there was a bailment for the benefit of the bailor, making Hugh liable to Herb for the damage resulting from Hugh's failure to use reasonable care.
   c. there was a bailment for mutual benefit, making Hugh liable to Herb for the damage resulting from Hugh's failure to use reasonable care.
   d. there was a bailment for the benefit of the bailee, making Hugh strictly liable to Herb for all damage to the dehumidifier.

8. Austin Tatious took his 1990 Mercedes to Risky Car Wash and asked the owner, Doyle Risky, to wash and wax the car. Tatious said that he would pick the car up after work. Risky asked for the keys; Tatious gave them to him. A sign at the car wash read as follows: "Risky not liable for loss or damage of whatever nature." While the car was in Risky's possession, it was stolen. The car was never found. Which of the following statements is accurate?
   a. No bailment was created between Tatious and Risky.
   b. Risky is liable for the value of the car because of the strict liability imposed on bailees.
   c. Risky must reimburse Tatious for the cost of the car wash (assuming he had pre-paid), but cannot have liability beyond that because of the disclaimer in the sign.

d. Risky will be liable for the value of the car if he failed to use reasonable care to safeguard the car and if that failure contributed to the car's being stolen.

9. When a bailee is in possession of bailed property,
   a. the bailee's duty of care as to the bailed goods may be somewhat higher if the bailment is solely for the benefit of the bailor than the duty of care would be if the bailment were for mutual benefit.
   b. the exact level of the bailee's duty of care toward the goods may vary somewhat, depending upon the sort of bailment involved.
   c. the bailee must use extraordinary care in guarding against damage to the property, if the bailment is for mutual benefit.
   d. both b and c are correct.

10. In a bailment for the sole benefit of the bailee,
    a. the bailor is liable for injuries suffered by the bailee, if the injuries were caused by defects in the bailed goods that the bailor would have known about if he had conducted a suitable inspection of the goods.
    b. the bailor must use reasonable care to inspect the bailed property to be certain that it is safe before delivering it into the bailee's possession.
    c. the bailor has a duty to warn the bailee of known defects in the bailed goods.
    d. none of the above is true.

Short Essay

1. Bud asked his neighbor Ruth to take care of his bicycle while Bud was on vacation, and Ruth agreed. Ruth stored the bicycle in her garage but a thief broke a window and entered the garage and stole Bud's bike. If Bud sues Ruth for damages, what standard of care will apply? Do you think he will be successful? Explain.

2. Shirley and LaVerne went to dinner at a fine restaurant. Shirley checked her mink coat at the coat check. Above the coat check was a sign that plainly stated "Management not responsible for lost or damaged articles." After dinner, when Shirley attempted to retrieve her coat, she discovered that the coat check attendant had spilled red fingernail polish all over the coat. The management denies liability based on the disclaimer. Is the disclaimer enforceable? Discuss.

3. The Nerdleys live next door to the Nimrods. One day, a package service attempted to deliver a package for Mr. Nerdley, but the Nerdleys were not home. Because the Nerdleys have no garage, the delivery person placed the package in the Nimrods' unlocked garage along with a note asking them to deliver the package to the Nerdleys. Both Mr. and Mrs. Nimrod were at work at the time and had no knowledge that the package was being stored on their property. During the day, the Nimrods' large and ill-mannered dog tore the package to shreds and destroyed most of its contents. If the Nerdleys asked you whether they had a good case against the Nimrods, what would be your legal analysis?

4. Chad took five suits, which together were worth $1,000, to Zeke's 36-Hour Dry Cleaning, Inc. He gave the suits to a Zeke's employee and paid, in advance, the charges for having the suits cleaned. He was then given a receipt by the Zeke's employee. After he arrived at home, Chad noticed that at the bottom of the receipt, the following statement appeared: "Any liability Zeke's may have for loss of or damage to customers' clothing is limited to the value of the clothing or $200, whichever is greater." The Zeke's employee with whom Chad dealt had said nothing to that effect. Chad had no previous knowledge that Zeke's employed such a policy. When Chad returned two days later to pick up his suits, he learned to his dismay that as a result of a Zeke's employee's negligence in operating the dry cleaning equipment, Chad's suits had been reduced to a pile of ashes. Zeke's agreed to pay Chad $200, but refused to pay anything more. Is Zeke's liable for the remainder of Chad's loss? State the reasons for your answer.

CHAPTER 35
REAL PROPERTY

Outline

I. The Nature of Fixtures

    A. A fixture is personal property that is so attached to or used with real property that it legally is considered part of real property.

    B. Test is the <u>intent</u> of the parties; a court will consider express agreement by the parties, attachment and use in determining whether an item is a fixture.

    Example: <u>Morse Signal Devices of California, Inc. v. City of Los Angeles</u> (Minor components of alarm system considered fixtures for purposes of personal property tax.)

    C. Additions by tenants for business purposes remain personal property of the tenant under the <u>trade fixture</u> doctrine.

II. Rights and Interests in Real Property

    A. There are different possible ownership interests in real property. These include fee simple (basic ownership interest), life estates, leasehold estates, and easements.

    B. An easement is a right to use or enjoy the land of another person. An easement can also be established by adverse possession.

    Example: <u>Kaufer v. Beccaris</u> (Discussing requirements to establish an easement by prescription.)

    C. Other interests in land include a license and private restrictions enforceable by parties to the agreement.

    Example: <u>Schwab v. Kelton</u> (No abandonment of the building restriction scheme.)

III. Co-Ownership of Real Property

    A. Different kinds of co-ownership discussed in Chapter 33 include tenancy in common, joint tenancy, tenancy by the entirety, and community property.

    B. Condominium ownership gives the purchaser title to the unit she occupies; in a cooperative, the entire building is owned by a group of people and the buyer holds his unit under a long-term renewable lease.

IV. Acquisition of Real Property

    A. Real property may be acquired through purchase, gift, inheritance, tax sale, or adverse possession.

    B. To acquire title by adverse possession, a person must possess land that belongs to another in such a way that the claim is hostile, open, and continuous for the statutory period of time.

    Example: <u>Appalachian Regional Healthcare Inc. v. Royal Crown Bottling Company</u> (discussing the requirements for obtaining title by adverse possession.)

    C. Brokers assist sellers in the sale and purchase of real property. Generally, they are entitled to a commission if they produce a "ready, willing, and able buyer."

    Example: <u>Lyons v. Shane</u>

    D. Real property is transferred by deed. There are different kinds of deeds, but the two most common are the general warranty deed and the quitclaim deed. In the latter case, the grantor makes no warranty of title in the conveyance.

    E. Today, most states recognize an implied warranty of habitability in the sale of new homes by a builder/vendor. One issue arising in sales of new homes is whether this implied warranty may be disclaimed. Another is whether the warranty runs to subsequent purchasers.

    Example: <u>Hershey v. Rich Rosen Construction Company</u> (Implied warranty of habitability ran to subsequent purchaser.)

V. Public Controls

    A. Nuisance may be private or public. Under common law, a court may enjoin an activity which is a nuisance.

        Example: <u>Hartford Penn-Cann Service, Inc. v. Zymbolsky</u> (A less drastic remedy than injunction is appropriate in this nuisance case.)

    B. Zoning ordinances are an exercise of municipal power to regulate use of property.

    C. The constitution permits the <u>taking</u> of private property for public use, but such taking must be compensated. Particular problems arise in determining when a regulation so impacts the use or value of property that it becomes a "taking."

        Example: <u>Nollan v. California Coastal Commission</u>

Learning Objectives

1. You should understand when personal property may be treated as real property, and the tests courts use for determining when an item of personal property becomes a fixture.

2. You should understand the kinds of interests a person may acquire in real property, and the differences between those interests.

3. You should note the different ways a person may acquire an interest in real property.

4. You should be familiar with the different steps required to acquire real property by purchase.

5. You should be familiar with various controls that society places on a person's ability to use her property—for example, public nuisance laws and zoning ordinances.

6. You should know what a trade fixture is and should know the special rules governing trade fixtures.

7. You should be able to describe the different kinds of easements.

8. You should know the distinguishing features of the different forms of co-ownership of real property.

9. You should know what is necessary to make a gift of real property.

10. You should know the meaning of the term "adverse possession" and what is necessary to acquire ownership of land by adverse possession.

11. You should know the general rights and obligations of real estate brokers.

12. You should know the various ways of discovering and protecting against defects in title to real property: title opinion based on abstract of title, title insurance, and the Torrens system.

13. You should know what the implied warranty of habitability is and should know the other duties a seller of residential real estate has with respect to defects in the property.

14. You should know what eminent domain is.

Learning Hints

1. It is not always easy to distinguish an item of personal property from a fixture. Generally, courts attempt to determine the intention of the parties, and consider different factors, such as the use of the item and the degree of annexation to the property, in making this determination.

2. Ownership of property actually consists of a bundle of rights with respect to property. The most complete ownership interest is called a fee simple. A life estate is less than complete ownership because the interest terminates on the death of the holder and thus cannot be devised (that is, inherited by an heir.)

3. Some interests in real property are less than ownership interests. For example, the right to use but not possess the land of another (affirmative easement) or to prevent the other person from doing something on his land that he would otherwise have the right to do (negative easement) is called an easement. An example of a negative easement would be one in which your neighbor agreed not to build a second story on his house so that he would not block sunlight to your solar collector.

4. There are different ways to acquire real property. The most common is by sale or purchase, and the transfer of ownership in property is accomplished through a deed.

5. Today, most courts recognize an implied warranty of habitability in the sale of a new home by a builder-vendor. This is one example of the erosion of the traditional common law doctrine of "caveat emptor," ("Buyer beware.") Today, the rule "caveat venditor" ("Seller beware") is more common, especially in sales of new residential property.

6. A license is temporary and limited permission to enter upon or use another person's land. When you invite a friend over for dinner, you give that person a license to enter your land. That means she can enter the land without liability for trespass.

7. Real property is capable of a number of forms of joint ownership, some traditional and some fairly modern. Among the traditional forms of co-ownership, an important distinction between the joint tenancy and the tenancy by the entirety and the tenancy in common is that the first two include the right of survivorship. This means that the share owned by a tenant who dies automatically passes to the surviving co-tenant(s) rather than to the deceased tenant's heirs. In a tenancy in common, the deceased tenant's share is distributed to his heirs rather than to the surviving co-tenant.

8. The difference between a cooperative and a condominium is that when you own a condominium, you own your individual unit in fee simple (or some other form of ownership) and you own your fractional share of the common elements of the condominium as tenants in common with all the other unit owners, whereas if you "own" a cooperative apartment, you really own stock in a corporation that owns the building. Technically, you do not have an ownership interest in real estate, but rather an ownership interest in a corporation. The "owner" of a cooperative gets a long-term lease of the unit she occupies.

9. Adverse possession is like "squatter's rights" with certain technical requirements. It means possessing land in such a way and for such a length of time that the possessor gets better rights to the land than the title owner.

10. To remember the requirements for adverse possession, think of the acronym POACH. P=possession for the statutory period, O=open and notorious, A=actual possession, C=continuous, and H=hostile to the real owner's title. Add to that the requirement in some states that the adverse possessor pay taxes on the land. By the way, "hostile" does not mean that there must be malice toward the owner. It means that the adverse possessor's use contradicts the owner's ownership. In other words, the adverse possessor is using the property without the owner's permission or after the owner has ordered the adverse possessor to leave.

True-False

In the blank provided, put "T" if the statement is True or "F" if the statement is False.

_____ 1. A trade fixture is an item of personal property that is considered real property because it is used in a business.

_____ 2. A temporary right to use another person's land for a limited and specific purpose is called a license.

_____ 3. Private restrictions on the use of real property are unenforceable.

_____ 4. If two people hold property as joint tenants, and one dies, the other party automatically owns the property.

_____ 5. Generally, if a real estate broker produces a ready, willing, and able seller, the broker is entitled to a sales commission even though the sale of the property did not go through.

_____ 6. The federal Real Estate Settlement Procedures Act (RESPA) requires that a buyer receive advance disclosure of the settlement costs that will be incurred in a settlement.

_____ 7. If taxes assessed on real property are not paid, they become a lien on the property that has priority over all other claims.

_____ 8. The U.S. Constitution allows the government to take property from private persons without paying for it, so long as the government uses the property for the public's benefit.

_____ 9. Title to property can be obtained through adverse possession by using the property for 20 years with the permission of the owner.

_____ 10. A seller of real property may be liable to the buyer for misrepresentation if he knowingly conceals some material fact relating to the quality of the property.

Multiple Choice

Circle the Best Answer.

1. A person who has a legal right to drive across another person's property most likely possesses:
   a. a fee simple estate;
   b. a life estate;
   c. an affirmative easement;
   d. a tenancy at will.

2. H and W are married and own property "as husband and wife." In many states, this form of co-ownership is called:
   a. tenancy in common;
   b. joint tenancy;
   c. tenancy by the entirety;
   d. tenancy in partnership.

3. Bill purchased a townhouse unit in a building containing other units. Bill has title to his unit and owns the common facilities as a tenant in common with other owners. This form of ownership is called:
   a. a condominium;
   b. a tenancy at will;
   c. a cooperative;
   d. none of the above.

4. Which of the following is not a requirement for obtaining title to real property by adverse possession?
   a. The possession must be open and visible;
   b. The possession must be hostile;
   c. The owner must have actual knowledge of the adverse possession;
   d. The possession must continue for a statutory period of time.

5. X sold real property to Y by "quitclaim deed." Under these circumstances:
   a. X has conveyed what ever title he had at the time he executed the deed;
   b. If X has no title, Y may not sue him under the quitclaim deed;
   c. X makes no warranties in conveying title;
   d. All of the above are correct.

6. An easement can be created by:
   a. adverse possession.
   b. necessity.
   c. purchase.
   d. all of the above.

7. Brendan told his dearest friend, Phillip, that he wanted to give Phillip his house. Two years later, Brendan died without ever having given Phillip a properly executed deed to the property. Phillip:
   a. now owns the property in fee simple.
   b. now has a life estate in the property.
   c. now has an easement on the property.
   d. has no ownership interest in the property.

8. Nash owned a commercial building which he leased for three years to Stickells for use as a restaurant. During the first winter of Stickells' lease, Stickells complained to Nash that the heating was inadequate. Stickells purchased an electric space heater, which he installed by bolting it to the ceiling. In the second year of Stickell's lease, Nash sold the building to Hopkins. In the third year of the lease Stickells decided to seek a larger space and elected not to renew the lease. A dispute arose between Stickells and Hopkins over the space heater. Which of the following is true?
   a. The space heater is a trade fixture, which Stickells is free to remove at any time, even after the leasehold has ended.
   b. The space heater is a fixture in the building which belongs to Hopkins by virtue of his purchase of the building from Nash.

c. The space heater is a trade fixture, which Stickells may remove so long as he does so before his leasehold terminates.

d. Stickells may remove the space heater and take it with him even if removing the heater would damage the building.

9. Which of the following is (are) true of the law concerning condominiums?

a. The owner of a condominium takes title to his unit individually and has title to common areas as a tenant in common with the owners of the other units.

b. The terms "cooperative apartments" and "condominiums" are different names for the same thing.

c. Condominium ownership means that a person owns stock in a corporation that owns a building and which permits the stockholders to rent units.

d. Two of the above are true.

10. Jim agrees orally to buy a parcel of real property known as "Blackacre" from John. John subsequently refuses to deed Blackacre to Jim. Jim sues for breach of contract. What result?

a. Jim wins because oral agreements are valid contracts.

b. Jim loses because the agreement was not in writing.

c. Jim wins because he intended to enter a contract.

d. None of the above.

Short Essay

1. The Smiths purchased a new home from JC Construction in "Sunnyvale" subdivision. They signed a standard purchase agreement which stated in "boilerplate language" that there were no warranties, express or implied, in the sale of the home. One year after they moved into the home, the basement began to flood as a result of substantial defects in the construction of the basement. It will cost the Smiths $10,000 to repair the basement. Is JC liable for that cost? Why or why not?

2. Roberts purchased a house from Bell. The contract of sale provided that Roberts was purchasing "all fixtures and permanent improvements" but did not specify which items were to be considered fixtures. When Roberts took possession of the house he was distressed to find that Bell had taken with him a large window air conditioning unit that had been installed and bolted in the living room window when Roberts viewed the home before making his offer. No mention of the air conditioner was made by either party at that time. Bell refuses to give the air conditioner to Roberts, and Roberts files suit against him in small claims court. Who wins, and why?

3. Maude moved onto a piece of property owned by Harold. She lived on the property as if it were hers for forty years, and even paid taxes on the property. Harold didn't like this, but he didn't do anything about it until after forty years, when he went to see her and ordered her off the property. Must she leave? Why or why not?

CHAPTER 36
LANDLORD AND TENANT

Outline

I. Nature of Leases

A. A lease is a contract for possession of property. A tenancy may be fixed, periodic, at will, or at sufferance.

Example: Melson v. Cook (When a lease is for an indefinite term, it is a tenancy at will.)

II. Rights and Duties of the Landlord

A. The landlord impliedly warrants that the tenant will have quiet possession; in most states, a residential lease also carries with it an implied warranty of quality or habitability.

Example: Solow v. Wellner (conditions in the apartment building constituted a breach of the implied warranty of habitability).

B. Housing Codes and other legislation may impose other duties on the owner of leased property.

C. A number of courts impose on landlords the duty to reasonable care in maintenance of leased property.

Example: Howard v. Horn (landlord not liable for injuries sustained by tenant where landlord was unaware of latent defect in premises causing injury to tenant.)

D. A landlord may be liable for negligently failing to protect a tenant from the criminal acts of third parties.

Example: Morgan v. 253 East Delaware Condominium Association (holding Association had not breached a duty to plaintiff who was attacked by gunman.)

III. Rights and Duties of Tenant

A. Tenant has the right of possession and duty to pay rent and not to commit waste.

B. The lease may generally be assigned; a subleasing occurs when the tenant transfers less than complete rights to possession to a third person.

IV. Termination

A. Constructive eviction occurs when a tenant vacates after giving the landlord a reasonable opportunity to cure a defect and he fails to do so.

Example: Gottdiener v. Mailhot

B. Today, many states require the landlord to attempt to mitigate damages if the tenant abandons the premises.

Example: Reid v. Mutual of Omoha Insurance Co.

Learning Objectives

1. You should understand when leases have to be in writing and when oral leases are effective.
2. You should understand the rights, duties, and liabilities of the landlord and tenant as a result of a lease agreement.
3. You should know the meaning of the implied warranty of habitability.
4. You should understand the circumstances under which a landlord may be liable for failing to protect tenants against criminal conduct of third parties.
5. You should understand the difference between an assignment and sublease.
6. You should know the difference between a periodic tenancy, a tenancy at will, a lease for a definite period of time, and a tenancy at sufferance.
7. You should know when a landlord is liable for injuries caused by dangerous conditions on the leased premises.
8. You should know the different ways in which a tenancy can be terminated.

195

Learning Hints

1. A lease is a contract, and thus is subject to the requirements of the statute of frauds. Generally, an oral short-term lease is enforceable.

2. As in the case of contract law in general, there has been an erosion of the traditional doctrine of "caveat emptor" in landlord-tenant disputes. Today, many courts and legislation protect tenants by imposing upon the landlord an implied warranty of habitability in leased premises. Further, many states regulate by statute provisions for lease termination and other lease provisions.

3. In leasing real property, a landlord and tenant will often agree that the tenancy is to last for a specified period of time. For example, a student signs a lease for nine months on an apartment in a college town. The lease will automatically expire at the end of the period specified in the lease. Also, neither party, acting alone, can terminate the tenancy during the lease period.

4. In other situations, the parties do not specify how long the tenancy will last, but they agree that the tenant is to pay rent at regular intervals of time: monthly, weekly, or even yearly. These are called <u>periodic tenancies</u>. They continue until one of the parties gives advance notice to the other party that he or she wants to terminate the tenancy.

5. If the landlord agrees that someone else may live on or otherwise possess the landlord's property but the parties do not have an understanding about how long the tenancy will last or at what intervals the tenant is to pay rent, a <u>tenancy at will</u> exists. For example, Father permits his son and his son's wife to live in the apartment above Father's garage. Such tenancies last until they are terminated by either party. Most states require the landlord to give some advance notice of termination.

6. A tenant who has retained possession of the leased property after his lease has expired is called a <u>tenant at sufferance</u>. For example, George signs a 9-month lease on an apartment until May 10. George does not move out on May 10, however, and stays in possession. George's landlord has two choices now. He can treat George as a trespasser and evict him, or he can accept rent from George and treat George as a periodic tenant or a tenant for a specified term. In the period between the time George holds over and the time the landlord takes action (either rejecting or accepting George as a continued tenant), George is a tenant at sufferance.

7. Although a tenant may often assign or sublease leased property, assignment or subleasing does not permit the tenant to escape his legal obligations under the lease. If the subtenant does not pay rent during the period covered by the lease, for example, the landlord can go after the tenant for payment.

8. A tenant who abandons leased property (moves out before the lease term has elapsed) breaches his legal obligations to the landlord. The tenant cannot escape the obligation to pay rent merely by moving out. However, many states now place the obligation on the landlord to make reasonable efforts to re-rent the property.

9. Constructive eviction is a doctrine that developed in the days when tenants had no legal protection with respect to the quality and safety of the leased property. If the leased premises (generally residential premises) became uninhabitable because of the landlord's act or failure to act, the tenant could move out without incurring liability for rent for the remainder of the lease term. The idea was that he had been <u>forced</u> to leave by the conditon of the property. For the doctrine to apply, there must be some <u>serious</u> defect in the property such as rodent infestation or inoperative plumbing—a Jacuzzi on the blink would not be enough. After giving the landlord a reasonable opportunity to fix the problem, the tenant must <u>move out</u> within a reasonable time in order to claim constructive eviction.

True-False

In the blank provided, put "T" if the statement is True or "F" if the statement is False.

_____ 1. If the parties to a lease do not specific a definite term, this is a tenancy at sufferance.

_____ 2. Because he owns the property, a landlord retains the legal right to possess the premises during the term of a lease.

_____ 3. A landlord may be liable for the criminal acts of third parties if the landlord's negligence substantially increased the likelihood of that criminal act.

_____ 4. Generally, a lease agreement cannot be assigned, but the tenant may usually sublease the premises.

_____ 5. Most states today recognize an implied warranty of habitability in a residential lease.

_____ 6. A lease can be created without an explicit agreement between landlord and tenant as to how long the lease will last.

_____ 7. A landlord is liable for all injuries suffered on leased premises.

_____ 8. Constructive eviction occurs when a landlord ejects a tenant for nonpayment of rent.

_____ 9. The tenants are responsible for keeping the common areas in repair and in a safe condition for tenants and visitors to the property.

_____ 10. The implied warranty of habitability means that the tenant has the obligation to return the property to the landlord at the end of the lease in the same condition in which it was rented, normal wear and tear excepted.

Multiple Choice

Circle the best answer.

1. In cases where there is no explicit agreement between the landlord and tenant as to how long the lease will last, the court will treat the tenancy as:
   a. periodic tenancy;
   b. tenancy at sufferance;
   c. tenancy at term;
   d. none of the above.

2. Rex rented an apartment from Mr. Landlord for one year, with rent of $500 payable on the first of each month. Two months after renting the apartment, Rex discovered the apartment was infested with rats. He notified Landlord, who has done nothing to correct the problem. What are Rex's rights in this situation?
   a. In most states, Rex may sue Mr. Landlord for damages for breach of implied warranty of habitability;
   b. In most states, Rex may move out and treat the lease as terminated under the doctrine of "constructive eviction";
   c. In most states, either remedy is available to Rex in this situation.
   d. In most states, Rex must continue to pay rent, but he may be entitled to a "set-off" for damages under these circumstances.

3. Which of the following statements concerning a tenant's rights is <u>not</u> correct?
   a. The tenant generally has the right to exclusive possession of the leased premises;
   b. The tenant generally has the right of quiet enjoyment of the property during the term of the lease;
   c. The tenant generally has the right to sublease the premises;
   d. The tenant generally may avoid liability to persons injured on the premises over which the tenant has control.

4. Ronnie visited his friend Steve at Steve's apartment. Ronnie slipped and fell on the stairway leading to Steve's apartment because the stair was broken. Under these circumstances:
   a. The landlord is liable to Ronnie for damages because the landlord is strictly liable for defects in common areas of the building, even if he had no actual or constructive knowledge of the defect;
   b. The landlord is liable to Ronnie for damages in negligence if Ronnie can prove the landlord breached a duty of reasonable care to persons like Ronnie;
   c. The landlord is not liable to Ronnie because Ronnie was not a tenant;

d. The landlord is not liable to Ronnie because the accident occurred in a common area.

5. If a landlord or tenant transfers all of her rights under a lease to a third person, this is called:
   a. a novation;
   b. a sublease;
   c. an assignment;
   d. constructive eviction.

6. Which of the following, if any, would create a tenancy at sufferance?
   a. Landlord leases property to Tenant on a month-to-month lease.
   b. Landlord orally leases property to Tenant for eight months.
   c. Tenant stays in possession of an apartment after her one year written lease has expired.
   d. None of the above would create a tenancy at sufferance.

7. Which of the following would create a periodic tenancy?
   a. A lease for a period of 9 months, from August 1, 1990 to May 1, 1991
   b. Rental of a furnished apartment on a weekly basis
   c. Tenant stays in possession after the expiration of a one-year lease and Landlord elects to treat him as a trespasser
   d. Father allows his son and daughter-in-law to live in a cabin on his land indefinitely, without any agreement about paying rent or the length of time they will remain there

8. Which of the following is true with respect to the implied warranty of habitability?
   a. It exists in every lease of real property for commercial use.
   b. It guarantees that property leased for residential use will be in habitable condition.
   c. If the warranty is breached, the tenant may be able to obtain a rent abatement reflecting the decreased value of the property.
   d. Two of the above are true concerning this warranty.

9. Which of the following is necessary for constructive eviction?
   a. The premises become uninhabitable because of acts of the landlord.
   b. The tenant must give the landlord a reasonable opportunity to correct the defect.
   c. The tenant must vacate the premises within a reasonable amount of time.
   d. All of the above are necessary for constructive eviction.

10. Which of the following is a true statement about the legal responsibilities of landlords?
    a. A landlord is liable for all injuries that occur on the property he has leased to a tenant for residential purposes.
    b. A landlord cannot be liable for trespass for entering leased premises without the tenant's permission because he owns the property.
    c. In many states, a landlord who leases residential property impliedly warrants that the leased premises will be fit for human habitation.
    d. Landlords have not yet been found liable for failure to protect their tenants from the foreseeable criminal conduct of third persons.

Short Essay

1. Delbert rented an apartment for one year from Property Plus and paid a $250 deposit. At the end of the year, Property Plus refused to return the deposit because it maintained that Delbert ruined the wallpaper in the apartment by printing the words "Delbert loves Millie" all over the walls. If it will cost $500 to replace the wallpaper, may Property Plus apply the security deposit to this cost?

2. Don rents an apartment near campus. He pays his rent on the first of each month. He and the landlord have no explicit agreement about the duration of the lease. What kind of tenancy is this? If Don wanted to move out, what would he have to do?

3. Adam leased an apartment from Phillips for a period of one year beginning April 1, 1983. On April 30, 1983, Phillips entered the apartment using a passkey while Adam was at work so that he could see whether Adam was keeping the apartment clean. Adam came home from work and found Phillips in the apartment. Does Adam have a suit against Phillips? Why or why not?

4. Horizon Properties, Inc. owns a large apartment complex in University City. On January 31, University City experienced heavy snowfall. Horizon cleared most of its walks, driveways and parking lots, but neglected to take any action to remove ice and snow in the parking lot and driveway leading to one of its buildings, X building. That night, Mrs. Smith happened to visit her son, who lives in X building. As she exited her car, which was parked in the lot outside of X building, she slipped on an icy patch that was hidden beneath the snow and fell, injuring her back severely. Mrs. Smith files suit against Horizon. Discuss Horizon's possible liability.

CHAPTER 37
ESTATES AND TRUSTS

Outline

I. Disposition of Property by Will

  A. A will disposes only of property belonging to the testator at his/her death.

    1. Requires capacity and legal age.

    2. Must meet statutory requirements. Some states recognize handwritten (holographic wills). *Example:* Estate of Rowell v. Hollingsworth (handwritten will not valid because not executed by testator.

    3. An oral will (nuncupative) will is only valid in some states and only under limited circumstances.

    4. There are limitations on disposition by will under state statutes.

    5. All wills are revocable.

    6. A living will is a document in which a person states his intention to forgo extraordinary medical procedures. In some cases, a person may protect that interest by giving another a durable power of attorney. *Example:* Cruzan v. Director, Missouri Department of Health

II. Intestate Succession

  A. Intestate succession (disposition of property in cases where person dies without a will) differs from state to state. *Example:* Hotarek v. Benson (example of application of intestate succession law in Connecticut.)

    1. Under a "uniform simultaneous death act" property of husband and wife may be distributed as if each survived the other.

III. Administration of Estates

  A. The will must be proven (probated), and an administrator of the estate. *Example:* In Re Estate of Pina (Executor removed for breach of fiduciary duty.)

  B. A trust is a legal relationship in which a person holds property for the use and benefit of another. *Example:* Green v. Green (Trust accounts were valid Totten trusts.)

  C. The recognizes resulting trusts, based on persumed intention of donor. A constructive trusts arises by operation of law. *Example:* Gaines v. Roberts (placing son's name on mother's savings account created a constructive trust.)

  D. The trustee owes a fiduciary duty to the beneficiaries of a trust.

Learning Objectives

    1. You should understand the laws governing distribution of assets upon death of a person who has no will.

    2. You should know the requirements for executing a valid will.

    3. You should recognize the most common grounds for challenging wills.

    4. You should know under what circumstances oral wills or documents not formally complying with requirements of a valid will will be recognized.

    5. You should know the limitations on disposition of property by will.

    6. You should know the meaning of the word "intestate."

    7. You should be able to describe the typical steps in the administration of estates.

    8. You should know what a trust is and what the requirements are for the creation of an express trust.

    9. You should know how resulting trusts and constructive trusts are created.

    10. You should know what a spendthrift clause is, as well as the situations in which creditors or assignees may have claims to such a trust.

Learning Hints

1. The laws governing intestate succession and requirements for a valid will are state laws. Consequently, these requirements will vary from state to state.

2. It is extremely important that a person comply strictly with the requirements for executing a valid will. If a person fails to so comply, the will may be invalid. In such cases, the laws of intestate succession of the state may apply, and the person's wishes for disposition of his/her property upon death may not be met.

3. Persons who are of legal age and have sufficient mental capacity may dictate who will get their property at their deaths by making a will that complies with all the formalities required by state law.

4. If a person dies without a valid will in effect, she is said to have died intestate. The property she owned at death will be divided according to the standards provided by her state's law of intestate succession (also called "descent and distribution"). An administrator will be appointed at administer the estate.

5. Generally, wills must be in writing, signed and acknowledged by the testator, and witnessed by a certain number of disinterested witnesses. Some, but not all, states recognize the validity of less formal wills, known as nuncupative and holographic wills. A nuncupative will is an oral will, whereas a holographic will is written and signed in the testator's own handwriting, but is not properly witnessed and not in compliance with other statutory requirements.

6. A person who makes a will is called a "testator" or "testatrix." Testators and testatrixes are free to revoke wills, even up to the moment immediately preceding death. A person who is named as a beneficiary in a will has no interest in the testator's/testatrix's property before the testator's/testatrix's death, because the testator/testatrix could always change his/her mind and revoke or change the will.

7. If the testator/testatrix wants to modify the will without executing an entirely new will, he/she can execute a codicil amending some provision of the will. The codicil must meet the same formal requirements mandated by statute for the execution of wills.

8. Many states now recognize, by statute, "living wills" or "durable power of attorney" by which a person may indicate his/her wish that extreme unusual medical care not be administered if that person is close to death and otherwise not able to make those wishes known.

9. A trust exists when a person who has some legal right to property also has the obligation to hold the property for the benefit of someone else. For example, Robert deeds property to a bank as trustee of a trust created to benefit Robert's wife, children, and grandchildren. The bank has legal title to the property, but also has the legal obligation to administer the property for the beneficiaries named by Robert.

10. The "settlor" or "donor" is the person who creates the trust. (In the example above, Robert is the settlor.) A trust that goes into effect during the settlor's life is called an inter vivos trust. A trust that is established by a will and goes into effect on the settlor's death is called a testamentary trust. Express trusts are usually quite detailed about the identity of the beneficiaries, the duties of the trustee, and the terms of the trust.

11. In some situations, trusts can be imposed by law to effectuate the intent of the settlor (resulting trust) or to avoid injustice (constructive trust).

True-False

In the blank provided, put "T" if the statement is True or "F" if the statement is False.

_____ 1. A holographic will is not enforceable in any state.

_____ 2. A nuncupative will is not enforceable in any state.

_____ 3. All wills are revocable at the option of the maker.

_____ 4. A living will is a will made by a person on behalf of someone else.

_____ 5. Under a "uniform simultaneous death act" property of husband and wife may be distributed as if each survived the other.

_____ 6. If the testator's will met all of the legal requirements, a later codicil to the will does not have to satisfy the legal requirements for a will.

_____ 7. When the powers of the trustee are not spelled out in the trust agreement, the trustee has all powers reasonably necessary to carry out the trust.

_____ 8. Generally, the beneficiary of a trust may assign, to another person, the beneficiary's right to the principal or income of a trust.

_____ 9. Publication of a will is a declaration by the testator, at the time of signing the will, that the instrument being signed is in fact his will.

_____ 10. Once a will has been made, it cannot be revoked unless the maker, by means of a special clause in the will, expressly reserves the right to revoke the will.

Multiple Choice

Circle the best answer.

1. Which of the following laws is most important in determining the requirements for a valid will?
   a. The "due process clause" of the U.S. Constitution;
   b. Federal estate tax laws;
   c. State statutory laws;
   d. Common law.

2. A will which is not executed with the formalities of law is:
   a. void;
   b. voidable;
   c. valid so long as all beneficiaries consent;
   d. illegal.

3. Which of the following statements concerning a holographic will is not correct?
   a. Holographic wills are wills that are entirely written and signed by the testator;
   b. Holographic wills are recognized in only about half of the states;
   c. In some states, a typed holographic will is valid if signed by the testator;
   d. All of the above statements are correct.

4. A person who makes a trust is called:
   a. The settlor;
   b. The trustee;
   c. The executor;
   d. The beneficiary.

5. If a person is given an interest or life estate in one third of her husband's property, regardless of the provisions of the husband's will, this interest:
   a. Is invalid;
   b. Is valid in most states as a "dower right";
   c. Is only valid if the husband did not revoke this right in his will;
   d. Is only valid if contained in a nuncupative will.

6. Justine executed a valid will that named her boyfriend, Boris, as her sole beneficiary. She became angry at Boris, so she destroyed the will. She informed her attorney that she no longer wanted the will to be operative. The next day, before she had a chance to make a new will, Justine died. Which of the following is an accurate statement?
   a. Justine had no right to revoke her will unless she specifically reserved the right in the will.
   b. Because Justine did not make a new will, Boris, as the beneficiary of the only will she had made, will still get Justine's property.
   c. Boris had present rights to Justine's property before she died, because he was the beneficiary of her will.
   d. Justine died intestate.

7. Gus died, leaving a valid will that bequeathed his home to his friend, Ingrid. The home was secured by large mortgage in favor of Solvent National Bank. Which of the following is an accurate statement?
   a. Because Ingrid's claim to the home is superior to the bank's, the bank can never foreclose on the mortgage, even if payments are not made.
   b. The home cannot pass to Ingrid, because it is subject to a mortgage.
   c. Ingrid will own the home subject to the mortgage.
   d. Ingrid will own the home free of the mortgage.

8. Which of the following is/are necessary for a valid will?
   a. The testator must give property to persons within his immediate family.
   b. The testator must be in perfect mental health.
   c. The testator must be of legal age.
   d. Both b and c.

9. Which of the following is/are accurate with regard to an administrator of an estate?
   a. She is responsible for filing estate tax returns.
   b. She may be required to post a bond to ensure that he or she will properly and faithfully perform his duties.
   c. She may be a relative of the deceased person.
   d. All of the above.

10. Under the intestacy laws of most states,
    a. the decedent's adopted children are not treated the same as nonadopted children, for purposes of intestate succession.
    b. the decedent's half-brothers and half-sisters are treated differently from brothers and sisters related by whole blood, for purposes of intestate succession.
    c. children born out-of-wedlock are not necessarily treated the same way, for purposes of intestate succession, as children born during wedlock, if the decedent was the father of the children born out-of-wedlock.
    d. all of the above are correct.

Short Essay

1. Peter wrote a statement of how he wished his property to be distributed upon his death. It was entirely written in his handwriting, but was not signed. He placed it in an envelop on which he had written "My last will," and put it in his safe deposit box at the bank. When Peter died, the document was found in the safe deposit box. Is the document just described a valid will? Explain.

2. Sandy went to a lawyer's office and asked to have a formal written will prepared. She signed the will in the presence of two witnesses as required by law. Later that year, Sandy married Bob. Sandy forgot to change the will to recognize her new marital status. If Sandy dies without changing her will, is Bob entitled to any property belonging to Sandy?

3. Lola, an elderly woman, knew that she was dying. She took out a pen and paper and scrawled these words: "I give all my property to my brother, Lamoine." She signed the paper, using her full legal name. Is this an enforceable will? Explain your answer.

4. Erma lived in Cedar Rapids, Iowa. She owned a home and a substantial amount of personal property, all located in Cedar Rapids. She also owned a vacation cabin in Montana and an oceanfront condominium in California. Erma died suddenly without leaving a will. What will happen to her property?

CHAPTER 38
INSURANCE

Outline

I.Life Insurance Contracts

A. The insurance contract is a valued policy (requiring the insurer to pay a fixed amount.)

    1. A Whole life policy creates a cash surrender value if the policy is terminated.

    2. Term life creates no cash surrender value.

B. Fire Insurance contracts are indemnity contracts, although some may be valued policies. Most fire insurance policies are open polices.

    1. A coinsurance clause may limit the insured's right to recovery. A pro rata clause determines the liability of a particular insurer in proportion to the total amount of insurance covering property.

II.Contract Law Applicable in Insurance Cases

A. General contract rules of offer and acceptance apply; a binder is an agreement for temporary insurance pending the insurer's decision to accept or reject the risk.

    Example: Independent Fire Insurance Company v. Lea (Submission of insurance application was an offer not accepted by insurance company.)

B. Misrepresentation by insured or agent may be basis for rescission or damages.

C. Warranties are express terms in the policy that operate as conditions on which insurer liability is based. Most states require life insurance contracts be in writing. Ambiguities are generally construed against the insurer.

    Example: State Farm Fire and Casualty Company v. Paulson (contract provision insuring "water damage" was not ambiguous.)

D. Life insurance policies are assignable because the identity of the insured remains unchanged; fire insurance policies are generally not assignable.

E. A person must have an insurable interest in the life or property being insured.

    Example: Herman v. Provident Mutual Life Insurance Company (former partners of insured may recover insurance proceeds.)

    Example: Crowell v. Delafield Farmers Mutual Fire Insurance Company (To have an insurance interest in a fire insurance policy, the party must suffer a loss of property interest that is substantial and real.)

III.Other provisions

A. Notice and Proof of loss are required to recover benefits under an insurance policy. Under the right of subrogation, an insurer obtains all of the insurer's rights to pursue legal remedies against a third party who may have caused the loss.

B. Cancellation of Lapse of the policy will terminate the policy.

    Example: Barney v. League Life Insurance Company (Insurance company had duty to provide insured with notice of past due premium or cancellation.)

Learning Objectives

    1. You should understand the contractual rules governing the creation of the insurance relationship.

    2. You should be able to explain how courts assess the liability of insurers.

    3. You should understand when and how an insurer may cancel an insurance policy.

    4. You should know the basic differences between whole life and term insurance policies, and should become aware of the advantages and disadvantages of each type of policy.

    5. You should understand what an indemnity contract is.

    6. You should become familiar with the types of fire insurance policies and should know the differences among them.

7. You should understand what a coinsurance clause is and how it may be applied.

8. You should understand how a pro rata clause in a fire insurance policy may operate when the insured has in force more than one insurance policy that would apply to a loss.

9. You should be aware of what constitutes acceptance in the context of an insurance contract, and should comprehend why courts might construe insurance contracts in ways other than was specifically intended by the insurer.

10. You should understand how courts will handle misrepresentations by the insured, and should be able to distinguish between representations and warranties.

11. You should be aware of the insurance contracts that can be assigned to a third party, as well as why those contracts are assignable and why others are not assignable.

12. You should understand what constitutes an insurable interest and should know why the insurable interest is a necessary element of an insurance contract.

Learning Hints

1. An insurance policy is essentially a contract between the company and the insured. As such, common law rules of contract law, such as offer and acceptance, and rules of contract interpretation apply. However, many states have adopted statutes regulating insurance contracts, and these may override common law rules.

2. A life insurance contract differs from a fire or casualty insurance policy in that the insurer is bound to pay a certain sum when the death of the insured occurs. Unlike most fire insurance policies, a life insurance policy is a valued policy with a face value.

3. Most fire insurance policies are open polices, permitting the insured to recover the fair market value of the property at the time it was destroyed, up to the policy limit.

4. It is important to remember that insurance law, like contract law in general, is in a state of flux. Its rules are taking on more and more of an equitable flavor in situations involving one party's possessing superior knowledge or bargaining strength. This is especially the case in most insurance contracts, because the insurer dominates the contracting process.

5. Insurance contracts are of special interest to the courts because of the weak bargaining position of the beneficiary after the insured's death or disability. The courts are aware of the fact that many insureds trust the company's representative as their agent, when in reality what resembles an arm's length transaction may have taken place. Further, some litigation has involved alleged strategies on the part of insurance companies to intentionally refuse payment on meritorious claims. Such strategies assume that the beneficiary will settle for a lesser amount or drop the claim entirely. In cases in which such strategies on the part of the insurer have been proved, the courts have been willing to award punitive damages against the insurer for its bad faith conduct.

6. Note that the law's treatment of misrepresentation by the insured resembles ordinary contract law's treatment of misrepresentation by a party to a contract. However, in some cases the law will not allow the insurer to avoid the contract, despite the misrepresentation. There is a presumption that the insurer would be willing to insure the insured person in most instances; the only question is the amount of the premium. Therefore, instead of rescinding a contract that has been in effect for some time, it is considered more reasonable to reform the agreement in a manner that avoids rewarding the insured for the misrepresentation. To totally invalidate the contract might reward insurance companies that ignore misrepresentations until the time when the benefits are due.

7. The policy of construing ambiguities in insurance contracts against the author (which in most cases will be the insurer) is consistent with the approach generally taken in contract law. It avoids rewarding a party for having confused the other contracting party.

8. The requirement of an insurable interest may be important in protecting against widespread destruction and even murder. The persons who qualify as possessing the interest fit within a group whose members should be less likely to injure the person or property that is the subject of the insurance contract. In a sense, those with an insurable interest merely are being compensated for the loss they have suffered. Persons who do not have an insurable interest might

have fewer reservations about doing away with the insured person or about damaging the insured property.

True-False

In the blank provided, put "T" if the statement is True or "F" if the statement is False.

_____ 1. If an insured makes regular premium payments on either a term life insurance policy or a whole life policy, she is entitled to a cash surrender value if she terminates the policy prior to death.

_____ 2. If a fire insurance policy is a valued policy, the insured may only recover the fair market value of the property destroyed, not the face amount of the policy.

_____ 3. A pro rata clause limits the amount recoverable upon death of the insured in life insurance contracts.

_____ 4. A binder is an agreement for temporary insurance pending the insurer's decision to accept or reject the risk.

_____ 5. Warranties are express terms in the policy that operate as conditions on which insurer liability is based.

_____ 6. Generally, both the insurer and the insured must have capacity to contract in order for an insurance agreement to be enforceable.

_____ 7. A fire that begins as a friendly fire may become a hostile fire, for purposes of determining whether a loss is covered by a fire insurance policy.

_____ 8. A typical misstatement of age clause will operate to invalidate the policy if the insured misrepresented his or her age in the application for insurance.

_____ 9. Coinsurance clauses apply only in cases of partial losses.

_____ 10. Without an insurable interest on the part of the purchaser, an insurance contract would be an illegal wagering contract.

Multiple Choice

Circle the best answer.

1. Stan offered to enter a fire insurance contract by completing an application provided by the insurer's agent and submitting it and the premium to the insurer. The application provided that submission of the application and premium to the agent constituted a "binder." If a fire occurs following submission of the application but prior to delivery of the policy to Stan, what result and why?
   a. There is no effective policy because there was no insurable interest in this case;
   b. There is no effective policy because there was no acceptance of the offer until delivery of the policy to the insured;
   c. There is an effective policy because a binder is an agreement for temporary insurance pending the insurer's decision to accept or reject the risk;
   d. There is an effective policy because submission of the application to the agent generally constitutes acceptance in insurance cases.

2. If an insured makes fraudulent statements about his medical history on an application for life insurance:
   a. This constitutes misrepresentation which makes the contract void;
   b. This constitutes misrepresentation which makes the contract voidable by the insurer;
   c. This constitutes undue influence which makes the contract voidable the insurer;
   d. This constitutes duress which makes the contract void.

3. An oral contract for life insurance:
   a. Is generally enforceable;
   b. Is unenforceable under the laws of most states;
   c. Is enforceable if the parties agree;
   d. Is illegal.

4. Which of the following statements concerning "insurable interests" in real property is <u>not</u> correct?
   a. Those who have an insurable interest in property must have that interest at the time the loss occurs.
   b. A life tenant or secured creditor of the property has an insurable interest in the property;
   c. The extent of a person's insurable interest in property is limited to the value of his or her interest in the property;
   d. All of the above are correct statements.

5. The right of subrogation:
   a. Arises when a party has a right to terminate or cancel a policy under its express terms;
   b. Arises when the policy expires upon default of the insured;
   c. Permits an insurer to pursue legal remedies against a third party for damages caused to the insured property;
   d. None of the above states are correct.

6. Which of the the following persons has/have an insurable interest in the life of Nerdley, a married person who has two children?
   a. Nerdley's business partners
   b. The bank to which Nerdley owes $23,000
   c. Nerdley's mother
   d. All of the above

7. Of the following statements concerning assignability of insurance contracts, which is/are correct?
   a. If the insured sells the property that is the subject of a fire insurance policy, the insurer automatically will be bound to insure the same property in favor of the purchaser, if the insured assigns the policy to the purchaser as part of the purchase agreement.
   b. Once a fire loss has occurred, the insured cannot assign to someone else the insured's right to receive payment under the fire insurance policy.
   c. If the beneficiary of a life insurance policy has been designated irrevocably, the policy ordinarily cannot be assigned without the beneficiary's consent.
   d. Both b and c.

8. At the time she purchased her home, Gabrielle purchased (from Heartless Insurance Co.) a fire insurance policy covering the home. The policy was a valued policy with a face amount of $113,000—the amount Gabrielle had paid for the property. Two years after the policy went into effect, the home was totally destroyed by fire. At the time of the fire, Gabrielle's home had a fair market value of $99,000, because of declining property values in the area where it was located. On these facts, how much must Heartless pay Gabrielle?
   a. $99,000
   b. $99,000 plus interest at the legal rate
   c. $113,000
   d. $106,000

9. Incontestability clauses
   a. generally bar the insurer from contesting its liability on the policy because of misrepresentations of the insured, if the policy has been in force for a specified period of time.
   b. bar the issuer of a life insurance policy from refusing to pay out the amount of the policy on the basis that the party who took out the policy on the insured person's life did so with the intent of murdering the insured person.
   c. prevent the insurer from arguing, once the policy has been in force for a specified period of time, that there was no insurable interest on the part of the person who took out the policy.
   d. do all of the above.

10. When the insured has purchased fire insurance policies from more than one insurer and there is a loss as to which each policy would appear to provide full coverage if it were the only policy in force at the pertinent time,
   a. the insured is entitled to collect the full amount of the loss from each insurer, assuming that the insured is current on the premiums for each policy.
   b. the loss must be paid by the insurer whose policy went into effect first.
   c. the loss must be paid by the insurer whose policy went into effect last.

d. the loss will be apportioned among the insurers in accordance with the relationships the respective amounts of the individual policies bear to the total amount of insurance on the property.

Short Essay

1. Bill purchased a fire insurance policy from ABC Insurance. The insurance policy covered his home and office and was a valued policy of $100,000. The office was destroyed by fire when a disgruntled employee, Ted, deliberately set fire to a waste paper basket. The fair market value of the office was $85,000. Under the fire insurance policy, what will Bill be entitled to recover? What rights and remedies, if any, does ABC have in this case?

2. Overbearing Realty, Inc. purchased a fire insurance policy from Tight Insurance Co. The policy covered the building that housed the Overbearing business. The policy contained a 70 percent coinsurance clause. Although the building had a fair market value of $500,000, Overbearing purchased a policy with a face amount of $300,000. A fire caused $77,000 worth of damage to the building. How much must Tight pay Overbearing on Overbearing's claim under the policy? Explain how you arrived at your answer.

3. Mona purchased a fire insurance policy to cover her home. The property was located in an area of the city in which land values had been in a state of gradual decline. After the policy had been in effect for a period of several years, a chimney fire totally gutted the property. The open policy Mona had purchased stated that it would cover all hostile fires. The policy had a face amount of $83,000, which was the original purchase price of the home. When Mona notified the insurer of the fire, the company denied liability, claiming that the fire was not hostile. Further, the insurer stated that if it was liable on the policy, it would be liable for only $67,000, which was the fair market value of the property as of the time of the loss. Discuss the insurer's responsibilities under the facts just stated.

4. Stan saw an ad in the newspaper concerning a new life insurance policy being written by a major insurance company. The ad indicated that no person, regardless of age or physical condition, would be denied the insurance. Stan sent for further information. The insurance company responded by mailing him a packet of information that included an application form. He filled out the application and mailed it to the company along with his first year's premium, which he calculated from a table included in the material he had received. Stan received no reply from the insurer. Finally, three months after he had mailed the completed application, Stan was killed in an automobile accident. Upon receiving notification of his death from the beneficiary Stan had designated on his application form, the insurance company replied that Stan did not have a policy in effect. The insurer indicated that the premium Stan had forwarded was not sufficient, because Stan apparently had misread the table. The company forwarded a check to Stan's estate to cover the amount of the incorrect premium that he had originally sent to the company. Should the beneficiary be entitled to recover on the policy? Why or why not?

CHAPTER 39
NEGOTIABLE INSTRUMENTS

Outline

I. Nature of Negotiable Instruments

  A. Commercial paper is a contract for payment of money: promises to pay and orders to pay are two basic types.

    1. Notes and certificates of deposit are promises to pay; drafts and checks are orders to pay.

  B. Articles 3 and r of the Uniform Commercial Code govern the law of commercial paper.

  C. A negotiable instrument is a special kind of paper because it can be accepted in place of money.

II. Kinds of Commercial Paper

  A. A promissory note is primarily a credit instrument

  B. A certificate of deposit is a promise to pay money.

  C. A draft is an order to pay money and a check is a draft payable on demand. The drawee of a check is always a bank.

III. Benefits of Negotiable Instruments.

  A. If the holder of a negotiable instrument is a holder in due course, he takes the instrument free of all defenses and claims to the instrument except those that concern its validity.

  B. Formal Requirements for Negotiability.

    1. There are different requirements for a note or check to be negotiable. If the instrument does not satisfy these formal requirements, it is nonnegotiable.

  C. The instrument must be in writing and signed.

  D. It must contain and unconditional promise or order, and must be to pay a sum certain in money.

    Example: Carnegie Bank v. Shalleck (Note containing a variable interest rate meets the Code's "sum certain" requirement.)

  E. The instrument must be payable on demand or at a specified time, and be payable to order or bearer.

  F. If the amount on a check differs from the amount written in words, the UCC retains the rule that words control the figures.

    Example: Yates v. Commercial Bank & Trust Co. (Words control figures under the Code).

Learning Objectives

  1. You should understand the special qualities and benefits of negotiable instruments.

  2. You should be familiar with the basic types of commercial paper.

  3. You should know the formal requirements that must be met for instruments to qualify as negotiable instruments.

  4. You should understand what happens when you receive a check in which there is a conflict between the amount set forth in figures and the one written out in words.

  5. You should be able to distinguish the rights of an assignee of an ordinary contract from the rights of a holder in due course of a negotiable instrument.

  6. You should know what promises or orders are conditional and, therefore, make a contract to pay money in which they are included nonnegotiable.

  7. You should know the effect of acceleration and extension clauses on the negotiability of a contract to pay money.

  8. You should know what is order language and what is bearer language, and whether an instrument contains order or bearer language.

Learning Hints

1. There are two basic kinds of commercial paper: promises to pay money and orders to pay money.

2. The promissory note and certificate of deposit are promises to pay money; drafts and checks are orders to pay money.

3. The significance of a negotiable instrument is that an assignee can obtain greater rights than the assignor. If a person qualifies as a "holder in due course," he takes the instrument free of all defenses and claims to the instrument except those that concern its validity.

4. Try to think of all the situations in which you have used negotiable instruments. You may have purchased groceries with a check, and you may have purchased a stereo on credit by signing a promissory note. You may have signed a promissory note with a bank to obtain money to pay your college tuition. You may have received a payroll check from an employer.

5. Note why negotiable instruments were used in these situations. They were used as substitutes for money because you did not have enough money or because it was too inconvenient or risky to carry large amounts of money with you. These examples explain why the law created negotiable instruments: to create a substitute for money. Negotiable instruments are not perfect substitutes for money, but they are as much like money as is consistent with our society's notions of fairness.

6. A promissory note is a two-party instrument. The maker promises to pay the payee.

7. A draft is a three-party instrument. The drawer orders the drawee to pay the payee.

8. A negotiable instrument is merely a special type of contract to pay money, one which a HDC may enforce despite any personal defenses the maker or drawer may have against the payee. Preventing a maker or drawer from asserting personal defenses to payment of a negotiable instrument works a hardship on the maker or drawer. Therefore, the law will not impose such a hardship unless the maker or drawer has issued a contract that is a negotiable instrument.

9. For a contract to be a negotiable instrument, it must meet each of the six requirements listed in the book. If any one of the requirements is not satisfied, the contract is not a negotiable instrument and assignees take the contract subject to all defenses. If all the elements of negotiability are met, the contract is a negotiable instrument and a HDC can hold it and enforce it free of personal defenses.

10. Note that a draft is an order to pay. That is, the drawer orders or commands the drawee to pay the payee. The order (or command) is the word "Pay" in "Pay to the order of Joe." This is the first of three uses of the word "order" in negotiable instrument law. To avoid confusion it is important that you understand these three uses of the word "order." The other two uses of the word "order" are discussed in Learning Hints 12 and 13 below.

11. If a promise or order to pay is conditional, the contract to pay money is nonnegotiable even if the condition is fulfilled. For example, a note says "Pay only if John delivers the goods." Even after John delivers the goods, the note is nonnegotiable. Why? Because the note is not like money. The note will not be easily transferred, because the condition included in the note requires a person to determine whether the condition has been satisfied. Such a determination is unnecessary when one takes money.

12. Likewise, if one cannot calculate the value of the instrument by merely looking at the instrument, it is not like money and is therefore not negotiable. However, a statement requiring the payment of attorney fees or the calculation of interest "at the judgment rate" does not make the instrument nonnegotiable.

13. For the instrument to be payable on demand or at a definite time, one must be able, by looking only at the instrument itself, to determine the latest date payment must be made or can be demanded. "On demand" means that payment must be made when a holder demands payment from the maker or drawee.
Acceleration clauses never prevent an instrument from being negotiable. Such clauses merely allow the holder to be paid earlier. One can calculate the latest date payment must be made. Extension clauses will destroy the negotiability of an instrument if the payment date is extended at the option of the maker for an unlimited time. This is because the maker may choose never to pay the instrument. However, any extension at the option of a holder will not

destroy negotiability, because the effect is the same as having it payable on demand. Giving a drawer any option to extend the payment date will make the draft nonnegotiable.

Extension clauses that delay payment for a definite time upon the maker's option do not destroy negotiability. This is because even if the extension is made, one can calculate the latest date that the instrument must be paid.

14. Every negotiable instrument must have order or bearer language. Order language usually includes the word "order," such as "Pay to the order of Joe." The order language is the word "order." This is the second use of the word "order" in negotiable instrument law. The first was discussed above in Learning Hint 8. Bearer language usually includes the word "bearer."

15. The third use of the word "order" in negotiable instrument law is its use in distinguishing order paper from bearer paper. This third use of the word order is discussed in Learning Hint 3 of Chapter 40.

16. When we decide a contract is a negotiable instrument, we mean that a HDC may enforce it free of personal defenses. A negotiable instrument is not necessarily enforceable or collectible. Real defenses may be asserted by the maker or drawer against a HDC, or the maker or drawer may have no money to pay the HDC.

When we decide a contract is nonnegotiable, we mean that it is an ordinary contract, that it cannot be held by a HDC, and that all defenses are good against the person seeking payment or performance. "Nonnegotiable" does not mean there is no contract. It does not mean that the contract is unenforceable or uncollectible. It means that the instrument is merely an ordinary contract.

True-False

In the blank provided, put "T" if the statement is True or "F" if the statement is False.

_____ 1. A note is an example of a promise to pay money.

_____ 2. The drawee of a check is always a bank.

_____ 3. Even if a person acquiring a negotiable instrument does not pay value for it, he becomes a holder in due course if he acquired it in good faith without notice of claims or defenses against it.

_____ 4. A non-negotiable note is not valid or collectible.

_____ 5. Under the UCC, words control figures if there is a conflict between numbers and written words on a check.

_____ 6. Negotiable instruments are used only by merchants.

_____ 7. A check is the most common type of draft.

_____ 8. A note is a two-party instrument.

_____ 9. A check may be payable at a specified future date.

_____ 10. A postdated check may be a negotiable instrument.

Multiple Choice

Circle the best answer.

1. Which of the following is <u>not</u> a requirement for negotiability of a promissory note or certificate of deposit?
   a. It must be in writing and signed by the maker;
   b. It must contain an unconditional promise to pay a sum certain in money;
   c. It must state in clear unambiguous language "This instrument is a negotiable instrument";
   d. All of the above are required for negotiability.

2. Which of the following statements concerning the requirement of a writing is <u>not</u> correct?
   a. The instrument has been signed if the maker or drawer puts a symbol on it regardless of whether that person intends to validate the signature;
   b. The writing does not have to be on any particular material, and could be made on waste paper;
   c. an instrument that is handwritten, typed, or printed is considered to be in writing;
   d. All of the above statements are correct.

3. If a note provides, "I promise to pay to the order of Kit Carson $1000 if he gives me his horse," (signed) Doc Holliday, dated Jan 1, 1993.
   a. This is a negotiable instrument;
   b. This is not negotiable because the sum is not certain;
   c. This is not negotiable because the promise is not unconditional;
   d. This is not negotiable because the note is not payable at a specified time.

4. If an instrument otherwise negotiable contains the statement: "Pay to the Order of Marcia Marshall"
   a. The instrument is order paper;
   b. the instrument is bearer paper;
   c. The instrument is nonnegotiable by the addition of the "order" language;
   d. none of the above statements is correct.

5. If a negotiable instrument contains the following: "The sum of ten hundred two dollars....$10,002.00":
   a. the instrument is not negotiable because it does not contain a sum certain;
   b. the amount of the check is $1,002.00 because that is the lower amount;
   c. the amount of the check is $1,002.00 because the words control the figures;
   d. the amount of the check is $10,002.00 because the figures control the words.

6. The person who writes a note is called:
   a. a maker.
   b. a drawer.
   c. a drawee.
   d. an issuer.

7. Which of the following is a consequence of negotiability of an instrument?
   a. Payment is assured.
   b. The instrument is valid.
   c. Subsequent transferees may become holders in due course.
   d. All of the above

8. Stella Starr is nicknamed "Kitty" by her friends. Which of the following is a valid signature for her for purposes of negotiability?
   a. Stella Starr
   b. S. Starr
   c. Kitty
   d. All of the above

9. A draft is:
   a. a three-party instrument.
   b. an I.0.U.
   c. a promise to pay money.
   d. a type of check.

10. Jim Smith gave Freda Field a piece of paper with the following writing on it. "I promise to pay $50 to Freda. /Signed/ Jim."
    a. This is a negotiable instrument.
    b. This is not a negotiable instrument because there is no payment date.
    c. This is not a negotiable instrument because it is not payable to order or to bearer.
    d. This is not a negotiable instrument because Jim's signature is invalid.

Short Essay
   1. Larry gave Jean a check. Larry wrote on the back of the check that by signing it, Jean acknowledged full satisfaction of any claim she had against Larry. Is this note negotiable? Explain.

2. Roy and Dale are cowboys. Dale agrees to sell 50 cattle to Roy. Roy gives Dale a note promising "to pay to the order of Dale $25,000 on June 1, 1983, unless Dale fails to deliver the cattle." Dale signs the note. Is this a negotiable instrument?

3. Lester sold Tammy a new car. Tammy did not have enough money to buy the car, so she gave Lester a note promising "to pay to the order of Lester $3,500 and to give to Lester or bearer my 1956 Volkswagen." Is this a negotiable instrument?

4. Hugh hired Carl's Home Repair Service to put a new roof on his house. Hugh and Carl's signed a contract for the reroofing. Hugh gave Carl's a note for the price of the reroofing. At the bottom of the note Hugh wrote, "subject to reroofing contract." Is this a negotiable instrument?

5. Is the following instrument negotiable?
April 16, 1983
To Jackson Creek Corp.
On April 1, 1984 pay to the order of Frampton Corp. $3000
Three Thousand and 00/100————————————————Dollars
Debit construction account for the amount of the bill.
Pay on November 15, 1983, if Frampton Corp. has completed subcontractor work by that date.
/Signed/ Anna Johnson

6. Is the following a negotiable instrument?

November 24, 1983

On November 30, 1983, I, Amanda Jones, promise to pay to the order of Pioneer Seed Company the sum of $12,000 out of the proceeds of the sale of my 1983 cotton crop. Payable at a later date to be determined by me if I cannot sell my crop.

/Signed/ Amanda Jones

CHAPTER 40
NEGOTIATION AND HOLDER IN DUE COURSE

Outline

I. Nature of Negotiation

A. Negotiation is the transfer of an instrument to a holder

B. Formal requirements are simple: If order paper, it can be negotiated by delivery after necessary indorsements; if bearer paper, no indorsement is necessary.

C. Indorsement is necessary to negotiate an instrument payable to the order of someone; second, indorsement generally makes a person liable on the instrument.

D. Kinds of Indorsement: special, blank, restrictive, and qualified

Example: Lehigh Presbytery v. Merchants Bancorp, Inc. (Bank is legally bound to follow restrictive indorsements.)

II. Holder in Due Course

A. A holder in due course (HDC) takes a negotiable instrument free of all personal defenses. A holder must have possession of an instrument issued to a him or her or indorsed and delivered to him or her.

B. A HDC must have a complete chain of authorized indorsements.

Example: La Junta State Bank v. Travis (Restriction on check "for deposit" meant that bank was obligated to handle it consistent with that restriction.)

C. A HDC must give value and take it in good faith.

In Re Nusor Parkhill v. Nusor (illustrating the factors a court may consider in determining whether a person should be on notice of possible adverse claims or defenses to an instrument.)
Example: Smith v. Olympic Bank (Bank not a HDC because it had notice of an adverse claim to the instrument.)

D. Any person who can trace his title to an instrument back to a holder in due course receives the same rights as the holder in due course under the "shelter provision" of the UCC.

III. Rights of a Holder in Due Course

A. HDC is not subject to any personal defenses; however, the HDC is subject to real defenses (defenses which go to the validity of the instrument.)

Example: Federal Deposit Insurance Corp. v. Culver

1. Some states have limited this rule, particularly as it affects consumers. The FTC also protects consumers by requiring a notice in the note or contract making the potential holder subject to all claims and defenses of the consumer.
Example: Ford Motor Credit Company v. Morgan (Consumers could assert personal defenses or claims against the Credit Company which financed the purchase of their automobile.)

Learning Objectives

1. You should understand the requirements for negotiating a check to someone else.

2. You should understand the circumstances under which a lost nstrument may be cashed by another.

3. You should understand the different kinds of indorsements and their effect.

4. You should know the requirements for a holder in due course.

5. You should understand the defenses that may be asserted against the holder in due course, and those defenses that may not be asserted against the holder in due course.

6. You should know how a person becomes a holder of an instrument.

7. You should know how to negotiate order and bearer paper.

8. You should know what is meant by irregular paper.

9. You should be able to distinguish real defenses from personal defenses.

10. You should know what changes in the holder in due course doctrine have been made by the FTC and the states.

Learning Hints

1. Negotiation is the transfer of an instrument in such a way that the person who receives it becomes a holder in due course. A holder acquires certain benefits in that he takes the instrument free of personal defenses that could have been asserted against the maker.

2. An indorsement is necessary in order for there to be a negotiation of an instrument payable to the order of someone else.

3. There are different kinds of indorsements with different effects. A special indorsement is the signature of the indorser along with words indicating to whom or to whose order the instrument is payable. An indorser who merely signs his name and does not specify to whom the instrument is payable is payable to the bearer.

5. Do not confuse the terms "negotiable" and "negotiation." Negotiable means that the instrument meets the six requirements of negotiability and can therefore be held by a holder in due course. Negotiation is the process by which a person becomes a holder of a negotiable instrument. Contracts become negotiable by complying with the requirements for negotiability. Negotiable instruments are negotiated by the process of negotiation.

6. Order paper is the third use of the word "order" in negotiable instrument law. (Refer back to Learning Hints 8 and 12 in Chapter 39.) Since order paper is payable to a specific person, that person's indorsement and delivery are necessary for negotiation; that is, necessary to make the next possessor of the instrument a holder. Bearer paper is negotiated by delivery alone.

7. Note that an instrument may be issued as order paper (to a specific person), be indorsed in blank (to no specific person), and thereby become bearer paper. It can then be indorsed specially (to a specific person) and thereby become order paper again. Therefore, it is possible that one instrument at different times in its life can be bearer paper or order paper. Note also that the word "order" need not appear in the special indorsement. "Pay to Alex" is a special indorsement and the instrument is order paper. It is order paper because it is payable to Alex.

8. Note that a restrictive indorsement, even though conditional, does not destroy the negotiability of an instrument. An indorsement never affects the negotiability of an instrument.

9. A qualified indorsement is designated as such because it qualifies the indorser's liability by eliminating his liability as an indorser and limiting his liability as a transferor.

10. You must understand completely what a holder in due course (HDC) is and why the law allows such a person to exist. The HDC is the most important person in all of negotiable instrument law. By allowing a HDC to take a negotiable instrument free of personal defenses, the law has created a substitute for money.
    Negotiable instruments are like money in that money is perfectly negotiable. If you receive money from Todd that Todd received from Jane, you do not need to worry about whether Todd cheated Jane when Jane gave the money to Todd. In fact, even if Todd stole the money from Jane, you receive clear ownership (title) to the money despite any defense Jane may have against Todd. This is the key aspect of money: it is transferred free of any defenses. This aspect is essential. Would a person be as willing to accept money if she took it subject to defenses a third party (Jane) had against her transferor (Todd)? Of course not.
    A negotiable instrument is as perfect a substitute for money as is consistent with our society's notions of fairness. If a person is a HDC, he takes the instrument free of personal defenses, but not real defenses. Our law states, in effect, that it is unfair for a person to be prevented from asserting a real defense against anyone. Real defenses are too important. Personal defenses are not so important, and the person who has the personal defense can always assert it against the person who harmed him. He merely cannot assert the personal defense against a third person not involved in creating the defense who is a HDC.
    Because the law allows a HDC to take a negotiable instrument free of personal defenses, people are more willing to accept negotiable instruments in commercial transactions. Less cash need be used. The result is safer commercial transactions and lower cost of credit, merchandise, and services.

11. Here is a handy formula to remember what value is: Value = consideration + antecedent claims - executory promises In contract law you learned that past consideration is not consideration. In negotiable instrument law, past consideration is value. If someone has owed you $5000 for two years and gives you a $5000 check today, you have given value for the check, because of your antecedent claim against the drawer.

    Executory promises, while consideration, are not value. Executory promises are unperformed promises. If you merely promise to do something, you have not given value. Once you perform the promise you have given value.

12. A person is a HDC only to the extent she has given the value she has agreed to give. So if you promise to give $5000 for a $6000 note but have given only $2500 so far, you are a HDC for only $2500. The other $2500 is an executory promise, not value. However, once you have given all the value you have agreed to give, you are HDC for the entire amount of the note. So if you gave $5000 cash for the $6000 note, you would be a HDC for $6000, unless the discount was too large to establish your good faith.

13. Note that all five requirements of a HDC must be met. If a person obtains notice of any defense (real or personal) before she becomes a holder or before she pays value, she is not a HDC. For example, you forget to indorse a note payable to your order and sell it to me for $1000 cash. A week later I discover a defense against the note. The next day you indorse the note. I am not a HDC, because I had notice of the defense before I became a holder.

14. To help you understand the distinction between real and personal defenses, think of the importance of the real defenses. These defenses exist because people are incapable of protecting themselves due to age or mental condition. It would be unfair to allow anyone to enforce a negotiable instrument against a minor, a drunk, or any insane person. Personal defenses are not so important, because the person could have better protected himself, but the young, the drunk, the insane, the unduly influenced, and those not given an opportunity to see what they are signing (as in fraud in the essence) cannot protect themselves.

15. Many consumers sign negotiable notes without knowing the effect of what they are signing: that they cannot assert their personal defenses against a HDC. This ignorance explains why most states and the FTC have eliminated the HDC doctrine in most consumer transactions.

True-False

In the blank provided, put "T" if the statement is True or "F" if the statement is False.

_____ 1. Indorsement generally makes a person liable on an instrument.

_____ 2. A restrictive indorsement is one where the indorser disclaims liability on the instrument if the maker or drawer defaults.

_____ 3. A forged indorsement is ineffective and prevents a person from becoming a holder in due course.

_____ 4. Any person who can trace his title to an instrument back to a holder in due course receives the same rights as the holder in due course under the "shelter provision" of the UCC.

_____ 5. A holder in due course take the instrument free of any defense arising from the minority or incapacity of the maker.

_____ 6. A note payable "to the order of Jonathan" is order paper.

_____ 7. A note with the payee's name misspelled must be indorsed with the payee's signature misspelled.

_____ 8. A customer's bank may supply a customer's missing indorsement on a check the customer deposits at the bank.

_____ 9. Bearer paper cannot be converted into order paper.

_____ 10. An indorsement may be blank and restrictive at the same time.

Multiple Choice

Circle the best answer.

1. If a check drawn "Pay to the Order of Steve Smith" is indorsed "Steve Smith" by Steve, what kind of indorsement is this?
   a. restrictive;
   b. qualified;
   c. blank
   d. special.

2. John Meyers was issued a check payable to the order of "John Myers." John may indorse the check:
   a. "John Meyers"
   b. "John Myers"
   c. Either (a) or (b);
   d. Neither, because this check is not negotiable.

3. A check drawn "Pay to the Order of Ted Pennington" was indorsed by Ted "pay to the Order of Sandy Pennington." Which of the following statements concerning this indorsement is correct?
   a. This indorsement is a restrictive indorsement;
   b. This indorsement is a special indorsement;
   c. This instrument remains order paper;
   d. Both (c) and (d) are correct.

4. If a person takes a negotiable instrument that is overdue:
   a. He is a holder in due course so long as he had no actual notice of the fact the instrument was overdue;
   b. He is a holder in due course so long as the instrument has not been dishonored;
   c. Both (a) and (b) are correct;
   d. He is not a holder in due course.

5. Which of the following is a real defense which may be asserted against a holder in due course?
   a. Discharge of the debt by the maker in bankruptcy;
   b. Failure of consideration;
   c. Breach of warranty in contract;
   d. All the above are real defenses.

6. Which of the following requires Joe's indorsement before negotiation may occur?
   a. A check payable "to order of bearer"
   b. A check payable "to Joe or bearer"
   c. A note payable "to order of Joe"
   d. All of the above require Joe's indorsement before negotiation may occur.

7. Which of the following is bearer paper?
   a. A check payable "to order of bearer"
   b. A check payable "to the order of Jim"
   c. A check indorsed "to Jim"
   d. A check payable "to Jim's order"

8. Which of the following is a special indorsement?
   a. "Without recourse. /Signed/ Jody"
   b. "Pay only if John delivers my stereo. /Signed/ Jody"
   c. "Pay to John. /Signed/ Jody"
   d. "/Signed/ Jody"

9. Which of the following is a restrictive indorsement?
   a. "Pay only if my shipment arrives."
   b. "Pay to any bank."
   c. "For deposit only."
   d. All of the above are restrictive indorsements.

10. Shana purchases a $7,000 used truck to use in her lawn care business. She gives her seller, Truck Sales, Inc., a negotiable note for $7,000 due in six months. Truck Sales sells the note to Talbott Factors, a holder in due course. Talbott agrees to pay Truck Sales $6,800 for the note, $800 in cash immediately and $6000 in four months. In one month the truck proves to be defective and Truck Sales refuses to repair it, despite the existence of an express warranty covering the defect. Shana tells Talbott that she will refuse to pay the note when it is due because of the unrepaired defect. Nevertheless, three months later Talbott pays Truck Sales the remaining $6000. On the note's due date Talbott demands payment, but Shana refuses. Which of the following is correct?
   a. Talbott cannot collect anything from Shana.
   b. Talbott can collect only $800 from Shana.
   c. Talbott can collect only $6,800 from Shana.
   d. Talbott can collect $7,000 from Shana.

Short Essay

1. Is the following writing a negotiable instrument? Decide and discuss.
   "Santa Rosa, California, May 1, 1993.
   I promise to pay to the order of Grace Hamilton the sum of $1,000 out of the proceeds of the sale of my 1986 Camarro.
   "/Signed/ Fronzel Pool."

2. Is this instrument negotiable? Explain.
   Louisville, Kentucky 6/1/92
   Six months after date I promise to pay to George Standley $300
   Three Hundred dollars
   Values received with interest at 6% after date.
   /Signed/ Ron Pool

3. Rob is a holder of a negotiable note with the following indorsements on its back: "Pay to Pam. /Signed/ Kerry"
   "/Signed/ Pam"
   Rob sells and delivers the note to Stan. Rob does not indorse the note. Has Rob negotiated the note to Stan?

4. Judy buys a properly indorsed negotiable note from Mark. Its face value is $1,000, due August 1, 1990. Judy buys the note for $700 on July 15, 1990. Is Judy a holder in due course?

5. When Mel bought a new typewriter for his business from Paul's Typewriter Sales, Inc., he gave Paul a check for $700. A month after the sale, the typewriter broke, and Paul refused to repair it. Henry, a holder in due course, has the check now. Mel has refused to pay Henry on the check, citing the defective typewriter as a defense. Can Henry collect from Mel?

6. Identify the following indorsements on a check originally payable to the order of Patrick. What are the effects of the indorsements?
"Without recourse. /Signed/ Patrick"
"Pay to Angela. /Signed/ Calvin"
"Pay only if Emily gives me her stereo. /Signed/ Angela"

CHAPTER 41
LIABILITY OF PARTIES

Outline

I. Contractual Liability

  A. Contractual liability on the instrument depends on the capacity in which the person signed. The terms of the contract are provided by law (UCC Article 3).

    1. A person may be primarily or secondarily liable.

    2. At the time a check or draft is written, no party is primarily liable. If the drawee bank certifies the check, it becomes primarily liable.

    3. The drawer of a check is secondarily liable unless she disclaims liability by drawing "without recourse."
    Example: First American Bank of Virginia v. Litchfield Company of South Carolina, Inc.

    4. A person who indorses a negotiable instrument is usually secondarily liable unless the indorsement is qualified.

  B. No person is contractually liable unless his signature appears on the instrument. The instrument can be signed by an authorized agent.

    Example: Valley National Bank v. Cook (Corporate treasurer was not personally liable on corporate checks she signed. NOTE: The court followed the minority rule in this case.)

  C. If a person's signature was unauthorized, the person is not bound.

    Example: Johnstown Manufacturing, Inc. v. Haynes

II. Contractual Liability in Operation

  A. The instrument must be presented. A note is presented to the maker when due. A check or draft is presented to the drawee.

  B. A person who transfers an instrument or presents it may incur liability on the basis of certain implied warranties called transferor's warranties and presentment warranties.

    Example: Garmac Grain Co. Inc. v. Boatmen's Bank & Trust Co. of Kansas City (Holding that a depository bank breached certain transfer warranties.)

  C. Other liability rules include common law negligence rules.

    Example: American Federal Bank, FSB v. Parker (A subsequent holder in due course may enforce an incomplete instrument as completed.)

  D. The Code establishes special rules for checks made payable to impostors and fictitious persons.

    Example: Merrill, Lynch, Pierce, Fenner & Smith, Inc. v. NCNB National Bank of North Carolina (Under the fictitious payee rule, the bank was relieved of liability for paying the check with a forged indorsement.)

  E. A person may become liable for conversion.

    Example: Stockton v. Gristedes Supermarkets, Inc.

III. Discharge of Neogitable Instruments

  A. Payment by the person primarily liable discharges all parties to the instrument.

  B. Discharge may also occur through cancellation or by alteration of the instrument.

    Example: Peterson v. Crown Financial Corp.

Learning Objectives

  1. You should understand the liability a person assumes when she indorses a check;

  2. You should understand the warranties made when a check is presented to a drawee bank for payment;

  3. You should understand the liability of a drawee bank to its customer if the check contains a forged signature;

4. You should know whether the drawee bank bears the loss if an imposter presented a check for payment;

5. You should understand the affect of materially altering a negotiable instrument.

6. You should be familiar with the ways that liability on a negotiable instrument may be discharged.

7. You should be able to distinguish primary liability from secondary liability.

8. You should know the effects of the certification of a check.

9. You should be able to determine the contractual liability of an accommodation party.

10. You should know what is meant by presentment, dishonor, and notice of dishonor.

11. You should know who makes which transferor's warranties, and to whom.

12. You should know who makes which presentment warranties, and to whom.

13. You should know the effect of a maker or drawer's negligent execution of a negotiable instrument.

14. You should be familiar with fictitious payees. You should know the special rule concerning forged indorsements when an imposter or fictitious payee exists.

15. You should know the extent of a drawee bank's liability for conversion when it pays a check with a forged indorsement.

Learning Hints

1. This chapter examines how a person becomes liable on a negotiable instrument and the nature of the liability incurred. Basically, liability may be based on the fact a person signed the instrument. In such cases, liability depends on the capacity in which the person signed the instrument.

2. Liability on a negotiable instrument can also be based on breach of warranty, improper payment, negligence, or conversion.

3. When a person signs a negotiable instrument, he generally becomes contractually liable on the instrument. That liability may be primary or secondary.

4. Note that the only way a person may become contractually liable on a negotiable instrument is to sign it. This explains why the forgery of your signature on a check does not make you liable, but makes the forger liable. Of course, your agent may sign for you and make you liable.

5. To aid your understanding of contractual liability, address each type of negotiable instrument separately. For example, a note has a maker, payee, indorsers, and perhaps accommodation parties. What is the contractual liability of each? An uncertified check has a drawer, drawee, payee, indorsers, and perhaps accommodation parties. What is the contractual liability of each? Do the same for certified checks, drafts, and accepted drafts.

6. Note that "accommodation" means help. This is why an accommodation maker has the liability of a maker, because the accommodation maker has helped the maker obtain credit.
Note that an accommodation maker is primarily liable. This means that the holder of the note can obtain payment from the accommodation maker before trying to obtain payment from the maker. As far as the holder is concerned, the accommodation maker is like any other maker. That a person is an accommodation maker is important only between the accommodation maker and the maker. If the accommodation maker pays, she can recover the payment from the maker.
The above analysis also applies to accommodation drawers and indorsers, except that in these situations, the liability is secondary.

7. Note that no one is primarily liable on an uncertified check or unaccepted draft. The drawee has no contractual liability, because the drawee has not signed the check or draft. The drawer has only secondary liability, because the drawer promises to pay only if the drawee does not pay.

8. Transferor's warranties arise because a person transfers an instrument. A person may have no contractual liability, yet have a transferor's warranty liability. A person may have both contractual liability and transferor's liability.

9. Transferor's warranties are based upon reasonable expectations. A person who receives a negotiable instrument expects five things to be true, because he expects to receive something very much like money. These five things are the five transferor's warranties. You must memorize them.

10. To help you understand transferor's warranties, make a chart setting forth the transferor's warranties made by the nonindorsing transferor, the indorser, and the qualified indorser, and to whom each of these parties makes transferor's warranties.

11. Presentment warranties are also based upon the reasonable expectations of the person who pays for the instrument.

12. It is easier to understand how contractual and warranty liability operate if you make a diagram of the transfer of the instrument. These schematics help you to see who held the instrument, and in what order. You can put notes next to each person's name indicating whether, for instance, he was a thief and whether he signed the instrument. Schematics also illustrate how the instrument eventually returns to its issuer.

13. The liability rules regarding negligence, impostors, and fictitious payees make good sense. The negligence rule places liability on the person who was negligent. Good examples of negligence are leaving unfilled spaces on the payee and amount lines of a check. A dishonest person could easily and skillfully raise the amount of the check and change the payee's name. The imposter rule places liability on the maker or drawer who failed to ascertain the true identity of the person to whom the instrument was written. It is fairer to impose liability on the drawer who dealt with the imposter than to impose it upon a holder who never met the imposter. The fictitious payee rule places liability upon the employer who should have better supervised the employee who made out the payroll checks to the fictitious payee. It is fairer to impose liability on the employer whose unsupervised employee did the wrong than to impose it upon a holder who was not aware of the fiction.

True-False

In the blank provided, put "T" if the statement is True or "F" if the statement is False.

_____ 1. If a bank certifies a check, it becomes primarily liable for paying the check.

_____ 2. If a drawer of a check adds the words "without recourse" under her signature as drawer, this effectively disclaims her liability on the instrument.

_____ 3. If a negotiable instrument is signed in the name of the organization followed by the name and office of an authorized individual, both the organization and the officer who signed the instrument will be bound.

_____ 4. If a note is dishonored, the holder can seek payment from any persons who indorsed the note before the holder took it.

_____ 5. A drawee bank has a contractual obligation to the payee to pay the check when it is presented.

_____ 6. Only a maker may be liable on a note.

_____ 7. No one is primarily liable on a check at the time it is written.

_____ 8. An indorser of a check is secondarily liable on the check.

_____ 9. An accommodation maker is secondarily liable.

_____ 10. Notice of dishonor may be made orally or in writing to hold a drawer liable on a draft.

Multiple Choice

Circle the best answer.

1. If a drawee bank refuses to pay a check:
   a. It is primarily liable to the presenter;
   b. It is secondarily liable to the presenter;
   c. It may be liable to the drawer for wrongfully refusing payment if there are funds in the account;
   d. All of the above are correct.

2. Which of the following statements concerning the contract of an accommodation party is correct?
   a. An accommodation party is a person who indorses an instrument with a qualified indorsement;
   b. An accommodation party is not contractually liable on a negotiable instrument;
   c. The contractual liability of an accommodation party depends on the capacity in which the party signs the instrument.
   d. An accommodation party may be contractually liable even though his signature does not appear on the instrument.

3. Sam stole Diane's checkbook and signed Diane's name to several checks. He cashed the checks at Bob's Big Boy. The bank has refused to pay the checks. From whom (if anyone) can Bob recover his loss?
   a. Bob cannot recover damages in this case because Sam's signature was unauthorized.
   b. Bob can only recover damages from Sam, who is liable on the check because he did sign it, even though he did not use his own name;
   c. Bob can recover damages from Sam and/or Diane, because Bob had no actual or constructive notice that the checkbook was stolen;
   d. Bob can recover damages from Sam, Diane, or the Bank, because Bob was a holder in due course.

4. Which of the following is not a transferor's warranty?
   a. That the person has good title to the instrument;
   b. That the signatures on the instrument are genuine;
   c. That no party to the instrument has a valid defense against the person transferring it;
   d. All of the above are transferor's warranties.

5. Normally, a check that has a forged indorsement of the payee:
   a. May not be charged to the drawer's checking account;
   b. May be charged to the drawer's checking account if there are sufficient funds in the account to cover the check;
   c. Must be charged to the drawer's account;
   d. None of the above statements is correct.

6. A signature on the back of a note is presumed to be by:
   a. a drawer.
   b. a maker.
   c. an indorser.
   d. an acceptor.

7. How should Abby Alston, president of Astra Corporation, sign checks on behalf of Astra, if her signature as an agent is required on the checks?
   a. Astra Corporation by Abby Alston, President
   b. Abby Alston, President
   c. Astra Corporation
   d. Abby Alston

8. Before an indorser may be held liable on a note:
   a. the note must be presented for payment.
   b. payment on the note must be refused.
   c. the indorser must receive notice of dishonor.
   d. all of the above must occur.

9. Hank holds a note issued by PC Corporation. The note has been indorsed and transferred by First Bank. SC Corporation is an accommodation maker. When Hank presents the note for payment, PC dishonors it. Hank gives appropriate notice to all parties. Who is contractually liable on the note to Frank?
   a. PC Corp., SC Corp., and First Bank
   b. PC Corp. and SC Corp.
   c. PC Corp. and First Bank
   d. SC Corp. and First Bank

10. In number 7, who has made transferor's warranties?
    a. SC Corporation
    b. First Bank
    c. SC Corp. and First Bank
    d. PC Corp., SC Corp., and First Bank

Short Essay

1. Amy issued his negotiable promissory note payable to the order of Buddy. Buddy indorsed the note, "Without recourse, Buddy," and negotiated it to Second Bank. At the time Buddy negotiated the note, Amy was insolvent but this was unknown to Buddy. The note was not paid. Is Buddy liable to the Bank on his indorsement?

2. Rose is the president of ABC Beverage and has the authority to sign negotiable instruments for ABC. Rose common signs the checks "Rose Red" on the signature line below where "ABC" is printed. Supply Company takes a check signed as above by Rose. The drawee bank dishonored the check because there were insufficient funds in the account. If Supply Company sues ABC and Rose to make the check good, is Rose personally liable to Supply Company?

3. Hank is a holder of a note originally issued by Diane to Paula. Diane is a minor. Paula has indorsed the note. Diane refuses to pay Hank on the note, citing her minority. On what grounds may Hank collect the amount of the note from Paula?

4. Frank, a traveling salesman, visited Mary's Stationery Store. Frank told Mary his name was Rick. Mary bought some supplies from Frank. She gave him a note payable to the order of Rick. Frank never delivered the supplies. Hanna now holds the note. Mary has refused to pay Hanna. Mary says that her defense is good against Hanna because Frank forged the name of Rick on the note, preventing Hanna from being a holder. Is Mary correct?

5. Dan wrote a check for groceries payable to the order of Gap's Grocery. Tim, an employee of Gap's, stole the instrument. Tim skillfully altered the check by writing "or Tim" in the space Dan had left on the payee line after "Gap's Grocery." Dan's bank paid Tim on the check. When Dan discovered Tim's alteration, he asked the bank to recredit his account for the amount of the check. Must the bank recredit Dan's account?

6. Helene owes Mildred $2000 for goods sold and delivered. To prevent Mildred from bringing suit to collect, Helene gives Mildred her negotiable note for $2000 payable to the order of Mildred and indorsed by Larry as an accommodation for Helene. The note is not paid by Helene when it becomes due. Proper notice is given to all parties. Is Larry liable to Mildred? If Larry pays, does Larry have recourse against Helene?

CHAPTER 42
CHECKS AND BANK COLLECTIONS

Outline

I. The Drawer/Drawee

A. The bank has a duty to pay as drawee if the check is properly drawn and there are sufficient funds in the account.

Example: Buckley v. Trenton Savings Fund Society (Bank liable to customer for wrongful dishonor of checks.)

B. A "stop payment" order must be given to the bank within reasonable time for it to comply. It is valid for only 14 days if oral unless confirmed in writing.

Example: Staff Services Associates v. Midlantic National Bank (Bank was not justified in paying check over the stop payment order.)

C. A bank's disclaimer of liability for negligence and breach of its duty of good faith will not be enforced.

II. The Drawee Bank

A. The drawee bank may charge a check to a customer's account even if this creates an overdraft.

Example: Pulaski State Bank v. Kalbe (Bank was legally entitled to pay a check that exceeded the balance in the drawer's account.)

B. A drawee bank is primarily liable for payment of a certified check. A cashier's check is a check on which a bank is both the drawer and the drawee.

C. A forged check is generally not properly chargeable to the customer's account. The customer has a duty to report forgeries to the bank.

Example: Rhode Island Hospital Trust National Bank v. Zapata Corp. (Bank is not liable for forged checks where customer failed to exercise reasonable care and promptness to examine the bank statement.)

Example: Knight Communications, Inc. v. Boatmen's National Bank of St. Louis

III. Funds Availability

A. Federal law limits check holds and specifies when funds are to be made available to customers by depositary institutions.

B. Use of electronic banking has raised new legal questions.

Example: State of Illinois v. Continental Illinois National Bank (Use of electronic funds transfers system constitutes the cashing of a check.)

Example: Kruser v. Bank of America NT & SA

Learning Objectives

1. You should know what happens if your bank refuses to pay a check even though you have sufficient funds in your account.

2. You should know whether your bank can create an overdraft in your account by paying an otherwise properly payable check;

3. You should know your rights and the bank's obligation if you stop payment on a check.

4. You should understand the right and labilities that arise if the payee on a check has it certified.

5. You should know the difference between a certified check and a cashier's check.

6. You should know the duties a drawee bank owes to its customer.

7. You should know what constitutes wrongful dishonor.

8. You should understand why a drawee bank has no liability to the drawer for disobeying a stop payment order when the drawee bank pays a person against whom the drawer has no defense to payment.

9. You should know the effect of a drawee bank's attempt to disclaim or limit its liability for disobeying a customer's instructions.

10. You should know when a drawee bank has the right to pay a check, especially forged and altered checks.

11. You should know when a drawee bank has the right to refuse to pay a stale check.

12. You should know the effect of certification on the liability of the drawer, the drawee bank, and the indorsers.

13. You should know the drawee bank's duty to report forgeries and alterations.

Learning Hints

1. The person who deposits money in a bank account becomes a creditor of the bank and the bank becomes that person's debtor. The bank also becomes an agent of the person who owns the checking account.

2. The obligations of the bank under banking law are established by the Uniform Commercial Code (Article 4).

3. A drawee bank may incur liability for wrongfully @T = failing to honor a check drawn on a drawer's account.

4. A customer may order the drawee bank to "stop payment" on a check. The bank is under the obligation to follow the order if reasonable and it has time to comply. Note, however, that a stop payment order does not necessarily relieve the customer of liability to a holder in due course.

5. Note that on an uncertified check, the drawee bank has no liability of any kind to anyone, except the bank's customer, the drawer. This means that when a drawee bank refuses to pay or to certify an uncertified check, the drawee bank cannot be sued successfully by the holder of the check for refusing to pay or to certify the check.

6. The drawee bank's only liability with respect to an uncertified check is to the customer-drawer. The basis of the drawee bank's liability to its customer-drawer is that the bank failed to follow the customer-drawer's instructions. As we saw in agency, so we see in banking law: the drawee bank, as an agent, must obey the instructions of the customer-drawer, the principal.

7. The two ways a drawee bank disobeys a customer-drawer's instructions are by paying a check when the bank should not pay the check and by not paying a check when it should. You should be able to organize the rules concerning wrongful dishonor, stop payment orders, stale checks, properly drawn checks, forged checks, and altered checks under these two categories.

8. Note why a bank need not recredit the customer's account when the bank disobeys a stop payment order and pays a holder against whom the customer does not have a good defense: the holder paid would have been able to collect on the check from the customer if the bank had obeyed the stop payment order. Either way, the drawer loses her money and the holder gets paid.

9. Understanding why certification at the request of a holder releases prior indorsers and the drawer from contractual liability is easier when you are aware of the reason for the rule: the holder is impliedly looking to the bank only for payment. When the drawer requests the certification, the holder makes no such choice. Hence, only the prior indorsers are discharged when the drawer requests certification.

10. Do not confuse cashier's checks and certified checks. Cashier's checks are drawn by bank cashiers. The bank is a drawer and drawee. Certified checks are certified by the bank. The bank is only a drawee.

11. To help the bank pay only properly drawn and indorsed checks, the customer owes the bank the duty not to assist a forgery or alteration by negligently drawing the check. Also the customer will help the bank reduce its loss if the customer quickly gives the bank notice of an altered or forged check the bank has paid. If given timely notice, the bank may be able to collect its loss from the forger or alterer. This explains why the customer will not be able to require the bank to recredit the customer's account when the customer negligently draws a check or fails to notify the bank of an alteration or forgery within a reasonable time.

True-False

In the blank provided, put "T" if the statement is True or "F" if the statement is False.

_____ 1. An oral "stop payment" order to a bank is ineffective.

_____ 2. A bank's disclaimer for failure to exercise ordinary care in paying a check over a stop payment order is not enforceable.

_____ 3. The drawee bank may charge a check to a customer's account even if this creates an overdraft.

_____ 4. A cashier's check is a check on which the bank is both the drawer and the drawee.

_____ 5. In general, a forged check is properly chargeable to the customer's account, but the customer may sue the forger to recover damages.

_____ 6. A bank has a duty to pay every check presented to it for payment.

_____ 7. A written stop payment order is valid for six months.

_____ 8. A bank may debit a customer's account for a stale check.

_____ 9. A drawer has no contractual liability after the bank has certified the check at the request of the drawer.

_____ 10. A bank has the right to pay the checks of a deceased customer until the bank has notice that the customer is deceased or for 10 days after the death, whichever is later.

Multiple Choice

Circle the best answer.

1. Which of the following statements concerning "stale checks" is correct?
   a. The bank may not pay a check that is more than six months old without authorization of the customer.
   b. A stale check is any check that is more than three months old;
   c. The bank may pay a stale check out of a customer's account and charge it to the customer's account.
   d. Both (b) and (c) are correct.

2. Bob requested that his bank certify his $100 check payable to Bob's father. Under these circumstances:
   a. The bank is legally obligated to certify the check if Bob has $100 in his account;
   b. The bank becomes both the drawer and the drawee if it certifies the check;
   c. If the bank does certify the check, it becomes primarily liable for payment.
   d. All of the above are correct.

3. Sally placed a "stop payment" order on a check he had written to Lois. Under these circumstances:
   a. The bank must follow Sally's order so long as it has time to comply;
   b. If the order was oral, it is only valid for 14 days;
   c. If the order was written, it is valid for six months;
   d. All of the above statements are correct.

4. Which of the following statements concerning a money order is correct?
   a. A money order is treated as a certified check;
   b. A money order is treated as an ordinary personal check;
   c. A money order is treated as a cashier's checks;
   d. The courts in various states are divided as to whether money orders should be treated as personal checks or cashier's checks.

5. Ricky stole Mike's checkbook and forged several checks over a period of three months. Mike received the first forged check from the bank in his bank statement on March 1. On March 5 the bank cashed 3 more forged checks. On March 18th, the bank cashed 3 more forged checks. On April 1, the bank cashed 3 more checks. On April 15, Mike notified the bank of the stolen checks. Under these circumstances, how many checks, if any, must the bank recredit to Mike's account?
   a. None, because the bank cashed all the forged checks before being notified of the forgery;
   b. All, because the bank wrongfully paid the checks from Mike's account;

231

    c. One, because after March 1, Mike should have notified the bank of the forgery;

    d. Four, because Mike had fourteen days after receiving the bank's statement revealing the forgery to notify the bank of the forgery.

6. Dan has $1,000 in his checking account at First Bank. Dan gives Paula a check for $50. When Paula presents the check for payment at First Bank, First Bank refuses to pay Paula and marks the check "N.S.F." First Bank has:

    a. issued a stop payment order.

    b. wrongfully dishonored the check.

    c. improperly debited Dan's account.

    d. done all of the above.

7. When a bank fails to pay a properly payable check, the customer may recover from the bank:

    a. the amount of the customer's check.

    b. direct damages only.

    c. direct and consequential damages.

    d. treble the amount of the customer's check.

8. Carla gave Peter a check in payment for a new battery for her car. In fact Peter did not sell Carla a new battery; instead, he put in an old battery. When Carla discovered this deception, she gave her bank a written stop payment order. A few days later when Hannah, a holder in due course, presented the check to the bank, the teller paid the check. Carla now wants the bank to credit her account. Must it?

    a. No, because Carla has no defense good against Hannah.

    b. Yes, because the bank must obey Carla's stop payment order.

    c. Yes, because Carla has a defense good against Peter.

    d. Yes, because the bank had an opportunity to act on the stop payment order.

9. When Tom opened a checking account at American Bank, American Bank required Tom to sign a form that released American Bank from liability for negligently disobeying any stop payment order that Tom might issue to American Bank. If American Bank negligently disobeys Tom's stop payment order, a court:

    a. will enforce the disclaimer because American's conduct meets the conditions of the form.

    b. will enforce the disclaimer because Tom voluntarily signed the form.

    c. will enforce the disclaimer because American Bank needs protection from this type of liability.

    d. will not enforce the disclaimer.

10. First Bank disobeyed Jaye's stop payment order. First Bank paid the check to Sam, a holder in due course. Jaye had a defense of lack of mental capacity. In an action by Jaye against First Bank to require First Bank to recredit her account:

    a. Jaye will win because the defense of incapacity is good against Sam.

    b. First Bank will win, if it was not negligent in disobeying the stop payment order.

    c. First Bank will win, because Jaye's defense of incapacity is not good against Sam, a holder in due course.

    d. First Bank will win, because payment to Sam by First Bank is final.

Short Essay

1. Eight days after Grace died, the bank received a check for $1000 drawn by Grace on her account before her death. The bank knew Grace was dead but paid the check even though it created an overdraft of $500 in the account. The bank then sued Grace's estate for the $500. Will the bank be successful? Explain.

2. Bryant, an employee of ABC Manufacturing, forged a series of checks on the ABC account at First Bank over a period of two years. When ABC discovered the forged checks, it requested the Bank to recredit its account for the total amount of the forged checks. Can ABC require the bank to recredit the account? Explain the rules governing your answer.

3. Oscar has $1,000 in his business checking account at Second Bank. Oscar wrote a check to Stella for $150. When Stella presented the check for payment, the teller at Second Bank made a mistake and refused to pay the check. Stella circulates rumors that Oscar cannot be trusted. Oscar's business suffers as a result. What recourse has Oscar against Second Bank?

4. Carl sold a stereo to Mike for $850. Mike gave Carl a check for that amount. Carl promised to deliver the stereo in a week. Carl never delivered the stereo. Mike gave his bank a stop payment order on the check. When Van, a holder in due course, presented the check for payment, the bank refused to pay it pursuant to the stop payment order. What recourse has Van against the bank and Mike?

5. Nan wrote a check for $100 to the order of Otto. Nan carelessly failed to use all the space on the payee line. Tim stole the check from Otto before Otto indorsed it. Tim skillfully added the words "or Tim" after Otto's name on the payee line. Then Tim indorsed the check with his own name on the back and received payment from Nan's bank. Three weeks later when Nan received her canceled checks from the bank, she discovered the alteration, notified the bank, and requested that her account be recredited. Must the bank recredit her account?

CHAPTER 43

INTRODUCTION TO SECURITY

Outline

I. Credit

A. Credit may be defined as a transaction where one party is obligated to pay consideration for the bargain at some future date.

B. Many transactions are based on unsecured credit.

C. In other cases, the creditor requires the debtor to convey a security interest on the debtor's property to secure payment.

   1. A surety is a person who is liable for the payment of another's debt. The surety joins with the person who is primarily liable. A guarantor makes a separate promise agreeing to be liable on the happening of a certain event.

   2. The creditor is required to disclose material facts affecting risk to the surety.
   Example: Camp v. First Financial Federal Savings and Loan Association (Surety was relieved of his obligation by bank's failure to disclose material facts.)

   3. A surety acquires rights of subrogation upon performance of the principal's obligation.

II. Liens

A. Liens on Personal Property

   1. Under common law, artisans improving property acquire a lien on the property until paid. Many states today recognize these liens by statute.

   2. Possessory liens permit a lienholder to keep possession of the property until paid.
   Example: Navistar Financial Corporation v. Allen's Corner Garage and Towing Service, Inc. (Defendant entitled to common lien for towing and storage of truck and trailer.)

B. Security Interests in Real Property

   1. A mortgage is a security interest in real property. Foreclose is the process of terminating rights of the mortgagor in the property. Other security interests include the deed of trust and land contracts.
   Example: Family Bank of Commerce v. Nelson (case involving foreclosure of a deed of trust.)
   Example: Looney v. Farmers Home Administration (Foreclosure of land sales contract.)

C. All states provide for mechanics liens to protect persons who furnish labor or materials to improve real estate.

   Example: In Re Skyline Properties, Inc. (Holding that mechanic's lien holder takes priority over the bank's mortgage.)

Learning Objectives

1. You should understand the difference between secured and unsecured credit, and the importance of that difference.

2. You should know different ways a creditor can obtain security in personal or real property.

3. You should be familiar with common law and statutory liens protecting artisans or tradespeople, innkeepers, and common carriers.

4. You should know what a mechanic's or materialman's lien is and how it protects laborers or suppliers of materials to the property.

5. You should understand the risks that attend unsecured credit, as far as creditors are concerned, and should recognize how difficult it is to recover from an unwilling or destitute debtor.

6. You should be aware of how secured credit minimizes the risks referred to in Learning Objective No. 1.

7. You should be familiar, in the context of surety and guarantor relationships, with what are personal defenses and what are defenses going to the merits, as well as with the significance of distinguishing between the two.

8. You should understand the duties the creditor owes the surety, along with the rights the surety has.

9. You should understand the mortgage relationship, as well as the rights of the parties upon default.

10. You should understand the importance of recording the mortgage.

11. You should be able to compare and contrast the deed of trust and the mortgage, and should understand why a deed of trust might be employed.

12. You should be able to compare and contrast the land contract and the mortgage, as well as the land contract and the deed of trust.

Learning Hints

1. Understanding the nature of a credit transaction is increasingly important for business people. In the event unsecured credit is extended to a debtor, for example, and the debtor fails to pay the debt, the creditor may be unable to recover the debt. For this reason, to minimize credit risk, a creditor can contract for security. In a secured credit situation, if the debtor defaults on the debt, the creditor may be able to foreclose his lien on the real or personal property of the debtor and recover some, if not all, of his loss.

2. There is a difference between a surety and a guarantor, but their rights and liabilities are very similar. A surety joins with the person who is primarily liable in promising to make payment or perform the duty, while a guarantor makes a separate promise agreeing to be liable on the happening of a certain event.

3. The rights and obligations of the surety or guarantor are easy to understand if one remembers that the relationship is basically contractual. Therefore, when the parties materially alter the terms without the surety's consent, one would expect the surety's performance to be excused. This also explains why defenses that go to the merits will excuse performance while the principal's personal defenses will not. Likewise, if the principal and the creditor do anything to increase the surety's risk, the surety's performance should be excused because the contract has been materially altered.

4. Notice that frequently a surety's right of subrogation will make the surety an unsecured creditor of the principal. However, the surety will be a secured creditor if property was also used to secure the original debt or the surety's promise.

5. The greatest weakness of the common law and statutory liens, from the standpoint of the creditor, is that they generally require the creditor to maintain possession of the security. Such a requirement does not necessarily facilitate smooth completion of the vast majority of consumer and commercial transactions that occur today.

6. Remember that foreclosure cannot take place without notice being given to the debtor and to the public before a sale is made. Notice to the debtor is essential in affording the debtor an opportunity to redeem by satisfying the debt. Notice to the public helps ensure that the creditor will receive the highest possible price at the foreclosure sale. The creditor's receiving the highest possible price works in favor of the debtor also, because the debtor could still be liable for any deficiency still owed after the foreclosure sale.

7. Recording a mortgage performs the role possession plays in the common law lien context. Third persons would often not be aware of security interests in property and might purchase from the debtor, since possession generally signifies ownership. Thus, in the common law lien situation, the creditor maintains possession in order to avoid the hardships that might arise if an unwitting buyer bought from the debtor. With real property, it is not practical for the creditor to take possession, because doing so would effectively deny the debtor use of the property. The recording statutes were designed to allow prospective buyers and prospective creditors to discover encumbrances on real estate before they purchase it or extend credit in reliance on it.

8. The debtor's right to redeem is his or her last chance to maintain possession of the property securing the debt. In order to redeem and thereby avoid sale of the property, the debtor must pay the debt and any costs or penalties in full.

9. All states have statutes protecting materialmen or mechanics who improve real property. The procedure for obtaining and foreclosing such liens varies from state to state. It is important to note, however, that a valid mechanic's lien may take priority over other lien-holders. No one should purchase real property without making a title search (search of title records) to determine the existence of liens on the property.

10. Even though a land sales contract may not expressly create a security interest in real property, some courts have held that the legal effect of such contracts is to convey equitable title in the property to the purchaser, with the seller retaining a security interest in the property. The practical effect of that holding is to require the seller to foreclose his or her security interest upon default by the purchaser, and to give the buyer rights to redeem the property in certain cases.

True-False

In the blank provided, put "T" if the statement is True or "F" if the statement is False.

_____ 1. If a creditor fails to disclose a material fact about the risk involved to the surety, the surety is relieved of liability as surety.

_____ 2. If a lienholder possesses goods and his charges are not paid, he has the right to sell the property without further notice to the owner.

_____ 3. A mechanic's or materialman's lien is an example of a statutory lien.

_____ 4. The most common security interest in real property is the deed of trust.

_____ 5. In strict foreclose, the creditor keeps the property in satisfaction of the debt and the owner's rights are cut off, but the creditor has no right to a deficiency.

_____ 6. Courts are more protective of compensated sureties than they are of accommodation sureties, because compensated sureties serve to expand commerce.

_____ 7. The owner of mortgaged property ordinarily cannot sell the property without the consent of the mortgagee.

_____ 8. In an unsecured credit transaction involving the sale of goods, the creditor gives up all rights in the goods being sold, in return for a mere promise by the debtor to make payment of the purchase price.

_____ 9. A mechanic's lien cannot be foreclosed, meaning that the holder of a mechanic's lien cannot realistically expect to be paid the amount of his lien until the owner of the property decides to sell the property.

_____ 10. A surety may use a breach of warranty defense against a creditor of the principal.

Multiple Choice

Circle the best answer.

1. If a surety has to perform or pay the principal's obligation:
   a. The surety acquires all the rights that the creditor had against the principal;
   b. The surety is entitled to recover her costs from the principal;
   c. The surety is entitled to contribution from any co-sureties;
   d. All of the above are correct statements.

2. Which of the following statements concerning a land contract is correct?
   a. Title to the property is usually conveyed from the seller to the buyer at the time the contract is executed;
   b. If the buyer defaults, the seller generally has the right to declare a forfeiture and take possession of the property;
   c. Most states give the buyer on a land contract a limited period of time to redeem his interest.
   d. Both (b) and (c) are correct.

3. Jane purchased a new couch from a local department store and charged it to her Mastercard account. If Jane defaults on payments:
   a. This is an unsecured credit transaction and neither the store nor Mastercard has a lien on the couch.
   b. The department store has a common law lien on the couch;
   c. Mastercard has a common law lien on the couch;
   d. Both (b) and (c) are correct.

4. Allen's father agreed to be a surety for Allen on his purchase of a new motorcycle. Allen defaulted on the loan and the seller sued Allen's father. Which of the defenses may Allen's father assert against the seller?
   a. Allen was a minor at the time of purchase and lacked capacity to contract;
   b. Because the motorcycle was defective the seller breached an express warranty in its sale;
   c. Allen recently discharged this debt in bankruptcy;
   d. Allen's father may raise all of the above defenses.

5. Under common law, what is (are) the essential element(s) of a possessory lien?
   a. Possession by the improver or provider of services;
   b. Debt created by the improvement or provision of services concerning the goods;
   c. Express contract for services between the improver and the owner;
   d. Both (a) and (b) are required.

6. Alf and Biff were co-sureties of their friend, Chloe, on a certain obligation on which Chloe was the principal. When Chloe defaulted, Biff paid the entire obligation. After having done so, Biff
   a. was automatically relieved from any liability for any other obligations on which he was a surety and Chloe was the principal.
   b. acquired all rights the creditor had against Chloe.
   c. acquired the right to call upon Alf to reimburse him for Alf's share of the obligation.
   d. acquired the rights referred to in answers b and c.

7. When a debtor defaults on a secured debt,
   a. the creditor cannot continue efforts to collect, from the debtor personally, the funds that are owed.
   b. the creditor may proceed against the security, in order to have it sold and the proceeds of the sale applied to the debt.
   c. the creditor must proceed against any surety on the obligation.
   d. all of the above are accurate.

8. If the mortgagee fails to record the mortgage,
   a. the mortgagor is still liable on the debt.
   b. the mortgage will not be effective against subsequent purchasers of the property who were unaware of the existence of the mortgage.
   c. the mortgage will not be effective against subsequent mortgagees who have no notice of its existence.
   d. all of the above are true.

9. Mechanic's lien statutes
   a. require that the mechanic who did work on the motor vehicle actually have possession of the motor vehicle.
   b. provide protection to suppliers who sell materials to general contractors for miscellaneous uses by the general contractor, regardless of whether the materials were sold for use on a particular project.
   c. contain provisions that must be strictly complied with if the claimed lien is to be valid.
   d. do not provide a workable remedy for the holder of such a lien, because they typically prohibit foreclosure.

10. A surety will generally be relieved of responsibility
    a. if the creditor allows the principal additional time to perform.
    b. if the principal lacked capacity to contract.
    c. if the principal and creditor agree to an increased interest rate.
    d. in any of the situations referred to above.

Short Essay
   1. Ron and Rhonda have hired Cheetum Contractors to construct a new home for them on a lot they acquired in a new subdivision. Cheetum has subcontracted with Eddie's Electrical Service to provide electrical wiring for the new home. If Eddie provides the wiring and is not paid, what remedies, if any, does Eddie have?

2. Briefly explain the difference between a mortgage and a deed of trust.

3. Bart purchased a home for $99,000. He paid $10,000 down and financed the rest through Solvent Savings & Loan, which obtained a mortgage on the property to secure payment of the debt. Because of a Solvent employee's error, Solvent failed to record its mortgage interest. Several years later, Bart sold the house to Seretha, who paid him $118,000. At the time of the sale to Seretha, Bart still owed Solvent $81,000. When Bart failed to make his monthly payment for the second consecutive month, Solvent discovered the sale to Seretha. After learning that Bart had squandered the $118,000 in Las Vegas, Solvent instituted proceedings to gain possession of the property from Seretha. Seretha defended on the ground that she was not aware of the prior security interest and was therefore the sole owner of the home. Discuss the strength, or lack of strength, of Solvent's position.

4. Earl performed some repairs on Skip's car. He charged Skip $433. Not having the cash to pay immediately, Skip promised to make payment within a week. Skip drove the car home. The next day, he sent Earl a check for $150, but paid Earl nothing more. Two weeks later, while Skip was at work, Earl towed the car and locked it in his (Earl's) garage. He informed Skip that he would sell the car in two days, in full satisfaction of the debt, if Skip did not pay the remaining $283 before that time. Earl claimed to have the right to do this pursuant because he held a common law lien on the car. Is Earl correct? Discuss the issues presented by the facts.

5. Gus agreed to be a surety for Lefty on Lefty's credit purchase, from Shaft Motor Co., of an automobile previously owned by an elderly woman who had driven the car only to church and back. Lefty subsequently failed to pay Shaft the amounts called for in the purchase agreement. It was then established that Lefty was insane, and therefore lacking in capacity to enter into a contract, at the time he agreed to purchase the automobile. Shaft then made demand upon Gus for payment of the purchase price, but Gus refused, claiming that as Lefty's surety, he had the right to raise Lefty's insanity as a defense. Is Gus correct? Explain your answer.

CHAPTER 44
SECURED TRANSACTIONS

Outline

I. Security interests in general

  A. A security interest in personal property or fixtures is governed by Article 9 of the Uniform Commercial Code.

  B. Security interests under the UCC include a broad class of interests.

  Example: In Re Parraway (rejecting university's claim that it had a secured interest in student transcripts.)

  C. Obtaining an interest: Attachment and perfection

II. Attachment is legal rather than physical. It requires a security agreement, for value, and an underlying debt.

  A. The agreement must be in writing and signed by the debtor.

  Example: In Re Hardage (Holding that sales slips constitute valid security agreement in particular collateral.)

  B. The agreement may cover future advances, after-acquired property, and proceeds of the collateral.

  C. Waiver of defenses clauses in consumer contracts has been severely limited. Thus, an assignee of the contract will be subject to claims or defenses of the buyer-debtor.

III. Perfecting the Interest.

  A. Attachment gives rights to the creditor vis a vis the debtor; perfection protects the creditor against other creditors.

  B. There are three ways to perfect the interest under the UCC: filing public notice, taking possession, or automatic perfection in certain transactions.

   1. A creditor who sells goods to a consumer on credit has a purchase money security interest in those consumer goods, and no filing is required.
   Example: General Electric Credit Corporation v. Allegretti (Perfected security interest in goods held by seller passed to credit corporation when the credit agreement was assigned.)

   2. The retailer who would otherwise hold a perfected security interest by attached does not have priority over the "BFP" (Bona Fide Purchaser).

  C. Other rules apply to motor vehicles (requiring notation on the certificate of title), and there are special rules for perfecting security interests in fixtures.

IV. Priorities

  A. Problems arise when different creditors claim a security interest in the same collateral. The UCC establishes rules for determining which interest takes priority.

  B. Basic rule is that the first interest to be perfected takes priority.

  C. There are exceptions—for example, a perfected purchase money security interest in inventory takes priority in some cases.

  Example: ITT Commercial Finance Corp. v. Union Bank & Trust Company of North Vernon

  D. A buyer in the ordinary course of business takes free from the security interest.

  Example: DBC Capital Fund, Inc. v. Snodgrass

V. Default and Foreclosure

  A. The secured creditor may, on default, sue on the debt, repossess the collateral and keep it in satisfaction of the debt, or repossess and foreclose on the collateral.

  Example: Wade v. Ford Motor Credit Co. (Repossession took place peacefully so there was no breach of peace entitling owner to damages for wrongful repossession of automobile.)

  B. Method of disposal of the collateral must be commercially reasonable. Creditor must comply with Article 9 requirements.

Learning Objectives

1. You should understand how creditors and suppliers of businesses can obtain security for the credit they extend.
2. You should know the steps that creditors must take to obtain maximum protection against the debtor and other creditors.
3. You should know the relative rights of creditors vis a vis each other in the event the debtor defaults.
4. You should know the rights of creditors vis a vis someone who buys from the business in the ordinary course of business.
5. You should remember that the creditor will usually lose her protection as a secured creditor under Article 9 if she does not strictly conform to the procedures established in Article 9.
6. You should understand the meaning and significance of attachment, the purpose of perfection, and the difference between attachment and perfection.
7. You should become familiar with the respective meanings of the terms <u>future advances</u>, <u>after-acquired property</u>, and <u>proceeds</u>, and should understand why they are important to the creditor and the debtor.
8. You should become able to recognize the various classifications of collateral and should know how they differ in their treatment by Article 9.
9. You should become familiar with the ways in which perfection occurs, and should understand not only why some security interests are perfected under one means as opposed to another, but also what the strengths and weaknesses of each method of perfecting are.
10. You should become familiar with the importance of priority, in the context of competing security interests, and should understand the basic priority rule and the exceptions to it.
11. You should know what a buyer in the ordinary course is, and should understand why the buyer in ordinary course concept is significant with regard to secured commercial transactions.
12. You should understand the special procedures that pertain to security interests in fixtures, and should know why fixtures are given special treatment.
13. You should understand the various paths open to the creditor upon default by the debtor, as well as why the creditor might choose one path over another.
14. You should know the various procedures the creditor must follow in order to protect not only his interests, but also the debtor's interests, when collateral is sold after default by the debtor.

Learning Hints

1. In many credit transactions, a creditor will take a security interest or lien in personal property belonging to the debtor. The law covering security interests in person property is contained in Article 9 of the Uniform Commercial Code.
2. There are many different kinds of collateral recognized by Article 9. Two important concepts underlie effectively securing transactions under Article 9: Attachment, and perfection. Attachment is required to secure a lien against the debtor; perfection gives the creditor priority vis a vis other creditors.
3. The security interest is a matter of concern, initially, to the debtor and the creditor. It is an acknowledgement that the debtor has given the creditor certain rights in the property of the debtor. The security interest is also of concern to third persons, however, as they may wish to buy or extend credit on the same property. Article 9, therefore, serves to help coordinate the rights of all of these potential parties in the property.
4. Attachment is a subject of relevance to the debtor and the creditor. It is an acknowledgement of the debt and the creditor's interest in the collateral. A security agreement generally is in writing; the only other way for attachment to be effective is for the creditor to take possession of the collateral. Sometimes it is not possible for the creditor to take possession (as with accounts receivable, for example) and frequently it is not acceptable to the debtor for the creditor to take possession.

5. The attachment and perfection rules for personal property are generally dependent upon the classification of the collateral. The classification into which the property falls is generally determined by the debtor's intended use at the time the security agreement is drafted. Some courts, however, classify the property on the basis of its actual use.

6. Proceeds are what the debtor has acquired in return for a sale or exchange of the collateral. Proceeds take the form of money most of the time, although proceeds may take the form of other kinds of property. In a sense, the debtor transforms the collateral into money if it is sold for cash, or the debtor transforms the collateral into a car if it is traded for another car. With after-acquired property, however, the debtor has gained something in addition to the original collateral. This gives the creditor extra collateral, whereas with proceeds, only the form of the collateral has changed.

7. Notice that perfection is of significance as between the creditor and third persons who might wish to purchase an interest in the debtor's property. Filing of a financing statement and possession by the creditor are clear ways of informing third persons of the creditor's superior interest in the property. Remember, however, that automatic perfection is allowed for purchase money security interests in consumer goods. Many, if not most, holders of purchase money security interests in consumer goods are sellers who sell their own goods on credit. If these sellers were required to file financing statements on their own goods that were sold on credit, the filing system would be overwhelmed and the cost of credit would likely rise.

8. Note the problems that can arise when the debtor removes the collateral from the state. Because each state has its own filing system, there is no easy way to discover whether property has been secured in another state. A diligent creditor will check the new debtor's prior address to determine if it was an out-of-state address and, after making a loan or credit sale, will attempt to monitor the account to discover an interstate move as quickly as possible. Creditors must be wary when dealing with a debtor new to the state, because a prior creditor who has perfected in the debtor's former state could have a "hidden lien" for four months.

9. The basic priority rule is "first in time—first in right." This means that the first creditor to perfect generally has the superior security interest. After perfection, all later creditors should have been placed on notice of the prior encumbrance. You may note that it is possible to file a financing statement prior to the actual attachment of the security interest. In this way, a creditor can protect his or her interest while the parties are still negotiating the precise terms of the agreement.

10. A purchase money security interest arises when a seller/creditor retains a security interest in goods that the buyer/debtor has bought on time. However, a creditor may also possess a purchase money security interest when it loans the debtor money to buy certain goods. If the creditor wishes to have the benefit of a purchase money security interest, the creditor must be certain that the very money it loans is used to buy the goods. Therefore, to protect itself, the creditor loaning purchase money to the debtor may wish to make the loan in the form of a check payable to the seller.

11. A buyer in the ordinary course of business takes free and clear of an encumbrance on the seller's inventory. The seller's creditor anticipates that sales will be made and expects to be paid with the proceeds of such sales.

12. An exception to the basic priority rule is given to perfected security interests in fixtures. This poses no real hardship to a mortgagee, because the mortgagee's interest attached to the real property before the addition of the fixtures. It would be a windfall to the mortgagee if he or she also gained superior rights over the fixture.

13. Artisans' liens are given a special priority because it is not believed that doing so will impose any additional burdens on the prior secured creditors. The artisan has enhanced the value of the goods by making the repairs. In theory, the other secured creditors' liens are improved in the sense that the liens cover property that now has greater value than it did before. Not to give the artisan a special priority would be to give the creditor a windfall and greatly curtail the performance of repairs that could not be paid for immediately with cash.

14. When the debtor has paid more than 60 percent of the purchase price or debt owed on consumer goods in which the creditor has a security interest, the assumption is that there would be a surplus if the goods were sold at a repossession sale. Therefore, the creditor cannot have a strict foreclosure in such a situation unless the debtor agrees to it in writing after the default. Otherwise, the chances would be great that the creditor could pocket a large surplus whenever the debtor defaulted in such a situation. Imagine, for instance, a creditor's making a strict foreclosure on a relatively new car when the balance of the loan was only a few hundred dollars. When the debtor has paid less than 60 percent of the purchase price or debt owned on consumer goods in which the creditor has a security interest, the chances of such an unconscionable result are lessened greatly. Note, however, that even in this latter case, the debtor can avoid the strict foreclosure by making a proper written objection to the creditor's proposal of a strict foreclosure.

True-False

In the blank provided, put "T" if the statement is True or "F" if the statement is False.

_____ 1. The retailer who would otherwise hold a perfected security interest by attached does not have priority over the "BFP" (Bona Fide Purchaser).

_____ 2. In order to attach a security interest in personal property of the debtor, the creditor must prove there the existence of an underlying debt.

_____ 3. Article 9 prohibits a security agreement granting a creditor a security interest in after-acquired property of the debtor.

_____ 4. In some cases, a creditor may perfect a security interest merely by attaching the property.

_____ 5. The Federal Trade Commission has limited the ability of a creditor to require the debtor to waive certain defenses in consumer contracts.

_____ 6. A purchase money security interest in inventory will defeat a prior recorded security interest encompassing inventory and after acquired property only if the prior creditor is given notice.

_____ 7. Even if he or she is actually aware of a prior recorded security interest in inventory, a buyer in the ordinary course will defeat such a security interest when buying from the dealer/debtor.

_____ 8. Possession of the collateral by the creditor generally eliminates the need to file for perfection.

_____ 9. Generally, the creditor whose security interest attached first will be given the priority over other secured creditors, regardless of when the respective security interests were perfected.

_____ 10. The debtor who has defaulted necessarily loses the right to redeem the collateral.

Multiple Choice

Circle the best answer.

1. Which of the following ways is not a method by which a creditor may perfect a security interest in personal property of the debtor under Article 9?
   a. By filing a public notice of the security interest;
   b. By taking possession of the collateral;
   c. By mere attachment of the interest;
   d. By agreement between the creditor and debtor.

2. Assume that Mr. D's Department Store sold a new refrigerator on credit to Roseanne. Assume that the credit agreement was sufficient to meet the requirements of attachment. What must Mr. D's do to perfect that interest?
   a. Mr. D's must file a notice of the security interest in the appropriate public office;
   b. Mr. D's must take possession of the refrigerator;
   c. Nothing—Mr. D's has a perfected purchase money security interest under these facts.
   d. Either (a) or (b) will perfect Mr. D's security interest in the refrigerator.

242

3. In a state which issues certificates of title for motor vehicles:
   a. The secured creditor must file a notice of its security interest with the Department of Motor Vehicles of the state;
   b. The secured creditor must note the security interest on the title;
   c. The secured creditor may perfect its interest either by (a) or (b) above;
   d. Nothing—the secured creditor perfects its security interest by attachment in such cases.

4. The basic priority rule under the UCC is:
   a. The first security interest to be perfected has priority over any that is perfected later;
   b. The first security interest to be attached has priority over any that is attached later;
   c. The first security interest to obtain a written agreement granting the creditor the security interest takes priority over any subsequent creditor;
   d. None of the above correctly states the basic priority rule under the UCC.

5. Which of the following is not a collateral recognized by Article 9?
   a. documents of title;
   b. chattel paper;
   c. transcripts of university students who are indebted to the university;
   d. all of the above are recognized as collateral by Article 9.

6. A purchase money security interest in inventory
   a. will be automatically perfected for four months.
   b. may defeat a prior recorded security interest covering inventory.
   c. is automatically perfected for 10 days.
   d. will usually be perfected by possession.

7. Of the following statements concerning proceeds, which is/are correct?
   a. If the creditor's security interest is to extend to proceeds, the creditor and debtor must enter into a special security agreement that is separate from the security agreement dealing with the primary collateral.
   b. No proceeds are generated if the debtor transfers collateral to another party in exchange for property other than money.
   c. Under the 1972 amendments to Article 9, proceeds automatically are covered by a security agreement unless the security agreement specifically states to the contrary.
   d. Both b and c.

8. Security interests in checks and promissory notes are perfected by
   a. possession.
   b. public filing.
   c. automatic perfection.
   d. any one of the above.

9. A financing statement dealing with a security interest in fixtures
   a. need not be filed in order to have a security interest that is effective against claims of third parties.
   b. must be signed by the creditor as well as the debtor.
   c. is not governed by Article 9 of the UCC.
   d. must be filed in the office where real estate mortgages are filed.

10. If a security interest is unperfected,
    a. the debtor's promise is unenforceable.
    b. the debtor is in default.
    c. the creditor has breached the contract underlying the debt.
    d. the creditor will not have a preferred status in bankruptcy proceedings.

Short Essay

1. Dan, owner of "Dan's Furniture Store," comes to the loan officer at First Bank and asks to borrow $10,000. He offers to put up his inventory as collateral for the loan. What steps should the loan officer take to protect a security interest in the inventory for bank?

2. Mickey purchased three built-in ovens from Bucky to use in his restaurant located in a building rented from Ralph. Ralph knew nothing of the transaction. Mickey defaulted and Bucky removed the ovens, and in doing so, damaged the building. Must Bucky pay Ralph for the cost of repairs?

3. Bulbous Corp. held a properly perfected security interest in all of the inventory of Alf's Appliances, Inc., whose business was retail sales of stoves, refrigerators, dishwashers, and other kitchen appliances. Fritz and Gert were customers of Alf's. They were aware that Alf's had acquired its inventory pursuant to a "floor plan" financing arrangement and that Bulbous held a security interest in what Alf's had available for sale to the public. Fritz and Gert purchased a refrigerator and stove from Alf's. At the time of the purchase, Alf's was in default on its obligations to Bulbous. Because of the default, Bulbous began attempting to repossess the secured property. Bulbous made written demand upon Frtiz and Gert, calling for them to give Bulbous possession of the stove and refrigerator and maintaining that its security interest gave it a superior claim to the items Fritz and Gert had purchased while Alf's was in default. Is Bulbous entitled to possession of the refrigerator and stove? Why or why not?

4. People's Bank loaned Hadley Construction Co. $215,000 and obtained a security interest in all of Hadley's present equipment, as well as any equipment Hadley might acquire in the future. The security interest was properly attached and perfected on the day the loan was made. Several weeks later, Hadley borrowed $38,000 from Local Loan for the purpose of purchasing a new tractor for the business. Hadley and Local entered into a security agreement giving Local a security interest in the tractor. Local made the check payable to the dealer and immediately filed a suitable financing statement concerning the new equipment. If Hadley should default on both loans, which creditor would possess the first priority security interest in the tractor? Explain.

5. Griese Sales & Service, Inc. sold Duane a big-screen color television, a dryer, and a portable dishwasher on credit. All three items were for use at Duane's home. Griese and Duane agreed that Griese would retain a security interest in the three items until the full purchase price had been paid by Duane. No financing statement was filed by Griese. Duane then borrowed money from Acme Finance Co., and agreed to give Acme a security interest in the big-screen TV and the dryer. Acme filed a proper financing statement. Duane also proceeded to sell the dishwasher to Sandy, who bought the dishwasher for her family's use. Sandy had no knowledge that Griese claimed a security interest in the dishwasher. When Duane defaulted on his payments to Griese and Acme, both Griese and Acme claimed a first priority security interest in the big-screen TV and the dryer. Upon learning that Duane had sold the dishwasher to Sandy, Griese contacted Sandy and made demand upon her for possession of the dishwasher. As between Griese and Acme, who has a first priority security interest in the big-screen TV and the dryer? Why? Is Griese entitled to possession of the dishwasher, or is Sandy entitled to keep it? State the reasons for your answer.

CHAPTER 45
BANKRUPTCY

Outline

I. Bankruptcy Proceedings

  A. The Bankruptcy Act covers several different types of proceedings.

  B. Liquidations are called "straight bankruptcies." At the end of the proceedings, the petitioner's debts are discharged.

  C. Other types of proceedings include reorganizations, family farms, and consumer debt adjustments.

II. Liquidation Proceedings (Chapter 7)

  A. Either a voluntary or involuntary petition may be filed. The filing of the petition operates as an automatic stay of various actions against the debtor or his property.

  B. The trustee takes possession of the property and precedes over the meeting of creditors.

  C. Certain property is exempt from creditors' claims under state law or federal law.

    Example: In Re Griffin (Sailboat was not exempt from the claims of creditors.)

    1. A debtor is also permitted to void certain liens against exempt property.

  D. The trustee may recover preferential payments made by the bankrupt person—those payments made within 90 days of filing of the bankruptcy petition are preferential payments. Likewise, a trustee may negate a preferential lien or fraudulent transfer.

    Example: In Re Kranich (Example of trustee recovering property on the grounds that the transfer was fraudulent.)

  E. Creditors must file proof of claim; Certain claims have priority over other claims. At the end of the proceedings, the bankrupt's debts are discharged. Some debts, however, are not dischargeable in bankruptcy.

    Example: In Re Hott (Discharge of a debt barred on the ground it was obtained through the use of a false financial statement.)

  F. The law permits a debtor to reaffirm a debt, but the reaffirmation is subject to court review.

    Example: In Re McCreless (Reaffirmation agreement not set aside by the court.)

  G. Bankruptcy courts may dismiss cases there determine are a substantial abuse of the process. *Example:* In Re Newson (stating criteria for dismissal under this theory.)

III. Chapter 11 Reorganizations

  A. Intended primarily for use by businesses, this proceeding requires the business to file a reorganization plan which is submitted to the creditors for approval.

    Example: Official Committee of Equity Security Holders v. Mabey (Court erred in ordering distribution of bankrupt's assets before the reorganization plan was approved.)

  B. 1987 Amendments to the law address concerns that some companies were using Chapter 11 to avoid collective bargaining agreements.

IV. Other Provisions of the Bankruptcy Code

  A. Chapter 12 establishes special rules for relief for family farms

  B. Chapter 13 provides for adjustment of consumer debt for individuals. It is similar to Chapter 11 in that the debtor submits a plan of payment which is submitted to the secured creditors for acceptance.

    Example: In Re Doersam (Plan was not filed in good faith and should not be approved.)

Learning Objectives

  1. You should understand how the federal Bankruptcy Act provides an organized procedure for dealing with the problems of insolvent debtors.

  2. You should know the different kinds of proceedings available to debtors under the Bankruptcy Act.

3. You should understand provisions of the Act that protect creditors against potentially unfair actions by the debtors and other creditors.

4. You should understand the significance of a discharge in bankruptcy, and the requirements for reaffirmation of debt.

5. You should be able to distinguish among liquidations, reorganizations, and consumer debt adjustments.

6. You should understand, with regard to liquidation proceedings, the difference between voluntary and involuntary proceedings, as well as the procedural safeguards that accompany each.

7. You should understand the duties of the trustee in a liquidation proceeding.

8. You should become familiar with the categories of property that are exempted by federal law in a bankruptcy proceeding, and should be aware of the kinds of property that may be exempted by applicable state law.

9. You should be familiar with the priority of claims in a straight bankruptcy, and should understand why it is so important, from the individual creditor's standpoint, to be a secured creditor.

10. You should be able to recognize a preferential payment and a preferential lien, and should know why the preferential payment and preferential lien provisions are in the Bankruptcy Act.

11. You should know and be able to recognize the types of debts that are not dischargeable, and should understand the responsibilities of the debtor for such debts even after a discharge in bankruptcy.

12. You should understand why a debtor may wish to pursue a reorganization instead of a liquidation, and should be familiar with the administrative procedures that govern a reorganization.

13. You should understand why a debtor may wish to secure a consumer debt adjustment, and should become familiar with what the prerequisites for a consumer debt adjustment are.

Learning Hints

1. Bankruptcy law is a matter of federal law, although the exemptions available to a debtor may be determined under state law.

2. The most common kind of individual bankruptcy is the Chapter 7 or "liquidation" proceeding. Under Chapter 7, a debtor is entitled to discharge debts and get a "fresh start."

3. Note that some kinds of debts are not dischargeable in bankruptcy. For example, child support payments and taxes are not dischargeable. Congress recently amended the law to provide that student loans are not exempt in bankruptcy proceedings.

4. Business reorganization plans are filed under Chapter 11. Under this chapter, a business may continue operating (and thus bring in money to pay creditors) while staying legal action against it by creditors. The plan is submitted to a trustee, who submits it to the creditors for their approval.

5. Recognize how the procedures governing an involuntary petition in bankruptcy are designed to protect the debtor from unfair treatment by an over-anxious creditor. If the debtor has many creditors, it will take more than one to start the bankruptcy forces in motion. If the debtor has a few creditors, an involuntary petition can only be imposed by one or more creditors with a sizeable amount of unsecured claims.

6. You should note the protection accorded the creditors in a bankruptcy proceeding. They select the bankruptcy trustee. This is important, because the trustee will be attempting to challenge the secured claims against the estate and thereby enlarge the pool of property available to the unsecured creditors. When voting among creditors takes place, the creditors' vote is determined both by their absolute numbers and by the amount of claims that each possesses.

7. This chapter should impress upon the student the importance of being a secured creditor. In a bankruptcy proceeding, the secured property is immediately separated from the property available to the general unsecured creditors. (Exempt property is also separated from the pool of unsecured property.) Secured property will only be available to satisfy the claims of unsecured creditors if there exists a surplus after the secured creditor is paid (assuming that the "excess" portion of the secured property is not otherwise exempt). Secured creditors, on the other hand,

can share in the pool of unsecured property if the secured property is insufficient to satisfy their claims against the debtor.

8. The exemption policy of the new Bankruptcy Act may be somewhat confusing. The list of federal exemptions is available to the debtor unless the debtor's state has prohibited use of the federal exemptions. In some instances, a state may permit the debtor to elect either the federal exemptions or a separate list drafted by the state. Hence, in terms of exemptions, debtors will not be treated the same from state to state.

9. Preferential payments and preferential liens are prohibited by the bankruptcy laws because of their generally unfair impact on the creditors who did not receive the benefit of the preferential treatment. By transferring large amounts of property for little or no consideration within 90 days of bankruptcy, the debtor removes property which might have been used to satisfy the claims of unsecured creditors. Likewise, by giving an unsecured creditor a lien immediately prior to bankruptcy, the debtor ensures that a favored creditor will receive a greater proportionate return than the other unsecured creditors. In such situations, the appearance of impropriety is so great that the transfer or lien is likely to be invalidated, so as to treat the other creditors more fairly.

10. Concern over debtor abuse of the bankruptcy privilege lies at the heart of the Bankruptcy Act's provisions making certain debts nondischargeable and the Act's provisions concerning actions that may prevent a debtor from obtaining a discharge. It would not be sound public policy to allow debtors to discharge any and all debts, regardless of nature or type, or to allow debtors who have been dishonest or have engaged in other reprehensible behavior to obtain the relief bankruptcy may afford.

True-False

In the blank provided, put "T" if the statement is True or "F" if the statement is False.

_____ 1. A straight bankruptcy results in a discharge of debts of the debtor, except those debts which are non-dischargeable.

_____ 2. The bankruptcy judge calls the first meeting of creditors.

_____ 3. An involuntary petition for bankruptcy may be filed against the debtor by her creditors.

_____ 4. A preferential payment is a payment made by an insolvent debtor within one year of the filing of the bankruptcy petition.

_____ 5. A debtor's purchase of more than $500 in luxury goods on credit within 40 days of filing a petition is presumed to be a nondischargeable debt in bankruptcy.

_____ 6. A farmer may obtain relief under Chapter 12 of the Bankruptcy Act regardless of whether he has regular income.

_____ 7. Secured creditors must file a proof of claim in a bankruptcy proceeding, but unsecured creditors need not do so in order to protect their rights to a distribution of assets.

_____ 8. In order to be able to file a voluntary petition in bankruptcy, the debtor must be insolvent.

_____ 9. In a bankruptcy proceeding, the debtor may be permitted to void certain liens against exempt property if the liens impair his exemptions.

_____ 10. Both the obligation to pay child support and the obligation to repay certain educational loans will not be affected by a discharge in bankruptcy.

Multiple Choice

Circle the best answer.

1. Which of the following debts is dischargeable in bankruptcy?
   a. provable debt to a spouse for alimony;
   b. provable debt for taxes owed to the state;
   c. grocery expenditures accumulated on a credit card;
   d. All of the above are dischargeable debts.

2. Which of the following statements concerning reaffirmation agreements is not correct?
   a. A court must approve a reaffirmation agreement on a loan secured by real property;
   b. A debtor may voluntarily pay any dischargeable obligation without entering into a reaffirmation agreement;

c. The reaffirmation agreement must be filed with a statement from the debtor's attorney that the agreement is voluntary.

d. The agreement must be made before the discharge is granted.

3. Under a Chapter 11 Reorganization Plan:
   a. Approval by the creditors must be unanimous;
   b. If approved by the creditors, court approval is not required;
   c. The bankruptcy court may distribute a portion of the bankruptcy assets to a portion of the unsecured creditors prior to approval of the plan;
   d. None of the above statements is correct.

4. Upon the filing of the bankruptcy petition:
   a. All debts of the debtor are discharged;
   b. All actions against the debtor or his property are automatically stayed;
   c. All creditors are required to continue extending credit to the petitioner;
   d. None of the above is correct.

5. The petitioner in bankruptcy is permitted to exempt in bankruptcy:
   a. Property exempted by state law;
   b. Property exempted by federal law;
   c. Either property exempted under state or federal law, at the petitioner's election;
   d. Both property exempted by state and federal law.

6. Assume that the trustee can show that an individual debtor's relative, knowing the debtor was insolvent, received a payment from the debtor. This payment can be recovered if it was made
   a. no more than 90 days from the filing of the bankruptcy petition.
   b. within one year of the filing of the bankruptcy petition.
   c. within five years of the filing of the bankruptcy petition.
   d. at any time before the bankruptcy petition was filed.

7. The automatic stay provided for by the Bankruptcy Act
   a. prohibits creditors from beginning new judicial proceedings against the debtor.
   b. does not prohibit creditors from continuing to prosecute judicial proceedings they had instituted against the debtor before the debtor filed his bankruptcy petition.
   c. does not bar creditors from pursuing the debtor for payment, if the means employed by the creditors falls short of instituting suit against the debtor.
   d. is accurately described in each of the above answers.

8. Tax claims against the bankruptcy estate are paid
   a. after all creditors' claims are satisfied.
   b. after administration expenses are paid, but before secured creditors realize on their security.
   c. before all other claims.
   d. after secured creditors realize on their security.

9. If a Chapter 13 proceeding is dismissed,
   a. all of the debtor's debts are discharged.
   b. all further bankruptcy proceedings are held in abeyance.
   c. straight bankruptcy proceedings may proceed.
   d. both a and b are true.

10. Which of the following is not/are not entitled to a discharge in bankruptcy?
    a. An individual debtor who received a discharge eight years prior to the present bankruptcy proceeding.
    b. An individual debtor who, among other debts, owes a debt that is a nondischargeable debt.
    c. A corporation.
    d. a, b, and c.

Short Essay

1. John and Marcia filed a joint petition for bankruptcy under Chapter 7. In their state, they were entitled to exempt $7500 each for real property and $5000 each for personal property. They listed their assets as follows:

   Home valued at $70,000. (Property encumbered by a mortgage of $50,000.) Personal property, including automobile, furniture, and $500 in bank account valued at $12,000.

   They listed debts as follows: $100,000 to the Valley Hospital; $50,000 in various credit card debt; $25,000 to Marcia's father Bill, and $15,000 in property taxes on the residence. Only the mortgage debt to the bank is secured. Which of these debts are dischargeable? What assets are available for distribution to the creditors? Discuss.

2. Identify and briefly discuss the provisions of the Bankruptcy Act that are designed to curb abuses of the bankruptcy privilege.

3. Fragile Corp. has filed a voluntary Chapter 7 petition. Included among its numerous debts are the following, all of which are provable and allowed claims: an unsecured debt in the amount of $10,000, owed to Barracuda Finance Co; a fully secured debt in the amount of $43,000, owed to Smalltown Savings and Loan; $7,000 in back income taxes, owed to the state government; an unsecured debt in the amount of $1,800, representing unpaid wages earned by a Fragile employee during the month preceding the filing of the bankruptcy petition; and an unsecured debt in the amount of $2,500, representing unpaid wages earned by another Fragile employee during the month preceding the filing of the bankruptcy petition. In what order should the above-referred to claims be paid? State the reasons for your answer.

CHAPTER 46
GOVERNMENT REGULATION OF BUSINESS

Outline

I. State Regulation of Business

A. States retain the power to regulate intrastate commerce, but the U.S. Constitution gives the federal government power to regulate interstate commerce.

Example: Taylor v. General Motors Corporation (Tort suit preempted by federal law authorizing installation of seat belts.)

B. States may regulate aspects of interstate commerce not preempted so long as that regulation does not place an unreasonable burden on interstate commerce.

Example: Healy v. The Beer Institute (Statute unconstitutional under the commerce clause.)

II. Federal Regulation

A. State action must exist for constitutional checks on governmental power to apply.

Example: N.C.A.A. v. Tarkanian (Due Process Clause affords no shield against arbitrary private conduct by N.C.A.A.)

B. The Due Process Clause guarantees procedural due process and certain substantive rights.

Example: Maryland Department of Human Resources v. Bo Peep Day Nursery (Utilizing a balancing analysis to determine whether procedural due process had been denied when a state agency revoked a child-care center's license.)

C. The Equal Protection Clause prohibits unfair discrimination against certain protected classes.

Example: MSM Farms v. Spire (Family farm measure does not discriminate in violation of the Equal Protection Clause.)

D. The First Amendment protects commercial speech in some cases.

Example: Posadas De Puerto Rico v. Tourism Co. (Legislation preventing advertising of gambling casinos does not unconstitutionally interfere with the casinos' commercial speech rights.)

III. Administrative Agencies

A. Agencies are established by law; their powers and duties are established by the enabling legislation creating the agency. Agencies may have legislative, judicial, and executive functions.

B. The Federal Trade Commission Act created the FTC to enforce federal antitrust policies and prevent unfair competitive practices in the marketplace.

Learning Objectives

1. You should understand the evolution of government regulation of business from a 19th century laissez faire approach to business activity to today's increasingly complex regulatory environment. You should understand the various forces that have triggered the enormous growth in government regulation during this century, and should recognize why, despite deregulation movements in some quarters, many of these same forces will not permit a totally free market economy.

2. You should be familiar with basic constitutional principles affecting business. One of the most significant questions is whether business activity affects interstate commerce. If so, state regulation of that activity may be preempted by the commerce clause of the U.S. Constitution. You should understand the Commerce Clause and the restraints it imposes on state regulation, as well as the diminishing impact of the Commerce Clause as a restraint on federal regulation.

3. Even if federal action does not preempt state regulation of a business activity, state regulation is prohibited if it places an unreasonable burden on interstate commerce.

4. Several constitutional protections are significant for businesses. Among these are the 14th amendment due process and equal protection clauses. You should understand what is meant by the rational basis test and why the likelihood of invalidating legislation under this analysis is slight.

5. You should become familiar with the meaning of strict scrutiny and the with kinds of situations that will trigger this more stringent analysis of a government regulation.

6. You should develop an awareness of what suspect classes and fundamental rights are, and of what significance each has with regard to the application of the equal protection clause.

7. You should understand the development of the first amendment, and in particular the different levels of protection given by it to commercial speech and political speech.

8. You should become familiar with the reasons for the tremendous growth of administrative agencies, and should understand the diverse functions the agencies perform, as well as the various limits on their powers.

9. You should understand why the FTC was created and be aware of its broad scope of authority.

10. You should understand the importance of enabling legislation in establishing an administrative agency's powers and duties.

Learning Hints

1. One of the most significant legal developments in this century for American business is the tremendous growth of administrative agencies. Agencies like the FTC (Federal Trade Commission) and EPA (Environmental Protection Commission) exercise enormous power and authority over business activities. These agencies are established by federal enabling legislation which establish their powers and duties, and which also limits their authority to act in some cases.

2. States also establish state agencies. State legislatures adopt enabling legislation establishing agencies with the power to adopt rules and regulations governing business activities. Significant state agencies include environmental protection agencies, state OSHA agencies (Occupational Safety and Health), and state Industrial Workman's Compensation Boards.

3. The tremendous growth of regulation is easily understood if one considers the economic notion of "externalities." Externalities are the things one does that have an impact on other people. Although in the abstract most people probably would favor more independence for themselves, they frequently lobby for regulation in order to control the behavior of others, when that behavior's external effects will have an impact on their lives. In a complex, interdependent world, one would expect these externalities to increase rather than decrease, meaning that regulation is not going to disappear.

4. The notion of externalities also explains the judicial interpretation of the Commerce Clause that has caused the clause to be a restraint on state acts. The activities of any state almost always affect the rest of the country. Hence, state acts having external effects that might undermine the solidarity of the nation as a whole will be struck down. Likewise, this notion has reduced the negative influence of the Commerce Clause on the federal government. Instead, the federal government is viewed as the only body that can address the needs of the whole nation. It is therefore considered to be better suited to regulate in the areas that have the greatest likelihood of affecting the nation as a whole.

5. When studying the due process clause and the equal protection clause, it is important to understand that they only limit government action. They are not addressed to private persons or businesses. The vast majority of statutes and regulations confronting the business community are instead based upon the federal government's authority to regulate interstate commerce. Through such statutes and regulations, the activities of private persons and businesses clearly can be reached.

6. In cases in which a violation of the equal protection clause is alleged, the notion of strict scrutiny is used only when fundamental rights have been interfered with or suspect classes have been singled out for discrimination. Normally, the court would not indulge in such exacting analysis because the court is not ordinarily inclined to second guess a legislative body. However, when the regulation discriminates against a suspect class (race, religion or national origin) or interferes with a fundamental right, the court feels compelled to act because the judiciary is the guardian of fundamental (constitutional) rights and of those persons against whom discrimination has been common throughout history. The strict scrutiny analysis is largely outcome-determinative, in that a decision by the court that strict scrutiny governs the case effectively

determines what the result of the case will be most of the time, because the government is hard pressed to prevail under such a rigorous standard.

7. Equal protection cases involving a claim of discrimination on the basis of one's sex are given a special degree of analysis that falls somewhere between strict scrutiny and the lenient rational basis test applied in cases involving most economic regulations.

8. Do not forget that there is no violation of one's first amendment rights if no government action created the alleged deprivation. (Government action is also required in order for there to have been a violation of the due process clauses or the equal protection clause.)

9. Be certain to note the distinction between the constitutional protection given to commercial speech and the constitutional protection given to political speech. Commercial speech, though entitled to first amendment protection, does not receive the full panoply of protection given to political speech. Remember, too, that corporations cannot be denied, simply on the basis of their corporate status, the political speech rights that a natural person would have. The cases in which first amendment protection has been extended to commercial speech have tended to be based on the idea that the public (listeners) has a right to hear the views of these speakers. At least in part, a similar rationale has been utilized in the corporate political speech cases.

True-False

In the blank provided, put "T" if the statement is True or "F" if the statement is False.

_____ 1. The states retain the exclusive power to regulate intrastate commerce.

_____ 2. If state law is preempted by the commerce clause of the U.S. Constitution, that law is unconstitutional.

_____ 3. A statue which arbitrarily violates an employer and employee's freedom to contract is unconstitutional under the equal protection clause of the 14th amendment.

_____ 4. The First Amendment of the U.S. Constitution protects political speech but does not protect "commercial speech."

_____ 5. The FTC (Federal Trade Commission) has the power to adopt rules prohibiting unfair trade practices, but has no power to levy fines for violation of those rules.

_____ 6. The Due Process Clauses contained in the U.S. Constitution prohibit the federal and state governments from taking the private property of citizens.

_____ 7. The Supremacy Clause gives the states the authority to legislate to promote the health, safety and welfare of their citizens.

_____ 8. Only the federal government can regulate activities that have an impact on interstate commerce.

_____ 9. The First, Fifth, and Fourteenth Amendments to the U.S. Constitution protect against infringements of certain basic rights, regardless of whether those basic rights are infringed by government action or private, nongovernment action.

_____ 10. Government regulation of business is a relatively new phenomenon that had its beginnings in the 1930's.

Multiple Choice

Circle the best answer.

1. Under federal law, the Federal Trade Commission:
   a. May issue cease and desist orders and punish violators by levying fines;
   b. may issue trade regulation rules and punish violators by levying fines;
   c. may enforce other federal statutes like the Federal Drug and Cosmetic Act;
   d. All of the above statements are correct.

2. As originally interpreted, the Due Process Clause:
   a. Guarantees procedural fairness by requiring reasonable notice, and the right to an impartial hearing;
   b. Guarantees a person's right to be free from unfair or unreasonable discrimination as a result of race, sex, or national origin;
   c. Protects the federal government's right to regulate interstate commerce;
   d. All of the above are governed by the Due Process Clause.

3. Which of the following requires that statutes differentiating between similarly situated persons or groups must bear a "rational relationship" to a legitimate state purpose unless the statute involves a "suspect" classification?
    a. The Due Process Clause of the 14th amendment;
    b. The Equal Protection Clause of the 14th amendment;
    c. The commerce clause;
    d. The First Amendment.

4. Which of the following provides constitutional safeguards protecting commercial speech, for example, in cases where states attempt to regulate commercial advertising:
    a. The Due Process Clause of the 14th amendment;
    b. The Equal Protection Clause of the 14th amendment;
    c. The commerce clause;
    d. The First Amendment.

5. Which of the following statements concerning administrative agencies is not correct?
    a. Administrative agencies perform executive, legislative, and judicial functions;
    b. Agencies are limited in conducting their affairs by legislative acts and constitutional guarantees;
    c. An agency decision that is unwise will be overturned by a court, because the court has the obligation to review cases to determine whether the agency has exercised good judgment in a particular case.
    d. Today, unlike in the past, there are many federal agencies exercising broad powers to regulate a wide variety of business activity.

6. State statutes may be found by courts to be in violation of the U.S. Constitution when
    a. they operate as impermissible infringements of First or Fourteenth Amendment rights.
    b. they create an impermissible burden on interstate commerce.
    c. they do not expressly conflict with federal law but nevertheless deal with a subject about which federal statutes and/or regulations have preempted state law.
    d. any of the above conditions exists.

7. Judicial interpretations of the Commerce Clause
    a. have greatly narrowed the reach of the clause since the 1930s.
    b. recently have focused on its negative impact on federal regulation.
    c. have been extremely expansive in recent times.
    d. consistently have prevented the states from regulating commerce in any respect.

8. Under the Due Process Clause, a court would be very likely to strike down state legislation that
    a. regulated the minimum age for employment.
    b. regulated the maximum hours that employees could work.
    c. dispensed with the right to a trial for criminal prosecutions.
    d. did any of the above.

9. A court would use the strict scrutiny analysis in examining a law if the law
    a. lowered the minimum wage for minors but not for older employees.
    b. treated black persons differently from white persons.
    c. regulated the amount of profit that a liquor retailer could make on a bottle of wine.
    d. did any of the above.

10. In light of the Supreme Court's rulings concerning corporate political speech, which of the following statements is/are accurate?
    a. The political speech of corporations is given a lesser degree of First Amendment protection than is the political speech of natural persons.
    b. A corporation's speech is protected under the First Amendment, but only if the speech pertains to matters affecting the corporation's property or business.
    c. Both a and b.
    d. Neither a nor b.

Short Essay

1. Assume a state passed a law prohibiting attorneys from advertising in the yellow pages of the telephone directory. Is such a statute constitutional? Discuss.

2. Assume a state passed a law requiring all people of Hungarian descent to register with the secretary of state in order to reside in the state. Is this statute constitutional? Discuss.

3. The Georgia legislature was concerned about pollution problems in its industrial areas. It therefore passed legislation under which owners of factories could be fined if their factories emitted more than certain maximum levels of pollutants. Several factory owners have complained that the standards are slanted in favor of the textile industry. They claim that textile producers unconstitutionally were given numerous exemptions from the law's operation and effect. Discuss and analyze the equal protection aspects of the dissatisfied factory owners' challenge of the statute.

CHAPTER 47
THE ANTITRUST LAWS

Outline

I. The Sherman Act

A. The Sherman Act prohibits contracts in restraint of trade and monopolization.

B. Private plaintiffs may be entitled to treble damages under the act.

C. Section I of the Act prohibits contracts in restraint of trade.

   1. One problem is determining whether there was an agreement—that is whether there was "joint action" rather than "unilateral action."

   2. In finding joint action, courts determine whether the action was per se or a rule of reason violation.

   3. Price-fixing is prohibited by Section I of the Act.
   Example: Atlantic Richfield Co. v USA Petroleum (Finding USA Petroleum was not entitled to antitrust damages.)

   4. Rule of reason trials involve complex attempts by the courts to valance anticompetitive effects of the defendants' acts against competitive justifications for their behavior.

   5. Join ventures and Strategic Alliances are protected under the National Cooperative Research Act.
   Example: Northwest Wholesale Stationers v. Pacific Stationery & Printing (Holding that Northwest did not commit a per se violation of the Sherman Act.)

B. Section 2 of the Act

   1. The government or plaintiff must show not only that the defendant has monopoly power, but also intent to monopolize.

   2. Joint action is not necessary to show violation of this section.

   3. In order to determine monopolization (70% or more of the relevant market), courts must determine geographic and product market.
   Example: Blaine v. Meineke Discount Muffler Shops (Discussing three essential elements to a successful monopolization action.)

II. The Clayton Act

A. Supplements the Sherman Act by preventing monopolies. There is no criminal liability, but treble damages are available.

B. Section 3 addresses anticompetitive behavior: tie-in contracts, exclusive dealing contracts, and requirements contracts involving commodities.

   1. Exclusive Dealing and Requirements contracts require courts to look at percentage share of relevant market foreclosed to competition.
   Example: Roland Machinery v. Dresser Industries (Finding no illegal exclusive dealing contract.)

C. Section 7 addresses horizonal, vertical, and conglomerate mergers.

III. The Robinson-Patman Act prohibits discrimination in price between different purchasers.

A. Defenses include sellers who can cost-justify its discriminatory prices, changing conditions, and meeting competitive demands in good faith.

IV. Limits of Anti-Trust

A. The Parker Doctrine (State action exemption) exempts actions of state officials under authority of state law and actions of private firms or individuals under state official supervision.

B. The Noeer Doctrine permits joint lobbying by business.

C. International limitations include the sovereign immunity doctrine, act of state doctrine, and sovereign compulsion defense.

Example: W.S. Kirkpatrick & Co. v. Environmental Tectonics Corporation (ETC's suit was not barred by the act of state doctrine.)

D. Substantive coverage of the European Community Competition Law is similar to that of the U.S. antitrust laws.

Learning Objectives

1. You should understand the kinds of behavior that the antitrust laws prohibit, and the harmful consequences flowing from the anti-trust regulatory scheme.

2. You should be familiar with the defenses that businesses may raise to protect them from antitrust liability.

3. You should understand international aspects of anti-trust legislation, including defenses and the recently enacted European Community Competition Law.

4. You should understand the ongoing debate between the Chicago School advocates and those who advocate traditional antitrust policy, and should become familiar with the basic tenets of each of the two views concerning the direction antitrust law should take.

5. You should know and understand the basic prerequisites to liability under Section 1 of the Sherman Act, and should remain conscious of the necessity of joint action in order for there to have been a violation of such section.

6. You should become familiar with the alleged violations of Sherman Act Section 1 that will be considered per se violations, as well as with the alleged violations that will be considered under a rule of reason analysis.

7. You should be able to distinguish the proscriptions of Section 2 of the Sherman Act from those of Section 1, and should understand the test used by the courts in determining whether Section 2 has been violated.

8. You should understand how the Clayton Act is designed to remedy some of the perceived shortcomings of the Sherman Act, as well as what the procedural differences between the two acts are.

9. You should become familiar with the kinds of activities reached by Section 3 of the Clayton Act, and should become able to compare the Clayton Act's treatment of such activities to the way they would be handled under Section 1 of the Sherman Act.

10. You should know the various types of mergers and how Section 7 of the Clayton Act deals with them.

11. You should understand the operation of the Robinson-Patman Act, along with understanding the three levels of price discrimination and the defenses to a price discrimination charge.

12. You should become aware of the various exceptions to the antitrust laws and the reasons that support each of the exemptions.

Learning Hints

1. Public outcries for legislation designed to preserve competitive market structures and to prevent accumulation of economic power in the hands of a few resulted in the passage of the Sherman Act in 1890, later supplemented by the Clayton and Robinson-Patman Acts.

2. The Sherman Act makes contracts in restraint of trade and monopolization illegal and provides criminal penalties and civil damages for violations. The Clayton Act supplements the Sherman Act by prohibiting certain practices that monopolists had used to gain monopoly power. The Robinson-Patman Act prohibits price discrimination between different purchasers of commodities of like grade and quality.

3. The Chicago School of economics is a major force in current antitrust law. This approach gives little regard to the desirability of any antitrust provisions other than Sections 1 and 2 of the Sherman Act. Further, within Section 1, it would greatly expand the vitality of rule of reason analysis, considering it applicable for all but horizontal restraints.

4. When an activity is per se unlawful, the courts will not allow the defendant to offer any excuse or economic justification for the restraint. It automatically will be prohibited. Horizontal activities nearly always fall into this category because the courts can think of no reason for their use other than to limit competition. Vertical restraints, on the other hand, may have effects that actually increase competition at the interbrand level despite their limitation of competition at the intrabrand (dealer) level. If interbrand competition is enhanced by the intrabrand restraint, the

courts are likely to allow the activity. You should read carefully the <u>Sylvania</u> decision, which appears in the text, in order to understand this discussion.

5. Oligopolies are largely beyond the reach of the Sherman Act. They never have to actually meet in order to engage in parallel behavior. Most of them are so large that they can regularly determine what the others are doing by following the newspapers. When a major steel producer raises prices, it is national news. If the other companies do not follow suit, it can roll back the price. This parallel behavior is also beyond the reach of Section 2 of the Sherman Act, because no one of the companies possesses monopoly power. Attempts to create antitrust violations for conscious parallelism have not been successful.

6. The inquiry into geographic scope and product line that is required by Section 2 of the Sherman Act is necessary to determine whether the defendant possesses monopoly power. If a seller has this power, the buyer will have no choice but to pay the seller's price or do without the product. Therefore, analysis is necessary in order to determine the seller's control of the product and all its substitutes in the area where the buyer could be expected to go in search of an alternate supplier.

7. Horizontal mergers are more likely to be proscribed than are vertical mergers, because invariably the former tend to limit competition by reducing the number of competitors. Vertical mergers, on the other hand, following the logic of <u>Sylvania</u>, may well enhance competition, because it may be less costly to produce and market a product through a single entity than it is for producers to sell the product to independent dealers who, in turn, sell it to the consumers.

8. The Robinson-Patman Act has been criticized by some observers as being contrary to the spirit of antitrust, because (in their view) the act merely protects small competitors rather than truly furthering competition. Note how the defense of meeting the low bid of a competitor in order to retain a current customer may tend to stabilize prices rather than lower them.

9. The <u>Parker</u> doctrine allows the states to exempt certain activities from the federal antitrust laws if the state intends to replace competition with regulation and if the state actually regulates the activity. The <u>Noerr</u> doctrine exempts lobbying efforts, even though they may have an anti-competitive intent or result. Combined, the two allow special interests to shield themselves from the rigors of competition by resorting to the regulatory processes of the state governments.

True-False

In the blank provided, put "T" if the statement is True or "F" if the statement is False.

_____ 1. The Sherman Act provides for civil, but not criminal, penalties for violation of the provisions of the Act.

_____ 2. The Sherman Act prohibits horizontal, but not vertical, price-fixing.

_____ 3. A plaintiff is not required to prove "joint action" in order to prove a violation of Section 2 of the Sherman Act (prohibiting monopolization.)

_____ 4. Unlike the Sherman Act, the Clayton Act contains no criminal penalties for violation of its provisions.

_____ 5. Under the Sherman Act, courts have the power to order companies to divest themselves of the stock or assets of other companies.

_____ 6. Indirect purchasers generally do not have standing to sue for their injuries resulting from antitrust violations.

_____ 7. Attempts by competitors to control prices are rule of reason violations of the antitrust laws.

_____ 8. In a case arising under Section 2 of the Sherman Act, the courts look to see how the defendant acquired monopoly power.

_____ 9. A single firm can unilaterally refuse to deal with whoever it chooses without violating Section 1 of the Sherman Act.

_____ 10. The Robinson-Patman Act, like the Clayton Act, only requires that there be a probable anti-competitive effect in order for there to be a violation.

258

Multiple Choice

Circle the best answer.

1. The Robinson-Patman Act:
   a. prohibits discrimination in price between different purchasers of commodities only;
   b. prohibits discrimination in price between different purchasers of goods or services;
   c. Like the Clayton Act, the Robinson-Patman Act only requires that price discrimination have a probable anticompetitive effect;
   d. Both (a) and (c) are correct.

2. The Parker Doctrine:
   a. Prohibits sellers from discriminating in the services they furnish to competing customers;
   b. Exempts many anticompetitive acts from antitrust laws by exempting actions of state officials and private firms under their control who act under the authority of state law;
   c. extends protection to foreign governments involved in commercial activities acting with sovereign immunity;
   d. None of the above is correct.

3. Private plaintiffs who seek to recover treble damages under federal anti-trust laws:
   a. Must have standing to sue;
   b. Must prove action by business engaged in interstate commerce;
   c. Both (a) and (b) are required;
   d. Neither (a) nor (b) are required.

4. Which of the following statements concerning "joint action" required by the Section 1 of the Sherman Act is <u>not</u> correct?
   a. Unilateral actions which have an anticompetitive effect violate Section 1 under the definition of "joint action" in the Act;
   b. "Joint Action" may be express or implied;
   c. If Joint Action occurs by parties joining together for the purpose of restraining trade, this constitutes conspiracy;
   d. Unlike Section 1, Section 2 of the act does not require proof of "joint action."

5. Schlemiel Co. manufactures fertilizer spreaders. It has entered into distribution agreements with various retail dealers of Schlemiel spreaders. Under these agreements, each dealer has its own sales territory. Each dealer has agreed (with Schlemiel) that he will stay within his sales territory and will respect the sales territories of the other Schlemiel dealers. If a proper plaintiff brings a civil suit against Schlemiel on the theory that these agreements violated Section 1 of the Sherman Act,
   a. the court will give the agreements rule of reason treatment, meaning that Schlemiel will not necessarily be held to have violated Section 1.
   b. proof that the agreements existed will be enough to establish liability on Schlemiel's part, because of the per se treatment given to agreements of this nature.
   c. Schlemiel may be forced to pay a fine of as much as $1 million to the government.
   d. both b and c are accurate.

6. Recent decisions by the courts have expanded rule of reason analysis to include
   a. horizontal price restraints.
   b. vertical non-price restraints.
   c. unilateral refusals to deal.
   d. none of the above.

7. Which of the following mergers is a court most likely to prevent?
   a. A horizontal merger.
   b. A vertical merger.
   c. A conglomerate merger.
   d. A hybrid merger.

8. A defense to a price discrimination suit is
   a. that the defendant was only giving discounts to bulk purchasers.
   b. that the discrimination was necessary to gain a new customer.
   c. that the discrimination was based on a difference in the cost of shipping goods to different customers.
   d. any one of the above.

9. A manufacturer that states a suggested retail price
   a. has committed per se price fixing under the Sherman Act.
   b. has engaged in price fixing that is given rule of reason treatment under the Sherman Act.
   c. has not violated the Sherman Act because its action was unilateral.
   d. has not violated the Sherman Act because price fixing is not a restraint on competition.

10. Marginal Co. and Average, Inc. were competitors in the retail sale of televisions. They set the prices of their televisions that within a range that included both an agreed minimum price and an agreed maximum price. Both parties abided by the agreement. Which of the following statements is/are accurate?
   a. Marginal and Average committed a per se violation of Section 1 of the Sherman Act.
   b. Only that part of the parties' agreement concerning minimum prices was a per se violation of Section 1 of the Sherman Act.
   c. The portion of the parties' agreement that fixed maximum prices did not violate Section 1 of the Sherman Act because consumers are benefitted by agreements on maximum prices.
   d. Both b and c.

Short Essay

1. Briefly discuss the difference between horizontal and vertical price-fixing, and explain under what circumstances these activities may violate federal anti-true laws.

2. Swineco, Inc. supplies pickled pigs' feet (in jars) to numerous grocery stores across the country. The normal price is $2.19 per jar. In some circumstances, however, Swineco will give a 20 percent discount to stores that are able to sell in excess of 100 cans per month as an inducement to push the product during times of economic uncertainty. Discuss the antitrust aspects of Swineco's actions.

3. Numerous manufacturers of widgets conspired to fix prices in violation of the antitrust laws, in order to ensure that widgets were not sold to retailers at a price less than the artificially inflated figure upon which they had agreed. Retailers who purchased widgets at the artificially inflated price passed along the costs to consumers, in the form of higher prices for widgets. Once he acquired information tending to show what had taken place, Myron, a consumer who had purchased numerous widgets from a retailer at the higher prices, filed antitrust actions against the manufacturers involved in the conspiracy and the retailer from whom he had purchased the widgets. Evaluate Myron's chances for success, stating in your answer the reasons for your conclusions.

4. Benevolent Co. has been manufacturing racing bicycles for many years. It distributes its products through a network of local retailers. The contracts between Benevolent and its retail dealers provide for strictly enforced marketing districts. This distribution system is extremely efficient. Benevolent presently controls over 70% of the market for racing bicycles. Discuss this marketing strategy in light of Section 1 of the Sherman Act.

CHAPTER 48
CONSUMER PROTECTION LAWS

Outline

I. The Federal Trade Act is the grandfather of consumer protection legislation.

  A. The FTC (Federal Trade Commission) has power to establish rules and enforce consumer protection laws under this Act.

    Example: Grolier Inc. v. F.T.C. (FTC has wide power in issuing orders so long as they are reasonable.)

II. Consumer Credit Laws

  A. The Truth in Lending Act protects consumers by requiring lenders to advise them of important terms of their credit transactions.

    Example: Lawson v. Reeves (Failure to disclose finance charge a violation of the TILA.)

    1. The consumer may cancel the contract within three business days after the purchase on credit if the debtor's home is used as collateral under this Act.

  B. Fair Credit Reporting Act ensures that information about a person's credit background is accurate and current.

    Example: Pinner v. Schmidt (FCRA requires a reporting agency to reinvestigate and delete inaccurate information from an account.)

  C. Consumer Leasing Act requires the creditor to disclose the costs of leasing goods.

  D. Fair Credit Billing Act provides protections for users of credit cards.

    Example: Walker Bank & Trust Co. v. Harlan (Consumer remained liable for charges on credit card because she failed to return all cards to the bank as required in the cardholder contract.)

  E. Equal Credit Opportunity Act prohibits discrimination in credit transactions.

  F. Fair Debt Collection Practices Act regulates debt collection practices.

    Example: Juras v. Aman Collection Service, Inc. (Defendant's tactics in collecting the debt violated the FDCPA.)

  G. The FTC Holder in Due Course Rule: This rule preserves a consumer's claims and defenses against a holder in due course.

III. Consumer Product Safety

  A. The Consumer Product Safety Commission has authority to promote product safety in consumer products under the Consumer Product Safety Act.

  B. A majority of states have now passed "lemon laws" designed to protect consumers from defects in motor vehicles.

    Example: Ford Motor Co. v. Barrett (Holding the Washington lemon law constitutional.)

Learning Objectives

1. As society has changed, so has the law has changed. In the past, the law reflected the position of "caveat emptor" (let the buyer beware) because the purchaser and seller were more often than not in an equal bargaining position with respect to goods and could more freely negotiate the terms of their contracts. Today, the law is more protective of the consumer/purchaser. You should be familiar with important federal legislation designed to protect consumer interests which reflect this change in the law.

2. Just as Congress has passed several laws protecting consumers, so many states have adopted consumer protection legislation. You should be familiar with some examples of such legislation—for example, state "lemon laws."

3. You should be familiar with the broad reach of the Federal Trade Commission Act, as well as with the numerous functions served by the Federal Trade Commission.

4. You should understand the purposes and provisions of the Truth-in-Lending Act, and should know how its provisions implement the purposes.

5. You should understand, with regard to the Fair Credit Reporting Act, the aims of the Act, along with the rights of a consumer who contests information in a credit report and the limitations the Act imposes on credit reporting agencies.

6. You should become familiar with the rights of the consumer under the Fair Credit Billing Act and with the procedures established by the Act for instances in which the consumer disputes the accuracy of a billing statement.

7. You should know the classes of persons protected by the Equal Credit Opportunity Act, and should understand when and why the law will sometimes allow a creditor to ask for the applicant's marital status.

8. You should become aware of the protections provided to debtors by the Fair Debt Collection Practices Act.

9. You should understand the rights and responsibilities of the debtor, the seller, and the holder in due course in situations to which the FTC holder in due course rule applies.

10. You should become familiar with the essential provisions of the Consumer Product Safety Act and should know the functions served by the Consumer Product Safety Commission.

Learning Hints

1. The Federal Trade Commission Act established the Federal Trade Commission (FTC) in 1914 which has authority to adopt rules and enforce federal consumer protection laws and regulations discussed in this chapter. Some have suggested that the importance and influence of the FTC has diminished in the last decade during the administrations of Reagan and Bush.

2. In order to better understand the powers and authority of the Federal Trade Commission, you may wish to review the portion of Chapter 46 that discusses the FTC.

3. The Truth in Lending Act (TILA) requires disclosure of all of the terms of credit transactions at or before the time the credit contract is signed.

4. You should note the correct application of the three day "cooling off" period provided by the Truth-in-Lending Act. Most persons mistakenly believe that this right of rescission has a broader application than it actually has. Note that it applies only when the creditor, as part of the credit transaction, secures a lien on the debtor's home (other than a first mortgage to finance the purchase or construction of the home).

5. The provisions of the Equal Credit Opportunity Act closely mirror the provisions and underlying assumptions of the antidiscrimination legislation that exists in the employment area. These laws are designed to prevent creditors and employers from rejecting certain applicants simply because they are members of a certain class concerning which the creditors or employers have generalized, preconceived notions. Instead, the laws seek to force such decisionmakers to examine the qualifications of each person individually, erasing the stereotypical assumptions that have developed over time.

6. Remember that the Fair Credit Reporting Act's provisions apply only in the consumer context, and do not apply in a situation involving an applicant's request for commercial credit or commercial insurance. Similarly, the FTC holder in due course rule applies only in the consumer credit setting, and not in the commercial credit context.

7. The FTC Holder in Due Course Rule is an important protection for consumers because it preserves their right to use claims and defenses against a holder in due course. Because credit contracts are often sold to third parties, without this rule the consumer would frequently be unable to assert a defense such as breach of warranty against the holder of the paper.

8. Laws of the sort discussed in this chapter tend to be restricted to the consumer setting because lawmakers often regard consumers as more vulnerable and more subject to being taken advantage of by creditors than are seekers of commercial credit. Debtors and potential debtors in the commercial arena are likely to have more sophistication and experience in the securing of credit, making them better able (at least in theory) to protect themselves.

True-False

In the blank provided, put "T" if the statement is True or "F" if the statement is False.

_____ 1. Under the FTC Holder in Due Course Rule, a consumer is prohibited from asserting contract defenses against a holder in due course.

_____ 2. The Fair Debt Collections Practices Act prohibits debt collectors from communicating with consumers under any circumstances.

_____ 3. The Consumer Product Safety Commission does not regulate motor vehicles and equipment.

_____ 4. State "lemon laws" have consistently been declared unconstitutional because the FTC has exclusive jurisdiction over defective motor vehicle cases.

_____ 5. The Federal Trade Commission Act was the first consumer protection legislation passed in this century.

_____ 6. After passage of the Truth-in-Lending Act, debtors have a limited right of rescission in connection with every consumer loan.

_____ 7. A consumer who objects to the accuracy of information included in his or her credit report may have his or her version of the dispute included in the report.

_____ 8. Under the Equal Credit Opportunity Act, the creditor must approve or reject a credit applicant within 30 days after the application is submitted.

_____ 9. The provisions of the federal Fair Debt Collection Practices Act would apply to a bank's loan officer who harassed a debtor concerning an overdue account, but would not apply to harassment of the debtor by an independent collection agency retained by the bank to collect a past-due debt.

_____ 10. The right of rescission contained in the Truth-in-Lending Act applies to transactions in which the creditor supplying financing for the purchase or construction of a home acquires a first mortgage on the home.

_____ 11. Creditors generally are not permitted to ask the marital status of a loan applicant who seeks a separate account.

_____ 12. The Fair Credit Billing Act prohibits the previously common practice of giving discounts to purchasers who paid in cash instead of making a credit purchase.

Multiple Choice

Circle the best answer.

1. A person denied credit must be allowed to challenge the information supplied under
   a. The Fair Credit Reporting Act;
   b. The Equal Credit Opportunity Act;
   c. The Fair Debt Collections Practices Act;
   d. The Holder in Due Course Rule.

2. Debt collectors may not contact a consumer at unusual or inconvenient times under
   a. The Fair Credit Reporting Act;
   b. The Equal Credit Opportunity Act;
   c. The Fair Debt Collections Practices Act;
   d. The Holder in Due Course Rule.

3. A creditor must accept or reject a credit application within 30 days under:
   a. The Fair Credit Reporting Act;
   b. The Equal Credit Opportunity Act;
   c. The Fair Debt Collections Practices Act;
   d. The Holder in Due Course Rule.

4. Which of the following products would be regulated by the Consumer Product Safety Commission?
   a. A doll with removable parts;
   b. firearms;
   c. drugs and cosmetics;
   d. all of the above.

5. Under the disclosure requirements of the Truth-in-Lending Act, the term "finance charge" includes
   a. charges for accident insurance required for the loan.
   b. fees for credit reports.
   c. loan fees.
   d. all of the above.

6. The Fair Credit Billing Act
   a. establishes maximum interest rates that can be charged by issuers of credit cards.
   b. provides procedures to be followed if the user and holder of a credit card disputes items appearing on the statement sent to him by the issuer of the card.
   c. gives the user of a credit card 21 days after receiving a statement to report, to the issuer of the card, alleged errors appearing in the statement.
   d. is accurately referred to in both b and c.

7. The Federal Trade Commission Act gives the FTC authority to
   a. decide whether specific sales practices are unfair.
   b. establish rules governing industry conduct.
   c. require corrective advertisements to offset the impact of deceptive advertisements.
   d. do all of the above.

8. Under the terms of the Consumer Leasing Act,
   a. the lease agreement must define the consumer's liability at the end of the lease term.
   b. the creditor must disclose the aggregate costs of the lease for all consumer leases, regardless of the duration of the lease.
   c. the creditor must disclose the aggregate costs of the lease for all consumer leases, regardless of the dollar amount of the obligation.
   d. all of the above are true.

9. Of the following statements concerning the Equal Credit Opportunity Act, which is/are correct?
   a. The act covers discrimination in credit transactions, but only discrimination on the grounds of sex, marital status, or race.
   b. The act specifies that if a creditor extended credit to a person who is now deceased, the creditor must continue to extend new credit to the widow or widower of the deceased debtor.
   c. The act does not guarantee credit to anyone.
   d. All of the above.

10. Under the Fair Credit Reporting Act,
   a. one who has been denied consumer credit has a right to obtain a copy of the credit report on which the denial of credit was based.
   b. one who has been denied consumer credit may require the credit reporting agency that prepared the credit report on which the denial was based to reinvestigate information disputed by the consumer.
   c. a consumer is entitled to insist that a credit reporting agency not release a credit report on her to anyone.
   d. all of the above are true.

Short Essay

1. Sue purchased a new refrigerator from ABC Appliances and signed a promissory note agreeing to pay the note in 24 monthly installments. ABC negotiated the note to Happy Finance Company. Six months later, ABC filed bankruptcy and went out of business. One month later, the refrigerator blew up because of a defective part. Sue refused to pay for the refrigerator, maintaining that the refrigerator was defective and in breach of implied and express warranties under law. ABC Appliances sued her for $600, the balance remaining on the note. Is Sue obligated to pay the finance company the balance of the note under these facts? Explain.

2. According to PTL Department Store, Tammy owed a large past-due balance on a PTL charge account. Tammy disputed this assertion. An employee of Jim's Collection Agency, Inc. (retained by PTL to collect the debt) began telephoning Tammy periodically at her home to inquire about when she expected to pay the debt. Tammy then sent Jim's a written notice in which she stated that she did not owe any debt to PTL and that she was refusing to pay the amount being demanded. After this notice was received by Jim's, the Jim's employee continued to telephone Tammy (at home and during the afternoon) once each week for the next three weeks. In each of these telephone conversations, the Jim's employee politely inquired about when Tammy would be making payment on the PTL debt. Tammy then sued Jim's, alleging a violation of the Fair Debt Collection Practices Act. Did Jim's violate the Act? Why or why not?

3. While Viola Hefty was away visiting her parents, a door-to-door salesman for Otto's Siding Co. persuaded Viola's husband, Vic, to allow Otto's to install new aluminum siding on the Hefty home. According to the terms of the agreement (signed by Vic and the salesman on Tuesday, October 1), the Heftys would pay Otto's a total of $3,700 in installment payments over the next eighteen months. The agreement also provided that during this time, Otto's would hold a lien on the Hefty home to secure the unpaid balance. Viola returned home on October 2 and learned what had taken place. She was less than pleased with Vic. Vic therefore telephoned Otto's on October 2 and informed the manager of Otto's that "the dadgum deal is off." The manager countered with a "no dice, Vic" response. He informed Vic that an Otto's crew would arrive to start work the next day (October 3). What are the parties' rights and responsibilities here? Explain.

CHAPTER 49
ENVIRONMENTAL REGULATION

Outline

I. The Environmental Protection Agency (EPA)

    A. Created in 1970 with responsibilities for administering provisions of various federal environmental laws.

    B. The National Environmental Policy Act requires an environmental impact statement be prepared for every major federal action significantly affecting the quality of the environment.

II. Air Pollution

    A. The Clean Air Act of 1963, amended in 1965 and 1967, and comprehensive legislation passed in 1970, amended in 1977 and 1990, is the basis for federal regulation of air pollution.

        1. The EPA sets national ambient air quality standards: (1) primary standards and (2) secondary standards.

        2. Each region of the country is required to adopt an implementation plan (SIP).

        3. Specific provisions were added in 1990 to address acid rain, and to add regulations for emission of toxic air pollutants.
        Example: United States v. Tzavah Urban Renewal Corporation (Renovation of buildings contaminated with asbestos is regulated under the Clean Air Act.)

    B. New stationary sources must install the best available technology (BAT) under the Act.

    C. The Act also mandates air pollution controls on transportation sources such as automobiles.

III. Water Pollution

    A. Amendments to the Federal Water Pollution Control Act, especially the 1972 amendments known as the Clean Water Act, comprise the federal legislative scheme for addressing problems of water pollution.

    B. The law set water quality standards and requires dischargers to obtain permits.

    C. The Act also protects wetlands.

    Example: Bersani v. U.S. Environmental Protection Agency (Developer was not permitted to drain and fill a wetland in order to build a shopping center.)

IV. Waste Disposal

    A. The Resource Conservation and Recovery Act (RCRA) governs the generation, treatment, storage, and disposal of hazardous waste "from cradle to grave," and specifically includes underground storage tanks. The Act also provides for civil and criminal penalties.

    Example: United States v. Johnson & Towers, Inc. (employees of a corporation held criminally liable for violation of federal hazardous waste law.)

    B. The U.S. Supreme Court has struck down states' attempts to prohibit the importation of solid waste originating outside the state.

    Example: Fort Gratiot Sanitary Landfill, Inc. v. Michigan Department of Natural Resources (Michigan waste import restrictions held unconstitutional because it discriminated against interstate commerce.)

    C. The Comprehensive Environmental Response Compensation and Liability Act (CERCLA or Superfund) establishes a scheme for cleaning up hazardous wastes sites throughout the nation. The 1986 amendments to Superfund (SARA) also include "community right to know" provisions.

    Example: United States v. Chem-Dyne Corp. (Persons who contributed hazardous wastes to a particular site may be held jointly and severally liable for the cost of cleanup under CERCLA.)

V. Regulation of Toxic Chemicals

    A. The Federal Insecticide, Fungicide, and Rodenticide Act (FIFRA) and Toxic Substances Control Act (TSCA) regulate new and existing chemicals.

    B. Under FIFRA, the EPA has the authority to register pesticides before they may be sold, and to suspend or cancel registration to protect the public from an imminent hazard.

Example: <u>Consolidated DDT Hearing Opinion and Order of the Administrator</u> (Administrator may cancel the use of DDT as an imminent hazard.)

C. Under TSCA, the EPA may regulate chemicals which present an unreasonable risk of injury to health or the environment.

Learning Objectives

1. You should understand the historical background and the evolution of government regulation of business activities affecting the environment.

2. You should be familiar with legislative controls on the emission of chemicals and other pollutants into the atmosphere.

3. You should be familiar with legislative controls on the emission of chemicals and other pollutants into rivers, streams, and lakes.

4. You should understand the legislative controls on the manufacture, storage, and disposal of toxic chemicals.

5. You should understand legislation addressing the cleanup of hazardous waste sites which exist as a result of past manufacturing or industrial activity.

6. You should come to recognize that for many businesses, compliance with environmental statutes and regulations is an expensive and time-consuming process that cannot be ignored.

Learning Hints

1. The scope of environmental regulation has increased drastically in the past quarter-century. Environmental notions are now firmly entrenched in the legal scene and are not about to disappear. Therefore, prudent business persons cannot afford to be indifferent to and unaware of the major provisions of environmental law.

2. In studying what the text has to say about the National Environmental Policy Act and its requirements concerning environmental impact statements for federal projects, do not forget that various state and local governments have passed their own NEPA-like laws that also require environmental impact statements for major public and private projects.

3. Note that under the Clean Air Act, both the federal government and the state governments have enforcement roles. The federal government (through the EPA) sets the relevant air quality standards. The states than have the primary responsibility for enforcing these standards, but the federal government has the authority to enforce them when the states have failed to do so. In a sense, private citizens may also have a role in enforcement as well. Private citizens may file suits to force industry or the government to comply fully with the Clean Air Act's provisions.

4. Note how the Clean Water Act's provisions on wetlands may significantly limit the uses to which a property owner may put his, her, or its property.

5. The Resource Conservation and Recovery Act (RCRA) and the Superfund legislation were products of a growing awareness during the past two decades of the potentially devastating problems associated with hazardous waste disposal and abandoned or uncontrolled hazardous waste sites. In studying your text's treatment of these statutes, note their differing functions. RCRA is proactive in the sense that it is designed to minimize the likelihood that environmental disasters involving hazardous wastes will occur. Superfund, on the other hand, is reactive, in that it provides a mechanism for dealing with an environmental problem that has already occurred—in the form of an abandoned or uncontrolled hazardous waste site—but is certain to become worse if ignored.

6. As you consider the various legislative attempts to address the problems of industrial pollution, you should consider the following questions: What is (are) the problems the legislation attempts to address? What is (are) the method(s) by which the legislation addresses those problems? (Note, many of these federal laws are "command and control" legislation—that is, they do not rely on economic incentives to accomplish their goals.) How successful is the legislation in meeting those goals? In what ways might business and industry better address the problems of industrial pollution utilizing a "cost-benefit" approach?

True-False

In the blank provided, put "T" if the statement is True or "F" if the statement is False.

_____ 1. Under NEPA, an EIS (environmental impact statement) is only required if a federal action is involved.

_____ 2. The Toxic Substances Control Act (TSCA) governs cleanup of existing hazardous waste sites.

_____ 3. Under CERCLA (Superfund) a person who owns a hazardous waste site may be liable for cleanup costs even though he did not contribute wastes to the site.

_____ 4. States are required to adopt a SIP (State Implementation Plan) under the federal Clean Air Act.

_____ 5. The Clean Air Act currently does not address the problem of acid rain.

_____ 6. Up to this time, federal and state regulatory efforts have dealt only with outdoor air pollution; indoor air pollution is as yet unregulated.

_____ 7. The Clean Water Act regulates dredging or filling in wetlands, except when the wetlands are privately owned and the activity is being carried out by the landowner.

_____ 8. Persons who dispose of hazardous waste in violation of the Resource Conservation and Recovery Act may be criminally, as well as civilly, liable.

_____ 9. A state must decide which activities must be regulated or curtailed so that air pollution emissions for a given air quality region do not exceed national ambient air quality standards.

_____ 10. Under the Clean Water Act, the federal government has the primary responsibility for preventing, reducing, and eliminating water pollution.

Multiple Choice

Circle the best answer.

1. Problems of nuclear reactor safety are currently under the jurisdiction of:
   a. The EPA
   b. The NRC;
   c. Both (a) and (b);
   d. Neither (a) nor (b).

2. Which of the following statements about the Clean Water Act is <u>not</u> correct? The Clean Water Act:
   a. Requires that all municipal and industrial dischargers obtain permits to discharge any pollutants;
   b. Requires discharges to keep records and install and maintain monitoring equipment;
   c. Permits citizens to sue anyone violating an effluent standard under the Act;
   d. Gives the federal government the primary responsibility for preventing water pollution.

3. RCRA (The Resource Conservation and Recovery Act):
   a. Regulates underground product storage tanks;
   b. authorizes EPA to set minimum standards for the disposal of household waste material;
   c. authorizes the EPA to seek criminal penalties for violation of the Act;
   d. All of the above are correct.

4. Which of the following requires preclearance of new chemicals and provides for the regulation of existing chemicals posing an unreasonable risk to health or the environment?
   a. Clean Air Act;
   b. Clean Water Act;
   c. Toxic Substances Control Act (TSCA).
   d. Resource Conservation and Recovery Act (RCRA);

5. The sale of a pesticide
    a. is governed by provisions of the Superfund law.
    b. cannot be prohibited by the federal government if the pesticide has a beneficial use.
    c. is an activity subject to registration requirements administered by the Environmental Protection Agency.
    d. is an activity presently regulated only under state law.

6. Which federal environmental statute does not permit private citizen lawsuits?
    a. Resource Conservation and Recovery Act
    b. Clean Air Act
    c. Clean Water Act
    d. None of the above.

7. Which of the following is an accurate statement concerning environmental regulation?
    a. Nuisance suits provide a comprehensive, across-the-board approach to pollution problems.
    b. Although the Safe Drinking Water Act calls for the EPA to set primary drinking water standards, the main responsibility for enforcing the federally established standards lies with the states.
    c. A weakness of current environmental law becomes apparent when the EPA incurs costs in cleaning up a hazardous waste site, because the EPA is not allowed to recover those costs from parties responsible for creating the problem.
    d. None of the above.

8. Superfund cleanup activity is financed primarily by
    a. a tax on chemicals and feedstocks.
    b. permitting fees.
    c. court judgments in environmental lawsuits.
    d. local and state tax levies.

9.. The Superfund legislation requires
    a. that a state prevent future environmental problems on sites which have been cleaned up.
    b. that responsible parties reimburse the EPA for its costs of cleaning up a hazardous waste site.
    c. that those responsible for contaminating a site be jointly and severally liable for the cost of cleanup.
    d. all of the above.

10. Under the Clean Air Act, the primary ambient air-quality standards are designed to protect
    a. the public health.
    b. the economic vitality of the local region.
    c. the vegetation and animal life of the U.S.
    d. all of the above.

Short Essay

1. Discuss the responsibilities and authority of the Environmental Protection Agency under the Superfund legislation.

2. Describe the scheme for enforcing the national ambient air quality standards established by the Environmental Protection Agency pursuant to the Clean Air Act.

3. Larry owned a landfill where various hazardous wastes were deposited. Moe's company transported hazardous waste from Curly's manufacturing plant to Larry's landfill. Larry subsequently sold the landfill to Pee-Wee. The EPA has listed the site as a hazardous waste site under Superfund. Who may be liable for the costs of cleaning up the site? Explain.

CHAPTER 50
INTERNATIONAL LAW

Outline

I.Sources of International Law

A. International compacts or codes

B. United Nations Convention on Contracts for the International Sale of Goods applies to countries, including the U.S., who ratified this convention.

    1. Applies only to commercial sales of goods.

    2. The Choice of Law Convention provides rules for determining which law applies in cases where the parties' countries have not adopted the CISG.

    3. Courts typically respect a choice of law agreement of the parties.
Example: Carnival Cruise Lines v. Shute (Forum selection clause in a form contract was enforceable.)

II.Sales Abroad of Domestically Manufactured Products

A. Sellers frequently structure such sales using a documentary irrevocable letter of credit. The issuing bank issues a letter of credit agreeing to pay when presented with a bill of lading. The confirming bank promises to pay the seller on the letter of credit.
Example: Texpor Traders v. Trust Company Bank (Issuing bank is normally obligated to honor the beneficiary's request for payment only when documents presented are in strict compliance with the letter of credit.)

B. Countertrade transactions involve linking two or more trade obligations in a product-for-product exchange.
Example: Pagnan S.P.A. v. Granaria B.V. (Where parties had neither agreed to the differential in prices nor to what type of export certificates would be available, neither party was contractually bound.)

C. Sales through a distributor (such as international franchising) involve contract agreements.

III.Licensing Technology to Manufacturers Abroad

A. A firm may acquire parallel patents in major countries maintaining a patent system. Gray Market Goods are goods that bear a valid U.S. trademark bought outside the United States and then resold in the U.S. by unauthorized importers and distributors.
Example: K Mart Corporation v. Cartier, Inc.

IV.Investment to Establish a Manufacturing Operation Abroad

A. There is a growing trend toward holding parent corporations liable for the activities of their foreign subsidiaries.

B. Some countries limit the amount of earnings that may be repatriated each year.

C. A politically unstable country raises the risk of expropriation—the taking of a foreign company's facilities by the host government. Insurance is the best protection in such cases.

V.Limitations on Trade

A. Tariffs are taxes assessed on imported goods. The GATT treaty (General Agreement on Tariffs and Trade) has resulted in significant tariff reductions and promoted reduction of trade barriers.

B. Other agreements such as the Generalized System of Preferences and Caribbean Basin Initiative determine the duty-status of goods.

C. Many countries impose tariffs to counteract dumping and subsidized goods. Countries also limit exports and imports for other policy reasons.

D. Today, a system of managed trade dominated by regional trading blocs appears to be replacing the global trading system administered under GATT.

    1. For example, the European Community, as originally planned was to become an integrated trade bloc.

Example: <u>Cinetheque SA v. Federation Nationale Des Cinemas Francais</u> (discussing whether French regulation unlawfully interferes with the free movement of goods within the EC.)

    2. NAFTA (North American Free Trade Agreement) between Canada, Mexico, and the United States would eliminate barriers to trade in goods and serves among those members.

E. The Foreign Corrupt Practices Act prohibits an American firm from promising to make payment or gifts to foreign officials to influence a governmental decision.

Learning Objectives

1. You should understand the nature of a licensing agreement and the risks associated with it.

2. You should understand how multinational businesses might reduce their risk of doing business in the international environment.

3. You should be familiar with different laws which govern international transactions.

4. You should understand the purposes of the Vienna Convention on Contracts for the International Sale of Goods (CISG) and should be aware of the major ways in which it differs from the Uniform Commercial Code.

5. You should understand the role of choice-of-law and forum selection clauses in contracts between parties from different countries.

6. You should be aware of why the use of arbitration has increased in international transactions in recent years.

7. You should understand how documentary exchanges facilitate transactions between U.S. sellers and foreign buyers.

8. You should be aware of the major advantages of, and problems associated with, international franchising.

9. You should know the major legal concerns associated with the licensing of technology to manufacturers abroad.

10. You should understand why U.S. firms that invest elsewhere in the world must be concerned about other countries' repatriation regulations and about the possible danger of expropriation.

11. You should understand how tariffs are used to restrict imports and protect domestic sales, and how tariffs may be employed to combat dumping and subsidized goods.

12. You should be aware of the major purposes of the EC.

Learning Hints

1. The United Nations Convention on Contracts for the International Sale of Goods (CISG) was created to unify and codify an international law of sales.

2. Though there are many similarities to the Uniform Commercial Code, the CISG differs from the UCC in a few important ways. One important difference is the fact that the CISG does not apply to consumer transactions but only applies in commercial sales.

3. The rules governing documentary irrevocable letter of credit transactions involving sellers and buyers from different countries will be easier to understand if understand the purposes underlying them: to give the seller reasonable assurance of payment and the buyer reasonable assurance that the purchased goods will in fact be provided. Carefully study your text's discussion of these rules and the related concept summary also found in the text.

4. Remember that a U.S. firm's actions in international transactions may be subject not only to U.S. antitrust laws but also to other countries' antitrust laws.

5. The possibility of expropriation is an ever-present concern of U.S. companies that have facilities located in politically unstable countries. Once expropriation occurs, it is usually an uphill battle for the U.S. company that, however rightfully, wishes to seek adequate compensation for the taking of its facilities.

6. Note how the EC (European Community) attempts to promote free trade within the boundaries of the relevant economic community. The single European market that will be created by 1992 will accelerate the amount of free trade and may well lead to the emergence of European multinational corporations that are capable of effectively competing with Japanese and U.S. companies in the world market.

7. The United States, Canada, and Mexico have been recently negotiating terms of a North American Free Trade Agreement (NAFTA). Passage of that treaty would eliminate barriers to the free flow of goods and services between those countries. Passage of the treaty, however, for political reasons is far from certain at this time.

True-False

In the blank provided, put "T" if the statement is True or "F" if the statement is False.

_____ 1. The Foreign Corrupt Practices Act prohibits any payments to government officials even if the recipient has no discretion in carrying out a governmental function.

_____ 2. The United Nations Convention on Contracts for the International Sale of Goods (CISG) applies to all international contracts even if the countries involved have not adopted it.

_____ 3. Under the CISG, a contract does not have to be in writing to be enforceable unless the contract itself requires a writing for modification or termination.

_____ 4. Choice of law clauses in international contracts are generally enforceable.

_____ 5. Sellers in international transactions frequently utilize irrevocable letters of credit to structure the sale of goods.

_____ 6. In recent years, courts have become less likely than they formerly were to impose liability on parent corporations in the United States for the actions of their foreign subsidiaries.

_____ 7. Generally, the law governing international business transactions in situations where choice of law is not spelled out in the parties' contract is the law of the country in which the seller's place of business is located.

_____ 8. The most common form of international transaction engaged in by U.S. firms is the export of products manufactured by the firms in the U.S.

_____ 9. Under the Uniform Customs and Article 5 of the Uniform Commercial Code, the promises made by the issuing bank and the confirming bank in a documentary irrevocable letter of credit transaction are dependent upon the seller's satisfactory performance of its obligation under the underlying sales contract.

_____ 10. In international contracts, arbitration is often the forum of choice.

Multiple Choice

Circle the Best Answer.

1. Which of the following statements concerning the United Nations Convention on Contracts for the International Sale of Goods (CISG) is not correct?
   a. The CISG applies to consumer as well as commercial contracts;
   b. Unlike the UCC, there is no specific requirement in the CISG that contracts for the sale of goods must be in writing;
   c. The CISG applies only to the sale of goods, not to the sale of land or provision of services;
   d. The CISG does not hold merchants to a higher standard than non-merchants.

2. In a documentary irrevocable letter of credit transaction where the seller is a resident of the United States, the issuing bank:
   a. Is located in the customer's country;
   b. Is the seller's bank;
   c. Issues the bill of lading to the confirming bank;
   d. Pays the seller on the letter of credit.

3. A genuine product bearing a valid U.S. trademark that is bought outside the United States and then resold in this country by unauthorized importers and distributors is called:
   a. A parallel patent;
   b. gray market goods;
   c. a process innovation;
   d. none of the above.

4. A distribution agreement between a U.S. firm and a distributor abroad
   a. is primarily governed by contract law.
   b. has as its forum of choice the U.S. court system.
   c. is exempt from U.S. and foreign antitrust laws.
   d. is unenforceable in the U.S. courts.

5. The biggest worry of a U.S. firm which establishes a manufacturing operation abroad is
   a. repatriation.
   b. res ipsa loquitur.
   c. expropriation.
   d. tariffs.

6. "Dumping"
   a. involves goods that are economically supported by the government of their country of origin and can therefore be sold for less than goods produced in the native market.
   b. involves the selling of goods at unfairly low prices.
   c. involves a tax or duty assessed on goods when they are imported into a country for the purpose of restricting imports and protecting domestic sales.
   d. involves the seizure of a U.S. firm's manufacturing facilities by the host government without compensation.

7. Obstacles to the extraterritorial application of U.S. antitrust laws
   a. are nonexistent in most of the major trading nations.
   b. can be easily overcome by the use of exclusive dealing agreements.
   c. include the requirement that the acts challenged be shown to have had a substantial effect on U.S. commerce.
   d. are eased by the doctrine of comity.

8. An exclusive dealing provision in a distribution agreement between a U.S. firm and a foreign distributor
   a. is virtually certain to be unlawful under foreign antitrust laws.
   b. will be governed primarily by the Foreign Corrupt Practices Act.
   c. will be subject to U.S. antitrust laws.
   d. is mainly intended to benefit the foreign distributor.

9. Which of the following is not a concern for U.S. firms that establish manufacturing facilities abroad?
   a. Local labor laws
   b. Local limits on repatriation of earnings and investments
   c. Expropriation
   d. None of the above

10. Countries impose import and export controls by
    a. using tariffs.
    b. controlling the licensing of technology.
    c. limiting exports of militarily sensitive technology.
    d. all of the above methods.

Short Essay

1. How is the Vienna Convention on Contracts for the International Sale of Goods (CISG) similar to and different from the Uniform Commercial Code?

2. What are three advantages of arbitration in international trade over other dispute settlement mechanisms?

3. What is the difference between repatriation and expropriation?